STEPS TO SUCCESS
THE FAIRLEIGH DICKINSON WAY

Revised Printing

■■■

Edited by

Judith Kaufman

Fairleigh Dickinson University

Kendall Hunt

publishing company

Cover image courtesy of the author

Kendall Hunt
publishing company

www.kendallhunt.com
Send all inquiries to:
4050 Westmark Drive
Dubuque, IA 52004-1840

ISBN 978-0-7575-9165-5

Printed in the United States of America
9 8 7 6 5

CONTENTS

PREFACE AND INTRODUCTION

■ Welcome to the Next Step on Your Journey to Success!

What's ahead? You are now ready to embark on your voyage to adulthood. You are now a student at Fairleigh Dickinson University, and are beginning your transition to independence and your future career. This step you are taking will help you move toward achieving your dreams. You have worked hard to get here, and you want to make your college years special. Accepting the challenge of learning, of making new friends, and having new experiences, you can make this time of your life productive, exciting, and fulfilling. Our Freshman Seminar program and this textbook, with its exercises, will give you the tools and information to help make a successful transition to college.

What's so different? High school and college are dramatically different experiences, particularly if you are living on campus. Scheduling, expectations, studying, "homework" and rules and regulations are not the same. You will be expected to manage your own time, develop your own course schedule (with advisement), have more unscheduled time, pay for textbooks and to regularly attend classes as grades may be penalized if you have frequent absences. Your instructors expect that you will become independent learners, think about issues, do a substantial amount of out of class work, and follow the course outline (syllabus) which lists assignments and class requirements without being reminded at each class session.

While there are some "have to" classes, most of the courses you take are those you choose. You will begin to take classes that develop the skills for your chosen major and future career.

You will also find that most of the people you have gone to school with for the past several years will no longer be in your day-to-day life and you will begin to negotiate new relationships which can be a challenge. You will be meeting people with backgrounds unlike your own; from other neighborhoods, people from across the country and from all over the world. While such diversity may be initially a challenge for you, getting to know all kinds of people can be the most enriching part of coming to college.

You will need to learn to take care of yourself, particularly if you are living on campus. Eating right, sleeping right, exercising, managing your stress and developing effective coping strategies are important in order to maximize your college experience. That does not mean that you can't have FUN or an active co-curricular life. But you will need to learn to make decisions that are in your best interests. Joining clubs, organizations, a fraternity or sorority, participating in campus activities, United Nations involvement and taking advantage of our global learning and study abroad opportunities (see Appendix for listings) help to make your college years important building blocks for the rest of your life.

What you can do.

- ■ Give yourself the freedom to explore new interests, new people and new ideas
- ■ Before committing to one group or direction, get to know what is going on and finding out where YOU feel most comfortable
- ■ Participate and prioritize. You cannot do everything at once and you need to remember that your grades are extremely important
- ■ Begin to take responsibility for yourself. While others are important, you must be important to yourself
- ■ Be patient, things take time to adjust to

- Expect ups and downs. Things don't always go exactly as we would like them to.
- If you think you are having a problem, academically or emotionally . . . ask for help. Challenges managed early may not become problems!
- Stay connected with those who can support you and assist you with your college life. Family and friends are important. Your professors are people you can talk to. Your Freshman Seminar instructor is there to guide and mentor you. Take advantage of the support services on the Metropolitan campus. They are there for you.

Our Freshman Seminar is a course that has been developed to help you and your fellow students in the transition to college and to assist you in negotiating your first semester at Fairleigh Dickinson University. As you will see in the chapters that follow and in your classroom assignments, many of the critical issues that concern students in their adaptation to the college environment are discussed and addressed. Your instructor also serves as your mentor and is available to assist you with any issue that you might have. Both formal and informal mentoring sessions will be scheduled throughout the semester. Take advantage of your Freshman Seminar experience . . . ask questions, discuss issues, find out about our campus and don't be afraid to express your concerns if you have any. If I can be of help in any way, please feel free to contact me.

ENJOY YOUR COLLEGE EXPERIENCE.
I WISH YOU WELL ON YOUR JOURNEY TO SUCCESS.

Judith Kaufman, Ph.D.
Freshman Seminar Coordinator.
Judith_Kaufman@fdu.edu

Section 1

College:
Why Are You Here?

CHAPTER 1
Expectations and Challenges

What Does It Mean to Have a College Education?

When asked what college means to them, students say such things as it's:

" . . . a means to a better job."
" . . . something to do instead of working."
" . . . my parents' dream for me."
" . . . something that comes after high school."

" . . . a place to learn."
" . . . a place to be irresponsible and have fun."

While a college experience may be any or all of the above for a student, a college education is not a product nor a "thing" one gets; it is a process one participates in. A college education:

- ■ is an exposure to a life and a way of looking at the world through many new and different lenses.
- ■ can provide a better understanding of the world in which we live and increase our ability for meaningful interactions within our environments.
- ■ expands and deepens an increasing awareness of our creativity.
- ■ provides an opportunity to grow in compassion and understanding of other people, to gain a new appreciation of differences, and a new sense of responsibility for our life.
- ■ helps develop effective problem solving skills and strategies that equip us for various employment, cultural, and interpersonal opportunities.

The comedian Woody Allen is reported to have said that 80 percent of success in life simply comes from "showing up." Unfortunately "showing up" is not enough to guarantee success in college. It's what a student chooses "to do" after "showing up" that makes the difference. The university furnishes the environment and the opportunities for success. The task for every student is to decide whether or not to take advantage of those opportunities. Attending class, completing assignments, interacting with professors, passing tests, and being involved in extracurricular activities are important parts of the next four years. Equally important are the decisions made, the goals set, and the relationships formed. In sum, what a college experience means depends on what one chooses to do now that they have shown up.

"Now, here, you see, it takes all the running you can do to keep in the same place. If you want to get somewhere else, you must run twice as fast as that."

Lewis Carroll
Through the Looking-Glass

Realizing that the freshman year is a challenging time, the university provides a wealth of resources to help its new students with the transition. Read carefully and think about the transition and what it means to you. Catalogs outline the campus offices, clubs, and opportunities for freshmen students. There are numerous clubs and organizations covering special interest groups, service clubs, religious groups, recreational clubs, and scholastic organizations. In addition, universities participating in the Greek system of fraternities and sororities, offer membership opportunities in many such groups.

New students are encouraged to join clubs and participate in campus activities. Campus involvement is one way of making a connection with the university and the larger student body. A word of caution: balance in life is an important ingredient of success. A careful examination of personal goals and use of time gives one a fairly good idea of how to balance the time between studies, work, and extracurricular activities.

What Is Expected of New Students?

"The freedom from work, from restraint, from accountability, wondrous in its inception, became banal and counterfeit. Without rules there was no way to say no, and worse, no way to say yes."

Thomas Farber

If the extent of personal freedom at the university is an eye-opening experience for new students, an equally important element of the transition equation is the personal responsibility that accompanies the new freedom. New students are expected to assume responsibility for their education and behavior. Among those expectations are the following:

Classroom Conduct

Appropriate classroom conduct is expected of all students. Students should arrive at class on time and be prepared with the necessary books, notes, paper, and writing supplies. Coming prepared to class also means having completed assigned readings, reviewed notes, and prepared questions.

Working on homework from another course, reading the campus newspaper during class, carrying on side conversations, and chatter during a lecture are not appropriate.

Cultivating Relationships with Faculty Is Important

Develop the interpersonal skills that promote interaction with professors and instructors. The first step is to find out what they expect of students and what students can expect from them. This information is usually found in the course syllabus and/or is discussed on the first day of class. Generally speaking, most professors expect students to:

- *Attend class regularly.* You lose when you skip a class. If you must miss a class arrange for another student to keep notes for you (don't expect the professors to give you theirs). Make sure you get any assignments that were announced.
- *Accept responsibility.* Don't make excuses; accept responsibility for your own learning.
- *Submit high quality work in both content and form.* Do the best you can in quality and neatness. Students who have difficulty writing papers should seek a tutor. Some instructors only accept typed papers, and students without personal computers should take advantage of the campus computer labs.
- *Turn assignments in on time.* Late assignments suggest a lack of enthusiasm and commitment. Habitually handing assignments in late is a bad habit that employers are less forgiving of.
- *Arrive on time and be attentive in class.* Late arrivals are a distraction to the entire class. If you must be late, find the nearest convenient seat and quickly and quietly sit down.
- *Participate in class discussions.* Participation in class is valued by some professors and not encouraged by others. Follow the preferences for each professor.
- *Meet with professors outside of class.* A good way to get to know your professor is to prepare some questions based on previous classes, readings and your own reflections that you can ask the professor before, after class, or in his/her office.

Academic Honesty

The faculty and staff expect students and faculty alike to maintain the highest standards of academic honesty. Dishonesty includes but is not limited to:

- Stealing a copy of the exam ahead of time
- Copying from someone else's paper
- Sending or receiving signals during an exam
- Using unauthorized notes during an exam
- Taking an exam for another student
- Letting another student take an exam for you
- Handing in a paper that you have not written

Plagiarism is a specific form of cheating in which a student fails to give proper credit for written work that belongs to someone else. It is trying to pass off the work of others as one's own. Students falsely assume that they will not be caught; however, professors are very adept at identifying work that has been incorrectly documented or "borrowed" from another source without proper citation. Knowingly representing the words or ideas of another as your own in any academic exercise or activity carries with it serious consequences.

■ Developmental Changes

"When we plant a rose seed in the earth, we notice that it is small, but we do not criticize it as "rootless and stemless." We treat it as a seed, giving it the water and nourishment required of a seed. When it first shoots up out of the earth, we don't condemn it as immature and underdeveloped; nor do we criticize the buds for not being open when they appear. We stand in wonder at the process taking place and give the plant the care it needs at each stage of its development. The rose is a rose from the time it is a seed to the time it dies. Within it, at all times, it contains its whole potential. It seems to be constantly in the process of change; yet at each stage, at each moment, it is perfectly all right as it is."

W. Timothy Gallwey
The Inner Game of Tennis

You can expect to go through a great number of changes during your college years. Most of these changes will not be noticeable to the naked eye because they take place inside of you. How you cope with these changes will be determined mainly by your personality, your past experience, and your current life situation. Many students glide right through this time of transition with little awareness that anything new has occurred. Others come through thrashing and kicking. Regardless, the one thing you can count on is that you will grow and change during the next few years.

As you begin to explore your personal values and set goals for your future, you will be creating a world view that is unique to you. This is good, and this is healthy. It is important to realize that there are some very normal developmental tasks which you will be completing during the next few years.

One of the most challenging tasks is redefining relationships with your family. The important thing to remember is that these next years will be a period of adjustment for you and your family. Your first trip home may start out as a hero's welcome and end in tears and disagreement. Be patient! Don't try to flex all of your new freedom at once. Give your family a chance to get used to the new you. And remember, your family hasn't been standing still while you have been gone. They may have changed and grown as well. Finding your new place within the family may take patience and time.

There is no way to predict how you will move through these next four years. To be sure, at times you will find yourself struggling and feeling out of sorts. At other times, life will seem wonderful, and you will be on top of the world. The important thing to remember is that normal developmental changes will take place. It will help to define some of the changes you are likely to experience. Just remember that the college years are a time of change and while you may not always be at ease as those changes unfold, you are OKAY!

■ Elements of Success

Success in all of its forms and varieties is a goal of every student who enrolls at the university. However, wanting to succeed and doing what is necessary to succeed are two very different things. This section details suggestions and ideas about how to bridge the gap between desiring and actually achieving success. We encourage you to read and make use of the ideas presented because they are only as helpful as you make them. There are no quick fixes, no easy answers.

> *"Two roads diverged in a wood and I took the one less traveled by, and that has made all the difference."*
>
> *Robert Frost*
> *The Road Not Taken*

The first step in succeeding at something is realizing that wanting to succeed is just the starting place. Additional factors in any successful college experience include: (1) attitude about school and life; (2) prior academic experience and ability; (3) ability to effectively manage time and to discipline oneself; (4) ability to relate to and get along with others; and, (5) the learning environment.

Attitude

Attitude is a combination of thoughts and feelings. Much of a student's attitude about college is determined by how and why they chose to be here and how they feel about that choice. Some students find themselves in college but are not aware how they arrived at the decision to attend. Do you want to be here? Are you in school because someone said you had to come? Enrolling in college because someone else said you should, may motivate you to enroll, but won't necessarily enable you to succeed. In order to succeed, you need to have your own reasons for attending; you need to "own" the decision to come to school.

There are many different (but no right) reasons for attending college. Some students pursue a degree in order to get a good job or to advance into a higher position in their current job. Others come to school for social reasons—high school was fun, so college will be even more fun! Some would rather go to school than work full-time. Others find it an easy way to move away from home and have their parents or others pay for it! Some students decide on a college education because they love learning and see college as an opportunity to pursue that love.

The reasons for choosing to go to college are as limitless as the persons attending. Reasons for attending also change over time as events and circumstances unfold. Be reflective, visit with yourself from time to time about why you are here. Are those reasons being fulfilled? What are you doing to fulfill them?

The thing to remember is that when the days are long and the nights are short your attitude about school will determine how hard you are willing to work to make it work!

Experience and Ability

Prior academic experience and ability play an important role in your success. Students who arrive at the university with a strong academic background have an advantage. New ideas are more quickly assimilated when they can be associated with prior knowledge. Don't rest on your laurels; however, professors expect a lot.

This is not to say that a lack of prior strong academic experience prohibits success, but it will take greater commitment and hard work to catch on in some of your classes. It is also a fairly common experience for "average" high school students to "catch fire" in the stimulating environment of the university.

Prior academic experience includes a knowledge of basic learning and life skills. Do you know how to study, how to manage time, how to set goals, and how to communicate effectively? Many students come to college unaware of the need for these skills. They register [...] buy their books, attend the first day of class, and begin to "study." They are [...] and their own abilities as the old habits that wo[...] now and the work piles higher and hig[...] d lower.

Handwritten note:
— Studying strategies, Tips about them...
— Knowing how to control time, Balancing time for school work / myself / & friends, family.

Success[...] arder, it is a matter of studying smarte[...] need to work harder and smarter to be a[...] more difficult than high school, and su[...] success in college. Taking the time to lear[...] of your classes is time well spent.

Your [...] study strategies on: listening and note-[...] memory. In addition, it explores some[...] uccess. We challenge you to examine a[...] e strategies you need to develop as scho[...] ful in learning how to successfully jug[...] s, and extracurricular activities are des[...] nd how you can best structure your ow[...]

Experiences are dynamic. Periodically [...] e to stop and reflect on yours. What's going right? Wrong? What can you do to sustain or alter the experiences you are having?

Self-Discipline

Self-discipline and effective time management are vital keys to success. Students who are self-disciplined are better able to handle the increased freedom that comes with college. One of the first things that is discovered about university life is that in many classes attendance is not required. Unfortunately, some students interpret this to mean that attendance is not important. Nothing can be farther from the truth. Skipping class is a poor strategy for achieving success. Having decided to enroll and having paid the tuition, deciding not to attend class is counterproductive and costly!

Self-discipline includes taking care of yourself physically, mentally, and emotionally. Many of these issues, including ways to enhance and improve existing strategies for self-discipline and effective time management are discussed in later chapters.

Interpersonal Skills

Another very important part of success at any university is the ability to relate to and get along with other people. This includes roommates, friends, other students, faculty, and family. Although satisfactory progress towards a degree is measured in grades, the sense of well-being and accomplishment may well be measured by the ability to make friends, relate to classmates, and interact with faculty.

Having significant people who support you in your decision to attend college is a big help in your success at the university. These are the people who remind you of your commitment and encourage you to continue on with your plans when you are tired and discouraged. They are the same people who share in your accomplishments and your success. These people comprise an important part of your support network. Although they cannot make you succeed, they can remind you of your goals and even help lighten some of the burden you carry. Recognize their support. "Good strokes for good folks" goes a long ways to ensuring their continued support.

Environment

Finally, success in college is determined by the learning environment which includes defining and setting up an area for studying. By following a few basic suggestions a supportive study environment can be created. Study in the same place at the same time and use a signal to tell roommates and yourself that you are studying.

Your learning environment also includes campus and community resources. The Chamber of Commerce is a good reference for information on the local community and surrounding areas.

In summary, the university defines a successful college student as one who is making satisfactory progress towards his or her educational goals. The rate of progress (time it takes) and the qualitative measurement of that progress (grades received) are determined by individual circumstances. Understanding the factors that impact on that success—attitude, prior academic experience, self-discipline, relations with others, and the working/studying environment—helps to bridge the gap between wanting success and achieving success.

CHAPTER 2
Motivate Your Way to Success

■ Welcome to College!

You have a lot of neat experiences ahead of you, some frustrating, and hopefully many rewarding. Are you excited about this new learning venture? Think back to your first day of elementary school. Do you remember how excited you were? Do you have that same enthusiasm today?

Unfortunately, many students associate learning with "school" and they don't have a lot of positive feelings toward school. Learning performance tends to drop as we go along in our academic pursuits. School is associated with "drudgery," and before we know it our attitude starts to be indifferent.

From *Practical Approaches for Building Study Skills and Vocabulary*, Second Edition by Funk et al. © 1996 by Kendall Hunt Publishing Company.

Let's try and start fresh with a good attitude like we had in first grade!

■ Why Are You Here?

This is an important question for you to answer. There are several reasons why students attend college. Fill out the exercise titled: Why Are You Here?

You need to stop and think about why you are in college. Are your reasons for being here due to others? Will these people be responsible for your success in life? Will they be attending class for you? Taking your tests? Receiving your diploma?

A recent study at a midwestern university revealed the top three reasons chosen for attending college were:

1. To increase the chances for a higher paying career

2. To expand knowledge

3. To help ensure success in life

This is a good time to examine your values and decide what you feel is important. Fill out the worksheet on clarifying your values. These values affect the choices you make in life.

The Coat of Arms Exercise will help you think about your personal feelings. Fill in this worksheet and think about the priorities in your life.

The student who is "educated" is the one who has learned how to learn. It is important to be aware of your values and goals because that will help motivate you to do your best. You need to recognize what is important to you, and strive to reach your potential. A college education can help you develop a flexible and open mind, sharpen your ability, and enrich your life.

■ What Is a Successful College Student?

We all want to be successful. There is not one college student that attends college to be unsuccessful. How can we be successful? There have been numerous studies done in this area. Most of these studies show that successful students tend to possess the following characteristics:

1. *They have a definite reason for attending college.*

   You must decide what *you* want out of college. After completing the Exercise, Why Are You Here, you have had the opportunity to think about what is important to you.

2. *They have selected a vocation and are pursuing this course.*

   Don't panic if you don't have a career chosen. But, be aware that it provides motivation to have a career goal. Spend this first year trying out several courses in varying fields. Maybe one will ring a bell! When you have chosen your career, you will be motivated by a clearer sense of direction.

3. *They realize the need for understanding the material in each class and envision the value of it.*

A successful student does not study just to pass a test. They usually have a three-pronged approach to the material.

   a. They master the basic facts. Without doing this, there is nothing on which to build.

   b. They take these basic facts and draw supporting details in for a total picture.

   c. They learn to "think" with the subject. Once you are able to explain a concept in your own words—it's yours!

This approach allows them to "learn" the subject matter, not just memorize it.

4. *They have a desire for success.*

The more success you experience, the more you will want.

"Success Breeds Success"

"Success Creates Interest"

What a wonderful feeling accomplishment can bring! Have you ever failed a class that you really liked? Probably not. Success can create interest, which further ensures success. One way we have of achieving success is the attainment of goals. Much more about that later!

5. *They have the will to succeed.*

Abraham Lincoln loved to read. It was told that he walked 20 miles to borrow a book. Would you exert that much effort? If we can't park close to the library, we probably will not bother to check out a book!

How can we develop this kind of will to succeed?

GOALS ⟶ SUCCESS ⟶ STRENGTHENS WILL ⟶ MORE SUCCESS

We can develop this will to succeed by the attainment of short-term goals. Small successes strengthen our will, and the strengthened will provides us with additional power to work even harder.

6. *They have developed good study skills.*

The definition of study skills is the efficient use of our mind and our time. The key word is "efficient." There are other phases of our life that need attention, and we need to develop study skills so we can accomplish the maximum in the minimum amount of time. Study skills are not instinctive, but something that we need to learn. The goal of study skills is independent learning. As long as you look to someone else for interpretation, you are not a free person intellectually.

7. *They know they must set priorities. "This is the time to learn."*

Rank your needs at this time. It is not necessary for school to be number one, but it must be extremely high on the list.

Consider this scenario:

Greg was studying for a physics test. Doug and Jeff were on their way for pizza and a movie. They stopped by Greg's room and invited him along. Greg's decision could be crucial toward a high grade on his test the next day. What would you do?

■ What Is Motivation?

Webster's Dictionary defines motivation as the condition of being motivated; an incentive or drive. How do we apply this to ourselves? Let's think for a moment about ourselves.

How many brain cells do you have?

Hint: A lot more than you think!

You have 13 billion brain cells. Do you feel smarter already? One thing you should be thinking about right now is how to use these 13 billion cells to their fullest potential. In this book you will be able to find several effective ways to learn; ways that are the best for *you*.

Let's imagine that we have an assembled computer sitting in front of us. This computer contains one million parts.

What is the first thing we would need to do in order to use it?

Hint: Think electricity.

O.K., we should plug it in to the electrical outlet. What do we need to make *our* 13 billion part computer work? Our electric current is called *motivation*. Motivation is what makes learning come alive!

What Is Your Source of Motivation?

Our source of motivation is human needs. The psychologist Abraham Maslow believed that all human beings have a need to grow, to develop abilities, to be recognized, and to achieve. He viewed human needs in hierarchical order. Some needs take precedence over others. We need to satisfy the lower needs in order to achieve the higher ones (see Figure 1). If we don't take care of our fundamental needs which are our basic physiological needs (hunger, thirst, sex) and our need to feel safe, then we have difficulty proceeding to the next level which involves our psychological needs. These in turn need to be fulfilled in order to reach the top which is our self-actualization needs. For self-actualized persons, problems become a means for growth. Wouldn't it be nice to view problems in this manner?

What Is the Difference between External and Internal Motivation?

1. *Internal Motivation*—These are motivational elements that are within ourselves. We have feelings of pleasure or disgust as we meet or fail to meet our own standards. This is the reinforcement level we should all strive to meet. We should try to find value in our work, enjoy success, develop an appropriate value system, and thereby reinforce ourselves for our efforts. People differ in what they think provides reinforcement.

2. *External Motivation*—These are motivational elements that come from outside stimuli. Rewards in the form of material things, privileges, recognition, trophies, praise, or friendship. These are a "public" way of saying a job is well done.

Critical Thinking

Todd felt he had prepared for his first major exam in geology. Science was difficult for him. He had attended all lectures, revised his notes, and read the chapters. He made an appointment with his professor to clarify some points that he didn't understand. He felt he was ready for the exam. When Dr. Jones returned the test, Todd had scored 94%. The reward of the high score was a real high! He felt successful, and knew he could continue to do well in this course. He called his parents that night and they were elated. Their praise echoed their feelings. Todd had received internal and external praise. Do you believe the external or the internal motivation that he received from the test score was the best motivator?

As you progress through school, internal motivators should become stronger. We should not always feel the need for external motivation. This doesn't mean we don't want external rewards, but its value should begin to lessen.

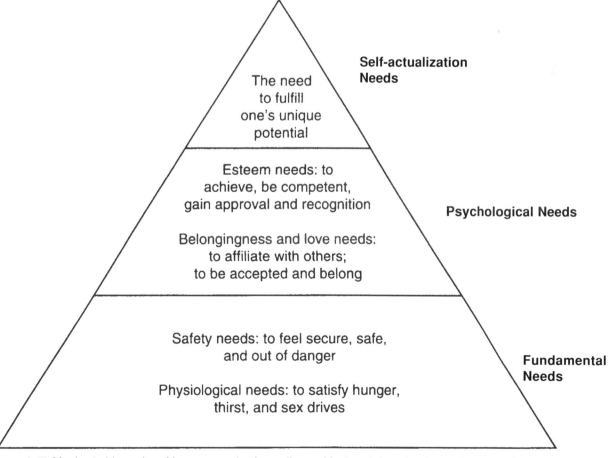

Figure 1 ■ Maslow's hierarchy of human needs. According to Maslow, it is only after satisfying the lower levels of need that a person is free to progress to the ultimate need of self-actualization.

■ What Are Your Goals?

Motivation is the first step in all goals. A goal should be something that you desire and that you will be motivated enough to try and reach.

Goals can be divided into three categories:

1. *Personal*—These will be determined by your value system. You have already filled out the Value exercise. This should give you an idea of what you feel is important to you. Personal goals can also include personal fitness, developing a positive attitude, and overcoming a bad habit.

2. *Academic*—You can be successful if you set your goals on what *you* want to get out of college. The exercise on reasons to attend college should also include some academic goals.

3. *Work Related*—What do you want from your chosen field of work? Improving your performance? Changing jobs? Learning new skills?

Why Do You Need Short-term and Long-term Goals?

It is necessary to have short-term and long-term goals. It is easy to lose motivation with only long-term goals. Short-term goals are necessary to act as our motivational elements. The accomplishment of these goals give us the will to succeed. Long-term goals clarify our direction.

What Are Some Important Characteristics of Goals?

There are four characteristics of goals that we will discuss. While you are reading about these characteristics, think about how you can apply these points to your life.

1. *Goals should be realistic*—A realistic goal is one you can reasonably expect to achieve given your abilities. If your goal is too high and you don't reach it, it can certainly affect your self-concept. If your goal is too low, when you attain this goal there is no real feeling of success.

   Amy attained a 3.0 (out of a 4.0) in high school. Her college goal was to attain a 3.0 average. Is this a realistic goal? Is Amy setting herself up for failure, or is this a possible goal?

   Bill was valedictorian of his graduating class. His goal in college was to maintain a C average. His goal was not high enough to give him the sense of accomplishment that he would need to make him feel successful.

2. *Goals should be measurable*—A measurable goal establishes a time frame and it also has a foreseeable outcome. You should have daily and weekly goals. Attaining these short-term goals will give you the successful feeling that you need to experience to keep you going. Semester, yearly, and other long-term goals (college degree, marriage, family) are also vital because they clarify your direction.

3. *Goals should be flexible*—Decide what you want to do and be willing to change your plans if necessary. Rarely do we set goals and follow through to completion without any problems. You might change your major, withdraw from a class, or experience any number of setbacks. Reassess your plan for reaching your goal. You might

---

Critical Thinking

Your long-term goal is to be a lawyer. Is that enough to motivate you to attend and be excited about the basic psychology class that you have at 8:00 a.m. on Monday, Wednesday, and Friday? Maybe at first, but as the semester rolls along there will be mornings that being a lawyer doesn't quite have the zip that it once did. The short-term goal of making a B in psychology that will complete three hours of general education requirements just might! (Hopefully your short-term goal will be to learn as much as you can about human behavior so you can effectively deal with people in your law practice.) It will help you to have a goal that you can accomplish in a short period of time to serve as an inspiration. An even better short-term goal would be to make a B on the first exam. Once this is accomplished, hopefully the adrenaline will flow!

---

need to revise it or make a new plan. It's alright to change your goals if you make a mistake or decide to change your plans.

4. *Goals should be specific*—The purpose of goals is to make us "act." In order for a goal to activate us, we must have specific objectives in mind. If we are too vague, we never receive the satisfaction of success that we should feel when we attain the goal.

Nancy's goal this semester is to attain a 3.0 grade point average. Peggy's goal this semester is to "do well" in her classes. Who will receive the greater satisfaction if they attain their goal? Who will know if their goal is met?

Goals do not have to be major events. Your goal for today may include:

Pick up cleaning
Read Chapter 3 in sociology
Do math problems 2.1 through 2.6
Clean the bathroom

These are specific goals. You will know at the end of the day if you have attained them. These are much more motivating than:

Run errands
Study
Catch up on housework

Is There a Relationship between Setting Goals and Academic Success?

After what we have learned to recognize about goals, this is an easy question to answer—Yes—Yes—Yes. Goals are activators, they provide a successful background that enables you to continue to strive. They are like gas to a car, food to our bodies, and rain to the grass.

The attainment of goals is also related to a positive attitude and high self-esteem. When we attain goals, we feel successful!

■ How Can You Develop a Positive Attitude?

Visualize yourself being successful. Jeni Burnett, a Pittsburgh State University basketball player, relates her success technique at the free throw line:

First of all, I block out the crowd noise. I dribble a couple of times and feel the ball. During this time I visualize my entire body. I think about my legs bent properly, my arms' and hands' position, my release, the ball being "up," the correct spin, the right arch, my follow-through. I see the ball "swish" the net.

It is amazing how powerful positive thinking can be! It is also very contagious. Of course, negative thinking is also contagious. It is unbelievable how a "down" person can pull others "down" with them. We all know some people that constantly dwell on the negative side of life. They sometimes do not even realize it—it has become a way of life.

Fred woke up with a headache. He had worked a double shift the previous day. His roommate, Jim, was on his way out the door to class. Jim had actually read his history chapter and he hoped it would help him take better notes. Fred noticed it was raining; he had worked a double shift the previous day. He rolled over and muttered that he wasn't going to fight the rain to listen to Dr. Smith's boring biology lecture. It was annoying enough that he had a headache. He could have gotten the notes from Sue, but he recalled after his remark about her sweater that she probably wouldn't share her notes. He told Jim that he couldn't understand why teachers always seem to enjoy frustrating students. There had to be more to life. Jim walked out the door to go to class. He was beginning to wonder why he got out of bed today.

■ What about That Negative Voice?

Should we look at the negative side of a situation? We don't like to because being a "positive" person is crucial to our success. We also need to be realistic (unfortunately or fortunately—life is "real"). What are you going to do if you fail the first test in one of your classes? That is a possibility (distant, of course). What will your plan be? Inside we have two voices that are always screaming to get out of us. One is a positive voice, the other is the dreaded negative voice. Unfortunately, the voice seems to have more volume at the most inopportune times.

Jane came to college from a large high school. She took college prep classes and maintained a B average. She was active in a lot of social activities in her high school. Studying was a concern, but certainly not a major one. She kept up in her classes with very little effort. Jane came to college and since she had experienced success in high school with very little effort, why should this change? The social scene was important to her in college (that's o.k.) and she knew everything would just fall in place. In sociology and biology her first exams fell on the same day. (Don't teachers ever get together and try to avoid this?) The night before the tests (as in high school), Jane sat down and started digging. "Surely, I won't need to know all of this, so I'll concentrate on my notes," she rationalized. "The notes are obviously what the teachers will think is important. After all, that is what they talked about!" A lot of the information didn't seem that vital, so Jane picked out what she thought would be on the tests. About midnight, after telling at least twelve of her friends how hard she was studying, she was ready to call it a night. After all, her biology test was at 11:00 and her sociology was at 1:00. There was a mild panic at 9:30 the next morning when she realized she had slept through her alarm. But, not to worry, she had plenty of time to shower and review once more. Food could wait until lunch.

The biology test was given to the class. How could it be that many pages? Where did he come up with these questions? She found a lot of questions that she thought she knew, but the wording was ridiculous! What a relief when that was finished! On for a quick lunch and the sociology test.

She thought, "These teachers must get together and decide to ask weird questions." She wondered if there was an upper level education class for teachers that taught them to ask sneaky questions. "Why don't they ask questions that come directly from the book? After all, they wanted us to read it."—were two thoughts that Jane had. Jane definitely needed a nap after these two tests. She wasn't very concerned until the tests were handed back. There must be a mistake! She had never made a D in her life! How could she have made a D on both exams? She quickly folded back the corner of the tests so no one could see. What voices were screaming to be heard?

This could and might very well happen to you. It's not important that it happened, but it's how you are going to react that is important. You can turn this experience into a productive event. Before you throw this book in the trash, let's analyze the situation. Which voices will be dominant?

"I'm not smart enough to be here!"
"The teacher is a jerk—he didn't cover this!"
"He tried to trick us!"
"I hate this class!"
"At least I did better than Sally."
"I didn't really understand, I just memorized."
"I could have used the book to help me understand the notes."
"Now I know the type of questions that he asks."

High school students are usually concerned with the "literal" meaning of their textbooks. This means they are interested in the exact meaning—the words that are obviously stated. In college it is important to have an understanding of the material so you can *apply* the information. Concepts or ideas should be the result of studying your text. Maybe this means one of our *goals* should be the understanding of what the author is trying to say along with your teacher's interpretation. What do you think?

■ Summary

It is important to think about *why* you are attending college. You should recognize your values and goals because they clarify your direction. Your motivation is directly related to achieving your goals. Success in our endeavors strengthens our will to succeed.

A good positive attitude is vital in achieving success in college as well as in life!

■ Exercise 2. Values

In the first column check 10 of the values that are most important to you. In the second column, rank from 1–10 the order of priority of these 10 values.

A world without prejudice	_____	_____
A satisfying and fulfilling marriage	_____	_____
Lifetime financial security	_____	_____
A really good love relationship	_____	_____
Unlimited travel opportunities	_____	_____
A complete library for your use	_____	_____
A lovely home in a beautiful setting	_____	_____
A happy family relationship	_____	_____
Good self-esteem	_____	_____
Freedom to do what you want	_____	_____
An understanding of the meaning of life	_____	_____
Success in your chosen profession	_____	_____
A peaceful world	_____	_____
Recognition as the most attractive person in the world	_____	_____
A satisfying religious faith	_____	_____
Freedom within your work setting	_____	_____
Tickets and travel to any cultural or athletic event as often as you wish	_____	_____
The love and admiration of friends	_____	_____
A chance to direct the destinies of a nation	_____	_____
International fame and popularity	_____	_____
The ability to eliminate sickness and poverty	_____	_____
A month's vacation with nothing to do but enjoy yourself	_____	_____

Write a brief paragraph describing what goals you are setting for yourself that reflects your top value choices.

_____

_____

_____

_____

_____

_____

_____

_____

_____

Exercise 3. The Coat of Arms

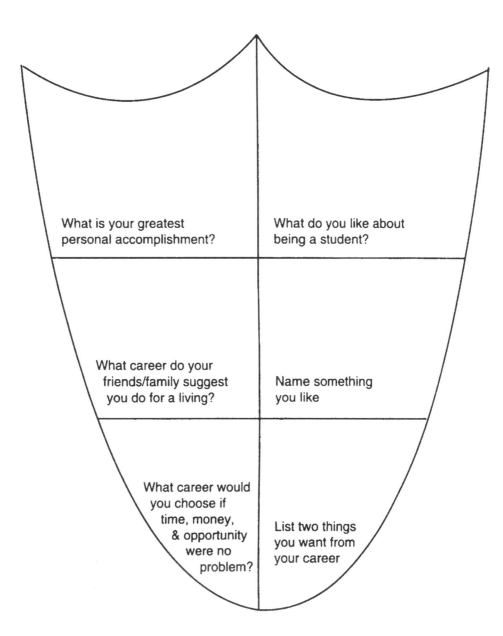

What is your greatest
personal accomplishment?

What do you like about
being a student?

What career do your
friends/family suggest
you do for a living?

Name something
you like

What career would
you choose if
time, money,
& opportunity
were no
problem?

List two things
you want from
your career

◼ Exercise 5. External or Internal Motivation?

Considering your experience in classes that you have taken, what has motivated ⟩ u to learn, to work, to achieve?

In the first column, put a check mark if the experience has been used to motivate ⟩u. In the second column, decide whether the motivation was *E* (external motivation) or *I* (ernal motivation).

_____ _____   1. Teacher paying attention to me

_____ _____   2. Not wanting to disappoint the teacher

_____ _____   3. Getting on the honor roll

_____ _____   4. Getting a job in the future

_____ _____   5. Wanting to learn and understand

_____ _____   6. Parents caring about me

_____ _____   7. Teacher caring about me

_____ _____   8. My satisfaction from receiving a high grade on an exam

_____ _____   9. Not wanting to disappoint parents

_____ _____   10. Being praised by classmates

_____ _____   11. Finally figuring out the correct answer

_____ _____   12. Putting words together that became concepts that mad ense

_____ _____   13. Helping other students

_____ _____   14. Pleasing my family

List below the latest internal motivator that you have experienced.

_____

List below the latest external motivator that you have experienced.

_____

Write a brief paragraph describing how you feel you became motivated. Do internal or external motivation factors seem to be the most important? Do you feel motivated at this time of your life? Why?

_____

_____

_____

_____

_____

_____

_____

_____

_____

_____

CHAPTER 3
Connecting Common Threads Across a Diverse World

We live in an increasingly complex world that requ.. es us to be adept in many life-skills (interpersonal communication/human ..ations, problem solving/decision making, physical fitness/health main¹ ..ance, and identity development/purpose-in-life). In a pluralistic society differences ..ist among and between various groups of people (e.g., ethnic, racial, religious, gende. .exual orientation, physical, and other groupings). While living in a pluralistic society ..n create tension as various groups attempt to sustain and develop their traditional c ..ure or special interests within the confines of a common society, the experience can ..o create a rich source of energy that can fuel the creative potential of a society and a.. ance it culturally and democratically. To fully develop as a person requires one to b. .ware of both the common threads that hold people together as a community, a natic ., and a world and the unique threads of various hues and textures that complete the ..apestry called humanity. It takes a multitude of skills to negotiate a diverse world.

■ Multiculturalism

*If we are to achieve a richer culture, rich in contrasting values, we must recognize
the whole gamut of human potentialities, and so weave a less arbitrary social fabric,
one in which each diverse human gift will find a fitting place.*

—Margaret Mead

Multiculturalism is a philosophical belief based on ideals of social justice and equity that recognizes not only that diversity does exist but that it is a valuable resource in a community. Proponents of multiculturalism believe that it is to each and every person's advantage to acquire a set of skills, knowledge, and beliefs about diversity. These life-skills are needed individually to help us achieve success in a multicultural world and collectively to move our society beyond a toleration of differences among people to a respect for cultural pluralism.

Multiculturalism challenges us to recognize multiple perspectives, and in doing so, we enhance our problem-solving and critical-thinking skills. While adopting a multicultural perspective can prepare us to live in a multicultural world, it can also create discomfort, fear, denial, guilt, and anger during the process. People often believe that their own standards are the right standards; this view is known as *ethnocentricity*. When you have different groups of people living close to one another, and each group is functioning quite well by its own set of standards, conflict can arise as groups try to figure out what set of standards is right for the society as a whole.

College administrators understand that change is inevitable and recognize the value of a multicultural education in helping students to develop multicultural competencies. College campuses are a part of this multicultural world, and many colleges require students to take a multicultural class and, in addition, offer multidisciplinary programs (e.g., women's studies and African studies). Activities that challenge your mind expand the number and strength of neural connections that learning is based on. Engaging in activities that are unfamiliar or different (e.g., talking with people from cultures different from your own and engaging in diverse cultural experiences) helps to create a more complex system of thoughts, perceptions, assumptions, attitudes, feelings, and skills that can lead to a greater learning potential.

Manning Marable (2000) informs us that the racial composition of the United States is based on immigration, and that about a third of the total growth rate in the U.S. labor force is supplied by legal and illegal immigration. Pragmatically, students as well as others need to learn how to deal with diversity because the world in which we live is becoming more diverse. It is inevitable that among your neighbors, teachers, fellow students, coworkers, friends, and teammates will be individuals with backgrounds quite different from your own. You will need effective interpersonal skills to interact with these people. As a college student, you are in a unique learning situation that offers numerous opportunities to increase your diversity skills. If you have not formed relationships with people who have dissimilar backgrounds from you, now is your chance. People who ignore or resist opportunities may find themselves both vocationally and personally deficient in a global, multicultural society.

■ Demographic Changes

The U.S. Census Bureau reported that in 2000 there were an estimated 281,421,906 million people living in the United States, an increase of 32.7 million people since the 1990 census. About 75.1 identified themselves as white only (down from 83% in 1990), 12.3% were black or African American only (down from 13% in 1990), 3.6% were Asian and Pacific American only, .9% were American Indian and Alaskan native only, and .1% were native Hawaiian and other Pacific Islander only. In addition, 5.5% identified themselves as some other race only, and about 2.4% selected more than one category. In response to a separate question on the census about ethnicity, 13% identified themselves as Hispanic or Latino, who may be of any race (up from 11% in 1990). The Hispanic or Latino population rose 58% since 1990 (from 22.4 million to 35.3 million). Projections for the year 2050 are that the percentage of white people living in the United States will continue to decline and the percentage of current minorities will increase. The Hispanic or Latino population will show the largest increase (24%) followed by African Americans (15%). Today, most immigrants in this country come from Latin America, followed by Asia, and most immigrants settle in the western and southern parts of our nation. Some cities like Miami, where more than 59% of the population is foreign born, are more diverse than other cities.

Along with racial and ethnic demographic shifts there have been dramatic changes related to gender and age. Females (143,368,000) outnumbered males (138,054,000) in the United States in 2000, and women and minorities were identified as the largest groups of people to enter the work force. The *World Almanac* (2002) refers to the United States as an "aging nation" with a median age of 35.3, the highest ever reported. In 2000, it was estimated that there were about 4.2 million (1.5% of the total population) Americans 85 years or older and about 50,454 centenarians (people aged 100 and older) living in the United States. Centenarians have increased 35% in numbers since 1990. The 2000 census identified South Dakota, Iowa, and the District of Columbia as the states having the largest percentage of centenarians among their populations. What do you think accounts for such longevity? Researchers are looking for the answers as you read this.

Unfortunately, with the rise in diversity has also come a rise in the number of incidents related to prejudice and discrimination. According to the National Institute against Prejudice and Violence (NIAPV), more than 250 of the nation's 3,300 colleges and universities have reported acts of violence against people due to their ethnicity since mid-1986. Additionally, many more incidents on many campuses have gone unreported (Kendall/ Hunt, 1999).

■ Living in a Pluralistic Society

Two primary goals of a college education are to help you develop life-long skills for continuous personal growth and to be a responsible community member. Today's college students do not believe that there are any quick fixes for our nation's social problems. One of the biggest social problems facing college students today on college campuses throughout the United States is racism. Racism is a form of discrimination based on biased assumptions about what people are and are not. It is a powerful force throughout the nation, weaving in and out of cultures, institutions, and individuals. Racism, ableism, sexism, heterosexism, ageism, and classism are all powerful discriminatory forces. These isms have the power to include, exclude, legitimize, and marginalize groups of people. Assumptions about what people are and are not enable prejudices and discrimination to flourish.

Throughout the world, countries are becoming more pluralistic. Diversity encompasses differences in educational level, gender, ethnicity, race, age, sexual orientation, religion, socioeconomic level, and physical ability. In the last 25 years there has been a dramatic shift in population trends in the United States, and the demographics of this country will continue to shift. The pluralities and complexities that exist between and among groups of people will also continue to change as differences in language, politics, regional differences, social class, religion and nationality further subdivide groups. Marable (2000) calls for a new and critical study of race and ethnicity to understand the changes that are taking place around us. He believes that one of the reasons that discussions about race and social diversity are so difficult is the complicated relationship between ethnicity and race.

■ Terminology

The terminology associated with multiculturalism is continually changing to more accurately reflect changing attitudes about diversity. Currently you will read about "people of color" rather than nonwhites; gays, lesbians, and bisexuals rather than homosexuals; and people with disabilities rather than disabled or handicapped. Even though many people, through a process like stereotyping, choose to define you rather narrowly, most people choose to define themselves in broad, diverse categories. What comes to mind when you think of a nontraditional student? A fraternity member? A gay student? A Hispanic or Latino student? An Asian student? A student with disabilities? Culture refers to a way of being, the way we define ourselves. If someone asks you to define your culture, you might choose a narrow definition and respond that you are Catholic, Baptist, American, or German. You might also choose a broader definition of culture and respond that you are a musician, a Southerner, an athlete, or a member of a sorority.

What about race? Is it a social concept used to discriminate against groups of people or is it a biological/genetic concept? There is a lot of controversy in the literature about the definition of race. Pedersen (1994) defines race as "a pseudobiological system of classifying persons by a shared genetic history or physical characteristics such as skin color" (p. x). Race is a topic that people struggle to talk about with one another. Talking about race can be especially challenging due to the political and emotional misapplications of the term. For the first time in the history of the census, respondents in 2000 were given the choice of selecting one or more race categories to identify their racial identity. About 2.4% (6.8 million) of the total population chose more than one category of race. Questions about being Hispanic or Latino were designated a separate category. As pointed out previously, there is often more diversity within a group of people who are regarded as having similar characteristics than there is between different groups.

Ethnicity exists within the broader category of race. Ethnic groups such as Japanese, Cambodian, Chinese, Korean, Filipino, Vietnamese, and Pacific Islander fall under the racial umbrella of Asian. Hispanics, or Latinos, as some people prefer, are Spanish-speaking people. Some Hispanic people may be from Puerto Rico, the Dominican Republic, Mexico, Cuba, Colombia, or Argentina. Hispanics are a very diverse group with varied customs, food, cultural patterns, and politics. People who refer to themself as black might look to Africa, Haiti, Jamaica, or the West Indies for their cultural heritage. People who identify with having a white ethnic background may look to Poland, Australia, Italy, Africa, Ireland, or Germany. Among the American Indian and Alaska native population, you will also find a multiplicity of cultural patterns.

What is your ethnicity? Exercise 1 at the end of this chapter is designed to help you to get in touch with your ethnic heritage. This exercise may be difficult for some of you whose relatives have moved away from the family's historical roots to assimilate into American culture. It may take some phone calls and digging to put your heritage into an ethnic perspective. Before you read about suggestions for developing multicultural competencies, in the next section, take a moment to become familiar with some of the terms associated with diversity and multiculturalism.

ableism	prejudice or discrimination against people with mental, emotional, and physical disabilities
ageism	prejudice or discrimination based on age
anti-Semitism	hostility toward Jewish people
classism	prejudice or discrimination based on economic background
culture	group of people bound together by traditions (food, language, religion) and values
discrimination	an action or policy that differentiates one group from another in terms of treatment
ethnocentrism	a belief that one's own culture is more correct or superior
homophobia	an irrational fear of gays, lesbians, or bisexuals
prejudice	preconceived opinion for or against someone or something
privilege	unearned access to resources due to membership in a particular social group
racism	discrimination based on skin color and ethnicity; a belief that a particular race is superior or inferior
sexism	prejudice or discrimination based on gender
stereotyping	overgeneralizing about groups of people based on biased assumptions

■ Developing Multicultural Competencies

We know that our attitudes and beliefs influence our perceptions. We assimilate attitudes and beliefs throughout our lives, forming assumptions about the way things are and are not, including judgments about people. Unfortunately, we tend to filter out information that does not affirm, or align with, our perception of the world, so we tend to rely on many biased assumptions to guide us through life. Biased assumptions distort the truth and give rise to prejudices that keep us confined in narrowly defined spaces. Is there any way for us to get out of our own little boxes to see what is truly going on around us? The answer is, emphatically, yes! Biases can be intentional or unintentional. They might be based on cultural isolation or ignorance. When you form a belief about an entire group of people without recognizing individual differences among members of the group, you are engaging in *stereotyping*.

We are all guilty of stereotyping because of the way in which the mind stores, organizes, and recalls information to reduce complexity and help us make quick decisions (Johnson & Johnson, 2000). Johnson and Johnson report that the term stereotype was initially used in the eighteenth century to describe a printing process that duplicated pages of type. According to Johnson and Johnson (2000) it was not until 1922 that Walter Lippman used the term to describe the process by which people gloss over details to simplify social perceptions. We tend to stereotype people to whom we do not pay much attention. The practice of stereotyping can lead to prejudice, which can lead to discrimination. Why does it endure? Read over the reasons given in Table 1.

What can you do to overcome biases that cloud your perceptions and create distortions? How do you move beyond intolerance and prejudice? These are questions that have no easy answers. Examining your own attitudes, becoming more aware of other cultures, and developing a multicultural view that will help you communicate, appreciate, and respect people from diverse backgrounds are steps in the right direction.

Table 1. Reasons Why Stereotypes Endure

1. People tend to overestimate the association between variables that are only slightly correlated or not correlated at all creating an **illusionary correlation**. Many people for example, perceive that being poor and being lazy are associated. Any poor person who is not hard at work at the moment you notice him or her may be perceived to be lazy. Low-power groups can easily acquire negative traits in this way, and once acquired, the stereotype is hard to shed.

2. Having a prejudice makes people notice the negative traits they ascribe to the groups they are prejudiced against, and they more readily believe information that confirms the stereotypes than evidence that challenges them. People tend to process information in ways that verify existing beliefs. This tendency to seek, interpret, and create information that verifies existing beliefs is known as the **confirmation bias**.

3. People have a **false consensus bias** when they believe that most other people share their stereotypes. They tend to see their own behaviors and judgments as quite common and appropriate, and to view alternative responses as uncommon and often inappropriate.

4. Stereotypes tend to be **self-fulfilling**. Stereotypes can subtly influence intergroup interactions in such a way that the stereotype is behaviorally confirmed. People may behave in ways that elicit the actions they expect from out-group members, thus confirming the stereotype.

5. People often dismiss individuals who do not match a stereotype as exceptions to the rule or representatives of a subcategory.

6. Stereotypes often operate at an implicit level below people's conscious awareness.

7. People often develop a rationale and explanation to justify their stereotypes and prejudices.

Source: Johnson, D., & Johnson, F. (2000). *Joining Together.* Boston: Allyn and Bacon. Adapted and reprinted with permission

Examine Your Attitudes

Your culture surrounds you. Culture influences the way you think, feel, and behave. Identities are forged within the cultural context in which you live. Society, the larger culture in which you live, sends both positive and negative messages about the self. Unconscious or conscious beliefs about the way you are suppose to be can create a great deal of pain for those who are excluded and marginalized by the majority members of society. If while you were growing up you received a constant stream of negative messages that you were not okay because your cultural rules were different from those in the dominant culture, you may have internalized feelings that you are not okay. Prejudice has a negative impact on the process of identity formation. Examine some of your own prejudices by answering the following questions.

◼ Activity

Assessing Cultural Influences

1. When were you first aware of differences among people?

2. When did you become aware of your own racial/ethnic heritage?

3. When did you first experience some form of prejudice? Do you remember your thoughts and feelings?

4. When did you become aware that you had certain privileges, or that you were denied privileges, based on your physical characteristics, socioeconomic background, or ability level?

5. How have others stereotyped you or members of your family?

6. What kinds of messages did you receive as a child that you were inferior or superior to others? Who or what sent these messages?

Attitudes can create barriers to interacting with people from diverse backgrounds. When you see someone walking toward you, what do you tend to notice? Gender? Weight? Skin color? Clothing? Hair? What kinds of assumptions do you make based on your observations? Student? Sorority girl? Nontraditional student? Professor? Athlete? Foreigner? Finally, what assumptions do you make about each kind of person? We all assume things about people. Just remember that your assumptions are often incorrect. Prejudice is a learned habit, and it takes a conscious effort to break it.

Sources of Prejudice

Where do these prejudices come from? They come from a variety of sources.

Economic competitiveness and scapegoating. Scapegoating is the process of displacing aggression or projecting guilt onto a group of people. When the economy is bad, accusations like "Those immigrants are taking away all our jobs" increase in frequency. Political candidates sometimes appeal to prejudices among voters. They may scapegoat immigrants, for example, in an effort to win votes from those who feel disempowered or frustrated with the economy.

Parents and Relatives. What messages did your parents send about other people? When you were young and found yourself near a person in a wheelchair, what messages did you receive about how to behave? Did you observe the adult look away or maybe address the person accompanying the person with the disability rather than communicating directly with the person who was disabled? What about when you asked a parent if a friend who was from another socioeconomic or cultural group could come home with you or if you could go to his or her house? Messages can be overt or covert. The effect is the same. When negative messages are attached to differences between people, prejudice takes root.

Institutions. Prejudice is learned through living in a society where prejudices are sustained. Who received the most privileges in your school? Did the gifted students get to engage in more creative learning situations than the other students? What about overweight children in your school? How were they treated? Who participated in sports and organizations with you? Were accommodations made for someone who was mentally or physically disabled? As a child, were you ever conscious of the fact that all U.S. presidents have been white males?

Media. What kinds of messages do you receive from magazines, movies, and television? What prejudices are perpetuated in the media? What groups of people are stereotyped? What types of misinformation about certain groups of people are broadcast? When you watch television or go to a movie, how are women depicted? How often are they depicted as sex symbols? Stereotyping is based on ignorance. Have you heard any disparaging remarks about others lately through the media? What about jokes about religion, sexual orientation, skin color, or weight?

Social Fragmentation. Levine and Cureton (1998) found that undergraduate students across the country described themselves more in terms of differences than similarities. Their study also revealed that students today are more socially isolated than previous generations; increasingly, they voluntarily segregate themselves to form small self-interest groups. Look around you. Gaps between socioeconomic groups in this country seem to be widening.

The sources that fuel prejudice come together to create a powerful, destructive force that can lead to discrimination and even violence. The number of reported incidents of prejudice and discrimination are reported to be on the rise throughout the country. The Anti-

Defamation League and the National Institute Against Prejudice and Violence (NIAPV) record and report incidents of prejudice, discrimination, and hate crimes. The brutal murders of Matthew Shepard, a gay, white man who was a student at the University of Wyoming, and James Byrd, Jr., a black man who was chained to the back of a pickup truck and dragged to his death, outraged the country. Yet *Life* magazine reported that at Matthew Shepard's funeral, a protestor appeared with a sign that read "God hates fags."

The Power of Prejudice

Ableism. Joy Weeber (1999), a person with a disability, has written about being discriminated against and described how painful it is. She wrote that her pain was caused by unconscious beliefs of a society that assume that everyone is, or should be, normal, . . . "capable of total independence and pulling themselves up by their own bootstraps'" (p. 21). She defined ableism as a form of prejudice and bigotry that has as its core a belief in the superiority of being nondisabled and an assumption that those who are disabled wished they could be nondisabled—at any cost.

Laura Rauscher and Mary McClintock (1998) offer the following comments to help educate people about disability and oppression.

- Disability is not inherently negative.
- Becoming disabled involves major life changes including loss as well as gain, but it is not the end of a meaningful and productive existence.
- People with disabilities experience discrimination, segregation, and isolation as a result of other people's prejudice and institutional ableism, not because of the disability itself.
- Social beliefs, cultural norms, and media images about beauty, intelligence, physical ability, communication, and behavior often negatively influence the way people with disabilities are treated.
- Societal expectations about economic productivity and self-sufficiency devalue persons who are not able to work, regardless of other contributions they may make to family and community life.
- Without positive messages about who they are, persons with disabilities are vulnerable to internalizing society's negative messages about disability.
- Independence and dependence are relative concepts, subject to personal definition, something every person experiences, and neither is inherently positive or negative.
- The right of people with disabilities to inclusion in the mainstream of our society is now protected by law, yet they are still not treated as full and equal citizens.

Hetcrosexism. Heterosexism is the belief that heterosexuality is the only acceptable sexual orientation. In recent years in the United States, there has been increased visibility, via news coverage, movies, advertisements, and television, of gay, lesbian, and bisexual people. Pat Griffin and Bobbie Harro (1997) point out that despite the increased visibility, most Americans continue to have contradictory feelings about gay, lesbian, and bisexual people, and that educators have been uncommonly reluctant to address the issue of homophobia in the schools. Silence about issues that minimize particular groups of people can have devastating effects. The Department of Health and Human Services Report on teen suicide (1989) indicated that lesbian, gay, and bisexual young people are two to three times more likely to commit suicide. Prejudice and discrimination are powerful forces that isolate and marginalize people in society. The first step to getting beyond prejudice and intolerance is to examine your own attitudes and beliefs about people. The second step is to develop an awareness of other cultures.

Developing an Awareness of Other Cultures. Educate yourself about issues related to multiculturalism. Make an effort to get to know people from dissimilar backgrounds. Your college probably hosts a variety of cultural events throughout the year. Many international student organizations sponsor cultural nights, which students and the community are invited to attend. Discover when they are and make a commitment to be there. Develop an open mind, like an anthropologist observing other cultures. As you begin to observe other cultures, be aware of your own cultural filters.

Colleges offer opportunities to study abroad. If your college does not offer a study program in a country you wish to visit, check with other colleges and see what they have to offer. Immerse yourself in different cultures. Ask lots of questions. Learn about different international organizations on campus and in your community. Also check with your local Chamber of Commerce for local cultural celebrations.

You can also educate yourself about other cultures by watching videos. Try renting some international movies the next time you pick up a video at your local video rental store. Having to read subtitles cannot be used as an excuse! Your aim is to become more immersed in another culture. You might also try attending a different place of worship or interviewing other students about their experiences living in a different culture. The more personal information you have about another person or another culture, the less likely you are to stereotype that person or culture.

Developing a Multicultural View

Developing a multicultural view requires the motivation to develop better diversity skills to interact with a wider range of people. For some people, the motivation to become multiculturally competent arises from a desire to become a social change agent in the community by helping other people develop more tolerant attitudes. Some people view this as a way of supporting their country, since democracy is a system based on mutual respect and equality of rights. There are things you can do to help build a healthier approach to living in a multicultural society.

Develop good critical-thinking skills. Learn to think through your assumptions about different groups of people. Remember that your assumptions are based on your experiences. Since your experiences are necessarily limited, your assumptions are going to have many biases where you filled in the gaps. The process of critical thinking can help you get beyond preconceived notions that have been formulated over the years and see the truth.

Part of the process of developing good critical thinking skills is becoming aware of the influence you have on other people. Starting with yourself, think of how you influence friends and family, people at work and school, and your community. What actions could you implement within each one of these spheres to combat sexism, racism, ableism, and other discriminatory isms? Complete Exercise 4 at the end of this chapter to identify some of those spheres of influence. How can you change your environment to encourage a multicultural view of the world?

Educate others about laws and policies. There are campus policies and laws to deal with acts of bigotry and discrimination. Become familiar with them. What kind of sexual harassment policy does your college or university enforce? In 1990 the Americans with Disabilities Act (ADA), a civil rights act for people with disabilities, passed into law. It states that all public facilities, including colleges, are required by law to make a serious effort to provide barrier-free access to all persons with disabilities. When you are eating out in a restaurant, do you ever wonder whether or not the restaurant you are dining in is accessible to all? Many restaurants and public places are not. How does your college respond to incidents of bigotry? Bigotry can appear in many forms: graffiti, physical violence, written and spoken remarks, and privileges. What about invited or uninvited outside speakers who come to campus to speak with students? Should a student newspaper be allowed to run an advertisement that provides misinformation about a group of people and promotes racism, sexism, anti-Semitism, or any other form of intolerance? What about running a cartoon that is demeaning to people with disabilities in a campus, local, or national newspaper?

The issue of political correctness (PC) has been debated on campuses and throughout society. Pedersen (1994) states, "Philosophically, PC means the subordination of the right to free speech to the right of guaranteeing equal protection under the law. The PC position contends that an absolutist position on the First Amendment (that you may slur anyone you choose) imposes a hostile environment for minorities and violates their right to equal education. Promotion of diversity is one of the central tenets of PC" (p. 5). Are you an advocate or proponent of PC? Why? Or why not?

■ References

Barron, W. G. (2002). United States population: Census 2000—The results start rolling in. In W. A. McGeveran (Ed.), *The world almanac and book of facts 2002* (pp. 374–385). New York: World Almanac Books.

Glauser, A. (1999). Legacies of racism. *Journal of Counseling & Development, 77,* 62–67.

Goodman, D., & Schapiro, S. (1997). Sexism curriculum design. In Adams, M., Bell, L., & Griffin, P. (Eds.). *Teaching for diversity and social justice: A sourcebook* (pp. 110–140). New York: Routledge.

Griffin, P. & Harro, B. (1997). Heterosexism curriculum design. In Adams, M., Bell, L., & Griffin, P. (Eds.). *Teaching for diversity and social justice: A sourcebook* (pp. 141–169). New York: Routledge.

Johnson, D., & Johnson, F. (2000). *Joining together.* Boston: Allyn and Bacon.

Kendall Hunt Publishing Company (1999). *First-year experience sourcebook.* Dubuque, IA: Author.

Levine, A., & Cureton, J. S. (1998). *When hope and fear collide.* San Francisco: Jossey-Bass.

Life: The year in pictures, 1998. (1999). New York: Time.

Marable, M. (2000, February 25, 2000). We need new and critical study of race and ethnicity. *Chronicle of Higher Education,* B4–B7.

Pedersen, P. (1994). *A handbook for developing multicultural awareness.* Alexandria, VA: American Counseling Association.

Princeton Language Institute. (1993). *Twenty-first century dictionary of quotations.* New York: Dell.

Rauscher, L., & McClintock, M. (1997). Ableism curriculum design. In Adams, M., Bell., L., & Griffin, P. (Eds.). *Teaching for diversity and social justice: A sourcebook* (pp. 198–230). New York: Routledge.

U.S. Department of Health and Human Services. (1989). *Report of the Secretary's Task Force on Youth Suicide.* Rockville, MD: Author.

Weeber, J. E. (1999). What could I know of racism? *Journal of Counseling & Development, 77,* 20–23.

Wijeyesinghe, C. L., Griffin, P., & Love, B. (1997). Racism curriculum design. In Adams, M., Bell, L. & Griffin, P. (Eds.). *Teaching for diversity and social justice: A sourcebook* (pp. 82–109). New York: Routledge.

■ Exercise 3. Why Do Stereotypes Endure?

Given below are several reasons discussed by Johnson and Johnson (2000) as to why stereotypes persist. What do you think are the most important reasons? Why? Explain your rationale on the second page of this exercise.

Reasons Why Stereotypes Endure
1. People tend to overestimate the association between variables that are only slightly correlated or not correlated at all, creating an **illusionary correlation**.
2. People tend to process information in ways that verify existing beliefs. This is known as the **confirmation bias** (the tendency to seek, interpret, and create information that verifies existing beliefs).
3. People tend to have a **false consensus bias** by believing that most other people share their stereotypes (e.g., seeing poor people as lazy).
4. People's stereotypes of others tend to be **self-fulfilling**. Stereotypes can subtly influence intergroup interactions in such a way that the stereotype is behaviorally confirmed.
5. People dismiss individuals who do not match their stereotype as exceptions to the rule or representatives of a subcategory.
6. Stereotypes often operate at an implicit level below people's conscious awareness.
7. People often develop a rationale and explanation to justify their stereotypes and prejudices.

Most important reasons

_____

2 _____

3. _____

Explanation

Exercise 4. Spheres of Influence

Consider the different spheres of influence that you have. Beginning with yourself, explain how you can influence your environment in a way that is more conducive to the development of multicultural world?

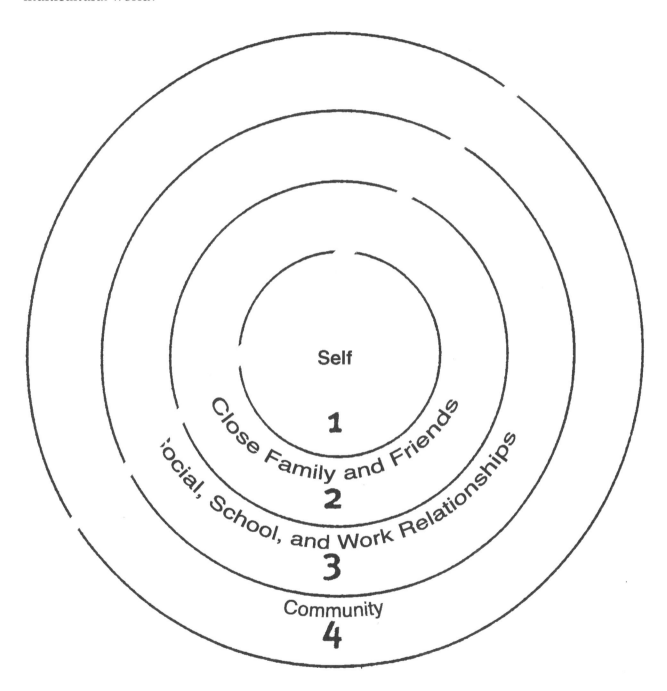

Self

1

Close Family and Friends

2

Social, School, and Work Relationships

3

Community

4

1. **Self.** Indicate how you could educate yourself, develop a deeper understanding of your values and feelings, and examine how you want to change.

2. **Close family and friends.** Explain how you could influence the people closest to you.

3. **Social, school, and work relationships.** Indicate how you might influence friends and acquaintances, coworkers, neighbors, classmates, people with whom you interact on a regular basis.

4. **Community.** Explain how you could influence people with whom you interact infrequently or in community settings.

CHAPTER 4
Appreciating Diversity

Chapter Focus

Read to answer these key questions:

- What is diversity and why is it important?
- How can an understanding and appreciation of diversity help me to be successful in school and in work?
- What is some vocabulary useful for understanding diversity?
- What are some ideas for communicating across cultures?
- What are some myths and facts about sexual orientation?
- How can I gain an appreciation of diversity?

Our schools, our workplaces, and our nation are becoming more diverse. Gaining an understanding and appreciation of this diversity will enhance your future success. Understanding yourself and having pride in your unique characteristics is the first step in the process. Self-knowledge includes information about your personality, interests, talents, and values. This chapter challenges you to examine some additional characteristics that make you a unique individual and to take pride in yourself while respecting differences of others.

■ Diversity Is Increasing

Another word for diversity is differences. These differences do not make one group inferior or superior. Differences are not deficits; they are just differences. Look around your classroom, your place of employment, or where you do business. You will notice people of a variety of races, ethnic groups, cultures, genders, ages, socioeconomic levels, and sexual orientations. Other differences that add to our uniqueness include religious preference, political orientation, personality, interests, and values. It is common to take pride in who we are and to look around and find people who share our view of the world. The challenge is to be able to look at the world from the point of view of those who are different from us. These differences provide an opportunity for learning.

The 2000 census showed a marked increase in the diversity of our schools and communities. In the United States, one in every five students has a parent born in a foreign country. Nationwide, non-Latino whites make up only 63 percent of the population. The current population includes 16 percent African Americans, 15 percent Latinos, and 5 percent Asians. California, one of the most populous states, is leading the nation in diversity. There is no single group in the majority: 43 percent are Latinos, 36 percent are non-Latino whites, 9 percent are African Americans, and 8 percent are Asian.[1] In New Mexico, Hawaii, and the District of Columbia, non-Latino whites are also in the minority.[2]

In our schools, places of work, and communities, we increasingly study, work, and socialize with people from different ethnic groups. This morning I talked with a student from Mexico and another from France. My classes have students from Mexico, Japan, Argentina, and Iraq. A colleague called on the phone and we spoke in Spanish. He invited me to a Greek café and deli where we ate Greek salad and purchased feta cheese and baklava. This diversity provides a different perspective and products from other countries enrich our lives. It requires an open mindedness and respect for differences for it all to work.

We also live in a **global economy**. Increased trade among the nations of the world requires an understanding and appreciation of cultural differences. The United States is in the center of the largest free trade area in the world. In 1994, the North American Free Trade Agreement (NAFTA) created a free-trade area that includes Canada, the United States, and Mexico. This act resulted in a freer flow of goods among these countries and an increase in international business. The success of this international business depends on increased cooperation and problem solving among these nations. Free-trade agreements will probably be expanded to other countries in Latin America in the near future.

Another major step toward the global economy was the creation of a single currency in Europe, the euro, which was successfully launched on January 1, 2002. The purpose of this largest money changeover in history is to establish a system in which people, goods, services, and capital can move freely across national borders. The European countries using the euro hope to make their economies more competitive and to encourage trade, travel, and investment.

International trade accounts for a quarter of all economic activity in the United States.[3] All we have to do is look around us to see that many of the foods and products we use in our daily lives come from other countries. For example, last night I made Chinese food with ingredients from Viet Nam, Thailand, Italy, Japan, and Mexico. These foods were purchased in my local grocery store. We ate on plates made in Malaysia. I got up this morning and dressed in a shirt made in the Dominican Republic and pants made in Mexico. I then put on my new walking shoes, made in Thailand. I put my CD player that was made in Japan in my backpack that was made in the Philippines. I listened to some Jamaican music while on my walk. For breakfast, I ate a banana grown in Honduras and drank coffee from Colombia. I then drove to work in a car that was made in Japan. Global trade not only brings us new and inexpensive products but also generates opportunities for employment in less developed nations. Of course, efforts need to be made to protect the workers in these countries from low wages and exploitation.

Awareness of diversity is also a result of technological changes. The world is becoming an **electronic village** connected by an array of communication and information technologies: computers, the Internet, communications satellites, cell phones, fax machines, and the myriad of electronic devices that are an integral part of our lives today. These devices make rapid communication possible all over the world and are essential for international business and trade. The Internet is like a vast information superhighway and each computer is an on ramp to the highway. Those who do not have a computer or lack computer skills will be left off the highway and have limited access to information and opportunities.

The increased use of the Internet offers both great opportunities and challenges. The Internet can help to break down barriers between people. When communicating with someone over the Internet, differences such as race, age, religion, or economic status are not obvious. The flow of information and ideas is unrestricted, and people with similar interests can communicate easily with one another. There is great potential for use as well as misuse of the Internet as well. Chat groups may share information about medical conditions or treatments, or hate groups can use the Internet to promote their political agendas.

The Internet presents new challenges for communicating since nonverbal cues are often missing. Looking at a person's face or listening to the tone of voice adds a great deal to communication. A new type of "netiquette" has evolved as a result. For example, using all caps is a form of YELLING! Increasingly words are shortened and changed for ease of communication resulting in a type of Internet grammar. Understanding Web pages in a different language is another new challenge.

Why Is Diversity Important?

Having an understanding and appreciation of diversity can help you to be successful at school and work. Here are some benefits:

Gain skills in critical thinking. Critical thinking requires identifying different viewpoints, finding possible answers, and then constructing your own reasonable view. Critical thinking skills are one of the expected outcomes of higher education. Many of your college assignments are designed to teach these skills. Whether you are writing an essay in English, participating in a discussion in a history class, or completing a laboratory experiment, critical thinking skills will help you to complete the task successfully.

Critical thinking skills are also helpful in finding good solutions to problems or challenges you might find at work. For example, for a business manager, an important task is helping employees to work together as a team. The critical thinking process results in greater understanding of others and better problem-solving skills. To stay competitive, businesses need to find creative solutions for building better products and providing good customer service. Critical thinking skills help people work together to come up with good ideas to make a business a success.

Have pride in yourself and your culture. Having pride in yourself is the foundation of good mental health and success in life. Sonia Nieto did research on a group of successful students. These students had good grades, enjoyed school, had plans for the future, and described themselves as successful. Nieto found that "one of the most consistent, and least expected, outcomes to emerge from these case studies has been a resoluteness with which young people maintain pride and satisfaction in their culture and the strength they derive from it."[4] Having pride in yourself and your culture is an important part of high self-esteem and can help you to become a better student and worker. Having good self-esteem provides the confidence to accept and care for others. The best schools and workplaces provide an environment where people can value their own culture as well as others. With respect between different cultures, ideas can be freely exchanged and the door is opened to creativity and innovation.

The world is constantly changing and we must be ready to adapt to new situations. Sometimes it is difficult to balance "fitting in" and maintaining our own cultural identity. Researchers have described a process called **transculturation**, in which a person adapts to a different culture without sacrificing individual cultural identity. One study of Native Americans showed that retention of traditional cultural heritage was an important predictor of success. A Native American student described the process this way: "When we go to school, we live a non-Indian way but we still keep our values. . . . I could put my values aside just long enough to learn what it is I want to learn but that doesn't mean I'm going to forget them. I think that is how strong they are with me."[5] Cultural identity provides strength and empowerment to be successful.

Gain an ability to network and learn from others. In college you will have the opportunity to learn from your professors and other students who are different from yourself. You may have professors with very different personality styles and teaching styles. Your success will depend on being aware of the differences and finding a way to adapt to the situation. Each student in your classes will also come from a different perspective and have valuable ideas to add to the class.

It is through networking with other people that most people find a job. You are likely to find a job through someone you know such as a college professor, a student in one of your classes, a community member, or a referral from a previous employer. Once you have the job, you will gain proficiency by learning from others. The best managers are open to learning from others and help different people to work together as a team. No matter how educated or experienced you become, you can always learn from others. Bill Cosby once told a graduating class at Washington University, "Don't ever think you know more than the person mopping the floor."[6] Every person has a different view of the world and has important ideas to share.

Improve interpersonal skills. A popular Native American proverb is that you cannot understand another person until you have walked a few miles in their moccasins. Being able to understand different perspectives on life will help you to improve your personal relationships. Good interpersonal skills bring joy to our personal relationships and are very valuable in the workplace. The Secretary of Labor's Commission on Achieving Necessary Skills (SCANS) identifies having good interpersonal skills as one of the five critical competencies needed in the workplace. Workers need to work effectively in teams, teach others, serve customers, exercise leadership, negotiate to arrive at a decision, and work well with cultural diversity.[7] Efficiency and profits in any industry depend on good interpersonal skills and how well workers can provide customer service.

Learn to be flexible and adapt to the situation. These two qualities are necessary for dealing with the rapid change that is taking place in our society today. We learn these qualities by successfully facing personal challenges. If you are a single parent, you have learned to be flexible in managing time and resources. If you served in the military overseas, you have learned to adapt to a different culture. If you are a new college student, you are probably learning how to be independent and manage your own life. Flexibility is a valuable skill in the workplace. Today's employers want workers who can adapt, be flexible and solve problems.

Develop cultural awareness. Cultural awareness is valuable in your personal life and in the workplace. In your personal life, you can have a wider variety of satisfying personal relationships. You can enjoy people from different cultural backgrounds and travel to different countries.

In a global economy, cultural awareness is increasingly important. Tuning into cultural differences can open up business opportunities. For example, many companies are discovering that the buying power of minorities is significant. They are developing ad campaigns to sell products to Asians, Latinos, African Americans, and other groups.

Companies now understand that cultural awareness is important in international trade. American car manufacturers could not understand why the Chevy Nova was not selling well in Latin America. In Spanish, "No va" means "It doesn't go" or "It doesn't run." Kentucky Fried Chicken found out that "Finger-lickin' good" translates as "Eat your fingers off" in Chinese! Being familiar with the culture and language of different countries is necessary for successful international business.

■ Vocabulary for Understanding Diversity

Knowing some basic terms will aid in your understanding of diversity.

Race. Race refers to a group of people who are perceived to be physically different because of traits such as facial features, color of skin, and hair.

Ethnicity. Ethnicity refers to a sense of belonging to a particular culture and sharing the group's beliefs, attitudes, skills, ceremonies, and traditions. An ethnic group usually descends from a common group of ancestors usually from a particular country or geographic area.

Ethnocentrism. Ethnocentrism is the belief that one's own ethnic, religious, or political group is superior to all others.

Culture. Culture is the behavior, beliefs, and values shared by a group of people. It includes language, morals, and even food preferences. Culture includes everything that we learn from the people around us in our community.

Gender, Sex. Gender refers to cultural differences that distinguish males from females. Different cultures raise men and women to act in specified ways. Sex refers to anatomical differences.

Sexism. Sexism is a negative attitude or perception based on sex.

Stereotype. A stereotype is a generalization that expresses conventional or biased ideas about people in a certain group. Stereotypes can lead to discrimination based on these ideas. They cause us to view others in a limited way and reduce our ability to see people as individuals.

Prejudice. A prejudice is a prejudgment of someone or something. Prejudices are often based on stereotypes and reflect a disrespect for others. Sometimes people who are prejudiced are insecure about their own identities.

Discrimination. Discrimination happens when people are denied opportunities because of their differences. Prejudice and stereotype are often involved.

Racism. Racism occurs when one race or ethnic group holds a negative attitude or perception of another group. It is prejudice based on race. Anthropologists generally accept that the human species can be categorized into races based on physical and genetic makeup. These scientists accept the fact that there is no credible evidence that one race is superior to another. People who believe that their own race is superior to another are called racists.

Cultural pluralism. Each group celebrates the customs and traditions of their culture while participating in mainstream society.

Genocide. Genocide is the deliberate and systematic destruction of a racial, political, or cultural group. It can include the destruction of the language, religion, or cultural practices of a group of people.

■ Understanding Diversity

There are over six billion people in the world today. Statistics provided by the Population Reference Bureau and the United Nations can give us a better understanding of diversity in the world today. By geographic area, the world's population can be broken down into these percentages:

61   Asians
13   Africans
12   Europeans
 9   Central and South Americans
 5   North Americans (Canada and the United States)

If visitors from outer space were to visit the earth and report back about the most common human being found, they would probably describe someone of Asian descent. Statistics also show that approximately 50 percent of the world population suffers from malnutrition and 80 percent live in substandard housing. Moreover, 6 percent of the population living in the United States, Japan, and Germany, own half of the wealth of the world. In addition, continuous wars and fighting among the people of the earth have contributed to human suffering and the flight of many refugees.

As children, we accept the values, assumptions, and stereotypes of our culture. We use our own culture as a filter to understand the world. Because of this limited perception, people often consider their culture to be superior and other cultures to be inferior.[9] The belief that one's own culture, religious, or political group is superior to others is called **ethnocentrism**. An example of ethnocentrism is the celebration in the United States of the 500th anniversary of the discovery of the new world by Christopher Columbus. In reality the Native Americans lived here long before Christopher Columbus arrived in 1492.

Ethnocentrism can lead to discrimination, interpersonal conflict, and even wars between different groups of people. In extreme cases, it can even lead to **genocide**, the deliberate and systematic destruction of a racial, political, or cultural group. History is full of examples of genocide. In the United States, Native Americans were massacred and their land was confiscated in violation of treaties. In Mexico and South America, the Spanish conquerors systematically destroyed native populations. During World War II, six million Jews were killed. Pol Pot and the Khmer Rouge killed millions of Cambodians. Unfortunately genocide continues today in various conflicts around the world.

An understanding of the harmful effects of stereotypes is necessary to improve our understanding and appreciation of diversity. A **stereotype** is an assumption that all members of a group are alike. For example, a tall African American woman in one of my classes was constantly dealing with the assumption that she must be attending college to play basketball. Actually she was very academically oriented and not athletic at all.

All of us use stereotypes to understand people different from ourselves. Why does this happen? There are many different reasons:

- It is a fast way to make sense of the world. It requires little thought.
- We tend to look for patterns to help us understand the world.
- We are often unable or unwilling to obtain all the information we need to make fair judgments about other people.
- Stereotypes can result from fear of people who are different. We often learn these fears as children.
- The media promotes stereotypes. Movies, magazines, and advertisements often present stereotypes. These stereotypes are often used as the basis of humor. For example, the media often uses people who are overweight in comedy routines.

The problem with stereotypes is that we do not get to know people as individuals. All members of a culture, ethnic group, or gender are not alike. If we make assumptions about a group, we treat everyone in the group the same. Stereotypes can lead to prejudice and discrimination. For example, a person who is overweight may find it more difficult to find a job because of stereotyping.

Psychologists and sociologists today present the idea of **cultural relativity** in which different cultures, ethnic groups, genders, and sexual orientations are viewed as different but equally valuable and worthy of respect.[10] These differences between cultures can help us learn new ideas that can enrich our view of the world. It can also promote greater understanding and better relationships among individuals and nations.

A New Look at Diversity: The Human Genome Project

Although the people of the world represent many racial, ethnic, and cultural groups, biologists are taking a new look at diversity by learning about human genes. The Human Genome Project began in 1990 as a multibillion-dollar government-sponsored research project to map all human genes. Genes are composed of segments of DNA that determine the transmission of hereditary traits by controlling the operation of cells. Cells are the basic building blocks of the human body.

Scientists have now completed a rough draft of the human genome, the catalog of all the genetic information contained in human cells. They have identified 2.69 billion of the approximately 3 billion DNA letters. The human genome is considered a biological treasure chest that will allow scientists to discover how a body grows, ages, stays healthy, or becomes ill. This knowledge is invaluable in discovering new medications and improving health.

Results of the human genome project show that we are all genetically similar while having unique individual differences. One of the interesting findings is that "as scientists have long suspected, though the world's people may look very different on the outside, genetically speaking humans are all 99.9 percent identical."[11] While we are genetically very similar, each individual can be identified by his or her genetic code. With the exception of identical twins, each individual human being is slightly different because of the unique combination of DNA letters inherited from one's parents.

Dr. Craig Venter, head of Celera Genomics Corporation, has stated that "race is a social concept, not a scientific one."[12] While it may be easy to look at people and describe them as Caucasian, African, or Asian, there is little genetic material to distinguish one race from another. Venter says, "We all evolved in the last 100,000 years from the same small number of tribes that migrated out of Africa and colonized the world."[13] Very few genes control traits that distinguish one race from another, such as skin color, eye color, and width of nose. These outward characteristics have been able to change quickly in response to environmental pressures. People who lived near the equator evolved dark skin to protect them from ultraviolet radiation. People who lived farther from the equator evolved pale skins to produce vitamin D from little sunlight. The genes responsible for these outward appearances are in the range of .01 percent of the total. Researchers on the human genome project agree that there is only one race, the human race.

The human genome project will be important for understanding the human body and will help us to find ways to prevent or cure illnesses. It may also provide new information for critical thinking about the idea of ethnocentrism and discover some basic ways in which all human beings are similar.

■ Communicating Across Cultures

Human beings communicate through the use of symbols. A symbol is a word that stands for something else. Problems in communication arise when we assume that a symbol has only one meaning and that everyone understands the symbol in the same way. For example, we use the word "dog" to stand for a four-legged animal that barks. However, if I say the word "dog," the picture in my mind probably doesn't match the picture in your mind because there are many varieties of dogs. I might be picturing a Chihuahua while you are picturing a German Shepherd. Language becomes even more complex when we have multiple meanings for one symbol. Consider the ways we use the word "dog":

- She is a dog. (She is unattractive.)
- He is a dog. (He is promiscuous.)
- He is a lucky dog. (He is fortunate.)
- It's a dog. (It is worthless.)
- Just dog it. (Just do enough to get by.)
- He went to the dogs. (He was not doing well.)
- He was in the doghouse. (He was in trouble.)
- Let sleeping dogs lie. (Leave the situation alone.)
- My dogs hurt. (My feet hurt.)
- He put on the dog. (He assumed an attitude of wealth or importance.)
- These are the dog days of summer. (These are hot days when people feel lazy.)
- The book is dog-eared. (The corners of the pages are bent.)
- He led a dog's life. (He was not happy.)
- May I have a doggy bag? (May I have a bag for my leftovers?)
- Doggone it! (I am frustrated!)
- I am dog-tired. (I am very tired.)

Imagine how a computer would translate the above sentences. The translations would be incomprehensible since there are so many variations in meaning depending on the context.

The problem of communication becomes even more difficult for those who are learning English. People who speak a different language might not understand the word "dog" at all because they use a different symbol for the object. Even after studying the language, it is easy to misinterpret the meaning of the word "dog." A recent immigrant was horrified when he was offered a hot dog at a ball game. He thought that this was a civilized country and was surprised that we ate dogs!

The symbols we use to stand for objects are arbitrary, complex, and dependent on our culture, language, and frame of reference. As a result, misunderstandings are common. When my son was very young, he was very frightened by noises on the roof of our house. He was afraid that aliens had landed. He said that he was certain there were aliens on the roof and that Dad said he had seen them too. I later found out that his father said that he had seen illegal aliens, or undocumented workers, in our neighborhood. It is strange that in the English language we use the word "alien" to refer to someone from outer space and someone from a different country. The "aliens" in my son's case turned out to be raccoons playing on the roof. The words that we use have a powerful influence on our lives and can make clear communication difficult.

Both verbal and nonverbal symbols have different meaning in different cultures. George Henderson in his book *Cultural Diversity in the Workplace*,[14] gives the example of the common thumbs-up gesture, which we commonly interpret as "okay." In Japan the same gesture means money. In Ghana and Iran it is a vulgar gesture similar to raising your middle finger in the United States. Another example is silence. In the United States, if a teacher asks a question and no one responds right away, the situation is uncomfortable. In Native American cultures, the person who remains silent is admired. Many Asian students listen more than they speak. According to a Zen proverb, "He who knows does not speak and he who speaks does not know." Think about how different our communications, especially business and sales techniques, would have to be in order to be effective in different cultures.

Here are some ideas to help improve your communications with people who are culturally different from you or speak a different language:

- Be sensitive to the fact that communication is difficult and that errors in understanding are likely.
- Remember that the message sent is not necessarily the message received.
- Give people time to think and respond. You do not have to fill in the silence right away.
- Check your understanding of the message. Rephrase or repeat the information to make sure it is correct. Ask questions.
- If you feel insulted by the message, remember that it is quite possible that you could be misinterpreting it. (Remember all the meanings for "dog" listed above.)
- If you are having problems communicating with someone who speaks a different language, speak slowly and clearly or use different words. Talking louder will not help.
- Remain calm and treat others with respect. Be patient.
- Find a translator if possible.
- Study a different language. This will help in understanding other cultures and the different ways that other cultures use symbols.
- Before traveling to a different country, read about the culture and learn some basic phrases in the language used. This will help you to enjoy your travel and learn about other cultures. Attempting to speak the language will show others that you care about and respect the culture.
- Sometimes nonverbal communication can help. If you are adventurous or desperate, smile and act out the message. Be aware that nonverbal communication can be misunderstood also.
- Don't forget your sense of humor.

■ Understanding Sexual Orientation

One of the causes of stereotyping and the prejudice and discrimination it can lead to is fear and lack of knowledge of those who are different. Prejudice and discrimination against gays and other minorities has sometimes led to hate crimes. For example, in 1998, Matthew Shepard, a gay student at the University of Wyoming, was lured from a bar, beaten, and tied to a log fence where he was left during cold weather. He died five days later. His murderers received life sentences in prison. At Matthew's funeral, protesters held up signs saying, "God hates fags."[15] (The term "faggot," which comes from the Latin word for a bundle of sticks, may refer to the time of the Inquisition when gays were burned at the stake along with witches.)[16]

Becoming educated about sexual orientation can help to diminish anti-gay prejudice and help people who are struggling with their sexual identity. It is highly likely that you go to school or work with gay men and lesbians. Test your knowledge about sexual orientation. Are these questions true or false?

_____ 1. Only one percent of the world's population is gay, lesbian, or bisexual.

_____ 2. Effeminate men and masculine women are always gay.

_____ 3. Homosexuality is a learned behavior.

_____ 4. You can always tell from a person's appearance if he or she is gay.

_____ 5. Approximately one out of every fifty families has a gay family member.

_____ 6. Lesbians and gay men never make good parents.

_____ 7. Gay men and lesbian women are often involved in child abuse.

_____ 8. The word "homosexual" is preferred over "gay" or "lesbian."

_____ 9. The term "gay" refers only to men.

_____ 10. Some cultures do not have gay men and lesbians.

_____ 11. Being gay is an emotional or mental disorder.

_____ 12. Through psychotherapy a gay person can be turned into a heterosexual.

_____ 13. A person is either completely heterosexual or completely homosexual.

_____ 14. Homosexuality does not exist in nature. It is dysfunctional.

_____ 15. Gay people should not be teachers because they will try to convert their students.

All of the above statements are false and represent myths about gay men and lesbians. The corrected information below is provided by PFLAG, which stands for Parents, Families and Friends of Lesbians and Gays. This organization provides information on its website at: www.pflagla.org. An organization called Rainbow Bridge also provides educational materials on gays and lesbians.

1. It is estimated that about ten percent of the world's population is gay, lesbian, or bisexual.

2. Effeminate men and masculine women can be heterosexual. Some gay persons fit this stereotype, but most look and act like individuals from the heterosexual majority.

3. No one knows how sexual orientation is determined. Homosexuality is not something that one chooses to be or learns to be. As children, gay men and lesbians are not taught or influenced by others to be homosexual. Various theories about sexual orientation have been proposed, including ones citing genetic or inborn hormonal factors.[17]

4. Most gay men and lesbian women look and act like individuals from the heterosexual majority.

5. Approximately one out of four families has a gay member.

6. Gay men and lesbians can make good parents. Children of gay and lesbian parents are no different in any aspects of psychological, social or sexual development from children in heterosexual families. These children tend to be more tolerant of differences.

7. Gay men and lesbian women are rarely involved in child abuse. In the United States, heterosexual men commit 90 percent of all sexual child abuse. The molesters are most often fathers, stepfathers, grandfathers, uncles, or boyfriends of the mothers.

8. The term "gay man" or "lesbian" is preferred over the term "homosexual."

9. The term "gay" refers to both men and women.

10. All cultures have gay men and lesbians.

11. Being gay is not an emotional or mental disorder.

12. Psychotherapy has not been successful in changing a person's sexual orientation.

13. Based on Dr. Alfred Kinsey's research, few people are predominantly heterosexual or homosexual. Most people fall on a continuum between the two extremes. A person on the middle of the continuum between heterosexual and homosexual would be a bisexual. Bisexuals are attracted to both sexes.[18]

14. Research suggests that homosexuality is "natural." It exists among all animals and is frequent among highly developed species.[19]

15. Homosexual seduction is no more common than heterosexual seduction. Most gay teachers fear they will be fired if it is found out that they are gay.[20]

■ How to Appreciate Diversity

Having an appreciation for diversity enriches all of us. Poet Maya Angelou has described the world as a rich tapestry and stressed that understanding this concept can enrich and improve the world:

It is time for us to teach young people early on that in diversity there is beauty and strength. We all should know that diversity makes for a rich tapestry, and we must understand that the threads of the tapestry are equal in value, no matter their color; equal in importance, no matter their texture.[21]

Here are some ways to appreciate diversity:

■ Educate yourself about other cultures and people who are different from you. Read about or take courses on the literature or history of another culture or learn another language.

■ Explore your own heritage. Learn about the cultures that are part of your family history.

- ◼ Value diversity and accept the differences of others.
- ◼ View differences as an opportunity for learning.
- ◼ Realize that you will make mistakes when dealing with people from other cultural backgrounds. Learn from the mistakes and move on to better understanding.
- ◼ Work to understand differences of opinion. You do not have to agree, but respect different points of view.
- ◼ Travel to other countries to discover new ideas and cultures.
- ◼ Think critically to avoid stereotypes and misconceptions. Treat each person as an individual.
- ◼ Avoid judgments based on physical characteristics such as color of skin, age, gender, or weight.
- ◼ Put yourself in the other person's place. How would you feel? What barriers would you face?
- ◼ Make friends with people from different countries, races, and ethnic groups.
- ◼ Find some common ground. We all have basic needs for good health, safety, economic security, and education. We all face personal challenges and interests. We all think, feel, love, and have hope for the future.
- ◼ Be responsible for your own behavior. Do not participate in or encourage discrimination.
- ◼ Do good deeds. You will be repaid with good feelings.
- ◼ Learn from history so that you do not repeat it. Value your own freedom.
- ◼ Challenge racial or homophobic remarks or jokes.
- ◼ Teach children and young people to value diversity and respect others. It is through them that we can change the world.

◼ Stages of Ethical Development

After much study, Harvard University professor William Perry developed the theory that students move through stages of ethical development.[22] Students move through these patterns of thought and eventually achieve effective intercultural communication.

Stage 1: Dualism

In this stage we view the world in terms of black or white, good or bad, "we" versus "they." Role models and authorities determine what is right. The right answers exist for every problem. If we work hard, we can find the correct answers and all will be well. Decisions are often based on common stereotypes.

Stage 2: Multiplicity

At this stage we become aware that there are multiple possibilities and answers. We know that authorities can disagree on what is right and wrong. We defend our position, but acknowledge that on any given issue everyone has a right to his or her own opinion.

Stage 3: Relativism

As we learn more about our environment and ourselves, we discover that what is right is based on our own values and culture. We weigh the evidence and try to support our opinions based on data and evidence.

Stage 4: Commitment in relativism

At this stage we look at our environment and ourselves and make choices. In an uncertain world, we make decisions about careers, politics, and personal relationships based on our individual values. We make certain commitments based on the way we wish to live our lives. We defend our own values but respect the values of others. There is openness to learning new information and changing one's personal point of view. This position allows for the peaceful coexistence of different points of views and perspectives. It is at this point that we become capable of communicating across cultures and appreciating diversity.

■ Student Perspectives on Diversity

The following are some student comments on the subject of diversity. Many students have faced incidents of discrimination and hope for a better future.

> I am always faced with problems because I'm black or my hair is long or because I am a large man. I wish people could be more sensitive and love me as a person and not judge me based on what I look like.

> I am frequently discriminated against because of my religion. I feel really bad when it happens and it hurts a lot.

> I have always faced discrimination because of my sexual orientation and will probably continue to experience discrimination in the future. If you are part of a minority, discrimination is inevitable. The key is to not let it drag you down so that you become a second-class citizen. That can be accomplished by taking pride in who you are and then working to fight against discrimination.

> I come from Japan. I noticed that people here think their culture is better than any other. I think it's not bad to love your culture, but it is important to be open to other cultures.

> There is a story I tell my children about words being nails. When we speak, we pound our nails into the other person's spirit. We can go back and apologize for hurtful words and maybe that removes the nail, but it still leaves a hole in the spirit.

> If you constantly hear people say that you are not as good as another, you eventually start to believe it.

> I've been discriminated against because I am female and a blonde. When I hear blonde jokes, I've learned to laugh with people most of the time, but it still hurts my feelings.

> Discrimination is passed on to the next generation because a child believes what a parent tells them. We need to teach our children tolerance for differences.

> Discrimination hurts people's feelings and doesn't allow them to become successful in life because they lose confidence and self-esteem.

> Because I am black, salespeople tend to follow me around in the store thinking I am going to steal something. People of different races call me "nigger."

> When I was younger, I used to wear thick glasses. People would call me names such as "four eyes," "nerd," "dork," and "geek." I can look back and laugh at this now, but it made me feel inferior. Discrimination is based on ignorance and hate.

Black kids used to mistreat me because I was not as black as them.

Once when I was ten years old, I was playing in the park. I noticed this Caucasian kid playing on the slide and he was about to fall off the slide. I went over to catch him and the mother ran over to me and told me to take my hands off of him and that she would rather have him fall than to have some "nigger" put her hands on him. I will never forget this incident!

When I was younger, my father frequently made negative comments about women. Because of his prejudice, I felt less worthy of getting equal treatment for equal education and work. Now my father is trying to overcome this mindset, and I plan to graduate from college to earn equal pay with men.

It is sad that humans can be so cruel to one another. I hope someday this will all end and we can live in peace with one another.

By celebrating diversity, all the people of the world could come together and have peace.

■ Diversity Is Valuable and People Are Important

In 1963 Dr. Martin Luther King, Jr., made a famous speech in which he said, "I have a dream that my four little children will one day live in a nation where they will not be judged by the color of their skin, but by the content of their character." Because of his message of brotherhood and understanding, his birthday is celebrated as a national holiday. Tragically, King was assassinated because of his strong stand against racism. We are still working toward his ideal of brotherly love.

When I ask students to describe what success means to them, they often talk about having a good career, financial stability, owning a home, and having a nice car. Some students mention family and friends and people who are important to them. Understanding diversity and appreciating other people can add to your personal success and enjoyment of life.

To gain perspective on what is important to your success, it is interesting to think about what people will say about you after you die. What will you think is important at the end of your life? If you can ponder this idea, you can gain some insight into how to live your life now.

Learn to understand, respect, and appreciate the different people in your life. Take time to love those who are important to you. Focus on cooperation and teamwork on the job. Don't forget about the people you meet on your road to success; they are important too. Having an understanding and appreciation of diversity will make the world a better place to live in too.

■ Notes

1. Robert Rosenblatt and Robert Duke, "A New Boom in U.S. Student Population, Census Finds; Count: Enrollment of 49 Million Equals 1970 Record. But Immigration Is a Concern, Especially in California," *Los Angeles Times,* 23 March 2001.

2. Brian Melly, "One in Three Californians is Hispanic; Whites Minority, Census Shows," *Associated Press,* 29 March 2001.

3. David Broder, "Congress Wants to Shape Trade Debate," *San Diego Union Tribune,* 7 November 2001.

4. Sonia Nieto, *Affirming Diversity: The Sociopolitical Context of Multicultural Education* (New York: Longman, 1996), 283.

5. Terry Huffman, "The Transculturation of Native American College Students," in *American Mosaic: Selected Readings on America's Multicultural Heritage,* ed. Young Song and Eugene Kim (Englewood Cliffs, NJ: Prentice-Hall, 1993), 211–19.

6. Richard Bucher, *Diversity Consciousness* (Englewood Cliffs, NJ: Prentice-Hall, 2000), 119.

7. Secretary's Commission of Achieving Necessary Skills (SCANS), U.S. Department of Labor, *Learning a Living: A Blueprint for High Performance,* 1991.

8. World population statistics from the Population Reference Bureau website: www.prb.org 2001, and the United Nations website: www.un.org/esa/population, 2001.

9. H. Triandis, "Training for Diversity," paper presented at the annual meeting of the American Psychological Association, San Francisco, 1991.

10. Benjamin Lahey, *Psychology: An Introduction* (Dubuque, IA: Brown and Benchmark, 1995), 20.

11. Sue Goetinck Ambrose, "First Look at Genome Data Leaves Scientists in 'Awe'," *San Diego Union Tribune,* 11 February 2001.

12. Natalie Angier, "Do Races Differ? Not Really, Genes Show," *New York Times,* 22 August 2000.

13. Ibid.

14. George Henderson, *Cultural Diversity in the Workplace: Issues and Strategies* (Westport, CT: Praeger, 1994.

15. "Mourners Gather to Honor Gay Murdered in Wyoming," *Bellingham Herald,* 17 October 1998, A8.

16. California Rainbow Bridge pamphlet, 2000.

17. American Psychological Association, from http://www.apa.org.pubinfo.html, 2001.

18. Ibid.

19. Ibid.

20. Ibid.

21. Maya Angelou, *Wouldn't Take Nothing for My Journey Now* (New York: Random House, 1993).

22. William G. Perry, "Cognitive and Ethical Growth: The Making of Meaning," in *The Modern American College* by Arthur Chickering and Associates (Jossey-Bass, 1981), 76–116.

23. Quoted in Rob Gilbert, ed. *Bits and Pieces,* 4 November 1999.

Name: _____ Date: _____

◼ Find Someone Who . . .

Walk around the classroom and find someone who fits each description. Have the person write his or her name on the appropriate line.

_____ Shares a favorite hobby

_____ Father or mother grew up in a bilingual family

_____ Parents or grandparents were born outside the United States

_____ Speaks a language besides English

_____ Is the first one in the family to attend college

_____ Enjoys the same sports

_____ Knows someone who has died of AIDS

_____ Has a friend or relative who is gay, lesbian, or bisexual

_____ Has a disability they have had to overcome

_____ Is struggling financially to attend college

_____ Has children

_____ Is a single parent

_____ Has your same major

_____ Was born in the same year as yourself

_____ Attended your high school

_____ Moved here from out of state

_____ Has been in the military

_____ Has participated on an athletic team

_____ Can play a musical instrument or sing

_____ Has played in a band

Exploring Diversity

Part 1. Answer the following questions about yourself.

1. What is your ethnic background?

2. Where were your parents and grandparents born?

3. How much education do your parents have?

4. What languages do you speak?

5. What is your biggest challenge this semester?

6. What is one of your hopes or dreams for the future?

7. What do you enjoy most?

8. What is your most important value and why?

9. What is one thing you are proud of?

10. What is one thing people would not know about you just by looking at you?

11. Have you ever experienced discrimination because of your differentness? If so, briefly describe this discrimination.

Part 2. Meet with two other students you do not know. Introduce yourself and share answers to the above questions. Your instructor will ask you to share your answers to the following questions with the class.

1. List three interesting things you learned about other persons in your group.

2. Did you change any assumptions you had about persons in your group?

Name: _____ Date: _____

■ Exploring Stereotypes

Part 1. We are all familiar with **common stereotypes** of certain groups. Think about how these groups are often portrayed in the media. Quickly complete each statement.

1. All athletes are _____

2. All lawyers are _____

3. All male hairdressers are _____

4. All construction workers are _____

5. All redheads are _____

6. All people with AIDS are _____

7. All people on welfare are _____

8. All young people are _____

9. All old people are _____

10. All men are _____

11. All women are _____

12. All A students are _____

Part 2. Your instructor will ask you to share the above stereotypes with the class. Then discuss these questions.

1. What prejudices result from such stereotypes?

2. What is the source of these prejudices?

3. What harm can come from these prejudices?

Exploring My Culture

Everyone has a unique cultural background based on many different factors. Answer these questions to explore your unique culture.

1. Describe where you grew up and the school you attended.

2. What beliefs did you learn from your family?

3. What beliefs did you learn from your teachers? How would your teachers describe you as a student?

4. How has your religious training or lack of religious training affected your beliefs?

5. If you are in a relationship, describe how your partner has affected your beliefs.

6. If you have children, how have your values and beliefs changed?

7. Are the beliefs you grew up with right for you today? Why or why not?

■ What Is Important?

Imagine that you are writing a eulogy for yourself. What would you say?

Section 2

Taking Care of Yourself

CHAPTER 5

Maintaining a Healthy Lifestyle

Healthy Lifestyles through Wellness

How are you? You probably answered "fine" without really thinking. But, how do you **really** feel . . . about yourself, your life, your lifestyle, your health? Chances are that you may not have considered all of the many facets that constitute your true well-being. Do you eat well? Do you exercise regularly? Do you smoke or drink? Do you have close friends with whom you can share your experiences, both good and traumatic? Are you under extreme stress to get good grades, perform well on the job, or be a good parent? Do you get regular medical checkups and do you practice self-care? Are you aware of safety and environmental factors that contribute to your health? This chapter will help you develop important strategies that will enable you to live life to the fullest, both physically and emotionally.

Traditionally, health was simply defined as the absence of disease or symptoms. This concept has gradually evolved over the past fifty years so that health is now defined by the World Health Organization as a continuous and harmonious balance of physical, mental, spiritual, intellectual, and social well-being. This continuum of a "balanced," healthy lifestyle has been defined as **wellness.** True wellness involves contracting with yourself to engage in healthy behaviors and attitudes that enhance the quality of your life and personal performance.

To achieve this state of wellness, you must maintain a balance of six continually changing dimensions that affect your overall health. These components of wellness are:

Physical

Physical wellness is the ability to maintain positive lifestyle habits to enable you to perform your daily tasks. Such components of the physical dimension of wellness entail eating healthy foods, maintaining appropriate weight and body fat, performing regular exercise to maintain cardiovascular fitness, and avoiding the abuse of tobacco, alcohol, and other drugs.

Emotional

Emotional wellness is the ability to manage stress and express your emotions appropriately by recognizing and accepting your feelings about the events in your life. Stress is part of everyone's life, but your ability to properly manage life's stressful events can greatly influence your overall health potential.

Spiritual

The belief in an abstract strength that unites all of your internal energies. This strength can include religion and/or nature, but also includes your values, ethics, and morals. Your personal sense of spirituality provides meaning and direction to your life, enabling you to learn, develop, and meet new challenges successfully.

Social

The skill to interact successfully with other people at work, school, and the community. This dimension of wellness encompasses your ability to handle relationships, both intimate and casual.

Intellectual

The ability to learn and use your knowledge effectively to enhance your overall health. Knowledge of self-care techniques, disease risk factors, as well as your family history of disease, are all important components to achieving intellectual wellness.

Environmental

The physical and social setting that influences your lifestyle. This dimension includes your personal safety practices, such as wearing seat belts, to your efforts to help promote a clean environment.

These six dimensions of wellness overlap, and components of one often can directly or indirectly affect factors in another. Some health parameters are under your direct control and some are not. For example, your lifestyle behaviors (diet, exercise, habits) constitute the greatest percentage of influences on the quality of your life.

Relationships involving family, friends, and the community are also important, as are factors pertaining to the quality of health care you receive by physicians and health care facilities. Approximately 85 percent of the factors influencing your health are within your control. The remaining 15 percent are beyond your individual control and consist of heredity predispositions. If your medical history reveals a family tendency toward a specific disease, such as heart disease or cancer, your lifestyle decisions can delay the onset, minimize the disease's effects, or possibly even prevent the disease from occurring. This is why a good knowledge of preventive medicine becomes so important.

■ Health Benefits of Wellness

You can achieve wellness through improving your knowledge about health, eliminating risk factors, practicing good self-care habits and preventive medicine, and maintaining a positive attitude. Some of the benefits of wellness include:

- a decreased risk of developing chronic diseases;
- a decreased risk of accidents;
- a decreased recovery time after injury and illness;
- an improved cardiovascular system function (heart efficiency and blood vessel diameter both increase);
- an increased muscle tone, strength, and flexibility;
- an improved physical appearance—less fat, greater muscle tone;
- an increased ability to manage stress and resist depression;
- proper nutrition for optimal growth, repair, immune function, and development;
- a higher self-esteem;
- an increased energy level, productivity, and creativity; and
- an improved awareness of your personal needs and the ways to achieve them.

■ Wellness as a Challenge

Your belief in your ability to perform healthy behaviors will influence your actual choices, your degree of effort to make the change, your persistence, and your emotional reactions to the new lifestyle. Your ability to turn your health-related goals into reality is dependent on formulating a plan of action. This lifestyle modification has several steps:

Step 1. Evaluate your personal health habits. Make a list of your behaviors that promote health and make another list of your behaviors that are harmful. Once you have compiled both of your lists, note which behaviors present the greatest threat to your overall well-being. These behaviors should be targeted for change first.

Step 2. Set realistic, specific, observable, and measurable goals. Don't expect miracles. Setting goals that are too ambitious leads to failure; the fear of failure may discourage future efforts. View lifestyle change as a lifetime change. Strive for moderation rather than striving for complete behavior reversal or abstinence. Behavior changes that are "slow-but-steady" are the ones most likely to result in permanent success.

Step 3. Formulate a strategy for success. Most people want to make positive changes, but too often find reasons why they cannot make changes. They may not have the time, are too tired, or simply feel embarrassed. What are some of your reasons? These barriers to change must be avoided if you are to achieve your healthy goals.

Step 4. Evaluate your progress. How well are you doing? The only way to consistently stick with your new healthy behavior is to receive feedback by monitoring your progress. This evaluation allows you to modify the program, enabling you to better achieve your goals. Initially, the evaluation periods should be frequent, such as daily or weekly. After periods of consistent success, the time interval between evaluation sessions could be lengthened to, perhaps, monthly.

Success does not have to be all-or-nothing. This manner of thinking can be detrimental to your overall motivation to change. When your goals are not fully realized, simply reshape your goals, set a more realistic time schedule, or formulate different intervention strategies, and **TRY AGAIN**. More importantly, answer these questions:

"What did I learn from this experience?"

"What can I do differently?"

Based on your answers, make a revised contract and begin immediately. Remember that lifestyle change is never easy but its rewards will last a lifetime. The exercise on the next page will assist you in planning for a healthier lifestyle.

■ You Are What You Eat

Dietary habits play a key role in both how long we live and how well we feel. A healthy diet is one that features a proper variety and balance of foods to supply our body with nutrients, essential dietary factors required for growth, energy, and repair. There are six nutrients: proteins, carbohydrates, fats, vitamins, minerals, and water.

Protein is necessary for growth and repair, forming the basic building blocks of muscles, bones, hair, and blood. Meat, poultry, fish, eggs, milk, cheese, dry beans, and nuts are excellent dietary sources of protein.

Carbohydrates provide the body with glucose, its basic fuel. There are two types of carbohydrates: simple and complex. Simple carbohydrates are sugars, which are responsible for providing short bursts of energy. Examples of dietary sugars include glucose, sucrose (table sugar), fructose (the sugar found in fruits), honey, and syrup. Complex carbohydrates consist of starches and fiber, important ingredients of cereals, breads, rice, pasta, fruits, and vegetables. Soluble fiber, found in oats, beans, apples, and citrus fruit, has been shown to lower blood cholesterol levels and decrease the risk of heart disease.

Fats are high calorie nutrients that come in two primary types: saturated and unsaturated. Saturated fats, found in animal products such red meat, egg yolk, and butter, have been shown to increase the blood cholesterol levels and increase the risk of heart disease. In contrast, monounsaturated and polyunsaturated fats are found primarily in foods of plant origin and have been shown to lower blood cholesterol levels. Polyunsaturated fats are found in safflower and corn oils, whereas canola and olive oil are monounsaturated fats. In contrast to protein and carbohydrates, which contain four calories per gram, fat contributes nine calories per gram when metabolized in the body. For this reason, a simple way to lose weight is to decrease the amount of dietary fat.

Vitamins are organic nutrients which work with the body's enzymes to enable biochemical reactions to take place. Vitamins C and E, as well as beta carotene, serve as antioxidants, substances that protect cells from dangerous free radicals produced by normal metabolic processes. Antioxidants have been shown to reduce the incidence of heart disease and certain types of cancer.

Minerals are inorganic substances found in food that are also essential for proper metabolism. Macrominerals (sodium, potassium, calcium, phosphorus, and magnesium) are required in larger amounts than are the trace minerals (iron, zinc, selenium, iodine, chromium, and fluoride). Calcium is the most abundant mineral in the body, responsible for bone integrity and prevention of osteoporosis, as well as for conduction of nerve impulses and cardiac contraction.

Exercise:

Do aerobic exercises (walking, jogging, swimming, cycling, etc.) for 30 minutes three to four times a week.

Incorporate exercise into your daily activities (e.g., take the stairs).

Always do warm-up and cool-down exercises and stretch before and after your aerobic session to improve flexibility and decrease risk of injury.

Nutrition:

Eat foods high in complex carbohydrates (breads, cereals, fruits, vegetables, pasta) to constitute 48 percent of your total daily calories.

Limit simple sugars (table sugar, soft drinks, candy); consume only with meals.

Limit saturated fat intake (animal fats, whole milk, etc.); consume more fat calories as monounsaturated (canola and olive oil) and polyunsaturated (vegetable oils) fats.

Drink at least eight glasses of water daily.

Stress management:

Improve your time management and organizational skills (set priorities, don't procrastinate, make a daily schedule with flexible time and follow it).

Practice progressive muscle relaxation, meditation, yoga, and deep-breathing exercises.

Self-care:

Don't smoke.

Only drink alcohol responsibly; (e.g. don't drink and drive, no more than two or three drinks in one sitting, etc.).

Perform breast or testicular self-exams monthly.

Have regular medical screenings and physical exams.

Know your blood pressure and cholesterol numbers.

Practice abstinence or safer sex (always use condoms).

Sleep at least seven to eight hours daily and develop a regular sleep-wake cycle.

Read about current health topics and medical discoveries; check the Internet.

Safety:

Always wear a seat belt.

Learn cardiopulmonary resuscitation (CPR).

Check smoke detectors in your home annually.

Figure 1 ■ Wellness Strategies for Top Performance: Academically and Athletically

I, _____, pledge that I will accomplish the goals listed below.

—Personal Goal: *Improve my fitness level.*

—Motivating Factors: *I want to have more energy and feel better.*

—Change(s) I Promise to Make to Reach This Goal: *Jog for 20–30 minutes at least three times a week.*

—Start Date: *January 1*

—Intervention Strategies:

1. *I will walk early in the morning before classes.*
2. *I will walk after classes on days when it is raining in the morning.*

Plan for Making This Change:

First week: walk for 10 minutes three times a week.

Weeks 2 to 4: Increase the amount of walking time by five minutes every week until I walk for 20–30 minutes each session.

Week 5: Evaluate my progress.

Weeks 5 to 9: Gradually increase my speed.

Week 10: Evaluate my progress.

After the first 10 weeks: Continue my morning jogs three times a week.

—Target Date for Reaching Goal: *March 15*

—Reward for Reaching Goal: *Buy a new, expensive pair of jogging shoes.*

—If I Need Help: *I can call my friend _____ to walk or jog with me.*

Signed: _____

Witness: _____

Date: _____

Figure 2 ■ A Sample Contract for Lifestyle Change

Approximately 60 percent of your weight consists of **water**. Water helps to digest foods, maintains proper body temperature, lubricates joints, and eliminates the body's waste products via urine. Water is necessary for survival, as we would die after only a few days without water. In contrast, we could survive for several weeks without food. You should drink at least eight glasses of water a day, not counting alcohol and drinks that contain the diuretic caffeine, such as coffee, tea, and certain soft drinks.

How Much Should I Eat?

According to the American Dietetic Association, 12 percent of your daily calories should come from protein; 58 percent from carbohydrates (of which 48 percent should be complex carbohydrates and only 10 percent simple sugars); and a total of 30 percent from fats (10 percent saturated fats, 10 percent monounsaturated fats, and 10 percent polyunsaturated fats). In contrast, the typical American diet consists of too much saturated fats and simple sugars, and lacks sufficient amounts of complex carbohydrates. To best help you determine what your daily nutrient intake is, you need to understand the food pyramid.

The Food Guide Pyramid

In 1992, the United States Department of Agriculture published the Food Guide Pyramid, a guideline to simplify the selections of foods that constitute a healthy diet. As shown in Figure 3, the Food Guide Pyramid incorporates five food groups plus fats, oils, and sugars. Foods in one category cannot replace those from another.

The foods at the base of the Food Guide Pyramid form the foundation of a healthy diet and consist of foods high in complex carbohydrates—breads, cereals, rice, and pasta. The foods at the Pyramid's base are high in fiber, iron, protein, and B vitamins, and should be consumed in the largest quantities, namely six to eleven servings daily. The second tier of the Food Guide Pyramid consists of vegetables and fruits—foods that are high in fiber, low in fat, and high in vitamins A and C. Scientific studies have revealed that vegetables and fruits may prevent cancers of the lung, colon, stomach, bladder, and breast. According to the Food Guide Pyramid, three to five servings of vegetables and two to four servings of fruits are recommended daily. Foods in the "Milk, Yogurt, and Cheese" group are high in calcium, protein, and vitamins A and B-12. Two servings per day are recommended. Foods in the "Meat, Poultry, Fish, Dry Beans, Eggs, and Nuts" group are excellent sources of protein, iron, zinc, phosphorus, and B vitamins. These foods are also high in fats and cholesterol; thus, you should choose low-fat varieties. Finally, foods at the apex of the pyramid (the smallest part of the pyramid) should be consumed in very small quantities. Fats, oils, and sweets are high in calories but supply little or no vitamins or minerals. Select foods from this category that are high in monounsaturated fats, such as canola or olive oils.

Using Your Resources

Visit the campus health center, a primary care physician, or a registered dietician to receive a personal nutrition consultation. A licensed health professional can help you lose weight or gain weight; prescribe a diet to help control blood pressure, diabetes, or high cholesterol; or provide guidance concerning dietary supplements.

Food Guide Pyramid

A Guide to Daily Food Choices

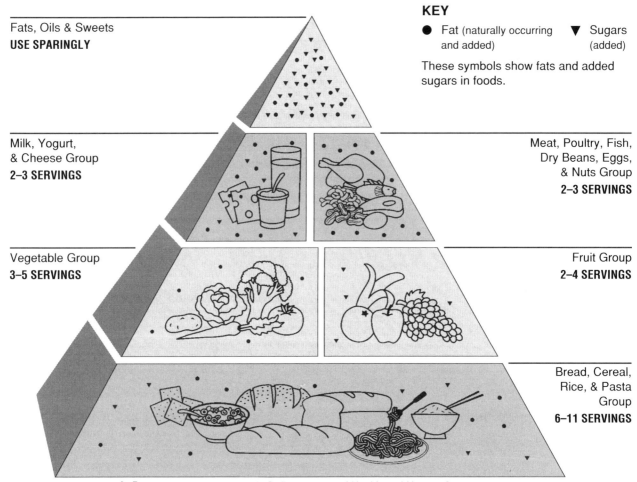

KEY
● Fat (naturally occurring and added) ▼ Sugars (added)

These symbols show fats and added sugars in foods.

Fats, Oils & Sweets
USE SPARINGLY

Milk, Yogurt, & Cheese Group
2–3 SERVINGS

Meat, Poultry, Fish, Dry Beans, Eggs, & Nuts Group
2–3 SERVINGS

Vegetable Group
3–5 SERVINGS

Fruit Group
2–4 SERVINGS

Bread, Cereal, Rice, & Pasta Group
6–11 SERVINGS

SOURCE: U.S. Department of Agriculture/U.S. Department of Health and Human Services.

What counts as one serving?

Bread, Cereal, Rice & Pasta Group	Vegetable Group	Fruit Group	Milk, Cheese Group	Meat, Poultry, Fish Group	Fats, Oils, Sweets Group
1 slice of bread	1 cup raw leafy veg.	1 medium fruit (apple, orange, banana)	1 cup nonfat milk	3 oz cooked lean meat+	butter, margarine*
1/2 cup of rice	1/2 baked white potato	3/4 cup juice	1 cup nonfat yogurt	3 oz sliced turkey+	corn, safflower oil
1/2 cup of pasta	1/2 baked sweet potato	1/2 cup canned fruit	1.5 oz natural cheese*+	3 oz chicken breast+	olive oil
1 oz of dry cereal	1/2 cup steamed veg.	1/2 cup grapes	1.5 oz processed cheese*+	1.5 cups kidney beans	canola oil
1/2 cup oatmeal	1 cup lettuce	1/2 cup melon chunks	1/2 cup low-fat cottage cheese*+	3 eggs	palm, coconut oil*+
1/2 bagel	1/2 cup carrot sticks			6 tbsp peanut butter	cakes, pies, cookies
				1.5 cups lentils	sugared drinks

* = foods that are high in fat
+ = foods that contain saturated fat or cholesterol

Figure 3 ■ Food Guide Pyramid

■ Responsible Drinking

According to a number of studies, abuse of alcohol is the number-one problem facing college students today. Although more students are choosing to abstain, approximately 85 percent of college students use alcohol. A small percentage of these students drink irresponsibly, either binge drinking (drinking five or more drinks at one sitting), drinking while under the legal drinking age, or driving under the influence of alcohol. The leading cause of death among college students is alcohol-related automobile accidents. The use and abuse of alcohol is also associated with most cases of campus violence, arrests, vandalism, rape, accidents, homicides, unwanted sex, sexually transmitted diseases and HIV/AIDS, unwanted pregnancies, poor grades, and drop-outs.

Alcohol can also impair your judgment. You may actually have sex with someone whom you would normally not even go out to lunch with! However, the consequences of your decision, such as an unintended pregnancy, a sexually transmitted disease, or an accident resulting in a lifelong disability, may last a lifetime.

By definition, any drink containing 0.5 percent or more ethyl alcohol by volume is an alcoholic beverage. However, different drinks contain different amounts of alcohol. For example, one drink is defined as any of the following:

- one 12 oz can of beer (5 percent alcohol);
- one 4 oz glass of wine (12 percent alcohol); or
- one shot (1 oz) of distilled spirits, such as whiskey, vodka, or rum (50 percent alcohol). The alcohol content is expressed as **proof**, a number that is twice the percentage of alcohol: 80-proof gin is 40 percent alcohol, etc.

To determine the amount that you can safely drink, you need to determine the blood-alcohol concentration (BAC), the percentage of alcohol in the blood. The BAC is usually measured from your breath. Most people reach a BAC of 0.05 percent after consuming one or two drinks; at this level, they do not feel intoxicated. If they continue to drink past this BAC level, they start to feel worse, with decreased reaction times, slurred speech, and loss of balance and emotional control. The legal BAC in most states is 0.08 percent. Persons driving a motor vehicle with a BAC of 0.08 percent or greater are cited for driving under the influence and are subject to severe legal penalties and fines. At a BAC of 0.2 percent, a person is likely to pass out and at a BAC of 0.3 percent, a person could lapse into a coma. Death is likely with a BAC of 0.4 percent or higher.

These factors will influence your BAC and response to alcohol:

- **How much and how quickly you drink.** If you chug drink after drink, your liver, which can only metabolize 0.5 oz of alcohol per hour, will not be able to keep up, resulting in a rapidly rising BAC.
- **The type of drink.** The stronger the drink, the faster the rise in BAC, and the consequent symptoms. If the drink contains water, juice, or milk, the rate of absorption will be decreased, slowing the rate of BAC rise. However, if you mix an alcoholic drink with carbon dioxide (e.g., champagne or a cola), the rate of alcohol absorption will increase.
- **The temperature of the alcoholic drink.** Warm drinks result in a faster rate of absorption.
- **Food.** Food slows the rate of absorption by interfering with the intestine's absorptive membrane surface. Certain high-fat foods can also prolong the time it takes for the stomach to empty its contents, resulting in delayed absorption times.

- **Your size.** Large people who have excessive fat or muscle tend to have a larger water volume, which dilutes the alcohol consumed. Therefore, large people can drink more alcohol and will get drunk more slowly than small or thin people.
- **Your gender.** Women tend to get drunk more quickly than men. Women possess smaller quantities of a stomach enzyme that metabolizes alcohol. The hormone estrogen also plays a role, as women are more sensitive to the effects of alcohol just prior to menstruation and when they are taking birth control pills that contain estrogen. One drink consumed by a woman will produce roughly the same physiologic consequences as two drinks consumed by a man.
- **Your age.** The older you are, the higher the BAC level will be after consuming equivalent drinks.
- **Your ethnicity.** Certain ethnic groups, such as Asians and Native Americans, are unable to metabolize alcohol as quickly as others including Caucasians and African Americans.
- **Other drugs.** Mixing alcohol with certain common medications, such as aspirin, acetaminophen (Tylenol), and ulcer medications can cause the BAC to rise more rapidly.

Prolonged alcohol consumption can lead to physical tolerance, as your brain becomes accustomed to a certain level of alcohol. You need to consume more alcohol to achieve the desired effects. This could lead to abuse and alcoholism.

Alcoholism

Alcoholism is a chronic disease with genetic, physiologic, and psychosocial consequences. Like other addictions, alcoholism is characterized by the following: drinking more alcohol than intended; persistent desire but unsuccessful attempts to stop drinking; frequent withdrawal and absenteeism; decreased performance at school or work; continued drinking despite the realization that his or her drinking is causing physical, social, or psychological problems; the presence of withdrawal symptoms when not drinking; and the need for increasing amounts of alcohol to achieve intoxication.

Drinking Responsibly

Abuse of alcohol is no longer the cultural norm, even in many segments of the college student population. Responsible drinking is always up to you. Alcohol does not need to be present to have a good time with friends. However, if you choose to drink alcohol, it is imperative that you also eat, to slow the rate of alcohol absorption into your body. Set a limit in advance on how many drinks you are going to have, and stick to it. Always go to a party with a designated driver, a friend who, in advance, commits to not drinking. Do everything possible to prevent an intoxicated friend from driving.

Don't rely on alcohol or other drugs as a means to relax; find alternative measures such as exercise, listening to music, reading, meditation, yoga, guided imagery, biofeedback, and hobbies to help you unwind.

Finally, don't drink alcohol just because you observe others drinking or because you believe "everyone else is doing it." According to national surveys, more students **believe** that others are using alcohol (95 percent) than what is actually reported (85 percent). Students who choose not to drink excessively report "second-hand" effects of the irresponsible use of alcohol by their friends. These non-drinking students are more likely to be physically abused or assaulted by their drinking friends, or become a victim to sexual harassment or assault. Academic performance may also suffer because of time spent caring for a roommate who had too much to drink; decreased study time, lack of sleep, and poor concentration may also be "second-hand" effects when friends or room-mates drink irresponsibly.

Using Campus Resources

The health center on most campuses sponsors student organizations which provide information and consultations concerning alcohol and drug abuse prevention. BACCHUS (Boost Alcohol Consciousness Concerning the Health of University Students) is a national student organization that provides programs on responsible alcohol use, including National Collegiate Alcohol Awareness Week and the Safe Spring Break campaign. To find out more information, contact your campus health center or counseling center. They may have physicians or mental health professionals who can assist you or refer you to a community organization for treatment.

HIV Infection and AIDS

We are experiencing an epidemic in the United States that is actually a worldwide pandemic. Infection with the Human Immunodeficiency Virus (HIV) has become the number-one challenging public health problem today, with far-reaching medical and psycho-social consequences. It is estimated that over 30 million people worldwide are infected with HIV, with approximately 16,000 new infections occurring daily. In the United States, it is estimated that over one million people are living with HIV infection, with about one-third having Acquired Immunodeficiency Syndrome (AIDS), the terminal phase of the continuum of HIV infection. States with the highest incidence of HIV and AIDS are California, New York, Florida, and New Jersey. The incidence of HIV infection is highest in individuals between the ages of 20 and 29 years, with the incidence of AIDS highest during the fourth decade of life (i.e., between 30 and 39 years of age). In the United States, AIDS is now the second leading cause of death among people aged 25 to 44, and in many parts of the country, AIDS is now the number-one cause of death among men in this same age range. Although the rate of infection is still highest in men, the incidence of infection is steadily rising in women. HIV infection is disproportionately higher among African Americans and Hispanics, when compared to Caucasians.

Epidemiology

The Human Immunodeficiency Virus is difficult to acquire. It is not spread through respiratory droplets or through casual contact, like the common cold or influenza viruses. You cannot acquire HIV by touching, simple kissing, hugging, or sitting next to someone who has the infection. HIV is not transmitted by sharing eating utensils, handshakes, using toilet seats, donating blood, or by mosquitoes.

There are only a few modes of HIV transmission. The virus is present in significant amounts only in blood, semen, vaginal secretions, and breast milk. The virus is present in very small concentrations in saliva, but there is essentially no risk of transmission via deep kissing. Transmission of HIV can occur as a result of:

- **Sexual activity.** HIV can be spread in semen and vaginal fluids during unprotected anal, vaginal, and oral sexual contact with an infected partner. Transmission is more likely to occur during anal intercourse than vaginal intercourse, and more likely to occur during vaginal intercourse than oral sex. Women are more likely to acquire HIV from an infected male partner than are men acquiring HIV infection from a female partner. The largest number of cases (55 percent) of HIV transmission involves homosexual sex, usually unprotected anal intercourse, between men; however, the incidence of heterosexual transmission has risen steadily over the past seven years, and is currently at 18 percent.
- **Injections using shared needles.** Any contaminated needle can transmit the virus, making steroid use, tattoos, and body piercing potentially risky unless sterile needles are used.
- **Perinatally.** A baby may **acquire** the virus before birth via the mother's circulation through the placenta, during the birth process via vaginal secretions, or after birth via infected breast milk. Mothers who are HIV positive have a 25 percent chance of infecting their unborn baby; this number decreases to less than 10 percent if the mother receives treatment during pregnancy.
- **Transfusions of blood, blood products, or organ transplants from HIV-infected individuals.** Since March 1985, the blood supply has been tested for the presence of HIV, significantly decreasing the incidence of HIV transmission via this means. Changes in the methods of screening blood donors have also helped with this decline. However, the risk still is present albeit very small.

■ Testing for HIV

The most widely used tests to determine the presence of HIV infection actually do not detect the virus itself, but measure the presence of antibodies that are formed in response to infection with HIV. The standard laboratory blood tests that are most commonly used are the Enzyme Linked Immunoassay (ELISA) and the Western Blot. The Ora-Sure is a type of ELISA test that detects the presence of HIV antibody in the mouth mucosa rather than in the blood; the accuracy of the Ora-Sure test is about the same as for the blood test.

The Western Blot is a more specific and expensive test and is therefore primarily used as a confirmatory test when the ELISA comes back as positive. The Western Blot is performed on the same blood specimen which resulted in the positive ELISA. If the ELISA is positive and the Western Blot is negative, the person does not have HIV infection. If the ELISA and the confirmatory Western Blot tests are both positive, then the person is diagnosed as having the HIV infection.

Since it takes at least two weeks to six months for the body to produce enough HIV antibodies to be measured by the tests, a negative result obtained on a test done too soon after the last risky behavior may not be accurate. It is imperative, therefore, that the ELISA be performed at least one additional time, preferably about six months later. Approximately 95 percent of people who have been infected with HIV will have positive blood tests within the first six months.

Anyone who feels they may be at risk should be tested for HIV. Early testing is important because treatments with AZT, ddI, ddC, and the powerful protease inhibitors suppress proliferation of HIV and, in most cases, lower the number of viruses in the bloodstream to undetectable levels, leading to a delay in the onset of AIDS symptoms. The use of AZT and the protease inhibitors, however, does not represent a cure. To date, there is no cure for HIV, and education remains the key ingredient in prevention.

> ■ *Always use a latex condom rather than a natural membrane condom.*
>
> ■ *Store condoms in a cool, dry place; never store them in the car or in your wallet.*
>
> ■ *Do not use condoms beyond their expiration date.*
>
> ■ *Only use water-based lubricants, such as K-Y Jelly; oil-based lubricants will break down the latex.*
>
> ■ *Use spermicide containing nonoxynol-9, as this compound inactivates HIV.*
>
> ■ *Know how to use a condom properly; practice if necessary.*
>
> ■ *Do not reuse a condom.*
>
> ■ *ALWAYS use one!*

Figure 4 ■ Guidelines for Condom Use

■ Limit Your Risk

NO ONE IS IMMUNE! Your risk of acquiring HIV infection is not dependent on who you are, but is dependent on your behaviors. The only absolutely safe way to protect yourself is by reducing or eliminating risky behaviors. If you do choose, for example, to have sexual intercourse, you should ALWAYS use a condom, even if you think that your partner is not infected. You can never be certain of your partner's past sexual history or drug use history, because he or she may have acquired HIV from a previous partner several years ago. Unknown to both of you, your partner may have slept with someone who slept with someone who once secretly abused injection drugs. Remember, once individuals become infected with HIV, they can remain completely asymptomatic for many years and may not even know that they have the infection! Next to abstinence, the safest way to protect yourself is to always use a latex condom with the spermicide nonoxynol-9. How confident do you feel that you will practice safer sex? Complete Exercise 2 to find out.

■ Summary

We discussed several important ways to enable you to live a balanced, healthy life. Health is something to be cherished. A healthy student is one who will excel academically, be more productive, and have time to pursue recreational pursuits and spend quality time with family and friends. A healthier student is a happier student, a happier employee, and a happier member of the community. Healthy decision making while in college will pay big dividends, with many benefits that will last far after you graduate.

■ Exercise 1. Wellness Lifestyle Assessment

DIRECTIONS: Using the following scale, answer each statement by placing the number that most closely corresponds to your lifestyle and feelings in the space preceding each statement.

KEY: 1 = "no/never" or "don't know"
2 = "rarely" or "1–6 times a year"
3 = "occasionally" or "1–4 times a month"
4 = "often, frequently" or "2–5 times a week"
5 = "yes/always" or "almost daily"

A. Physical Assessment

_____ 1. I perform aerobic exercises for twenty minutes or more per session.

_____ 2. When participating in physical activities, I include stretching and flexibility exercises.

_____ 3. My body fat composition is appropriate for my gender. (Men: 10–18 percent; Women: 16–25 percent)

_____ 4. I have appropriate medical checkups regularly and keep records of test results.

_____ 5. I practice safer sex or abstinence. I never have sex when intoxicated.

B. Nutritional Assessment

_____ 1. I eat at least 3 to 5 servings of vegetables and 2 to 4 servings of fruits daily.

_____ 2. I eat at least 6 to 11 servings daily of foods from the bread, cereal, rice, and pasta group.

_____ 3. I choose or prepare foods that tend to be lower in cholesterol and saturated fat.

_____ 4. When purchasing foods, I read the "Nutrition Facts" labels.

_____ 5. I avoid adding salt to my food.

C. Alcohol and Drugs Assessment

_____ 1. I avoid smoking and using smokeless tobacco products.

_____ 2. I avoid drinking alcohol or limit my daily alcohol intake to two drinks or less.

_____ 3. I do not drive after drinking alcohol or after taking medications that make me sleepy.

_____ 4. I follow directions when taking both prescription and over-the-counter medications.

_____ 5. I keep a record of drugs to which I am allergic in my wallet or purse.

D. Emotional Wellness Assessment

_____ 1. I feel positive about myself and my life. I set realistic goals for myself.

_____ 2. I can effectively cope with life's ups and downs in a healthy manner.

_____ 3. I do not tend to be nervous, impatient, or under a high amount of stress.

_____ 4. I can express my feelings of anger.

_____ 5. When working under pressure, I stay calm and am not easily distracted.

E. Intellectual Wellness Assessment

_____ 1. I seek advice when I am uncertain or uncomfortable with a recommended treatment.

_____ 2. I ask about the risks, benefits, and medical necessity of all medical tests and procedures.

_____ 3. I keep informed of the latest trends and information concerning health matters.

_____ 4. I feel comfortable about talking to my doctor.

_____ 5. I know the guidelines for practicing good preventive medicine and self-care.

F. Social and Spiritual Wellness Assessment

_____ 1. I am able to develop close, intimate relationships.

_____ 2. I am involved in school and/or community activities.

_____ 3. I have recreational hobbies and do something fun just for myself at least once a week.

_____ 4. I know what my values and beliefs are and I am tolerant of the beliefs of others.

_____ 5. My life has meaning and direction. I have life goals. Personal reflection is important.

■ Analyzing Your Wellness Assessment

For each of the six wellness sections, add the total number of points that you assigned to each question. Place the totals of each section below:

TOTALS for each of the six sections:

A. Physical Assessment _____

B. Nutritional Assessment _____

C. Alcohol and Drugs Assessment _____

D. Emotional Wellness Assessment _____

E. Intellectual Wellness Assessment _____

F. Social and Spiritual Wellness Assessment _____

TOTAL POINTS _____

Then, divide the Total Points by six to get the
"Average Wellness Score" = _____

What do your results mean? The results apply to each of the six individual sections, as well as for determining your overall wellness assessment (after dividing your total score by six).

Total for each section (or Average Wellness Score)	RESULTS (for each individual section and for the overall assessment)
23–25	Excellent Your lifestyle choices and attitudes can significantly contribute to a healthy life. You are to be commended!
19–22	Good You engage in many health-promoting behaviors and attitudes. You care about your health. However, there are some areas that you could improve to provide optimal health benefits and wellness.
11–18	Average You are typical of the average American who tends to not always practice the healthiest of behaviors, despite having the knowledge which would suggest the contrary. Now is the time to consider making changes in your lifestyle to foster a healthier future.
5–10	Needs immediate improvement You are to be commended for being concerned enough about your health to take this assessment, but your behaviors and attitudes may be having a detrimental effect on your overall health. Now is the time to take action to improve your health!

■ Exercise 2. Can You Practice Safer Sex?

Most people know how HIV is transmitted and what behaviors are necessary to reduce their risk of acquiring the virus. However, some of these behaviors are not always easy to do. Your confidence in yourself to perform these protective sex behaviors is as important as simply knowing what the behaviors are. Assess your safer sex confidence level by answering these questions honestly, according to the key below:

KEY: A = I always could do this in all situations.

B = I could do this occasionally.

C = I could not do this.

_____ buy condoms at a store.

_____ discuss using a condom with a new sex partner before having sex.

_____ refuse to have sex with a person if he or she did not want to use a condom.

_____ talk to a new sex partner about his or her past sexual experiences and number of sexual partners.

_____ ask a new sex partner whether he or she has ever had sex with another person of the same sex.

_____ ask a potential sex partner about the use of intravenous drugs and sharing of needles.

_____ be able to avoid using alcohol on a date to help make a decision about sex easier.

_____ be able to clearly express what my sexual expectations and limits are before beginning any sexual activity.

_____ be able to resist an unwanted sexual advance or stop sexual activity if a condom wasn't available.

_____ be able to resist an unwanted sexual activity even when slightly intoxicated after a few drinks.

What do my results mean?

1) Multiply the number of responses you answered with "C" by 2.
2) Add to the result, the number of responses you answered with "B."
3) Responses answered with "A" do not count as points.
4) Add the answers from 1) + 2) above to get the "Confidence Score."
5) Circle your overall confidence score on the continuum below to determine your risk.

0	2	4	6	8	10	12	14	16	18	20

LOW RISK   HIGH RISK

If you scored between 10 and 20 points, you tend to doubt your ability to behave in a way that would protect you from acquiring HIV. You should evaluate your own beliefs and attitudes concerning safer sex in the four areas assessed: condom use, self-protection, sex under the influence, and sexual limits.

CHAPTER 6

Stress
Accentuate the Positive

Everyone knows when he or she is experiencing stress, and each one of us can discuss various stressors that confront us each week. A **stressor**, according to Hans Selye, is anything that produces tension in your life, which may be of a physical nature (e.g., starvation brought on by a drought in east Africa, restricted access to a friend's house caused by a broken leg in a cast) or a psychological nature (e.g., being involved in interpersonal conflict, being frustrated in a second attempt to pass a required course). Of these two categories, it seems that psychological stressors are forever present, even in the best of times, for most students. Psychological stressors confront us all regardless of how healthy, powerful, or rich we are, although these stressors differ in the degree to which they "stress us out."

Stress often arises when we have choices to make. In most cases we would rather deal with selecting between two goods than two evils, but conflict can be experienced when one is selecting between two attractive outcomes. Such an **approach-approach** type of conflict might involve having to select between two high-paying jobs after graduating from college. While approach-approach conflicts are unlikely to end like the one in the example known as "Buridan's ass," where a donkey caught between two equally attractive piles of hay dies from being unable to decide which pile to eat, conflict is conflict, and even selecting between two desirables can be stressful.

Memories concerning our struggle to choose between two evils seem to be vivid and lasting. For example, a person choosing between taking out a student loan with a high interest rate or asking his or her parents for additional help knowing they can ill afford the assistance is in this situation. Having two dreadful choices is commonly referred to as being caught "between a rock and a hard spot." The person is experiencing an **avoidance-avoidance** type of conflict. No matter what the cause, psychological frustration can be profoundly stressful and may even cause us to respond aggressively. We might scream at our roommate or even become physically violent in extreme cases of stress.

If asked, all of us could easily list stressful events or periods in our life (e.g., death of a pet, moving from one school or town to another, loss of a close family member through death, divorce of parents, loss of some prized possession, enrolling in college classes for the first time). Stress can be defined as a personal experience of physical or mental strain that results in numerous physiological changes (e.g., heart-rate increases, increase in the force of one's heart-beat, digestive disturbance, blood-vessel constriction, elevated blood pressure, noticeable sweating, rise in muscle tightness). In this chapter we will discuss the causes and symptoms of stress and how you can develop effective ways to cope with stress.

■ What Is Stressful?

While we all experience stress, we are usually surprised to learn it has many faces and a subtle aspect that we are not always aware of, as if it is a companion that hides in the shadows.

■ What Is Stress Exactly?

The items listed on the assessment tool developed by Holmes and Rahe help us understand what the term stress encompasses in everyday language. Simply stated, **stress** is a reaction to the various things that happen to us, both negative and positive. Interestingly, while most of us readily think of negative events as stress-provoking (e.g., jail term, death of a close friend, being fired at work), in reality events that are very positive in nature can also be stressful (e.g., change in residence, vacation, marriage). Even though we might be able to cite exceptions, in the vast majority of cases one's wedding day is a joyful event marked by celebration. Marriage also introduces many changes for both people involved. Issues can range from who pays for which day-to-day living expense to the "correct" way to squeeze toothpaste from a tube. Changes associated with marriage can generate a lot of stress.

A meaningful and useful way to conceptualize stress is given in the following formula.

Stress = Number of Resources – Number of Changes

Thus, high levels of stress are due to changes exceeding resources, and low levels of stress are due to resources exceeding changes.

Holmes and Rahe's list of stressful events covers a wide range of the adult life span, although several of the items would not apply to many undergraduates. In a college environment one would expect to find certain changes not listed by Holmes and Rahe to be just as stressful as those listed. These could include dropping or being withdrawn from a class with a "W," receiving a $20 ticket from campus police for a parking violation, changing from one major to another, not being able to enter a major because of one's grade point average, being withdrawn from a course with a "WF," joining a sorority or fraternity, transferring to another college (leaving this college or coming to this college as a transfer student), failing a course in one's major with a "favorite" professor, first dismissal from college, and being accused of academic dishonesty. In the above equation, note that the word "change" is important. Frequently we are forced to deal with changes that wear us down physically and psychologically because we lack the necessary resources at the time to cope. Our store of coping resources can fluctuate. Remember the last time when you had the flu and experienced a drop in your ability to cope with the demands placed on you?

Not all change is bad; in fact, there is evidence to suggest that we need a certain amount of change to maintain our physical and psychological balance. Psychologists and other researchers once studied the effect of relatively unchanging surroundings (referred to as sensory deprivation studies). Participants were required to wear blindfolds or the equivalent, to stay still by lying down in soundproof rooms or large containers, to have their arms restrained in special devices to avoid experiencing tactile sensations, and so forth. The effects were profound in some cases; some participants even reported hallucinations. While too much change is bad, too little can also be bad. Apparently, too few external changes result in the body creating self-induced changes (hallucinations). But we are all individuals, and it is important to recognize that individuals differ in how much change they can tolerate.

■ Psychological Hardiness and Personality Differences

In *Man in Search of Meaning*, Victor Frankl describes how an individual can confront a truly unusual degree of change (incarceration in a concentration camp) and not only survive but come out stronger as a result. Perspective is very important in explaining outcomes, and we all differ in the degree to which we like change, or seek change in our lives. Some people seem to be revitalized by changes, and some even seek out high-pressure positions because of the constantly changing demands. Many presidents of the United States likely fall into this category of stress-hardy individuals. People such as Jimmy Carter, Elizabeth Dole, John Glenn, Hillary Clinton, Dianne Feinstein, George W. Bush, and Christine Whitman who are serving or have served in high-profile positions in politics probably all possess a high level of psychological hardiness. For example, when Senator Feinstein was asked whether she would consider running for president, she said:

> I've been the first [woman] four times now: once as president of the Board of Supervisors [in San Francisco], as mayor, as the first gubernatorial candidate in my state, the first woman Senator from my state. What I've learned is there is a testing period that goes on—particularly in an executive capacity. I think it [takes someone] with the ability to run a campaign well, put together a platform that resounds with the American people and someone with the stamina, the staying power, the determination and enthusiasm to carry it off. (Ciabatti, 1999, p. 6)

Psychological hardiness is reflected in individuals who like and seek change and challenges, possess a clear focus or goal, and perceive themselves as having control.

Stressful events can be short in duration (e.g., writing a speech) or long (e.g., a difficult job with a lot of responsibilities), but it is not always the magnitude of the event that determines how well we cope. The same stressors might be tolerable for one person but overwhelming to another. Our personal level of psychological hardiness is very important. Salvatore Maddi and Suzanne Kobasa (1994) studied executives in stressful situations, primarily due to an organization undergoing reorganization with the possibility of lost employment. Such periods of reorganization are associated with ill health (increases colds, influenza, backaches, and migraine headaches). Maddi and Kobasa found that some individuals were not as susceptible to the reorganization stressor. These resilient individuals were able to maintain a sense of control over most events encountered in life. The psychologically hardy displayed few of the effects found in others. The researchers found that the psychologically hardy (PH) possess

- An open attitude toward change, assessing *change as a challenge* rather than a threat to one's self.
- *A high degree of commitment* to what the person is involved in. This commitment is tied to goals and objectives. Subjects low in commitment tended to display evidence of being alienated from work, people, and things.
- *A sense of control over most events* rather than a sense of helplessness. High PHs are convinced they can influence the course of their future. In their eyes, effort makes a difference at work, in school, and in relationships. Low PHs felt they had little if any power to influence outcomes. For this latter group, outside forces controlled their future.

One of the lessons to be learned from the work of Maddi and Kobasa is that individuals confronted with stress can meet it head on (take active steps) or let the situation roll over them (take a passive approach). In the latter case, the person does not see the situation as a challenge, but rather as a threat beyond his or her control. In some cases, rather than being able to call upon a sense of commitment to sustain them during a difficult period, individuals low on hardiness worry and try to escape; they may deny what is occurring or even blame others. The following list summarizes the differences between high PH and low PH.

High PH	Low PH
Sees a challenge	Sees a threat
Commitment	Alienation
Active coping	Passive coping
Seeks change	Avoids change
Feels invigorated	Feels helpless

Martin Seligman (1995) has coined the term **learned helplessness**. Specifically, Seligman used the term to refer to situations where a person (or animal, since a lot of studies in this area use animal subjects) acts in a helpless manner if exposed to situations that are harmful or painful *and cannot be avoided*. The unavoidability of these situations seems to inhibit learning how to escape a harmful or painful situation in the future—a situation that could be avoided. In one early study on learned helplessness, dogs were placed in one of two treatments. Those in treatment A were confined to a harness and given electric shocks without any possibility of escape. Those in treatment B were exposed to the same exact conditions except if the animal struggled it could escape. Treatment A led to the dogs becoming less competitive, less aggressive, and less able to escape painful situations in the future. Treatment B resulted in dogs who were more competitive, aggressive, and better capable of escaping painful situations in the future. Other animal experiments on mice and rats produced animals in the learned helplessness group who were less active, displayed greater difficulty learning, and gave up sooner when confronted with challenges. Human participants in similar studies were found to be affected adversely in terms of problem-solving ability.

In general, from the numerous studies conducted it appears that some humans, due to certain experiences in and outside the academic world, "learn to be helpless." The effects of learned helplessness follow.

■ The ability to effectively solve problems is reduced. A drop in motivation, energy, and the will to struggle and survive occurs.

■ Learning becomes much more difficult. People ignore or seem unable to profit from information.

■ An elevation of emotional or physical distress occurs. Individuals are likely to show outward signs of anxiety and depression. If conditions are not altered, the person may become sick or develop an illness (similar to Holmes and Rahe's findings that also uncovered a relationship between stressful conditions and illness).

Finally, an individual's personality type influences how much stress the person may experience. For example, while anxiety can be a symptom of stress and anxiety, levels vary from day to day and week to week (called state anxiety), individuals also display somewhat consistent patterns (called trait anxiety). Charles Spielberger (1972) identified these two categories and uncovered some interesting findings. While the announcement of an important test can be expected to alter one's level of state anxiety, individuals differ in how much it affects them. These differences are related to the personality of the individual. Individuals with low trait anxiety usually seem calm and laid-back, while individuals with high trait anxiety typically seem high-strung and are frequently worried. Keep in mind that anxiety is not in and of itself bad—it serves to motivate us to study. Both high-anxiety and low-anxiety individuals may experience performance problems but for different reasons; in the former case, the high level of anxiety hinders processing of information, and in the latter, there is too little anxiety to motivate the person to study adequately.

Another type of personality that has been linked to stress is the **Type A personality**. Type A personalities are stress generators, creating stress in addition to what is placed on them from the outside. Type A personalities are driven to work (often working long hours, weekends), very goal conscious (frequently thinking of goals that need to be achieved and tasks that need to be completed), and find it very difficult to relax. This type of person always seems to be in a rush and may tend to finish others' sentences. Type A personalities find it very difficult to settle for less than perfection. Behind the wheel of a car, Type A personalities are likely to become agitated or angry because other drivers are "moving too slow," preventing the Type A from getting to his or her destination. The advantage of being a Type A is achievement (higher grades); the disadvantage is poor health (they tend to be more susceptible to heart attacks).

■ Prolonged Stress and Impairment of Functioning

Clearly, stress can be generated in many different ways, and we know from Holmes and Rahe's work that high levels of stress can result in illness and dysfunction. Does this happen overnight? The good news is no. The effects tend to accumulate over time, which means we have a period of time to take action to prevent the worst-case scenario from occurring. According to Hans Selye, when responding to stress, we go through a series of stages called the General Adaptation Syndrome (GAS).

Stage 1: Alarm

Stress leads to physiological changes in your body (e.g., heart rate and respiration increase, adrenaline levels rise, and digestive functions drop). The body is gearing itself up to take action. The person prepares to either *"fight or take flight,"* that is, run from a perceived danger.

Stage 2: Resistance

Our "fight or flight" response has its origins in our early history as humans two million or more years ago. The problem is we are no longer literally fighting or running from saber-toothed tigers. We can neither punch the rude, unreasonable professor nor run out of his required class. Often we must stay put and endure the stressors in our life and suffer the consequences (in the twenty-first century the "fight or flight" response we are physiologically and mentally prepared to carry out is no longer appropriate in many situations). When we are stuck between fight and flight, the physiological changes that occur in the alarm stage still occur but at a lower level. But this level is still strong enough to wear us down psychologically and physically.

Stage 3: Exhaustion

At this point our resources are low and physical deterioration can set in (possibly contributing to conditions such as heart disease, hypertension, asthma, colitis, and, according to some researchers, ulcers and some forms of cancer). These diseases of adaptation or psychosomatic illnesses are the result of the person being blocked from reacting to a problem in a manner that can reestablish his or her equilibrium.

Too much adrenaline is associated with a drop in white blood cells, which impacts the immune system. For many students, prolonged stress results in symptoms such as fatigue, boredom, less restful sleep, loss of appetite (or eating much more), agitation, and becoming prone to making mistakes and having accidents. It has been estimated that over 45% of headaches are stress related.

■ What Can Be Done?

Many students (and nonstudents) respond to stress in self-defeating ways, by using drugs and alcohol, withdrawing from the things that are important but cause stress, and using psychological defenses such as denial, projection, or fantasizing. In fact, there are many things that can be done to relieve and prevent stress. Here are several suggestions that we have found effective and relatively easy to apply.

■ Everyday Techniques for Reducing Stress

Check your gauges (psychological/emotional, behavioral, and physical). Periodically stop and determine how much stress you are experiencing. Is it high or low? Whatever the level is, is the stress having a negative impact on your academic performance, your personal life, or your ability to just enjoy life? Sometimes such self-examination leads to the awareness that there are some unnecessary sources of stress in your life. For example, perhaps an acquaintance is always putting you down in subtle ways but denies doing so; no one should go through life maintaining such an association. If confronting the person does not change the situation, it is probably better to break off the relationship.

Feed yourself psychologically and emotionally. Read that book you have wanted to get to, listen to your favorite music, go to a movie or the local mall, start a hobby, or get involved in a community service such as Habitat for Humanity. It is important to take time to get away. While a stressed-out student may find it difficult to find the time to get away, such time-outs can replenish one's depleted energy and help break the cycle of lingering stress (i.e., GAS).

Feed yourself physiologically and behaviorally. Exercise. Spend 30 minutes three times a week. Take advantage of the college exercise facility if one is available; play tennis, racquetball, handball, basketball, and learn mountain climbing. Joining a team also helps to establish a support system. If you are on a tight schedule and cannot take time to travel somewhere, walk or run a mile or more a day near your residence (walk or run with a trusted partner so you are not out alone), or ride a bike on campus and climb the stairs in a campus building rather than riding the elevator. Not only is health improved by exercise, but exercise has been proven to reduce stress levels. Of course, adequate sleep and good nutrition are necessary ingredients in managing anxiety and stress.

Breathe deeply. During periods of stress take a moment to close your eyes. Breathe in two or three times in a slow and deep manner, allowing your stomach to rise as you breathe in. Slowly exhale through your lips. Increasing one's oxygen level in this manner can help relieve stress.

Divert your attention. Waiting for the professor to distribute a test to the class or to be called on to make a presentation can elevate your anxiety and stress level. Instead of sitting there thinking negative thoughts ("I am not sure I am prepared"), bump the negative thought aside with a pleasant image (visualize your favorite vacation spot) or focus on an available image (the tree outside the window that is swaying in the breeze). A simple refocusing from negative thoughts to something more pleasant in nature has been found to reduce anxiety and stress.

Visualize success. When feeling anxious due to some stressor (e.g., a major course paper that is due), visualize yourself as being successful. Visualize the various steps necessary in a task and actually picture yourself being successful each step of the way. A student teacher might go to the classroom where he or she will be teaching and go through the lesson plan without students there. He or she might use the chalkboard, read from the text, and so forth, all the while imagining a positive outcome. Such an activity has proven to be effective in reducing one's level of anxiety and stress.

Apply environmental engineering tactics. Make your apartment, dorm room, or house a relaxing environment. Decorate the walls with favorite posters or pictures, place objects around that elicit pleasant memories or feelings, purchase a tropical fish tank, which can help to create a soothing environment. Have a place that can be your place to escape to and fill it with items that make you feel good.

Techniques for Periods of High Stress

During periods of high stress we typically find it much more effective to develop an ongoing routine that involves cognitive restructuring, muscle relaxation, meditation, or sequential imagery. Such techniques are intended to be learned and practiced on a regular basis.

Cognitive Restructuring. Sometimes students are aware they are their own worst enemy because of negative self-talk. These are messages that a person repeats to himself or herself that negatively affect both performance and quality of life. Both test-anxious and non-test-anxious students say negative things to themselves (e.g., "I am going to fail this test!"), but test-anxious students make such remarks much more frequently and tend to believe them more. Albert Ellis, the creator of rational emotive behavior therapy, has had considerable success in having people tackle their stress-producing thoughts using an A-B-C approach to modifying behavior.

> **A = activating event,** which can be thought of as the stressor ("I have an important test Tuesday"). The event in and of itself is not the problem; it is how we perceive the event that is crucial.
>
> **B = belief** about the activating event. If my belief is that I will fail the test, then I will experience unnecessary stress.
>
> **C = consequence.** If I perceive myself as failing, I will experience stress and thus become anxious and not perform at my optimum level. We can alter the process at point B by forcefully injecting more positive thoughts to push out the self-defeating ones we have come accustomed to speaking silently to ourselves.

Ellis emphasizes that our irrational thinking generates a great deal of stress that simply does not reflect reality. This view is captured in the story of the man who discloses the following when reflecting back about his long life: "I am an old man who has had many worries in my life, few of which ever came true."

Imagery. Imaging exercises can also break the cycle of negative self-talk but do so with images, not words. For example, a person may practice sequentially going through a certain set of positive images for 10 minutes or longer. During a period of stress (e.g., waiting for a test to be distributed in class), the person can call upon one of the images used to reduce anxiety on the spot.

An example of imaging exercise follows. Read over the following images and then close your eyes and imagine the scene described.

> It is a beautiful spring day.
> Out my window I can see a crystal-clear, deep-blue sky.
> Almost as in a dream I go to my front door and step outside.
> There is a gentle breeze.
> The smell of flowers and the sound of singing birds are very pleasant.
> I walk out onto the fresh, green grass.
> I slowly kneel down and decide to lie back on the fresh, spring grass.
> The temperature is just right.
> I start to daydream about a trip to my favorite beach.
> I see myself on the beach and the sun is not too bright, just nice and warm.
> The water is a beautiful aqua color that I can see through to the bottom.
> The sand on the beach is a beautiful white, and coconut trees are spread out up and down the beach.
> I start to walk on the beach.
> The sound of the waves is very soothing.
> The saltwater smell is refreshing.
> I stop when I notice a seashell embedded in the sand. It has many bright colors.
> Reds.
> Yellows.
> Blues.

I bend over and pick up the beautifully colored shell.

The feel of the water-worn shell is comforting.

The sun is going down and is near the horizon.

I sit down on the sand to watch the sun set.

It is a beautiful sunset with various shades of reds, and I feel warm and at peace.

A deep sense of peace flows over me, and I have no fears or worries.

I return from my imaginary trip to feeling both very relaxed and revitalized, as if I just enjoyed a long, restful sleep from which I open my eyes and feel great and optimistic about the world.

Deep Relaxation. For this exercise it is recommended that you practice approximately 20 minutes per day for about two weeks to master the technique. In a quiet, disturbance-free location, you are to go through the following muscle groups, tensing and relaxing them. The technique teaches a person, without going through the whole procedure, to quickly scan the body in approximately 10 seconds to locate pockets of muscle tension, which are then relaxed. The resulting state of relaxation can bring about a significant reduction in anxiety and stress allowing the person to focus his or her attention without having negative thoughts intrude. Keep in mind that when practicing this technique, you should not strain any part of the body that has been injured or is recovering from injury.

Lie back in a bed (or on the floor). Place a pillow under your head. After taking three deep breaths as described earlier, do the following:

Close your eyes.

Clench both your fists. Study the tension.

Relax the fingers of your hands and study the difference.

Enjoy the feeling of just lying there relaxed.

Again, clench both hands tighter and tighter. Study and focus on the tension you created in this part of your body.

Allow yourself to become relaxed all over.

Bend your elbows. Feel the tension created by bending your elbows. Dwell on the tension. Get to know how the tension feels in this part of the body.

Allow yourself to become very relaxed all over.

Become more and more relaxed. Imagine that you are so relaxed that you are sinking into the surface beneath you.

Straighten your arms out. Feel the tension created by pushing your arms straight out.

Now relax you arms and let them find their own place.

Wrinkle your forehead. Exam how the wrinkles feel and picture how they look. Now relax. Let the wrinkles go and picture in your mind the way your forehead now looks without the wrinkles.

Squeeze your eyes shut. Experience the tension you created using your eyes. Relax your eyes.

Relax all over.

Stay as relaxed as possible for about a minute.

Relax.

Relax.

Now clamp your teeth together. Study the tension created by biting your teeth together. Tension is being created in the jaws. Picture in your mind how the muscles in this area are tight.

Relax.

Now press your head back—push back on the pillow. Now stop and allow your body to become comfortable all over. Picture your body melting into the surface of the bed (or floor). Your body is so relaxed it is sinking down.

It is like you are a big rag doll just lying there.

Relax.

Move your head down so it is now against your chest. Study the tension that this movement created.

Relax.

Bring your shoulders up. Study the muscle tension created when you try to touch your ears with your shoulders.

Relax.

Now pull in your stomach, tighter and tighter. Now relax.

Relax.

Create a small arch in your back. Feel the tension in your muscles when you arch your back. Relax and allow your back to settle into a comfortable position as you do when you go to sleep at night.

Point your toes up toward the top of you head. Maintain this for 20 seconds. Now relax.

Relax.

Point your toes away from the top of your head. Maintain this position for about 10 seconds. Now relax.

Relax.

Raise one leg. Keep the leg up until the tension starts to become uncomfortable. Now lower that leg.

Relax.

Now lift the other leg. Keep it up for about the same length of time. Okay, now relax.

Become as relaxed as you are capable of becoming. Release all the muscle tension in your body. Relax more and more until you reach a very relaxed state—a very, very deep state of relaxation.

Lie there in a relaxed state for a while.

Now *imagine* getting up (*do not move*—just imagine getting up.) Notice the change in muscle tension even when you just picture in your mind that you are getting up.

Go back to a deep state of relaxation. Let any tension you find pour out of your body as if you were a bucket with many, many holes and the tension is water.

After about a minute permit yourself to come out of your relaxed state. You will feel refreshed upon getting up from where you were lying.

Meditation. There are various meditation techniques that can be used. A basic ingredient is to clear one's mind of thoughts and to concentrate on breathing, for example. As a person breathes in, he or she should count *one* for the *breath in*, *two* for the *breath out*, *three* for the next *breath in*. Continue all the way to the number ten. The trick is not to allow stray thoughts or images to occupy your mind. If this occurs, you must start over with the number one. It sounds easy—it is not. Try this exercise. It will take a period of practice (sometimes a long period) before you can reach the number ten without some sort of intrusion into your mind. Emptying one's mind is difficult.

In part, meditation is a way to slow us down. The mind is sometimes described as "a bunch of monkeys jumping from tree to tree," a metaphor to reflect how cluttered our mind can be with all the thoughts that enter its domain, disturbing its peace. As early as the 1970s, Herbert Benson and his colleagues at Harvard Medical School (see *The Relaxation Response*, 1975) found that by passively clearing the mind during meditation, oxygen requirements drop, heartbeat slows, blood pressure lowers, and we experience a mental and physiological calmness.

■ References

Barrios, B. A., Ginter, E. J., Scalise, J. J., & Miller, F. G. (1980). Treatment of test anxiety by applied relaxation and cue-controlled relaxation. *Psychological Reports, 46,* 1287–1296.

Benson, H. (1975). *The relaxation response.* New York: Morrow.

Ciabattari, J. (1999, January). Women who could be president. *Parade Magazine,* 6–7.

Ellis, A., & Grieger, R. (Eds.) (1977). *Handbook of rational emotive therapy.* New York: Springer.

Friedman, M., & Rosenman, R. H. (1974). *Type A behavior and your heart.* New York: Knopf.

Maddi, S. R., & Hess, M. J. (1992). Personality hardiness and success in basketball. *International Journal of Sport Psychology, 23,* 360–368.

Maddi, S. R., & Kosaba, D. M. (1994). Hardiness and mental health. *Journal of Personality Assessment, 64,* 265–274.

Seligman, M. E. P. (1975). *Helplessness: On depression, development, and death.* San Francisco: W. H. Freeman.

Selye, H. (1953). *The Stress of Life.* New York: Knopf.

Spielberger, C. D. (Ed.). (1972). *Anxiety: Current trends in theory and research.* New York: Academic Press.

◼ Exercise 1. Stress Assessment

If you are not sure of the level (degree) of stress being experienced in your life, the following exercise will help you obtain a more precise measure of how stress is affecting you in three categories.

Physical Symptoms

How many of these symptoms have you experienced during the last six months? Is your body trying to tell you something? Are you at risk? Go over this list and rate yourself on each item using a scale of 1 to 5, with 1 being "not a problem" and 5 being "I experience this all the time."

_____ 1. tension or migraine headaches

_____ 2. back, shoulder, neck, or joint pain

_____ 3. hypertension

_____ 4. excessive tiredness and chronic fatigue

_____ 5. white knuckles or cold, clammy hands

_____ 6. grinding teeth

_____ 7. rapid or irregular heartbeat, tightness in the chest or chest pain

_____ 8. shallow breathing or shortness of breath

_____ 9. excessive perspiration

_____ 10. digestive disturbances including abdominal pain, nausea, upset stomach, diarrhea, frequent urination, or constipation

_____ 11. ulcers

_____ 12. trembling, nervous tics, shaking hands, or voice tremor

_____ 13. heartburn and indigestion

_____ 14. increased blood pressure

_____ 15. acne, psoriasis, dermatitis, hives, rashes, and other skin problems

_____ 16. allergy and asthma attacks

_____ 17. blurry vision

_____ 18. frequent colds, cough, or flu

_____ 19. weakness or dizziness

_____ 20. speech problems

_____ 21. excessive weight changes, either gain or loss

_____ 22. tight muscles or muscular aches

_____ 23. jaw ache or pain

_____ 24. changes in body temperature

_____ 25. excessive thirst

_____ 26. choking sensations

_____ 27. hyperventilation

_____ 28. increased or decreased appetite

_____ 29. impotence or decreased sex drive

_____ 30. infertility

_____ 31. menstrual problems

_____ 32. loss of consciousness

_____ 33. palpitations

_____ 34. mononucleosis

_____ 35. increase adrenaline flow

Emotional or Psychological Symptoms

How many times in the last six months have you had these feelings? Review this list, and rate yourself on a scale of 1 to 5, with 1 being "never feel this way" and 5 being "feeling this way all the time."

_____ 1. depression

_____ 2. hopelessness or helplessness

_____ 3. mood swings

_____ 4. loss of interest

_____ 5. dissatisfaction

_____ 6. feelings of guilt

_____ 7. preoccupation

_____ 8. mental distraction

_____ 9. boredom

_____ 10. sadness

_____ 11. loneliness

_____ 12. fear

_____ 13. worry

_____ 14. feeling overwhelmed

_____ 15. frustration

_____ 16. confusion

_____ 17. forgetfulness

_____ 18. burnout

_____ 19. panic

_____ 20. thoughts of escape (e.g., "I wish I could run away")

Behavioral Changes

Have you noticed any of these kinds of changes in your behavior in the last six months? Go over this list and rate yourself on each item using a scale 1 to 5, with 1 being "not a problem" and 5 being "I experience this all the time."

_____ 1. overeating or undereating

_____ 2. increased use of alcohol

_____ 3. sleeping too much

_____ 4. insomnia

_____ 5. nightmares

_____ 6. overspending

_____ 7. increased reliance on prescription drugs

_____ 8. increased smoking

_____ 9. impulsive behavior

_____ 10. inability to concentrate on task

_____ 11. irritability

_____ 12. accident proneness

_____ 13. compulsive or repetitive behavior

_____ 14. inefficiency

_____ 15. excessive anger

_____ 16. aggressive behavior

_____ 17. use of nonprescription drugs

_____ 18. increase in risk taking behaviors (e.g., speeding)

_____ 19. difficulty making decisions

_____ 20. stuttering or speech difficulties

_____ 21. loss of productivity

_____ 22. mood swings

_____ 23. instability

_____ 24. nervous laughter

_____ 25. restlessness

_____ 26. poor memory

_____ 27. poor judgment

_____ 28. apathy, loss of interest

_____ 29. chewing fingernails

_____ 30. withdrawal

Scoring

Tally your score for each category, and write your scores on the lines below.

Physical   _____

Emotional/Psychological   _____

Behavioral   _____

Grand Total   _____

- If your grand total is *below 150*, you are probably able to manage your stress. If you are not sure this interpretation is correct, feel free to discuss your uncertainty with the instructor of this course.

- If your score is *150 or above*, you may want to meet with the instructor to develop a stress-reduction plan or to get suggestions from the instructor as to what resources are available on campus.

Note: This assessment is not a perfect measure of your stress level. We recommend that you seek some type of assistance, regardless of your actual score, if you believe stress is interfering with the quality of your life.

Coping with Stress

Indicate what category of stress seems most prevalent in your life at this time (physical, emotional/psychological, or behavioral). Based on what was discussed in class and in this chapter, indicate four steps you can take to reduce this stress. Finally, select one step and indicate the date you plan to initiate it.

- Type of stress most prevalent at this time _____

- Four steps to reduce this stress:

1.

2.

3.

4.

- I plan to use step _____ to reduce stress in my life. I also plan to initiate it on _____.

CHAPTER 7
Creating Time through Effective Time Management

Frequently, a student's reason for not succeeding at a college is attributed to such things as not being able to devote sufficient time to studying, overloading himself or herself with too many tasks, putting things off to the last minute, or having difficulty utilizing time that has been set aside to complete academic tasks. In the last instance, the problem may be one of concentration, an often cited complaint that may result from anxiety, sleep deprivation, stress, personal problems, or any number of interfering factors. All these reasons for not doing well are related to time management or, more accurately, time mismanagement. The major areas of discussion in this chapter are time management strategies tied to one's personal values, getting organized via a schedule, utilizing a to-do list, and effectively carrying out what you have planned.

■ Seeing the Big Picture in Relation to Time Management: Achieving Values-Congruence

To accomplish major tasks (the "big picture") in one's personal, academic, social, and professional life requires consideration of one's values. When goals are in line with our values, they have **values-congruence**. Achieving a values-congruent perspective will help you maximize your academic performance and your overall potential. Another outcome is likely to be greater general happiness.

Steps necessary to achieve values-congruence are the following:

1. Identify the most significant values in your life (e.g., financial security, working with others, utilizing creative ability, supervising others, influencing others, working with computers).

2. Identify how your academic preparation and choice of a major ties to your values.

3. Identify all the steps, activities, and academic opportunities involved in accomplishing lifelong educational and career objectives.

Now, identify, apply, evaluate, and modify your time-management plan for academic and career success. Simply stated, you should develop your own personal model of time management to accomplish what is of true value to you. The basic ingredients of this model are fourfold.

- Tie your plans to specific objectives (e.g., "I think I will take a survey course to decide what area of a particular career I want to enter.").

- Invest the necessary time to establish how you will implement, evaluate, and effectively modify, if necessary, your personal model (e.g., "I will take the survey course in the spring, visit a career counselor after completing the course, and discuss the major I am interested in to determine if this is the correct career path for me.").

- Manage your time in a way to reach your goals, but do this in a flexible manner without losing your focus on key objectives—objectives that are based on your personal values (e.g., values such as wanting to have a career in an area where you will be allowed to creatively express your ideas as well as being able to work with others, so you can apply your people skills).

- End each day (or some other specifically designated period of time such as once a week) by achieving at least one positive step to meet your objectives. The positive step can be a major step or a minor step, the most important thing is to be moving in a direction that results from values-congruence.

■ Three Keys for Creating and Utilizing an Effective Time Management Model

Keys for putting this model in effect involve the following areas: getting organized, the to-do list, and the carry-through.

Getting Organized

The following are points to consider when scheduling or structuring your time.

- Be reasonable. Construct a schedule you will actually live by. Do not try to change everything in your life to "finally get organized, once and for all." Keep this jingle in mind: "Inch by inch, it's a cinch. Yard by yard, it's too hard."
- Time-management is really self-management. There are 24 hours in a day, 168 hours in a week and 2,520 hours in a semester (i.e., 15 weeks). Use it or lose it.
- Maintain flexibility when scheduling. Allow for mishaps. Schedules that are too tight with no buffers for the unexpected can create stress once the person is off track because of the interruption.
- Establish time limits for tasks being scheduled. Move on to the next task when the established time limit is up. (If you are not allowing enough time for tasks, learn from the experience and in the future allow yourself more time.)
- At the end of your efforts (usually at the end of the day), reward yourself for accomplishing a step toward reaching a big goal. Visit downtown and walk around, purchase that DVD you've been wanting, eat at your favorite restaurant. Just take a break and enjoy your accomplishment.
- When getting organized and setting your schedule, think in terms of prioritizing. Periodically ask yourself, Is this the best use of my time now?
- Use a planner or appointment book with a daily, weekly, and monthly calendar. We advise purchasing the type of planner sold at the college bookstore because these note important academic calendar dates, such as when the residence halls open, new student orientation is scheduled, classes begin, the midpoint of the academic session falls, classes end, the reading day is assigned, final exams are given, commencement ceremonies are scheduled, holidays fall, and special exams are given.
- Always allow time for breaks. Breaks of at least 10 minutes after studying for an hour will rejuvenate you and help to maintain a higher level of efficiency of learning.
- When working on a task, concentrate on the task. Do not allow yourself to be distracted.
- When setting up your schedule, be sure to break tasks into manageable units. Spending 1 hour or 2 hours per evening studying a topic is much more efficient than trying to cram in 10 straight hours of studying. Avoid marathon study sessions.
- Plan in terms of specific and realistic goals.
- Schedule time to relax. This is an extended period (e.g., an hour) when you set aside time for yourself. Allow time for creative incubation to occur; sometimes serious students are studying so hard they forget to take time to just think.
- Complete a task. Finish each task before moving on (unless you misjudged the time required). Finishing a task creates a sense of accomplishment and psychological closure. Researchers have found that unfinished tasks tend to linger in our minds, contributing to a sense of frustration and possibly stress.

■ Know what resources are available and use them as part of your time-management efforts. For example, if you are taking a difficult course, schedule time to take advantage of any free tutoring offered through your college's academic assistance services.

■ Organize your schedule to allow yourself to review difficult curricular material soon after being exposed to it (e.g., stop and look over the notes taken in the psychology class where the professor lectures in a rapid manner; aim to achieve an overview and fill in gaps left in the notes while the lecture is still fresh in your mind). Even in cases where there is a delay (you have classes scheduled back to back and have to wait to review the material), aim to review the material within 24 hours of first being exposed to it, even if for no longer than 10–15 minutes. Failure to review in this manner might result in up to 50 to 60% of the information (understanding) being lost. Keep in mind that the sooner the review takes place, the better the result.

■ Know when to stop. Some individuals work past the time scheduled or needed. The result, if this becomes an established pattern, is decreasing return for the effort and possibly even stress because the work never seems to end. Find ways to stop yourself if you have to (use a kitchen timer to remind yourself to stop).

■ Before going to sleep at night, use five minutes to visualize your future and see yourself as moving toward the goals you are striving to reach. Such visualizations can serve as motivation boosters.

■ Some individuals find it helpful to make an oral (or written) contract with another person (e.g., significant other, study partner) concerning an important task. Knowing this other person is watching can foster and maintain motivation. Sometimes even writing a contract to ourselves can provide added initiative to meet a goal.

■ Write reminders and post them if need be. Jotting down one's most important time-management goals on a note and sticking the note on your computer, bathroom mirror, or textbook can help you stay on task.

■ Periodically review your goals (from small intermediate goals to large end goals you are working toward), reassess the steps you are taking, and make appropriate changes when necessary.

■ Schedule the things you like to study last. The importance of this is illustrated by the typical behavior of math-anxious students. Math-anxious students frequently study for the math course they are enrolled in at the end of their study time. By this time they are getting tired, so they become easily frustrated and thus do not devote the needed time to a subject they are having trouble with.

■ Plan to carry your schedule with you. In questioning students over the years, we have found that some good organizers forget important tasks simply because they have forgotten to carry their schedules with them.

■ To-do List

This is not to be confused with a schedule that is set up in a planner. The to-do list can stand alone or be incorporated into the planner. Many individuals have found a to-do list to be an indispensable time-management technique. In its simplest form, a to-do list is a list of things that must be accomplished that have been prioritized. Some people mistake a simple list of things to do for a to-do list; the two are not the same. A genuine to-do list keeps a person on track. A random, unprioritized listing of tasks can keep us off track.

If you simply list items to do (e.g., go to library to read a reserved book, study two hours for next week's history test, buy a new pair of shoes at the mall, drop off CD at friend's house), you may wind up spending too much time on items that could have been put off (you go to the mall and decide to also see a movie, or you spend three hours at the friend's house because of a spontaneous invitation to stay for some barbecue being cooked) and not devoting enough or any time to important tasks and then rationalizing your mismanagement of time ("I can study the night before the test."). Thus, to have a genuine to-do list, you should list and prioritize the items. Mark the most important task with a star, an asterisk, the letter A, or the number 1.

Another tip is to have a variety of things to accomplish that are not all top priorities (some items should be things you will get to if you can, but if you do not, it is not really a problem). Follow the 20/80 rule. In a list of 10 items, aim to have 2 (maybe 3) that are top-priority items. Think of it this way: we never read everything in a newspaper, only certain sections (20%) and leave much of it unread (80%); office workers refer to a few filing drawers in an office (20%) and not the others (80%) except on rare occasions; and we walk mostly on a small amount of floor space where we live each day (20%) but do not walk on the rest (80%). While there is not always a clear 20/80 breakdown, the point is that when we list things to accomplish, the top priority items should be fewer in number.

Adding the use of a to-do list to your repertoire of time-management skills can increase your efficient use of time dramatically. The effectiveness of a to-do list is reflected in the world of business where whole-day workshops on time management are often sponsored by major companies to get employees to be more effective users of time, which, of course, adds to earnings. It is unlikely that large corporations would invest in such workshops if there were not a monetary return. For people in the business world, time-management techniques can become almost second nature. To-do lists are constructed for important tasks automatically. Review the two examples of to-do lists in Figure 1. Which example represents a poorly constructed to-do list? Why is this an example of a poor to-do list?

The Carry-through

A vital part of being an effective time manager is to be able to carry through on what you have planned. Your scheduling skills and to-do lists may be impeccable, but the perfect schedule and perfect to-do list will do nothing for you if you cannot achieve what you have planned. Here are some points to consider.

- Think of the place you study as a **study territory** to be defended. The notion that all that is needed to establish a place to study is a neat desk with a cup to hold sharpened pencils is antiquated. In many ways a place to study is more of a frame of mind that fits your needs and unique personality. But regardless of the place, it should be one you can claim as your property. If you mark this place as yours, others are less likely to intrude on your study time. Interestingly, this sort of response to another territory cuts across many life forms.

  Dogs protect their territory (e.g., a student's apartment) from strangers and other dogs. The protector in this case is likely to win in a battle with an even stronger dog because fighting in one's territory provides a competitive edge. This is even true in some wars between countries where stronger countries have attempted to invade and take over weaker countries only to lose the war to the weaker country defending its home territory.

  Having areas that we claim as ours is more common than most people realize. For example, early in the academic term, part of settling into a classroom is finding a chair. Students frequently mentally mark a chair as theirs. Think of those times when you entered a classroom where you have sat in the same chair since the first day for several weeks only to find another student seated in "your" chair. You felt irritated because you had come to view that particular chair as your territory.

Example A   Example B

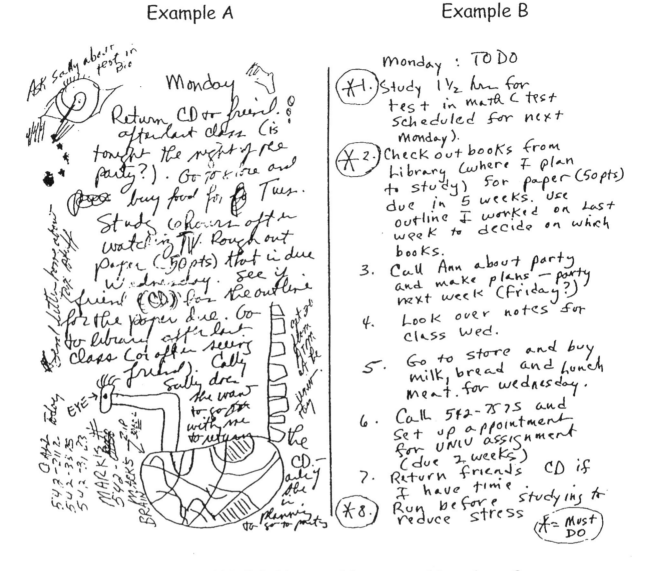

Which TO DO List would you want to rely on?

Figure 1 ■ Two Examples of To-Do Lists

Interestingly, we even have portable territories that we carry around with us. It is as if we all move about with an invisible bubble that shields us from others. This invisible bubble extends out to differing distances depending on the environment and on who is approaching. On a dark street at night it extends out so far that seeing a stranger walk toward us might cause us to cross the street. And even though during the day the bubble's boundary is much smaller (extending only a few feet from our bodies), think of those times when another student whom you did not know crossed this invisible boundary by standing too close. During such "invasions," we maneuver to reestablish the boundary. We step back or look away (similar to what occurs on crowded elevators where eveyone looks at the door). Such intrusions, coming within a few inches of our face or body, are rare because most people understand innately that territories (stationary and portable ones) are not to be violated.

The point is to have a place to study that is yours. For example, if a person knocks on your door to visit at a time when you must study for an important test, you should stand at the door (the boundary) and tell the person you are studying and will see or call him or her later. Use assertiveness skills if necessary. Learn to say no to requests that involve invasion of your scheduled time. Mark the territory with a sign on the door such as "Do not disturb" or "Back in three hours." The reader of the latter sign does not need to know you are behind the door and really mean that you will be back from studying in three hours.

■ Cut down or eliminate possible distractions. If you live in a noisy dorm or apartment, schedule time to go to one of the college's libraries. If phone calls keep occurring, unplug the phone. Anticipate possible distractions, and take steps to block the interference before it occurs.

■ Sometimes the distraction is from within. In such cases the persistent thought (e.g., about meeting friends later or the upcoming Florida vs. Georgia game) can sometimes be put aside by using an old Zen Buddhist trick. Welcome the intrusive thought, and honor its presence by writing the thought down on a scrap of paper (e.g., write "Prepare for trip to Gainesville, Florida, in two hours") and put the slip aside saying to yourself, I'll get back to you after I study for two hours.

■ Another possible contributor to distractibility from within is a low energy level. Are you a morning person, afternoon person, night person? When does your energy peak? If at all possible, and in many cases it is (at least more than we sometimes realize), we should schedule difficult, or mentally taxing, tasks at peak times and simple tasks that require little mental effort (e.g., shopping for groceries) at those times of low mental energy. When we mismatch a task with our energy level, we are going to be either over taxed or under taxed. Neither condition is an efficient use of our energy or time.

■ Sometimes the internal distraction is of such a nature that we give it a label—procrastination. We put off doing something that we perceive to be unpleasant until a future date. (In extreme cases of procrastination the future date never arrives.)

■ Activity. Procrastination Scale (PS)

Completing this assessment will provide you with a better sense of whether you should make reducing procrastination a top priority.

Indicate how you feel about each statement by writing the appropriate value in the blank.

4 = That's me for sure
3 = That's my tendency
2 = That's not my tendency
1 = That's not me for sure

1. _____ I needlessly delay finishing jobs, even when they're important.

2. _____ I postpone starting in on things I don't like to do.

3. _____ When I have a deadline, I wait till the last minute.

4. _____ I delay making tough decisions.

5. _____ I stall on initiating new activities.

6. _____ I'm on time for appointments.

7. _____ I keep putting off improving my work habits.

8. _____ I get right to work, even on life's unpleasant chores.

9. _____ I manage to find an excuse for not doing something.

10. _____ I avoid doing those things which I expect to do poorly.

11. _____ I put the necessary time into even boring tasks, like studying.

12. _____ When I get tired of an unpleasant job, I stop.

13. _____ I believe in "keeping my nose to the grindstone."

14. _____ When something's not worth the trouble, I stop.

15. _____ I believe that things I don't like doing should not exist.

16. _____ I consider people who make me do unfair and difficult things to be rotten.

17. _____ When it counts, I can manage to enjoy even studying.

18. _____ I am an incurable time waster.

19. _____ I feel that it's my absolute right to have other people treat me fairly.

20. _____ I believe that other people don't have the right to give me deadlines.

21. _____ Studying makes me feel entirely miserable.

22. _____ I'm a time waster now, but I can't seem to do anything about it.

23. _____ When something's too tough to tackle, I believe in postponing it.

24. _____ I promise myself I'll do something and then drag my feet.

25. _____ Whenever I make a plan of action, I follow it.

26. _____ I wish I could find an easy way to get myself moving.

27. _____ When I have trouble with a task, it's usually my own fault.

28. _____ Even though I hate myself if I don't get started, it doesn't get me going.

29. _____ **I always finish important jobs with time to spare.**

30. _____ **When I'm done with my work, I check it over.**

31. _____ I look for a loophole or shortcut to get through a tough task.

32. _____ I still get stuck in neutral even though I know how important it is to get started.

33. _____ **I never met a job I couldn't take care of.**

34. _____ **Putting something off until tomorrow is not the way I do it.**

35. _____ I feel that work burns me out.

Scoring

This assessment is scored by summing the values you entered for each item.

Before you sum the values you must "reverse score" the following items: 6, 8, 13, 17, 25, 27, 29, 30, 33, and 34. All of these items appear in bold type. When reversing the values, remember that $4 = 1$, $3 = 2$, $2 = 3$, and $1 = 4$.

After you reverse the scores for the items indicated, you add up all the values to obtain a total procrastination score.

Your Procrastination score is _____

General Interpretation

The higher the score, the greater the tendency to procrastinate, delay, or completely avoid an activity that you should be able to complete.

Look over the items again. What does this assessment tell you about your own unique style of procrastination? Is it only occasional? Is it frequent? Is it happening more often than before? Is it creating academic problems?

Procrastination deserves special attention because it is often the identifying problem presented by students who are having difficulty managing their time. Rita Emmett (2000) suggests that two "laws" should be considered in relation to complaints about procrastination. Careful consideration of these laws can help you discover ways to address habitual procrastination.

Source: Tuckman, B. W. (1991). The development and concurrent validity of the Procrastination Scale. *Educational and Psychological Measurements, 51,* 473–480.

■ Emmett's Two Laws Governing Procrastination

First Law: The dread of doing a task uses up more time and energy than doing the task itself.

Second Law: Obsession with perfection is the downfall of procrastinators.

In her second law Emmett uses the words "obsession with perfection" to refer to various fears that block us from starting on a project, task, or assignment. A number of fears are listed next which Emmett believes can cause procrastination.

Fear of . . .
Imperfection
Unknown
Judgment (What will others think or say?)
Making mistakes
Success
Having to live up to a high standard
Change
Too much responsibility
Feelings (e.g., not doing something because you fear the reaction of another person)
Finishing (e.g., "Once I finish this project, I have to start that other project—the project I am dreading.")
Being rejected
Making the wrong decision

Emmett believes the best way to manage procrastination is to identify your fear and then face your fear. "Once you identify your fear and face it, once you magnify that fear and decide you'll survive it and perhaps even learn from it, you can start moving and do whatever it is you've been putting off—-and start taking control of your life." (Emmett, 2000, p. 94)

Procrastination is not an unusual event. Everyone procrastinates from time to time (e.g., scheduling a doctor's appointment may be consistently put off), but procrastination can become a vicious cycle. This vicious cycle can become a mental and behavioral prison. Individuals caught in such a cycle reveal its strength when they say things such as, "There's no point in getting started—I can't get anything done," "I feel overwhelmed and stressed out and don't know where to start." Such self-defeating thoughts and behaviors tend to intensify the problem and frequently contribute to lower self-esteem. For example, a student puts off doing math homework because he does not like math. Because less time is being devoted to math, the student starts to do poorly in math. This drop in performance leads to longer delays and increased avoidance of the topic, which results in another drop in grade average. The student now repeatedly states self-defeating messages about math whenever confronted with the topic. Sometimes these statements are made to others, but most of the time they are simply repeated silently, as if a taped message were playing over and over inside this person's head. According to David Burns (1980), a **mind set** has been established.

Mind sets interfere with motivation and can be fueled by many different things, according to Burns. A syndrome is created, in which a group of signs are found together. The procrastination mind set is characterized by a feeling of hopelessness, a sense of being helpless, magnification of events leading to feeling overwhelmed, a tendency to jump to conclusions, negative self-labeling ("I am a loser"), undervaluing rewards due to perceiving outcomes as not worth the effort, self-coercion in the form of shoulds and oughts (e.g., "I should do X; otherwise I am a rotten person"), low tolerance of frustration, and a general sense of guilt and self-blame.

According to Burns, procrastination can be effectively dealt with. He suggests taking actions such as these:

1. **Use a schedule.** Prioritize tasks and do so using a weekly/monthly/annual planner.

2. **Keep a record of dysfunctional thoughts.** Record the self-defeating language you are feeding yourself and use cognitive restructuring techniques to break this pattern. This involves changing the negative scripts in your head and creating and using self-affirming scripts ("I am a capable person, so I can find ways to learn math!")

3. **Endorse one's self.** If you find yourself operating from a perspective of "what I do doesn't count," you should argue with yourself. Turn the old perspective around. ("I have always thought others were more deserving, but there is no reason to not place myself in the deserving group of people. The people I have been placing on a pedestal also have strengths and weaknesses. I am just as deserving as they are!")

4. **Avoid the oughts and shoulds that are governing your behavior.** Albert Ellis has referred to the destructive impact on one's quality of life because of absolutes ("I must always be the A student. Less than an A means I am a failure.") by saying we are performing "*must*erbation."

5. **Use disarming techniques.** If something or someone is contributing to a negative mind set, disarm it or the person by taking its or the person's power away. In cases involving others, you can call upon assertiveness skills to change the situation.

6. **Think about little steps.** Seeing too far into the future sometimes leads to procrastination. If you have to write a 25-page term paper for an early American history class, you might see the finished product in your mind and become overwhelmed, wondering "How can I ever write that 25-page paper?" When this takes place, stop and think about the task a step at a time. Break up what you see as the end product into manageable smaller stages.

7. **Visualize success.** Envision yourself completing the task. See yourself as succeeding when you start to experience self-doubt.

8. **Test your can'ts.** When you say you cannot do something, stop and do a specific assessment of what is involved in completing something. Often when we carefully assess what is required, we start to understand exactly what steps are needed to succeed, and the feeling of "I can't" loses its power.

■ Closing Remarks

This chapter covers many tips and concepts that deserve careful consideration. Above all, you should leave this chapter knowing you possess valuable tools for gaining control over your time. Keep in mind the information and skills discussed are to be used when needed. Using time-management tactics should not gobble up a lot of your time. If you are spending hours each week getting organized, that in itself is a time-management problem. Start using those things suggested in this chapter that seem to fit your time-management needs best, and add other tactics when appropriate.

■ References

Burns, D. D. (1980). *Feeling good: The new mood therapy.* New York: Morrow.

Emmett, R. (2000). *The procrastinator's handbook: Mastering the art of doing it now.* New York: Walker.

Lakein, A. (1973). *How to get control of your time and your life.* New York: New American Library.

Schmitt, D. E. (1992). *The winning edge: Maximizing success in college.* New York: HarperCollins.

Taylor, H. L. (1981). *Making time work for you.* New York: Dell.

Tuckman, B. W. (1991). The development and concurrent validity of the Procrastination Scale. *Educational and Psychological Measurements, 51,* 473–480.

Name: _____ Date: _____

■ Exercise 1. Where Does My Time Go?

Estimate the amount of time you typically devote to each activity listed below in a full week. After entering your estimates, record the exact amount of time spent on each activity during one week. Then answer the questions posed at the end.

	Estimated Hours/Minutes	Actual Amount of Time
Attending classes	_____	_____
Working at job	_____	_____
Sleeping (include naps)	_____	_____
Showering/bathing	_____	_____
Traveling to and from work	_____	_____
Eating (include snacks)	_____	_____
Studying for test(s)	_____	_____
Completing homework	_____	_____
Socializing (include time just talking to friends)	_____	_____
Organizational activities (band practice, fraternities/sororities, clubs, special groups, etc.)	_____	_____
Time devoted to physical fitness	_____	_____
Shopping (clothing, groceries, other)	_____	_____
Religious/spiritual activities	_____	_____
Time with family	_____	_____
Other (list)	_____	_____

a. _____

b. _____

c. _____

d. _____

Totals   _____   _____

How accurate was your estimated total compared to the actual total?

Look over the list. Which three activities are of greatest importance to you? Does the actual amount of time you are devoting to each seem to be enough?

How might you change the manner in which you manage time to boost your time-management skills to a higher level? Provide five ways to do this.

1. _____

_____

2. _____

_____

3. _____

_____

4. _____

_____

5. _____

_____

■ Exercise 2. Constructing a To-do List

List 10 items that need to be done by this date: _____. Use A, B, and C to indicate each task's importance (A = top priority).

Importance	Check if completed on time	List tasks here
_____	_____	1. _____
_____	_____	2. _____
_____	_____	3. _____
_____	_____	4. _____
_____	_____	5. _____
_____	_____	6. _____
_____	_____	7. _____
_____	_____	8. _____
_____	_____	9. _____
_____	_____	10. _____

Were any of the items you listed not completed by the specified date? Explain why for each item. Briefly discuss any feelings of accomplishment or frustration you experienced in completing or not completing the tasks listed. Suggest at least one change you would make in the future when you use a to-do list.

Name: _____ Date: _____

■ Exercise 3. Effective Planning for the Week

Select Option A or B.

Option A. Create a plan for the week starting next Monday. Use the blank calendar on the following pages. At the end of the week, evaluate what you planned. Were you able to follow the plan? The evaluation section appears on the last page of this exercise. What did you learn about your strengths and areas needing improvement?

Option B. Create a plan for a typical week using the blank calendar that follows. Then, evaluate your time-management skills by completing the evaluation section at the end of this exercise. What did you learn about your strengths and areas needing improvement?

Note: You may use an arrow to indicate when an activity carries over into another box at a different time or when an activity is repeated at the same time on another day. Do not leave any of the boxes empty. Account for all of the 168 hours that make up your week.

Example

	Mon	Tue	Wed	Thu	Fri	Sat	Sun
11	Work on Project for FINA →		Prep for Class	Study for STAT Exam →		Speak with Mom/Dad about sum.	Call Fred G. about tickets
12pm	Attend Class (STAT)	Meet with Fred G. about project	Attend Class (STAT)	↓	Attend Class (STAT)	Lunch with family →	
1	Go to Lunch	Attend Class (FINA)	Go to Lunch	Attend Class (FINA)	Go to STAT LAB (tutor)	↓	Start packing to go back

133

Plan
Option Selected: _____

	Mon	Tue	Wed	Thu	Fri	Sat	Sun
5 am							
6							
7							
8							
9							
10							
11							
12 (noon)							
1 pm							

■ Exercise 3. *Continued*

	Mon	Tue	Wed	Thu	Fri	Sat	Sun
2 pm							
3							
4							
5							
6							
7							
8							
9							
10							

	Mon	Tue	Wed	Thu	Fri	Sat	Sun
11 pm							
12 am							
1							
2							
3							
4 am							

Evaluation

1. Discuss the strengths of your time-management approach based on the plan you completed.

2. Discuss ways you may plan each week differently in the future to increase your effective use of the 168 hours in a week.

▮ Exercise 4. Understanding Procrastination

1. List three situations in which you typically find yourself procrastinating, or, putting off what you need to do.

   a. _____

   b. _____

   c. _____

2. How do you feel about putting off what needs to be done in these situations (e.g., guilty, angry, depressed)? What thoughts come to mind when you think about these situations (e.g., "I tell myself I'll get started, but I never do")?

3. What steps should you consider using to overcome procrastination (e.g., "I need to divide the work up into amounts I can handle")?

4. You know what to do, based on question 3, so what obstacle prevents you from doing what needs to be done (e.g., "I feel like a failure in math, so I delay doing homework")? What specific action will you take to overcome the obstacle that prevents you from doing what you need to do?

   The obstacle is

   The specific action I will take is

   The date I will initiate this specific action is _____.

Name: _____ Date: _____

■ Exercise 5. Plot Your Energy Level

Review the example below. Then plot your typical pattern of mental energy for a day.

Changes in Mental Energy Level during a Typical Day (example)

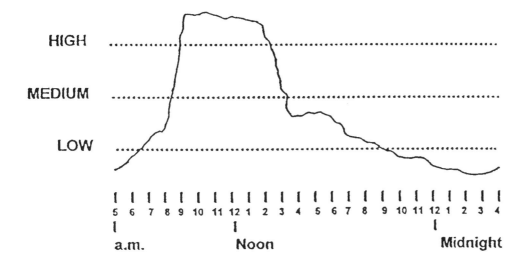

HIGH   ···

MEDIUM ···

LOW   ···

```
I  I  I  I  I  I  I  I  I  I  I  I  I  I  I  I  I  I  I  I  I  I  I
5  6  7  8  9 10 11 12 1  2  3  4  5  6  7  8  9 10 11 12 1  2  3  4
I                      I                               I
a.m.                  Noon                          Midnight
```

How might you use the information and understanding you obtained from plotting your changing energy level? Specifically, how could you schedule some activities differently to take full advantage of your periods of peak mental energy?

Section 3

Making It Work Interpersonally

CHAPTER 8
Developing Relationships

"Never doubt that a small group of committed individuals can change the world; indeed, that is the only thing that ever has."

—*Margaret Mead*

Developing Relationships

Going to college is perhaps the most difficult step that you have ever taken. It is difficult because of the many changes which will occur simultaneously in your life. Relationships will change too. You will change and others close to you will change.

There are reasons why change comes at this time in your life. First, there is a big difference between "going to school" and "attending college." It may immediately appear that there are no differences because you may be doing things in the same ways you did in high school: getting up, driving to school, going to classes, driving home, studying, and doing homework.

You will quickly discover, however, that university classes are probably larger than those you attended in high school. Some lecture sections may have as many as 200 students in class; this means the professor may not provide the same time and attention to you as a student. Some may not even know your name. You may know some people in your class or you may see no familiar faces. Further, no one but you will monitor what you do in and out of class. **You** will decide whether to attend or not. **You** will decide whether or not to buy your textbooks. **You** will decide whether or not to complete assignments and turn them in on time.

This new independence is difficult for some students who find the added responsibilities too challenging. In high school, others watched out for you; in the university, you watch out for yourself. As you begin to explore your new freedoms and choices, you are likely to make some good decisions and some poor decisions. Important relationships in your life will begin to change as you learn to handle each situation.

You will meet people who do not view the world in the same ways you and your family do. Some of these people will be students and some will be professors. You will make choices about your openness to new experiences and new people. If college is about learning, it includes what we learn from others about ourselves, our values, and our beliefs.

In this chapter, we will explore some of the ways in which your relationships with others will change during your time in college. We will also consider questions of difference and openness to change.

Living with Parents

New college students who continue to live at home almost immediately find a change in various long-standing relationships in their lives. As students begin to assert a new-found independence, many find that relationships with parents become strained. For students, the freshman year is a time for meeting new people, developing new ways of managing day-to-day decisions, and becoming more independent in the choices made. It is a rite into adulthood. For parents, this first year of college is a time to let go and establish new relationships with you as a young adult.

The problem is, however, that some parents have difficulty letting go. The problem is magnified when you continue to live at home. Parents often assume that you will keep the same hours as you maintained in high school, be available for family-related activities, and continue to perform certain household chores or manage family responsibilities. They may not realize that students really do study in the library past midnight, attend events on campus that don't begin until 10:00 p.m., and have classes that begin or end at unusual times.

You probably want your parents to be there to listen, but not tell you what to do. Your parents may say they want you to be independent but then don't seem to trust your judgment when you make your own decisions. What is needed is compromise on both sides. Be patient and allow your parents to adapt to the changes you are making and the new demands placed on your time. They are not being difficult; they are just accustomed to the way things have been at home for many years.

How are your relationships at home right now? Over the years, most students have developed a level of trust with their parents. As you have grown and matured, the trust and corollary freedoms given to you have increased. Open and honest discussion with your parents before you encounter problems is a good way to begin exploring what changes may be needed now that you are in college. Anger and confrontation create hostilities on both sides and rarely lead to any productive changes for either of you.

Remember that your adjustment to college and its demands, if you continue to live at home, is almost as difficult for your parents as it is for you. They are beginning to realize that you are finally a "grown-up" and that you have begun the process of leaving home for good. Subconsciously, they know that in just a few years, you will graduate, join the professional working world, and be on your own with your own family and responsibilities!

■ Living on Campus

Most college campuses provide some type of on-campus residence halls or apartments for students who either live too far away to commute from home or who want the experience of living away from home. Living on campus provides more freedom and independence but also carries more responsibility; for some students, it proves to be more difficult than living at home. Every year, there are students who move into college residence halls and do not make it through the first night without calling home or, in some cases, returning home without ever attending a class!

Living on campus can be an exciting, challenging experience which provides many opportunities to learn about living on your own within a supportive environment. Roommates, resident assistants, other students, and professional staff can provide assistance and encouragement as you make the transition to college. There are people with whom you can talk about what you're experiencing. Better still, there are other students who share some of the same experiences and feelings.

For many students the biggest change from home to campus living is learning to live with others. At home, relationships were established over many years of living together. Once you move into a residence hall, you have to start developing a new set of relationships, often with people who are total strangers. Living with another person presents wonderful opportunities and, sometimes, presents serious problems.

Don't wait for little problems to reach crisis proportions! As soon as possible, sit and talk with your roommate about each other's idiosyncrasies. In a living situation, compromise is essential. If you are a night owl and your roommate likes to go to sleep right after the 11 o'clock news, you need to discuss how the two of you can compromise so that you don't argue every night about one another's habits.

There are many possible points of conflict that you can anticipate and discuss up front such as cleanliness, sharing cleaning duties, taking phone messages, having overnight guests, and adhering to university and housing rules and regulations. You will find that if you discuss differences, you can head off many potential problems. You can also find ways to compromise so that each of you feels "at home" and can maintain your preferred personal and academic routines. Keep in mind that early discussions are more likely to resolve issues than waiting until there is a problem and you or your roommate is angry.

Should you find that all your efforts fail and that you just can't get along with your roommate, don't allow the situation to have a negative effect on your academics. Make an appointment with a housing staff member to discuss the problem and what attempts have been made to alleviate the situation. You will receive advice as to what to do next, including a possible move to another room. Leaving college or moving back home should be a last resort! Learning to cope with others different from you is part of your education and will be invaluable in your future endeavors.

Living on campus can be a rewarding experience and will allow you to continue your growth and maturation to independent adulthood. While it is not always easy to live in a college residence hall, students who have this experience often form friendships that last for the rest of their lives.

■ Having a Boyfriend/Girlfriend

Just when you think everything is going well—you made an "A" on your first college examination, you got a raise at work, and you won a pair of free tickets to a sold-out concert—you get a phone call from your boyfriend or girlfriend telling you that he/she wants to break up with you. Your world suddenly comes crashing down.

There is never a good time for a break-up, but during college, broken relationships often have a negative impact on academics. A relationship takes time, energy, and commitment, all of which are also required to be a successful student. Losing an important relationship can send you into a downspin that, if you are not careful, may cause you to hit bottom. Grades may drop and you may feel overwhelmed by all of the pressures.

The same recommendations suggested for dealing with roommates are useful in relationship problems. You should discuss the possible effects that college attendance may have on your relationship even if you have been dating for a long time and feel you know one another very well. If attending the same university, or living in the same town, share your class schedules and the amount of time you each may need for studying. Add time for extra-curricular activities, work, and other time commitments that may not involve time together. Your relationship doesn't have to suffer if you plan ahead and are clear with regard to your expectations.

The situation changes if your boyfriend/girlfriend lives elsewhere. The relationship may become strained simply because of distance. You will each meet new people and develop lives apart from one another. Be prepared for this potential problem and openly discuss your expectations. Is it okay to go out with other people? How often will you try to see one another? Talk on the telephone? Send e-mail or write letters?

Regardless of what your personal situation is, a sour romance can really put you down in the dumps. Believe it or not, it will pass! As the old song says, "breaking up is hard to do," but you will get over it. College is one of the best places to meet new people if you are interested. You can strike up a conversation with someone in class, in the library, or in the cafeteria; you can join a club or play intramural sports. From there, you are on your own!

If things are not going well, don't hurt in silence. Talk to a friend or relative; make an appointment with the university counseling center to speak with a staff member. It is perfectly normal to discuss your problems with another person, whether it is a friend or a staff member who is professionally educated to work with students. If you do decide to talk with a counseling center staff member, all conversations are confidential.

During the coming years, you will form a number of relationships and friendships. Some will be more serious than others; some will develop into life-long friendships, while others will fade away. One of these relationships may even develop into the "love" of your life! You will face challenges, particularly in your first year of college when you are feeling most alone and are, perhaps, separated from your family and friends. Learn from the challenges; use the campus resources available to assist you as you gain new experiences.

■ Differences Are Valuable

A college or university campus is one of the few places where every facet of society can be found, and every conflicting voice has a right to be heard. There may be times when you will be offended by what you see or hear on campus; realize that these occasions, too, are a part of your education! While you may not agree with or condone what others do or say, it is an opportunity for you to understand others better. On campus, open dialogue and discussion of issues is important to the academic process known as "academic freedom."

In the classroom, faculty members have the right to present materials and differing points of view and to delve into controversial areas openly and honestly. You will sometimes find a class uncomfortable because the views presented are different from your own; you may even feel that the professor has crossed the boundary of good taste or is talking about matters not appropriate to a college classroom. When you find yourself in this situation, ask yourself what is happening. Are your beliefs being challenged? Is the topic one that is never discussed at home?

In fact, if your education is to be genuinely valuable to you, you should encounter differing views; you should feel a little uncomfortable. More important, you should be open to hearing what professors and other students have to say! Be open to learning from others and you will learn a lot. You may not change your values or beliefs but you will have consciously chosen them from among a range of options.

■ Non-Traditional Students

Most of the students in this class are recent high school graduates who are considered "traditional" college students. In fact, many students are older when they begin college. Some have worked or served in the military; others have been raising children or have retired from their job; some are single parents; some are in school "just for the fun of it!" Many are attending college part-time while they hold full-time jobs or balance home and family responsibilities; some attend classes only at night or on the weekends. These are considered "non-traditional" students. They make up a growing segment of every university campus today.

As you sit in your classes, look around and see if there are any non-traditional students. Older students often have knowledge and expertise that can be valuable in and outside the classroom; yet, traditional students are often reluctant to approach them. It is difficult to return to college or begin college after a long absence from a classroom; don't be afraid to introduce yourself to a non-traditional student. Invite him or her to participate in a study group or to join you for coffee after class.

■ Students with Disabilities

Another growing population on college campuses is students with disabilities. While some are visible, many more are invisible because of the nature of the disability. Many students come to campus with little knowledge of the various disabilities and little experience in dealing with a person who is disabled in some way.

The most visible of the disabilities are those which are physical: the student in a wheelchair; the student using a guide dog or a cane; the student wearing a hearing aid. Many other students, however, have some form of learning disability that may not be apparent to the casual observer. On the first day of class, for example, a professor may ask for volunteer note takers to assist one or more students whose disability makes note taking difficult. You could volunteer and, as a result, become acquainted with a student who requires some accommodation in order to meet course requirements. This will broaden your experience and provide assistance to another student.

Most campuses have offices that provide assistance to students with disabilities to assure that the campus and all of its programs and services are accessible, regardless of the accommodation required. Under requirements of the Americans with Disabilities Act, any student should be able to participate in any activity or academic program offered to all students. Over the years, campuses have modified their buildings to include ramps, elevators, visual as well as audio fire alarms, and wheelchair seating in athletic arenas and theaters. Access on campus has made it possible for more students with disabilities to attend their college of choice and to successfully complete their degree of choice.

■ Race and Ethnicity

Race and ethnic background are among the most common differences on a college campus. For many students, college is the first place they will meet people who are different from themselves in ways that are very apparent to the casual observer. Race is one of these differences and ethnic or cultural background is another.

You will probably meet people from other countries who have come to the campus to study; you will also meet people from other parts of this country whose backgrounds are different from your own. Each person you meet who is culturally or racially different from you presents an opportunity to learn about another culture or their race. In addition, the campus offers many opportunities to learn about other cultures through clubs and organizations, through programs and social activities, and through formal classes for which you might register.

■ Sexual Orientation

Another visible population on many campuses are gay, lesbian, and bisexual students. College is a place where many students openly explore and question their sexual identity or orientation. It is generally accepted that approximately 10 percent of the general population is gay or lesbian, so it is likely you already know someone who is gay. Consider this as another opportunity to expand your appreciation for differences.

For many students, college is the place where they discover they are sexually attracted to someone of the same sex. Some students have been aware of such feelings for years but have never acted on them. These feelings may be unsettling because they are often in direct conflict with family beliefs, religious teachings, and attitudes of friends. To admit one might be gay or lesbian may mean being rejected by family or friends. Worse yet, it might mean being subjected to verbal harassment or physical attack.

Other students who are not gay may learn for the first time that a good friend or family member is lesbian or gay. This, too, can be unsettling and challenge one's beliefs. What does it mean if my friend is gay? How will others perceive me? How will I feel about that? What if a parent or sibling "comes out?" What will this mean to the family's relationships? These are difficult questions for which there are no simple answers.

There are many resources available to assist students who are dealing with questions of sexual orientation, whether it is their own or someone close to them. Gay and lesbian student organizations exist on many campuses; counseling centers have trained staff to provide assistance. Some campuses offer gay/lesbian studies or gender studies courses that provide an academic perspective on sexual orientation. Students who are harassed may use services available under the campus sexual harassment policy or other non-discrimination policies.

The biggest question for you is knowing who you are, understanding and accepting your feelings, and being open to others who may hold different views. You don't have to agree with someone's personal choices to be caring and supportive as a friend.

Understanding Diversity

Most students do not consider diversity on a day-to-day basis. Some simply are unaware; others have limited contact with certain groups, have no friends who are different from them, and see no reason to make changes in friendship patterns or relationships. Let's consider a context in which the importance of awareness and broadening one's knowledge of others might become more important.

According to information published by the United Nations in an **Information Bulletin (December 1997)**, there are approximately 5.8 billion people in the world. Think about this population as it might be represented on a campus of 100 students. The campus population would include (based on world demographics) the following mix of students:

57 Asians
20 Europeans
7 North Americans
7 South Americans
9 Africans

Seventy percent of our group would be non-white and 30 percent white; 65 percent would be non-Christian and 35 percent would be Christian; 70 percent would not be able to read; 50 percent would suffer from malnutrition; 80 percent would live in substandard housing. The odds are only one would complete a university degree! Students in this university would know that half of the entire wealth in the world is controlled by six people, three from the United States, two from Japan, and one from Germany.

Is there a reason to become more aware of the diversity which exists around you? Keep this mythical university in mind because it represents the world in which you live and will work.

Let's go back for a moment and ask how all of this diversity is affecting **YOU**. To create new visions and missions, isn't it necessary for everyone to consider the impact of diversity at the individual and personal levels? If we are to become change agents and allies, don't we first have to become aware of our own inherent beliefs about others? And in the process, don't we also have to become aware of how these beliefs affect the day-to-day choices we make about our behavior?

Valuing diversity begins with understanding yourself. It means taking a closer look at your own experiences, background, and culture. What are the messages from your background that you embrace? That you feel might be hindering you in some way? How do you view others? Are you aware of your own stereotypes and biases? How do you view others who are different from you?

Once you have faced the first challenge, AWARENESS, you are ready to continue exploring some additional concepts regarding diversity.

■ Stereotypes

John Glenn, the first man to orbit the earth (1962), participated in another space flight when he was 77 years old. Reactions were positive, for the most part, but gave rise to many questions. Should a 77-year-old man participate in a space flight even for scientific purposes? Is he crazy or just trying to recapture his youth? Could he manage the grueling physical, psychological, and emotional stress? Is this good for a person of his age? Are the skills and abilities required for this mission found in an older person?

Think about your reactions for a moment and be honest with yourself! What are the assumptions we often make about "older" people? Are they viewed as less productive? Less physically able? Slower? Not as able to learn new things? What John Glenn did by participating in a space flight at age 77, violates our **stereotypes** about older people.

Stereotypes are views and attitudes based on our assumptions about certain groups of people. These assumptions may or may not accurately represent the group but may guide our actions toward that group or our beliefs about that group. Let's consider another situation and look at how stereotypes might influence thinking.

You are at the library and see a pregnant woman checking out a number of books on parenting. What are your assumptions? You might make the assumption that she is pregnant for the first time and wants to learn all about parenting. Your brain has interpreted some limited information by using your past experiences and beliefs about what you have observed to make a decision about this woman. Your assumptions might even be correct.

What you do not know, however, is that the woman you observed has a younger brother who recently adopted a young child and became a single parent. She is checking out the books for him because she thinks he will find them useful. She found them useful when her first child was born.

Missing information changes your view of the situation, doesn't it? Now you might ask yourself about your stereotypes regarding single men who adopt children!

Some common forms of stereotyping include the following:

Abelism: A system of exclusion and discrimination that oppresses people who have mental, emotional, or physical disabilities.

Anti-Semitism: Systematic discrimination against, condemnation, or oppression of Jews, Judaism, and the cultural, intellectual, and religious heritage of the Jewish people.

Classism: Individual, institutional, and societal beliefs and practices that assign differential value to people according to their socio-economic class.

Heterosexism: Individual, institutional, and societal beliefs based on the assumption that heterosexuality is the only normal and acceptable sexual orientation.

Sexism: Individual, institutional, and societal beliefs and practices that privilege men, subordinate women, and denigrate values and practices associated with women.

Racism: The systematic subordination of members of targeted racial groups who have relatively little social power in this country. This subordination is supported by individual, institutional, and societal beliefs and practices.

What are your stereotypes? What views based on limited information have you formed about others? How did you acquire these views and attitudes? Have you encountered exceptions, that is individuals who do not fit the stereotype? The following exercise will help you in exploring your stereotypes.

Prejudice and Discrimination

There are two more concepts which are important if you are to fully understand and begin to value differences. These are **prejudice** and **discrimination**.

Prejudice refers to a negative attitude toward members of some distinct group based solely on their membership in that group. Prejudice has behavioral, cognitive, and affective components. In other words, prejudice affects our choices, the way we see the world, the way we interpret information, and the way we feel. All of these components can cause one to take actions that may discriminate against others.

We learn prejudice just like we learn everything else: by hearing the views expressed by our parents, teachers, friends, and the media. In some cases, children are rewarded for adopting the views of their elders and punished in some way if they do not.

To begin combating prejudice, your own and that of others, the following steps are useful:

1. Become aware of your own prejudices and their origins.

2. Educate yourself about the customs and beliefs of other cultures and peoples.

3. Challenge others' prejudicial statements, ideas, and beliefs.

4. Increase contacts with individuals and groups you might otherwise avoid or with whom you might not interact on a regular basis.

Discrimination involves negative actions toward another person. Actions may be mild or severe. Avoidance, for example, is a mild form of discrimination. Not inviting someone of a different race, age, or with a disability to join a study group could be considered a form of discrimination. This form of discrimination is subtle and often denied by those who engage in it.

The most severe forms of discrimination include outward aggression and violence. Consider the pictures you've seen of the civil wars in Bosnia or in the Middle East that, in part, are linked to religious and ethnic differences among people in those regions. Consider the Civil Rights movement in this country during the 1960s or, more recently, the reports of attacks on people who are gay or lesbian. These, too, are examples of violence directed at one group by another group.

In order to combat stereotypes and discrimination, it is important to be open-minded, ask questions, and become a good listener. You need to confront your own feelings and attitudes, become better informed about people different from yourself, and challenge others who use stereotypes or discriminate in some way. Finally, become aware of media images and the possible biases presented, both positive and negative. A good way to begin is with your own campus environment.

Summary

The next time you come to class, look at the classmate sitting to your right and to your left. Look at the person seated in front and behind you. These classmates are experiencing similar problems in adjusting to college. They are questioning their old habits, beliefs, and attitudes. They, too, are meeting new people different from themselves and are learning more about themselves in relation to others.

How many of your classmates have you met? Have you elected to sit with someone you already know, perhaps a friend from high school? Have you introduced yourself to anyone who appears to be different from you in some way? Someone who is older? Of a different race? With a disability? New relationships and friendships are an important part of this exciting time in your life; welcome them as learning experiences that will expand your horizons, make you a better student, and better prepare you for the world of work. The first step is the most difficult; why not start with those four people seated near you?

■ Exercise 1. Parent Relationships: An Assessment

Relationships with parents or other individuals who have been involved in raising you can become difficult as you approach and enter college. This is a time during which both you and they are undergoing some major life changes. Let's take a few minutes to assess what has been happening and what you would like to see happen in the next few months.

Part I. My Current Situation

1. Right now, I am living: _____ at home with my parents and siblings.

    _____ at home with one parent and siblings.

    _____ on campus in a residence hall.

    _____ in my own apartment or home.

2. There are other family members living in our house: _____ yes _____ no _____ sometimes

3. I share a room with: _____ a brother or sister.

    _____ another family member or spouse.

    _____ a roommate in the residence hall.

    _____ no one. I have my own room.

4. With regard to transportation to school: _____ I have my own car.

    _____ I drive a car my parents own.

    _____ I share a car with a sibling.

    _____ I use public transportation.

    _____ I live on campus and have no car.

5. Most of my school expenses are paid by: _____ me.

    _____ my parents.

    _____ financial aid.

    _____ a combination.

6. For spending money, I: _____ have a part-time job.

    _____ have a full-time job.

    _____ use savings.

    _____ get money from parents or relatives.

7. In my living situation: _____ I decide when I come and go.

    _____ There are some rules I have to follow.

    _____ We discuss what I can and can't do.

    _____ Rules are very restrictive for me.

8. I am the: _____ oldest child _____ middle child _____ youngest child

9. I am the first child in my family to go to college. _____ yes _____ no

Summary Statement: In my living situation, I feel . . .

Part II. Thinking about My Relationship with Parents

As you think about your living situation and your family, what thoughts do you have about yourself and your relationships with parents and siblings or other family members?

1. As I thought about my living situation, I became aware that . . .

2. My parents sometimes surprise me when they . . .

3. I wish my parents understood about . . .

4. If I could say anything to my parents right now it would be . . .

Summary Statement: I see my relationships at home as . . .

Name: _____ Date: _____

■ Exercise 2. Cultural Pursuit

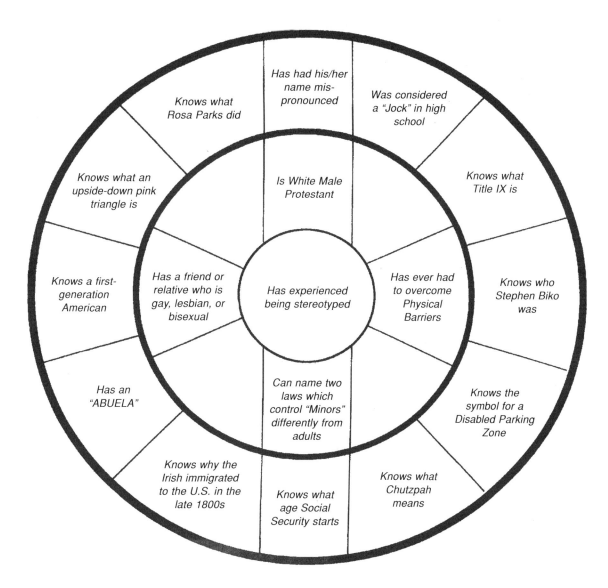

Directions: Locate an individual in the class who knows the answer to a question on the circle. Write that person's name in the block. Use each person only once.

■ Exercise 3. What Do You Know about Minority Groups?

1. A dulcimer is:
   a. An Appalachian folk instrument
   b. One who is low in spirits
   c. An Italian term of endearment
   d. A Native American weapon

2. The meaning of "Wounded Knee" is that:
   a. Native Americans in the 19th century viewed this as the last battle and a significant break in relationships with whites
   b. It was a rallying point for Native American militancy in the 1960s and 1970s
   c. None of the above
   d. Both a and b

3. A barrio is a:
   a. Political organization
   b. A small donkey
   c. Spanish speaking community
   d. None of the above

4. The letters "AME" are an abbreviation for:
   a. Anti-migration Effort
   b. American Muslim Enterprises
   c. African Methodist Episcopal
   d. Association of Moderate Encounters

5. Puerto Rico is an independent territory of the United States with self-governing powers.
   a. True
   b. False

6. A noted Chicano labor organizer and leader was:
   a. Pancho Villa
   b. Manuel Cortez
   c. Cesar Chavez
   d. Simon Bolivar

7. Name three prominent African-American writers:

8. According to most studies, what portion of the population in the United States is gay or lesbian?
   a. 1 in 50
   b. 1 in 10
   c. 1 in 100
   d. 1 in 5

9. The gay student organization on campus is called "Stonewall." What is the significance of this name?

10. Major league baseball did not allow any Black players until:
    a. 1925
    b. 1961
    c. 1947
    d. 1938

11. Match the following names with their achievements:

    _____ Arthur Ashe   a. wrote *Frankenstein*
    _____ Jim Thorpe   b. Gay author and activist
    _____ Jackie Robinson   c. Pilot who set speed records
    _____ Thurgood Marshall   d. First Black man to win US Open
    _____ Mary Shelley   e. First Black to win Academy Award
    _____ Frances Perkins   f. Native American Olympic athlete
    _____ Hattie McDaniel   g. First woman to hold Cabinet office
    _____ Randy Shilts   h. First Black Supreme Court justice
    _____ Henry Cisneros   i. First Hispanic mayor of major city
    _____ Jackie Cochran   j. First Black major league baseball player

Name: _____ Date: _____

■ Exercise 4. Who Are We?

The questions below are intended to help you think and talk about your background and experiences, and learn about the experiences of other students in your class.

Instructions:

1. Form a **random** group of three students.
2. Each student should take a few minutes to complete the chart below.
3. When everyone in the group completes the chart, have each person read his/her responses to the members of the group (members should feel free to ask questions, share experiences).
4. Each student will share with the remainder of the class something interesting learned about another student's background.

Who are we?

My full name:	
The name I prefer to be called:	
The cultural meaning of my name:	
My ethnic identity:	
Place(s) my grandparents and parents were born:	
The language(s) I speak:	
My family's educational achievements:	
A person I admire:	
An attribute I like about myself or am proud of:	
A characteristic I like about my culture:	
A challenge I would like to conquer this semester:	
A challenge I would like to achieve in my lifetime:	

Adapted from materials created by The National Conference's "Actions Speak Louder: A Skills-Based Curriculum for Building Inclusion," 1995.

CHAPTER 9
Communications and Relationships

Chapter Focus

Read to answer these key questions:

- What is my personal communication style?
- What are some problems in communication?
- What are some techniques for being a good listener?
- What is the best way to communicate in a crisis situation?
- How does language affect behavior?
- What are some conflict management techniques?
- What are the qualities of a good friendship?
- How can I get along with my roommate?
- How can I improve my relationships?

How is failure an opportunity for learning?

When you look back on your college experience, what you are most likely to remember and value are the personal relationships established while in college. These relationships can be a source of great pleasure or disappointment. What makes a good relationship? The answer to this question is complex and different for each individual. Good relationships begin with an understanding of personality differences and the components of effective communication. These skills can be useful in establishing satisfying friendships, happy marriages, effective parenting skills, and good relationships in the workplace.

■ Understanding Your Personal Communication Style

Becoming familiar with personality types can help you better understand yourself and others. Personality has a major impact on our style of communication. While we can make some generalizations about personality types, keep in mind that each individual is unique and may be a combination of the various types. For example, some people are a combination of introvert and extravert. The following descriptions will help you begin thinking about your own communication style and understanding others who are different. Remember that each personality type has positive and negative aspects. Knowledge of these differences can help individuals accentuate the positives and keep the negatives in perspective.

Introvert and Extravert Types

Communication Styles

- Introvert
- Extravert
- Sensing
- Intuitive
- Feeling
- Thinking
- Judging
- Perceptive

Extraverts are very social types who easily start conversations with friends as well as strangers. They know a lot of people and have many friends. They like going to parties and other social events and are energized by talking to people. They like to talk on the telephone and can read while watching TV, listening to music, or carrying on a conversation with someone else. They find talking easy and sometimes dominate the conversation. They find it more difficult to listen. They tend to talk first and think later, and sometimes regret that they have put their foot in their mouths.

In personal relationships, extraverts are fun to know and get along well with others. It is easy for them to make a date and do the talking. When extraverts are in conflict situations, they just talk louder and faster. They believe that the argument can be won if they can say just one more thing or provide more explanation. If there is a problem, extraverts want to talk about it right away. If they cannot talk about it, they become very frustrated.

The **introvert** is the opposite of the extravert. Introverts want to rehearse what they are going to say before they say it. They need quiet for concentration and enjoy peace and quiet. They have great powers of concentration and can focus their attention on projects for a long period of time. Because they tend to be quieter than extraverts, they are perceived as great listeners. Because they need time to think before talking, they often find it difficult to add their ideas to a conversation, especially when talking with extraverts. They often wish they could participate more in conversations. Because they are reserved and reflective, people often label the introvert as shy. In American society, introverts are the minority. There are three extraverts to every introvert. For this reason, the introvert is often pressured to act like an extravert. This can cause the introvert a great deal of anxiety.

The introvert often finds it difficult to start conversations or invite someone on a date. Introverts are often attracted to extraverts because they can relax and let the extravert do the talking. In conflict situations, the introverts are at a disadvantage. They will often withdraw from conflict because they need time to think about the situation and go over in their minds what to say. Introverts become stressed if they are faced with a conflict without advance notice.

Introverts and extraverts can improve their relationship by understanding each other and respecting their differences. The extravert can improve communication with the introvert by pausing to let the introvert have time to speak. He has to make a conscious effort to avoid monopolizing the conversation. Introverts can improve communication by making an effort to communicate. Introverts sometimes act like extraverts in social situations. Since this takes effort, they may need quiet time to relax and recharge after social events.

Imagine that two roommates are opposite types, extravert and introvert. The extravert enjoys talking and making noises. She will have guests, take telephone calls, and play music in the background while studying. These actions will cause the introvert to withdraw and leave the room to find a quiet place to study. These two roommates need to talk about their differences and do some compromising to get along with one another.

Sensing and Intuitive Types

Sensing types collect information through the senses. Their motto could be, "Seeing is believing." They are practical and realistic. They like communication to be exact and sequential. They want details and facts. They ask specific questions and want concrete answers. About 70 percent of the population of the United States is the sensing type.

In a dating situation, the sensing type focuses on actual experience. A sensor will describe the date in terms of what his or her companion looked like, how the food tasted, how the music sounded, and the feelings involved. In a dating situation, sensors talk about concrete events such as people they have known, experiences they have had, and places they have visited. Sensing types are generally on time for the date and get irritated if the other person is late. In conflict situations, sensing types argue the facts. They often don't see the big issues because they are concentrating on the accuracy of the facts.

Intuitive types gather information from the senses and immediately look for possibilities, meanings, and relationships between ideas. They are often ingenious and creative. Sensing types often describe intuitives as dreamers who have their heads in the clouds. They represent about 30 percent of the population.

In social situations such as dating, the intuitive person starts to fantasize and imagine what it is going to be like before it begins. The fantasies are often more exciting than the actual date. Conversations follow many different and creative trains of thought. Intuitive types are more likely to talk about dreams, visions, beliefs, and creative ideas, skipping from one topic to another. Sensing types sometimes have difficulty following the conversation. Intuitive types are less worried about being exactly on time. They believe that time is flexible and may not be on time for the date, much to the annoyance of sensing types. In conflict situations, intuitive types like to make broad generalizations. When sensing types remind them of the facts, they may accuse them of nit-picking.

Having both sensing and intuitive types in a relationship or business environment has many advantages, as long as these types can understand and appreciate one another.

Sensing types need intuitive types to bring up new possibilities, deal with changes, and understand different perspectives. Intuitive types need sensing types to deal with facts and details.

Feeling and Thinking Types

Feeling types prefer to make decisions based on what they feel to be right or wrong based on their subjective values. They prefer harmony and are often described as tender-hearted. Other people's feelings are an important consideration in any decision they make. The majority of women (60 percent) are feeling types. In a conflict situation, feeling types take things personally. They prefer to avoid disagreements and will give in to reestablish a harmonious relationship.

Thinking types are logical, detached, analytical, and objective and make decisions based on these characteristics. They like justice and clarity. The majority of men (60 percent) are thinking types. In a conflict situation, thinking types use logical arguments. They often get frustrated with feeling types and think they are too emotional.

In a dating situation, the differences between feelers and thinkers can cause much misunderstanding and conflict. Thinking types strive to understand love and intimacy. Feeling types like to experience emotions. Thinking types process and analyze their feelings. For the thinker, love is to be analyzed. For the feeling types, love just happens.

Remember that while most women are feeling types and most men are thinking types, there are still 40 percent of women who are thinking types and 40 percent of men who are feeling types. Unfortunately because of gender stereotyping, feeling-type men are often seen as less masculine and thinking-type women are seen as less feminine.

There is much to gain from understanding and appreciating the differences between feeling and thinking types. Feeling types need thinking types to analyze, organize, follow policy, and weigh the evidence. Thinking types need feeling types to understand how others feel and establish harmony in relationships or in a business environment.

Judging and Perceptive Types

Judging types prefer their environment to be structured, scheduled, orderly, planned, and controlled. Judging types even plan and organize their recreation time. They need events to be planned and organized in order to relax. They are quick to make decisions and once the decisions are made, they find it difficult to change them. In the social scene, judging types schedule and plan the dates. When traveling, judging types carefully pack their suitcases using a list of essential items to make sure that nothing is forgotten. In conflict situations, judging types know that they are right. They tend to see issues in terms of right and wrong, good and bad, or black and white. It is difficult to negotiate with a judging type.

Perceptive types are very much the opposite of the judging types. They prefer the environment to be flexible and spontaneous. Perceptive types find it difficult to make a decision and stick to it because it limits their flexibility. Perceptive types like to collect information and keep the options open. After all, something better might come along and they do not want to be restricted by a plan or schedule. In a social situation, these types are playful and easygoing. They provide the fun and find it easy to relax. They often feel controlled by judging types. In a conflict situation, this type sees many options to resolve the situation. They have trouble resolving conflicts because they keep finding many possible solutions.

The preference for judging or perceiving has the most potential for conflict between individuals. Judging types can drive perceptive types crazy with their need for schedules, planning, and organization. Perceptive types drive the judging types crazy with their spontaneous and easygoing nature. In spite of these differences, judging and perceptive types are often attracted to one another. Judging types need perceptive types to encourage them to relax and have fun. Perceptive types need judging types to help them be more organized and productive. These two types need understanding and appreciation of each other to have a good relationship. They also need excellent communication skills.

It is often asked whether two people should consider personality type in establishing relationships or choosing a marriage partner. There are two theories on this. One theory is that opposites attract. If two people have opposite personality types, they will have the potential for using the strengths of both types. For example, if one marriage partner is a judging type, this person can manage the finances and keep the family organized. The perceptive type can provide the fun and help the other to relax and enjoy life. A disadvantage is that opposite types have great potential for conflict. The conflict can be resolved by understanding the other type and appreciating different strengths the opposite type brings to the relationship. The relationship cannot work if one person tries to change the other. Good communication is essential in maintaining the relationship.

Another theory is that like types attract. If you have a relationship with another person of the same type, your basic preferences are similar. However, even matching types will be different depending on the strength of each preference. Communication is easier when two people have similar views of the world. One disadvantage is that the relationship can become predictable and eventually uninteresting.

Quiz—Communication Style

Test what you have learned by selecting the correct answer to the following questions.

1. Extraverts can help introverts improve communication by
   A. clearly explaining their point of view.
   B. pausing to give the introvert time to think and respond.
   C. talking louder and faster.

2. In a dating situation, sensing types are likely to talk about
   A. concrete events such as the weather or personal experiences.
   B. dreams and visions.
   C. creative ideas.

3. In a conflict situation, feeling types
   A. use logic to analyze the situation.
   B. engage in debate based on logical arguments.
   C. take things personally.

4. Perceptive types
   A. find it difficult to make a decision and stick to it.
   B. tend to decide quickly in order to finish the project.
   C. find it easy to be on time and meet deadlines.

5. In choosing a marriage partner it is best to
   A. choose a person with the same personality.
   B. choose a person with the opposite personality.
   C. be aware of each other's personality type to appreciate each other.

How did you do on the quiz? Check your answers: 1. B, 2. A, 3. C, 4. A, 5. C

OURNAL ENTRY #1
Consider how these terms affect your communication style: extravert, introvert, sensing, intuitive, feeling, thinking, judging, perceptive. What is your personal communication style?

Write your Journal Entry on page 187.

Communication for Success

To be an effective communicator, it is important to be a good listener and speaker. Practice the techniques of good listening and use language that helps you enhance your success and establish good relationships.

Problems in Communication

Effective communication involves a loop in which a sender sends a message and a receiver receives the message. Communications are disrupted when

- the receiver doesn't receive the message.
- the receiver hears the wrong message.
- the receiver doesn't care about the message.
- the receiver is more interested in talking than listening.
- the receiver only hears part of the message.
- the receiver only hears what she or he wants to hear.
- the receiver feels threatened by the sender.
- the sender didn't send the message correctly.
- the sender left out part of the message.
- the sender talks so much that nobody listens.
- the sender is not someone you want to hear.
- the sender is annoying.
- the sender was upset and did not mean to send the message.
- the sender assumes that you should know the message already.

There is a joke circulating on the Internet:

A man is driving up a steep, narrow mountain road. A woman is driving down the same road. As they pass each other, the woman leans out the window and yells, "Pig!" The man replies by calling the woman a name. They each continue on their way. As the man rounds the next corner, he crashes into a pig in the middle of the road. If only people would listen!

As you can see, there are many ways to disrupt communication. Just because a message was sent, does not mean that it was received. The first step in communication is to be a good listener. Many factors interfere with good listening. Do you recognize some of these reasons for not listening?

Message overload. There is so much communication going on today that it is difficult to keep up with it all. There are stacks of paper, multiple e-mail messages, voice mail, television, radio, and people who want to talk to you. Introverts may find this overwhelm-

Factors That Interfere with Good Listening

■ Message overload
■ Worries and anxiety
■ Rapid thought
■ Being tired
■ Noise and hearing problems
■ Faulty assumptions
■ Talking too much

ing, while extraverts may find it exciting. Both find it challenging to keep up with all these communications and to focus on the messages.

Worries and anxiety. It is difficult to listen to other people when you are preoccupied with your own thoughts. You may be thinking about an upcoming test or paper that is due or worried about a personal relationship. While others are talking, you are thinking about something else of more immediate concern to yourself.

Rapid thought. People think faster than they speak. We are capable of understanding speech at about 600 words per minute, but most people talk at 100 to 150 words per minute.[1] People use the spare time to become distracted. They daydream, think about what they will do next, or think about their reply.

Listening is hard work. It takes effort to listen. It requires paying attention and striving to understand. People can't listen effectively if they are tired, overloaded, or distracted.

Noise and hearing problems. Our world is becoming noisier. As people get older, many suffer from hearing loss. Younger persons are suffering hearing loss from listening to loud music. It is more difficult to get your message across when people can't hear everything you are saying.

Faulty assumptions. People often make faulty assumptions. They may assume that other people also know the information, and therefore they do not communicate well. People listening may assume that they know the information already or that the information is easy, so it is not necessary for them to pay attention. Or they may assume the material is too difficult to understand and block it out.

Talking too much. Since listening involves effort, people consider what they have to gain before they invest the effort in listening. They might think that there is more to gain in speaking than in listening. The speaker often feels that he or she has control. You might feel that in speaking you gain the attention or admiration of others. If you are speaking or telling a joke and everyone is listening, you feel important. Also, through speaking people release their frustration and think about their problems. They need to stop speaking in order to listen.

How to Be a Good Listener

To Be a Good Listener

■ Talk less
■ Minimize distractions
■ Don't judge
■ Look for main point
■ Ask questions
■ Feed back meaning
■ Be careful with advice

Being a good listener takes practice and effort. Here are some tips on becoming a good listener:

Talk less. It does no good to talk if no one is listening, if no one understands your message, or if your message is irrelevant to the situation. To have a better chance of communicating your message, it is important first to listen to gain an understanding of the other person and then to speak. In marriage counseling, a common technique is to have one person talk and express his or her point of view. Before the other person can talk, he or she has to accurately summarize what the previous person said. Too often people do not really listen; instead they are composing their own message in their head. It is a Native American custom that when members of the group assemble to talk about an important issue, a talking stick is used. Persons can only talk when they have the talking stick. When the person holding the talking stick is finished, it is passed to the next person who wants to talk. In this way only one person can talk at a time, and the others listen.

Minimize distractions. For important conversations, turn off the TV or the music. Find quiet time to focus on the communication. Manage your internal distractions as well. Focus your attention on listening first and then speaking.

Don't judge too soon. Try to understand first and then evaluate. If you judge too soon, you may not have the correct information and might make a mistake. People are especially vulnerable to this problem when their ideas do not agree with those of the speaker. They focus on defending their position without really listening to the other point of view.

Look for the main point. You may become distracted or impatient with people who talk too much. Try to be patient and look for the main points. In a lecture, write these points down.

Ask questions. You will need to ask questions to make sure that you understand. Each person looks at the world in a different way. The picture in my mind will not match the picture in your mind. We will have a better idea of each other's pictures if we ask for more information.

Feed back meaning. This communication technique involves restating the speaker's ideas in your own words to check the meaning. This is important because speakers often

- say one thing and mean something else.
- say something but don't mean it, especially if emotions are involved.
- speak in a way that causes confusion.

Feeding back meaning has two important benefits. It helps speakers to clarify their thoughts. It helps listeners make sure that they have received the correct message. Here are several ways to feed back meaning:

1. Restate what has been said. Sometimes this is called parroting. It is useful for clarifying information, but sometimes it annoys people if you use it too much.

   Statement: Turn right at the light.

   Feedback: Okay. So you want me to turn right at the light?

2. Ask for clarification.

   Statement: Take the next exit on the freeway.

   Feedback: Do you mean this exit coming up now or the next one?

   Statement: Pig! (referring to the joke about the man and woman on the mountain road)

   Feedback: What do you mean by "pig"?

   Statement: Be careful. There is a pig in the road ahead.

3. Reword the message to check your understanding. First, restate what you have heard and then ask for clarification. This is called active listening.

   Statement: Turn in the draft of your paper next week.

   Feedback: You want the draft next week. Does that include the outline, the draft of the entire paper, and the bibliography? Should it be typed, or is handwritten okay?

Statement:	Don't worry about your grade on this quiz.
Feedback:	You said not to worry about my grade on this quiz. Does that mean that the grade won't count or that I can make up the quiz?
Statement:	I need this project completed by Friday.
Feedback:	So this project needs to be done by Friday. What parts do you want included and how would you like me to do it?

4. Listen for feelings. Feelings get in the way of clear thinking. A person may say one thing and mean something else.

Statement:	Just forget about it!
Feedback:	I'm confused. You ask me to forget about it, but you sound angry.

5. Use your own words to restate what the speaker has said. In this way, you help the speaker to clarify his or her thoughts and hopefully to come up with some solutions.

Statement:	I wish I didn't have to work so much. I'm getting behind in school, but I have bills to pay. I have to work.
Feedback:	You seem to be caught in a bind between school and work.
Statement:	That's right. I just can't keep working so much. Maybe I should go check out financial aid and scholarships.

Be careful about giving advice. Whenever possible, listen closely and be an active listener. In this way, the person speaking to you has a way to clarify his or her thoughts and think about alternatives. When you listen, it is tempting to offer advice because you may have had similar experiences. You can share your experiences and offer suggestions, but beware of giving advice for these reasons:

- If you give advice and it turns out badly, you may be blamed.
- If you give advice and it turns out right, the person may become dependent on you.
- People are unique individuals with unique life situations. Something that works for one person may not work for another person at all.

Helpful Communication in a Crisis Situation

Most people have been in a situation where their friends or family are in distress and need immediate help. If you become aware of a dangerous or critical situation, seek professional help. Go to your college counseling center, a community service organization, your doctor, or a religious leader for help. Here are some general ideas for being a helpful listener:

- Let the person talk. Talking helps to clarify thinking.
- Paraphrase or feed back meaning.
- Avoid being critical. Comments such as "You asked for it" or "I told you so" do not help. They just make the person angry.
- Help the person analyze the situation and come up with alternatives for solving the problem.
- Share your experiences but resist giving advice.
- Ask questions to clarify the situation.
- Offer to be supportive. Say, "I'm here if you need me" or "I care about you."

■ Let people express their feelings. It is not helpful to say, "Don't feel sad," for example. A person may need to feel sad and deal with the situation. The emotion can be a motivation for change.

■ Don't minimize the situation. Saying, "It's only a grade (job, promotion)," minimizes the situation. It might not be important to the listener, but it is causing pain for the speaker. Give him or her time to gain perspective on the problem.

■ Replace pity with understanding. It is not helpful to say, "You poor thing."

Quiz—Communication for Success, Part I

Test what you have learned by selecting the correct answer to the following questions.

1. *One of the biggest problems with communication is that the message sent is not always the message that is*
   A. *appreciated.*
   B. *intended.*
   C. *received.*

2. *To be a good listener, it is important to remember that*
   A. *it is important to listen first, so that you can understand before speaking.*
   B. *it is important to talk first to make sure the other has heard your point of view.*
   C. *it is important to assume that the other knows what you are talking about.*

3. *Feeding back meaning is*
   A. *responding to questions.*
   B. *restating what has been said to check understanding.*
   C. *unnecessary because some people find it irritating.*

4. *Giving advice is*
   A. *generally not a good idea.*
   B. *only a good idea if you know what is best.*
   C. *a good idea if the other person does not know what to do.*

5. *In a crisis situation, it is best to*
   A. *tell the person not to feel sad.*
   B. *show your pity for the person.*
   C. *let the person talk in order to clarify thinking.*

How did you do on the quiz? Check your answers: 1. C, 2. A, 3. B, 4. A, 5. C

■ The Language of Responsibility

The way we use language reflects our willingness to take responsibility for ourselves and affects our relationships with others. Knowing about "I" and "you" messages, as well as how we choose certain words, can help us to improve communications. We can become aware of how our thoughts influence our behavior and communication. We can choose to use cooperation in dealing with conflicts.

"I" and "You" Statements

When communicating, watch how you use the pronouns "I" and "you." For example, if you walk in and find your apartment a mess, you might say to your roommate, "Just look at this mess! You are a slob!" Your roommate will probably be angry and reply by calling you an equally offensive name. You have accomplished nothing except becoming angry and irritating your roommate. Using the pronoun "you" and calling a person a name implies that you are qualified to make a judgment about another person. Even if this is true, you will not make any friends or communicate effectively.

"You" statements label and blame. They demand a rebuttal. They cause negative emotions and escalate the situation. How would you react to these statements?

> You must be crazy.
> You are really a jerk!

You would probably get angry and think of a nasty reply in return. When you use an "I" message, you accept responsibility for yourself. You might say something like this:

> I don't understand.
> I feel angry.

There are many ways to make "I" statements. Instead of calling your roommate a slob, you could:

1. Make an observation. Describe the behavior:
   Your things are all over the floor.

2. State your feelings. Tell how you feel about the behavior:
   I get angry when I have to step over your things on the floor.

3. Share your thoughts. Say what you think about the situation, but beware of disguised "you" messages such as, "I think you are a slob."
   I think it is time to clean up.

4. State what you want:
   Please pick up your things.

5. State your intentions. Say what you are going to do:
   If you do not pick up your things, I will put them in your room.

Here are some examples of "I" statements that can be used to express various feelings:

To express anger	*To express sadness*
I don't like	I feel disappointed
I feel frustrated	I am sad that
I am angry that	I feel hurt
I feel annoyed	I wanted
I want	I want
To express fear	*To say you are sorry*
I feel worried	I feel embarrassed
I am afraid	I am sorry
I feel scared	I feel ashamed
I do not want	I didn't want
I need, I want	I want

A complete "I" message describes the other person's behavior, states your feelings, and describes the effect of the other's behavior on you. For example, when your things are all over the floor (behavior), I feel angry (feeling) because I have to pick up after you (how it affects me). A variation on the "I" message is the "we" message. The "we" statement assumes that both persons need to work on the problem. For example, "We need to work on this problem so that we don't have to argue."

Words Are Powerful

The words that we choose have a powerful influence on behavior. One of the least powerful words is the word "should." This word is heard frequently on college campuses:

>I should do my homework.
>I should go to class.
>I should get started on my term paper.

The problem with "should" is that it usually does not lead to action and may cause people to feel guilty. If you say, "I should get started on my term paper," the chances are that you will not start on it.

If you say, "I might get started on my term paper," at least you are starting to think about possibilities. You might actually get started on your term paper. If you say, "I want to get started on my term paper," the chances are getting better that you will get started. You are making a choice. If you say, "I intend to start on my term paper," you have at least expressed good intentions. The best way to get started is to make a promise to yourself that you will start. The words "should," "might," "want," "intend," and "promise" represent a ladder of powerful communication. As you move up the ladder, you are more likely to accomplish what you say you will do. This ladder moves from obligation to promise, or a personal choice to act:

The Ladder of Powerful Speaking

"I promise" or "I will"

"I intend to"

"I want to"

"I might"

"I should"

Next time you hear yourself saying that you "should" do something, move one more step up the ladder. Move from obligation to making a personal decision to do what is important to you. For example, if a friend wants to borrow money from you, which response is the most powerful?

- I really should pay the money back.
- Well, I might pay the money back.
- I really want to pay the money back.
- I intend to pay the money back.
- I promise to pay the money back.

Negative Self-Talk

Self-talk is what you say to yourself. It is the stream of consciousness or the little voice in your head. This self-talk affects how you communicate with others. If your self-talk is negative, you will have lower self-esteem and find it more difficult to communicate with others. There are some common irrational beliefs that lead to negative self-talk. Becoming aware of these beliefs can help you to avoid them.

- **I have to be perfect.**
  If you believe this, you will think that you have to be a perfect communicator and deliver flawless speeches. Since this goal is unattainable, it causes stress and anxiety. If you believe in this idea, you may try to pretend or act as if you were perfect. This takes up a lot of energy and keeps others from liking you. Everyone makes mistakes. When people stop trying to be perfect and accept themselves as they are, they can begin to relax and work on the areas needing improvement. They can write papers and make speeches knowing that they will probably make mistakes, just like the rest of the human population.

- **I need the approval of everyone.**
  A person who believes this finds it necessary to have the approval of almost everyone. Much energy is spent in gaining approval from others. If approval is not obtained, the person may feel nervous, embarrassed, or apologetic. It is not possible to win the approval of everyone because each individual is unique. Those who constantly seek approval will sacrifice their own values and what they think is right just to please others.

- **That's always the way it is.**
  People who believe this statement are making a generalization. They take a few events and use them to predict the future or exaggerate their shortcomings. Here are some examples:

  > ### Beliefs that Lead to Negative Self-Talk
  >
  > - *I have to be perfect.*
  > - *I need everyone's approval.*
  > - *That's always the way it is.*
  > - *You made me feel that way.*
  > - *I'm helpless.*
  > - *If something bad can happen, it will.*

  - I'm not a technical person. I can't install my computer.
  - I'm not good at numbers. I'll never to able to pass algebra.
  - Some husband (wife) I am! I forgot our anniversary.
  - You never listen to me.

Notice the absolute nature of these statements. Absolute statements are almost always false and lead to anger and negative thinking. Remember that with a positive attitude, things can change in the future. Just because it was one way in the past does not mean it has to be the same in the future. Beware of "always" and "never" statements.

- **You made me feel that way.**
  Your own self-talk, rather than the actions of others, is what causes emotions. No one can make you feel sad or happy. You feel sad or happy based what you say to yourself about an event. If someone makes a negative comment about you, you can say to yourself that it is only the other person's opinion and choose how you react. Your reactions and emotions depend on how much importance you decide to attach to the event. People tend to react strongly to a comment if it is from someone they care about.

  People also do not cause the emotions of others. Some people do not communicate honestly because they are afraid of causing negative emotions in the other person. They may hesitate to tell someone how they really feel. This lack of honesty leads to increasing hostility over time and difficulties in communication.

■ **I'm helpless.**
If you believe that what happens to you is beyond your control, you will be unlikely to do something to make the situation better. Here are some examples of helpless self-talk:
- ■ I'm a shy person. It is hard for me to talk to people.
- ■ I won't consider that career. Women are always discriminated against in that field.
- ■ It's difficult for me to meet people.

Believing such statements, shy people don't attempt to talk to others, women limit their career options, and people give up trying to make friends. Believe that there is a way to change, and you can make your life better.

■ **If something bad can happen, it will happen.**
If you expect the worst, you may take actions that make it happen. If you expect that your speech will be a disaster, you may not prepare or you may forget your notes or props. If you believe that you will not pass the interview and will never get hired, you may not even apply for the job or attempt the interview. If you believe that your personal relationships will not get better, you will not invest the effort to make things better. There will be times when you make a poor speech, get turned down for a job, or have a relationship fail. Learn from these mistakes and do better the next time.

■ Barriers to Effective Communication

We all want to communicate effectively and get along with people whom we care about. We want to get along with our families, be a good parent, have friends at school, and get along with the boss and our coworkers on the job. Life is just more enjoyable when we have good communication with others. Watch for these barriers to effective communication:

■ **Criticizing**
Making negative evaluations of others by saying, "It's your fault" or "I told you so," causes anger, which gets in the way of communication.

■ **Name-calling and labeling**
If you call someone a name or put a label on them, they will attack you rather than communicate with you in any meaningful way.

■ **Giving advice**
Giving advice may be viewed as talking down to a person. The person may resent your advice and you as well.

■ **Ordering or commanding**
If you order someone to do something, they are likely to sabotage your request.

■ **Threatening**
Trying to control someone by making threats causes resentment.

■ **Moralizing**
Preaching about what a person should or should not do doesn't work because it causes resentment.

■ **Diverting**
Changing the subject to talk about your own problems tells the person that you do not care about them.

■ **Logical arguing**
Trying to use facts to convince without taking feelings into account is a barrier to communication. Present your facts and state your point of view, but respect the other person's feelings and different point of view.[3]

Quiz—Communication for Success, Part II

Test what you have learned by selecting the correct answer to the following questions.

1. *The following is a good example of an "I" statement.*
   A. I think you need to explain.
   B. I do not understand.
   C. I think you are crazy.

2. *"You" statements*
   A. put the blame where it needs to be.
   B. results in anger and rebuttal.
   C. are effective communication tools.

3. *Which statement is the most powerful?*
   A. I should get started on my paper.
   B. I want to get started on my paper.
   C. I will get started on my paper.

4. *The following statement is an irrational belief.*
   A. I have to be perfect.
   B. I don't need the approval of everyone.
   C. I make mistakes sometimes.

5. *This technique is used in effective communication:*
   A. moralizing.
   B. logical arguing.
   C. listen and then respond.

How did you do on the quiz? Check your answers: 1. B, 2. B, 3. C, 4. A, 5. C

■ Dealing with Conflict

There are several ways to approach a conflict. In every conflict there is the potential to be a winner or a loser.

■ **Win-Lose**
With this approach to conflict management, one person wins and the other loses, just as in a game or sport. Competition is part of the win-lose approach. In competition, power is important. In sports, the best and most powerful team wins.

Approaches to Conflict

■ *Win-Lose*
■ *Lose-Lose*
■ *Compromise*
■ *Win-Win*

There are many kinds of power, however. Power may be based on authority. Examples might include your boss at work, your teacher, or even your parents. Another kind of power is based on mental ability or cleverness. Sometimes battles are not won by the strongest, but by the cleverest person. Another kind of power is majority rule. In many settings in a democratic society, the person with the most votes wins.

In many situations, we cannot avoid the win-lose approach. Only one team can win, only one person can get the job, and only one person can marry another. In some circumstances the person you are communicating with does not want to cooperate but to compete.

The problem with this approach is that there is only one winner. What happens to the loser? The loser can feel bad, resent the winner, give up, or try again for victory. These are not always the best alternatives.

■ **Lose-Lose**

Lose-lose is another option for resolving conflicts. Both parties lose. Both parties strive to be winners, but the struggle causes damage to both sides. Wars are often lose-lose situations. In World War II dropping an atomic bomb caused the surrender of Japan, but it contaminated the environment with radioactive material and set a dangerous precedent for nuclear war. Recently Russia was able to stop a civil war by destroying Grozny, the capital of Chechnya. The city became nearly uninhabitable. Everyone lost. On an interpersonal level, divorce can be a lose-lose situation if the struggle becomes destructive to both parties.

■ **Compromise**

Another approach to solving conflict is compromise, where both parties to the conflict have some of their needs met. Both make some sacrifice in order to resolve the situation. For example, the buyer and seller of a used car may agree on a price somewhere between what the seller wants to get and the buyer wants to pay. As long as both parties are satisfied with the outcome, the results are satisfactory. Difficulties arise when people are asked to compromise their values. If they must compromise on something that is truly important, they may be dissatisfied with the outcome.

■ **Win-Win**

In a win-win approach, both parties work together to find a solution that meets everyone's needs. There is no loser. To reach a win-win solution, set aside competition and replace it with cooperation. This is often difficult to do because emotions are involved. Put aside emotions to discuss the issue. This may mean waiting until both parties have had the opportunity to calm down. This approach can be impossible, however, when one person wants to cooperate and the other person wants to win.

These are the steps in a win-win approach:

1. **Identify the problem.** Identify the problem as your own. If your roommate is having a party and you cannot study, it is your problem. You need to find a quiet place to study.

2. **Set a good time to discuss the issue.** When you are feeling angry is usually not a good time to discuss issues. Set a time when both parties can focus on the problem. A good rule is to wait twenty-four hours to let the emotions cool down and gain some perspective.

3. **Describe your problem and needs.** Use "I" messages. Resist the temptation to label and call names. Goodwill is important.

4. **Look at the other point of view.** Understand the other person's needs, and make sure the other person understands your needs.

5. **Look for alternatives that work for both parties.**

6. **Decide on the best alternative.**

7. **Take action to implement the solution.**

The win-win approach is a good tool for effective communication and maintaining good relationships.

JOURNAL ENTRY #2

Think of a conflict that you have had recently. How could you have applied the steps of a win-win approach to resolving that conflict?

Write your Journal Entry on page 187.

Friendships

College provides the opportunity to make new friends. These friends can broaden your perspective and make your life richer and more enjoyable. What do you value in a friendship? How can you establish and maintain good friendships?

■ Activity

Friendship is a relationship that involves trust and support. Beyond this basic definition, we all have different ideas about what is important in a friendship. Here is a list of common qualities of friends. Place a checkmark next to those qualities that are important to you in establishing your personal friendships.

A friend is a person who

_____ can keep information confidential.   _____ spends time with me.

_____ is loyal.   _____ has a sense of humor.

_____ can be trusted.   _____ is independent.

_____ is warm and affectionate.   _____ has good communication skills.

_____ is supportive of who I am.   _____ is an educated person.

_____ is honest.   _____ is an intelligent person.

_____ is a creative person.   _____ knows how to have fun.

_____ encourages me to do my best.   _____ cares about me.

What are the top three qualities you would look for in a friend? List them below.

1. _____

2. _____

3. _____

The friends that you choose can have a big influence on your life, so it is important to choose them wisely. In college and in the workplace, you will have the opportunity to make new friends who can add a new dimension and perspective to your life. For example, if your friends have goals for the future and believe that completing college is important, you will be more likely to finish your own education. If your friends distract you with too many activities outside of school, your college performance may suffer.

Some students naturally make friends easily, others find making new friends more difficult. Here are some ideas for making new friends:

- **Be a good listener.** Spend equal time listening and talking. If you are doing all the talking, the other person is likely to feel left out of the conversation. Show interest in the other person's interests and ideas.

- **Talk about yourself.** Let others get to know you by sharing your interests, where you come from, and what is important to you. In this way, you can find mutual interests to enjoy.

- **Be supportive and caring.** We all have good days and bad ones. Help your friends to celebrate the good days and be supportive through life's challenges. Showing that you care is the basis of developing trust and friendship.

- **Be a friend.** Treat your friends the way you would like to be treated.

- **Spend time with your friends.** It is difficult to maintain relationships if you do not spend time sharing activities. Make spending time with friends a high priority.

- **Accept your friends for who they are.** Everyone has good and bad qualities. Accept the idea that you are not going to be able to change people to match your expectations.

- **Show appreciation.** Say thank you and make honest compliments. Think of something positive to say.

- **Be assertive.** This means that you ask for what you want and that you don't give in to doing something that you don't want to do. Being assertive means that you have the right to your feelings and opinions. There is a fine line, though, between being assertive and being aggressive. Aggressive behavior is domineering, rude, and intimidating. Aggressive individuals act without consideration of other people's rights and feelings.

- **Be selective.** Not everyone makes a good friend. Make friends with people you respect and admire. Stay away from people who are critical or make you feel unhappy. Avoid those who cause you to do things that you do not want to do. Choose friends that make you happy and encourage you to do your best.

OURNAL ENTRY #3

What are the qualities you look for in a good friend?

Write your Journal Entry on page 188.

■ Roommates

Getting along with a roommate can be a challenge. It can be your best or worst college experience or somewhere in between. The key to getting along with a roommate is to understand differences and to work on compromise or win-win solutions. Making a wise choice of a roommate can make the situation much easier. Below are some areas of possible disagreement for roommates:

- **Neatness.** Some students like to keep their rooms neat and others can tolerate messiness.
- **Smoking.** Some students like to smoke and others are offended by smoking.
- **Noise.** Some students need quiet for study while others like to study with music and friends.
- **Guests.** Some students like to have guests in the room, others do not want guests.
- **Temperature.** Some like it warm and some like it cold.
- **Studying.** Is the room a place to study or to have fun?
- **Borrowing.** Some think that borrowing is okay and some do not.
- **Sleeping.** Some go to bed early and some go to bed late. Some need quiet for sleeping.

If you have a choice of roommates, it is a good idea to discuss the above issues in advance. Even best friends can part company over some of these issues. If you are assigned a roommate, discuss the above issues to avoid conflict later on. Aim for win-win solution or at least a compromise. If there is some conflict, following these guidelines may help.

1. Discuss problems as they arise. If you do not discuss problems, it is likely that anger and resentment will increase, causing a more serious problem at a later date.

2. Ask for what you want. Subtle hints often do not work.

3. Be nice to your roommate and treat him or her as you would want to be treated.

4. Be reasonable and overlook small problems. No one is perfect.

■ Relationships

A relationship starts as a friendship and then moves a step further. A relationship involves emotional attachment and interdependence. We often get our ideas about good relationships through practice and trial and error. When we make errors, the results are often painful. Although we all have different ideas about what constitutes a good relationship, at a minimum it includes these components:

- Love and caring
- Honesty
- Trust
- Loyalty
- Mutual support
- Acceptance of differences

Relationships between Men and Women

According to John Gray, popular author of *Men Are from Mars, Women Are from Venus,* men and women have such different values and needs in a relationship, it is as if they came from different planets.[4] He states that men generally value power, competency, efficiency, and achievement. He says, "A man's sense of self is defined through his ability to achieve results." While women are fantasizing about romance, a man is fantasizing about "powerful cars, faster computers, gadgets, gizmos, and new and more powerful technology."[5] The worst thing that women can do to men, according to Gray, is to offer unsolicited advice or to try to change them. These actions conflict with men's needs for power and competence and imply that they don't know what to do or can't do it on their own. We can communicate our honest feelings about our partner's behavior and ask for what we want and need. However, we should not use our feelings and requests to manipulate another person to change. Gray identifies the most important needs for men as trust, acceptance, appreciation, admiration, approval, and encouragement.

Gray says that women generally value love, communication, beauty, and relationships. Their sense of self-worth is defined through their feelings and the quality of their relationships. The worst thing that men can do to women is to offer solutions too quickly when women are talking about their feelings, rather than listening and understanding those feelings. When this happens, women get frustrated and feel a lack of intimacy. It is possible to listen carefully and understand these feelings without necessarily agreeing with them. The most important needs for women are caring, understanding, respect, devotion, validation, and reassurance.

Gray's ideas about men and women parallel the thinking and feeling dimensions of personality presented earlier. Men are 60 percent thinking types and women are 60 percent feeling types. His ideas are interesting for discussion and apply in many relationships, but it is important to be aware of gender stereotypes. Remember that 40 percent of women are thinking types and 40 percent of men are feeling types, so not all individuals will fit into the same categories that Gray describes.

Although Gray proposes that men and women generally differ in what they consider most important, he lists the following twelve components of love.[6] Men and women can improve their relationships when they demonstrate the following:

1. **Caring.** Show that you are interested and concerned about each other.

2. **Trust.** Have a positive belief in the intentions and abilities of each other.

3. **Understanding.** Listen without judgment and without presuming that you understand the feelings of the other person. In this way both men and women can feel free to discuss what is important to them.

4. **Acceptance.** It is probably not a good idea to marry a person if you think you can change him or her into the ideal person you have in mind. Love your partner without trying to change him or her. No one is perfect; we are each a work in progress. The key is to trust the people we love to make their own improvements.

5. **Respect.** Have consideration for the thoughts and feelings of each other.

6. **Appreciation.** Acknowledge the behavior and efforts of your partner. Appreciation can be in the form of a simple thank you or sending cards or flowers.

7. **Devotion.** Give priority to the relationship so that the other person feels important.

8. **Admiration.** Show approval for the unique gifts and talents of your partner.

9. **Validation.** Do not argue with feelings. Each person has a right to his or her own feelings. We can acknowledge, try to understand, and respect the feelings of another without necessarily agreeing with them.

10. **Approval.** Show approval by acknowledging the goodness and satisfaction you have with each other.

11. **Reassurance.** Show reassurance by repeatedly showing that you care, understand, and respect each other.

12. **Encouragement.** Notice the good characteristics of each other and provide encouragement and support.

How to Survive the Loss of a Relationship

Relationships require work and good communication to keep them going strong. Relationships also change over time as people grow and change. As we search for our soul mates, we may need to end some relationships and start new ones. This process can be very painful.

Following the break up of a relationship, people generally go through three predictable stages:

1. Shock or denial

2. Anger or depression

3. Understanding or acceptance[7]

Dealing with pain is a necessary part of life. Whether the pain is a result of a loss of a relationship or the death of someone important to you, there are some positive steps you can take along the road to acceptance and understanding.

■ Recognize that a loss has taken place and give yourself time to adjust to this situation. The greater the loss, the more time it will take to feel better. In the meantime, try to keep up with daily routines. It is possible to feel sad and to go to work and to school. Daily routines may even take your mind off your troubles for a while.

■ It is healthy to feel sad and cry. You will need to experience the pain to get over it. It is not helpful to deny pain, cover it up, or run away from it because it will take longer to feel better.

■ Talk to a friend or a counselor. Talking about how you feel will help you to understand and accept the loss.

■ Don't punish yourself with thoughts that begin "If only I had . . ."

■ Realize that there is a beginning and an end to pain.

■ Get plenty of rest and eat well.

■ Accept understanding and support from friends and family.

■ Ask for help if you need it.

■ Don't try to get the old relationship going again. It will just prolong the pain.

■ Anticipate a positive outcome. You will feel better in the future.

■ Beware of the rebound. It is not a good idea to jump into a new relationship right away.

 OURNAL ENTRY #4

What are the qualities you look for in a good relationship?

Write your Journal Entry on page 188.

- Beware of addictive activities such as alcohol, drugs, smoking, or overeating.
- Take time to relax and be kind to yourself.
- Use exercise as a way to deal with stress and feel better.
- Keep a journal to help deal with your emotions and learn from the situation.[7]

Key to Success: Failure Is an Opportunity for Learning

Everyone makes mistakes and experiences failure. This is the human condition. There is also a saying that falling down is not failure but not getting up is. If you can view failure as an opportunity for learning, you can put it into perspective and continue making progress toward your goals. It has been said that the famous inventor Thomas Edison tried 9,999 times to invent the light bulb. When asked if he was going to fail 10,000 times, he answered, "I didn't fail. I just discovered another way not to invent the light bulb." Failure allows you to collect feedback about how you are doing.

Imagine that your life is like a ship heading toward a destination. Sometimes the sailing is smooth, and sometimes the water is choppy and dangerous and knocks you off course. Failure acts like the rudder of the ship. It helps you to make adjustments so that you stay on course. Too often we do not learn from failure because shame and blame get in the way. Gerard Nierenberg, author of Do It Right the First Time, *advocates the "no shame, no blame" approach to dealing with errors, mistakes, or failure.[9] The first step is to identify the mistake that has been made. What went wrong? Then you look at how much damage has been done. The next step is to take an honest look at what caused the problem. The last step is to figure out a way to fix the problem and see that it does not happen again. There is no shame or blame in the process. Following this approach results in fewer errors and failures.*

Harold Kushner has another view about failure:

> *Life is not a spelling bee, where no matter how many words you have gotten right, if you make one mistake you are disqualified. Life is more like a baseball season, where even the best team loses one-third of its games and even the worst team has its days of brilliance. Our goal is not to go all year without ever losing a game. Our goal is to win more than we lose, and if we can do that consistently enough, then when the end comes, we will have won it all.[10]*

Like a baseball player, if you lose a game, analyze what went wrong and keep on practicing. Remember that you will eventually be a winner. Everyone remembers that Babe Ruth was a great baseball player and that he had 714 home runs. People do not remember that he also struck out 1,330 times. If you can look honestly at your mistakes and learn from them, you can have many winning seasons.

JOURNAL ENTRY #5

Describe a situation in which you have been disappointed with the results. Was there an opportunity to learn from the situation?

Write your Journal Entry on page 189.

Success over the Internet

Visit the College Success website at www.cuyamaca.edu/collegesuccess/

The College Success website is continually updated with new topics and links to the material presented in this chapter. Topics include

■ *Expectations in relationships*

■ *Common mistakes in relationships*

■ *Beginning, enhancing, and ending relationships*

■ *Dealing with anger*

■ *Personality and relationships*

Contact your instructor if you have any problems in accessing the College Success website.

Endnotes

1. A. Wolvin and C. G. Coakley, *Listening*, 3rd ed. (Dubuque, IA: W. C. Brown, 1988), 208.
2. *Care of the Mentally Ill* (F.A. Davis, 1977).
3. T. Gordon, *Parent Effectiveness Training* (New York: McGraw-Hill, 1970).
4. John Gray, *Men Are from Mars, Women Are from Venus* (New York: HarperCollins, 1992).
5. Ibid., 16.
6. Ibid., 133–37.
7. Melba Colgrove, Harold Bloomfield, and Peter McWilliams, *How to Survive the Loss of a Love* (New York: Bantam Books, 1988).
8. Adapted from Colgrove, Bloomfield, and McWilliams, *How to Survive the Loss of a Love.*
9. Gerard Nierenberg, *Doing It Right the First Time* (New York: John Wiley and Sons, 1996).
10. Harold Kushner, *Becoming Aware* (Dubuque, IA: Kendall Hunt).

Name: _____ Date: _____

■ Communication and Relationships Journal Entries

1 Consider how these terms affect your communication style: extravert, introvert, sensing, intuitive, feeling, thinking, judging, perceptive. What is your personal communication style? Explain.

_____

_____

_____

_____

_____

_____

_____

_____

_____

_____

2 Think of a conflict that you have had recently. How could you have applied the steps of a win-win approach to resolving that conflict?

_____

_____

_____

_____

_____

_____

_____

_____

_____

_____

3   What are the qualities you look for in a good friend?

_____

_____

_____

_____

_____

_____

_____

_____

_____

_____

4   What are the qualities you look for in a good relationship?

_____

_____

_____

_____

_____

_____

_____

_____

_____

_____

_____

5   Describe a situation in which you have been disappointed with the results. Was there an opportunity to learn from the situation? Explain.

_____

_____

_____

_____

_____

_____

_____

_____

_____

_____

_____

_____

_____

_____

_____

_____

_____

_____

_____

_____

_____

_____

Interview

Find at least three people over the age of 40. Ask them these three questions and write your notes below. Your instructor may ask you to share your answers with the class.

1. If you were 18 years old again, what would you do differently?

2. What is the best decision that you made between the ages of 18 and 22?

3. What advice would you give to a person who is 18 years old?

■ Your Personal Communication Style

1. How does being an **introvert or an extravert** (or combination) affect your communication style?

2. How does being a **sensing or intuitive type** (or combination) affect your communication style?

3. How does being a **thinking or feeling type** (or combination) affect your communication style?

4. How does being a **judging or perceptive type** (or combination) affect your communication style?

■ "I" and "You" Messages

Part 1.

"You" messages label, judge, and blame; they help demand counterattack.

"I" messages describe yourself and improve understanding.

Examples:

You are rude.
You make me mad.
You must be crazy.

I feel upset.
I feel angry.
I don't understand.

Change the following statements from a "you" message to an "I" or "we" message.

1. Your class is boring.

2. That was a stupid joke.

3. You gave me an F.

4. You don't understand.

Part 2.

For each situation below, state the behavior, the consequences, and your feelings in any order.

> *Example:* When you play your stereo this loud after midnight (behavior), I can't sleep (consequence) and I get really irritable (feelings).

1. Your date, who is supposed to arrive at 6:00, arrives at 7:00. The dinner you have fixed is ruined and you won't have time to catch that late movie after dinner. What do you say?

   _____

   _____

2. A student who sits next to you in class constantly asks you questions and tries to talk to you during the lecture. You find it difficult to concentrate and take notes. What do you say?

   _____

   _____

■ Rewrite the Script

Rewrite the script in the following scenario using "I" messages to try to improve the situation and come up with a win-win solution.

Eric and Jason are roommates who have known each other since childhood. Because they are good friends, they decide to be roommates in college. They rent an apartment together and sign a one-year lease.

Eric: Look at this place. It's trashed! You're really a pig! There are pieces of leftover pizza and empty beer bottles everywhere from that party you had. Your stupid friends spilled soda on the floor and broke the lamp. Are you going to pay for that?

Jason: Why do you always have to be so hostile? We were just having some fun. I was going to clean it up in the morning but I accidentally slept in. Then I had to go to class. Do you want me to miss class and fail? I'm still going to clean it up. Chill out!

Eric: Maybe I wouldn't be so irritated if you guys didn't keep me up all night. I had a test this morning at 8:00. You don't think of anyone but yourself. How can you be so irresponsible?

Jason: Whatever, dude.

■ Communication Exercise

List 10 ideas from this chapter that will help you to improve communication with others who are important to you.

1.

2.

3.

4.

5.

6.

7.

8.

9.

10.

◼ Rating Relationships

Relationships can be rated from 1 (very rocky, almost nonexistent) to 10 (exceptionally wonderful, virtually no rough areas).

Directions: Write the name, initials, or some symbol identifying a person with whom your relationship is a five or below. _____

Now write down what makes this relationship so rough.

_____

_____

_____

_____

_____

_____

_____

Now write the names of three people with whom you rate your relationship as five or better.

_____

_____

_____

What makes the relationships work?

_____

_____

_____

_____

_____

_____

_____

_____

Friendships

1. What is your definition of friendship?

2. What are the five most important qualities of a good friend?

3. Join with some other students in the class to share your ideas.

■ Relationships

1. For five minutes, brainstorm your ideas about what constitutes an ideal relationship. Remember that a relationship involves caring and interdependence.

2. What are the five most important qualities of an ideal relationship?

3. A good relationship requires the cooperation and caring of two people. What steps can you take to improve your present relationships?

Section 4

Making It Work Academically

CHAPTER 10
Understanding the Way You Learn

Introduction

Why does learning new skills and information seem to come so easily for some people, while others struggle? Is there one "right" way to learn something? Is there anything you can do to increase your personal learning power? The answers to these questions come from understanding how people learn, and especially, how *you* learn. This chapter will:

■ Explore some of the typical learning styles students have and then suggest techniques to enhance learning for each different style.

■ Help you to evaluate your own academic strengths and figure out how to compensate for your weaknesses.

■ Explain Howard Gardner's theory of multiple intelligences and what they mean to you.

■ Describe some of the instructional styles your teachers may use.

But what happens if you figure out your preferred learning style and your teacher's instructional style and find they don't match? Should you drop the class in despair? No, just keep reading this chapter. At the end, you should be equipped with several ideas on how to make college a great learning experience.

Pretest

Choose either a, b, or c to indicate which answer is most like you, or which is true more often than the other responses:

1. If I need to remember a phone number:
   a. I look at it long enough so I can visualize it in my mind.
   b. I repeat it to myself several times.
   c. I write it several times or remember where the numbers are on the keypad.

2. In math class, I would prefer to:
   a. read and follow the examples in the book.
   b. have the instructor explain how to do the problem.
   c. have the instructor show me the problem, then have me work one on my own.

3. When I started to drive, I could find where I was going if:
   a. I had a good map or written directions that included landmarks I should see along the way.
   b. someone told me exactly how to get there.
   c. I had driven there previously.

4. If I had to put something together, I would:
   a. read the directions or watch the instructional video first.
   b. ask an expert to tell me how to do it.
   c. take out all the pieces and start trying to put it together. I read the directions/ask for help only as a last resort if I can't figure it out.

5. If I wanted to learn more about the Civil War, I would:
   a. read about it on my own.
   b. get a Civil War book on tape or listen to an interesting documentary.
   c. take part in a Civil War reenactment.

6. I do well in classes where:
   a. the teacher uses visual aids and writes things on the board or overhead.
   b. the teacher lectures on the important things to know.
   c. there is some kind of lab or hands-on component where I can learn by doing.

7. When I need to spell a difficult word:
   a. I picture the word in my mind and mentally spell it, or I have to see it to know if it is correct.
   b. I spell it aloud.
   c. I must write it out.

8. When teaching other people things:
   a. I use pictures, diagrams, charts, etc. to show them what to do.
   b. I tell them what to do.
   c. I demonstrate how to do something and let them try it.

9. In a casual setting where I'm listening to an interesting speaker:
   a. I visualize the people, places, and events being described.
   b. I listen to the speaker's words and tone of voice to derive meaning.
   c. I like to doodle or engage in some other type of physical movement (such as swinging my foot, tapping, etc.) to help me concentrate.

10. When I shop for groceries I always get just what I need if:
    a. I make a list and refer to it while I'm in the store.
    b. I verbally go over my list or talk to myself as I'm shopping.
    c. I walk through the store and remember what I need as I go.

11. When it comes to music videos:
    a. I like to watch the video; it enhances my enjoyment of the song.
    b. I don't usually pay attention to the video; sometimes I'd rather just hear the song on the radio or a CD.
    c. I enjoy music most if I can dance to it/sing along with it. Or, I like to choreograph my own version of the video and get involved with the song.

■ What's Your Style?

- ■ If you answered A for most of the items, you are probably a **visual learner**.
- ■ If you chose B the most, you are probably an **auditory learner**.
- ■ If your answers were mostly C, it's likely you are a **tactile/kinesthetic learner**.

Psychologists and educators have done a lot of research on learning styles and have tried to find out how students learn best. It's useful information, especially now that you're in college, paying tuition, and are serious about your education. One of the easiest theories to understand describes three main ways people take in and remember information. These are called *learning modalities*. The first is visual, the second is auditory, and the third is tactile or kinesthetic.

Actually, everyone uses all three of these modes for learning, but most people have a stronger preference for one or two. Using a preferred learning style is kind of like using your right or left hand to write. Some people are ambidextrous and can use either hand equally well. However, most develop a greater skill with one or the other. When you're using your preferred hand, it's easier to write. You can do it without a lot of conscious effort. It comes naturally. In the same way, your preferred learning mode may make it easier and more natural to grasp the content of what you are studying. Let's consider some examples and see which one really seems most like you.

Victor

Victor Visual learns best by seeing how things are done. He has always liked to read. Ever since he was little he was always aware of his surroundings. When he was a baby he liked to look at mobiles and the interesting toys his mother placed in his crib. His mom always said she could take him anywhere; he would sit there quietly, staring at the people and things around him. When he went to school Victor loved the brightly colored posters and bulletin board displays hanging on the walls of his classroom. He learned the ABCs by staring at the alphabet posted above the board. His teachers were impressed at his ability to recognize words at an early age. In fact, learning to read sight words was no problem for Victor.

In fourth grade when the class was studying planets, he suggested to the teacher that they hang models of the planets from the ceiling. He really did not want to construct the models, but he did make sure they were labeled correctly. In the sixth grade he qualified for the pizza party by reading more books than anyone else in his class. For his birthday when he received toys that needed to be assembled, he always read the instructions before trying to put them together.

In high school Victor did well. He read his textbooks faithfully, but he really disliked classes where the teachers just lectured without using the board or providing handouts. When the teacher asked questions about the reading assignments from the night before Victor was the only one who raised his hand, except for Vanessa Vision. When Victor learned to drive, he got 100% on the written exam, but it took him three times to pass the behind-the-wheel portion of the test. Even now when Victor is going to drive somewhere he has never been before, he needs a good map with landmarks. In fact, Victor prefers written instructions for everything. In computer class Victor was one of the few students who actually read the manual.

As a community college student Victor continues to do well in classes where the teacher uses the overhead projector or writes on the board. In lab classes he prefers that the instructor or another student do the experiments so he can watch. When Victor is at home watching TV, he becomes really annoyed when his younger brother stands in front of the TV. If he goes to an assembly or any kind of performance, he likes to sit in full view of the stage. He gets more out of the performance if he is able to see the speaker directly.

Annie

As a baby Annie Auditory could always be soothed with a lullaby. She liked to listen to her mother talk on the phone or with friends. Her favorite toy was a stuffed teddy bear that played music. She loved to have the radio or television turned on, and by the time she was three she had memorized all the commercials. She even knew the Empire Carpet phone number. She learned the alphabet by singing the ABC song. She learned her numbers in Spanish from hearing them sung on *Sesame Street*.

In school Annie learned by listening closely to the teacher. She needed to have everything explained. If the teacher did not read the directions at the top of the page, Annie had a hard time getting started on her seatwork. As she got older her teachers praised Annie for her participation in class discussions. She always knew what was going on in school because she paid attention when the announcements were read over the loudspeaker. Annie's favorite birthday present was a cassette player/recorder. She loved to record her own voice and play it back.

In high school Annie used the tape recorder to help her study. She made audio study guides and read her textbook onto a tape so she could listen to it again. She understood the chapters better if she could hear them. She enjoyed getting her friends together to study for an exam by discussing the material for the test. She became proficient in foreign language classes because she was able to pick up the inflections and the accents. When Annie started to drive, her instructor usually had to tell her where to turn and when to stop. Even now when Annie gets lost, she needs to ask someone for directions. Giving her a map would not do her any good.

Annie enjoys lecture classes in college; she hates long reading assignments. She did well in Music Appreciation, but had difficulty with her Introduction to the Visual Arts course. If it were not for the Visual Arts course, Annie would have a 4.0 G.P.A. In fact, Annie has considered becoming a college instructor because she likes to talk and conduct class discussions.

Kenny and Terry

Kenny Kinesthetic and Terry Tactile are best friends. They have been together since their sandbox days. In the sandbox they built roads, houses, and elaborate castles. As babies they always had to have something in their hands. They clung to their bottles and pacifiers long after other kids had given them up; but, as his mom liked to point out, Kenny was walking by eight months. The boys both learned the alphabet by playing with blocks.

In grammar school they loved working with play dough and messy art projects. Learning to read was a little more difficult for Kenny and Terry. They fidgeted if too much time was spent doing seatwork. If they really needed to concentrate, it helped to be able to color, cut and paste, or at least drum a pencil on the desk. The teachers thought they were hyperactive and always told them to sit still. They spent a lot of time in the hall.

When Victor suggested making models of the planets, Kenny and Terry were the first to volunteer to do the job. They enjoyed those science experiments in junior high and for the first time felt good about learning.

In high school they were chemistry lab partners who always got an A on their experiments (except when they blew up the lab because they just had to see what happened when they mixed the pink stuff with the green stuff). Shop classes were their specialty. Their mothers had more knick-knacks, spice racks, and towel holders than any other moms in the PTA. Kenny and Terry had a flair for fixing things, and never had to read the directions to assemble anything. They learned to drive one day by taking Terry's father's car to an empty parking lot while he was taking his Sunday afternoon nap. They both had to take the written test over, though, before they actually got their licenses. It's a good thing PE counts as a high school requirement. They really needed those credits to graduate.

At the community college both Kenny and Terry do well in lab classes, technical courses, and art courses where there is not too much written work. In English they never read a book if there is a movie version available. They signed up for the fitness center immediately and will probably try out for sports. These two guys are pretty much alike. Terry is better at hand/eye coordination and working with his hands, while Kenny is better in athletics and physical activities.

The Three Basic Learning Modalities

From our stories about Victor, Annie, Kenny, and Terry, we have illustrated some of the strengths of the three distinct learning modalities: visual, auditory, and tactile/kinesthetic. Now let's look at each one in greater detail.

Visual Learners

These are the people who use their vision or sense of sight as their primary way of learning new information. They may like to read instructions or watch someone else do something before they try it on their own. They like to see pictures or illustrations, especially when reading. When they have to listen to a speech, they may seem like they're daydreaming when, in fact, they may be trying to get a mental picture of what is being said. Visual learners are attracted to colorful, bright things. They can often remember things if they are able to make strong visual associations.

Visual learners are at an advantage in most school systems, and often people have adopted many visual learning strategies as a result of their early school experiences. Walk into a typical elementary school anywhere in the country and ask the principal if you can visit the classroom of the best teacher in the building. As you look at the walls, you will be surrounded with visual stimuli. No matter where a child looks, there should be something to engage his/her mind. From the alphabet over the board to the spelling words or science display or reading corner, a good teacher will provide plenty of material for the visual learner's attention. That level of providing extra visual stimulation often continues through middle school and junior high. Sometimes in high school a few teachers will have current displays that reflect the topics of study in their classes. In college, however, most professors or instructors don't have a classroom of their own. Instead, they may teach in several classrooms or labs. Your classroom may be used for math, sociology, psychology, English, or a variety of other subjects including non-credit general interest classes. The walls tend to be sterile without much to engage your interest.

At the same time the classrooms start to lose their visual appeal, though, the slack gets picked up by the students' ever-increasing ability to read. Visual learners can thrive in classes where the textbook or outside readings are a primary source of course content. Teachers may use the board, overhead projector, or PowerPoint presentations to visually display important points of information. In lab classes there will often be demonstrations to watch, and in math classes the teacher may write out all the steps to the problem as s/he explains it.

Strong Visual Learners should try the following strategies to enhance their learning:

- *Sit near the front so you can see the teacher and the board clearly.*
- *Read the chapter before class so you will be familiar with the content to be covered.*
- *Pay close attention to pictures, illustrations, charts, and other visual aids in the textbook.*
- *Take notes in class so you will have something to review later.*
- *Use all hand-outs given to you by the teacher as learning tools.*
- *Highlight important information, and take notes as you read.*
- *Create your own visual aids such as flow charts, diagrams, sample problems, etc.*
- *Use flash cards to review things you need to memorize.*
- *Visualize the information as you read or listen to the lecture. See it in your mind's eye.*

Auditory Learners

People who prefer to listen and use their sense of hearing to learn new content or remember information are called auditory learners. They may also like to talk since hearing themselves saying something is a primary way the information is retained in their brains. They may have a hard time getting repetitive TV or radio jingles out of their head, but could use that as a learning strategy by making up their own songs, raps, or rhymes to memorize information for a test. Reading aloud, talking things out, even to themselves or perhaps the family pet, and repeating important instructions or information are signs of an auditory learner.

In grade school and high school, teachers may have really appreciated the auditory learners because they actually listened to directions and announcements. They have an advantage in lecture and discussion-type courses because information is presented in the way they receive it best. However, they may not do well if the instructor fails to explain things fully or expects the students to read the text, hand-outs, syllabus, etc. on their own without giving verbal reminders about assignments or up-coming tests.

Strong Auditory Learners may benefit from using the following techniques:

- *Sit near the middle of the class where you can hear everything that is said in lectures or class discussions.*

- *Ask well-thought-out questions in class.*

- *Go over class material with a friend or fellow student.*

- *Organize a study group with people from your class to talk about what you are learning.*

- *Tape-record your classes; then listen to the tapes at night before you go to sleep, while you're exercising, or when you're driving your car.*

- *As you read your textbook, stop after every section and recite out loud what you have just learned (main points, new vocabulary, important names and dates, how to do the problem, math or science formulas, etc.).*

- *Read your textbook out loud or into a tape recorder to play back later.*

- *Get the audio versions of books you have to read for literature and listen to them before you read. Be careful about movie versions because they often do not follow the story line closely enough.*

- *Read each chapter after you've heard the instructor explain the concepts in class.*

Tactile/Kinesthetic Learners

Actually, if you were studying this topic in depth, you'd discover that there are some slight differences between tactile and kinesthetic learners. Tactile deals more with the sense of touch, and kinesthetic is more of a whole body movement kind of thing. For our purposes we're going to combine these two very similar styles. The tactile/kinesthetic (TK) learner is someone who prefers hands-on learning or learns best by doing. They like to jump right in and try something. They need to be actively involved to make the information stay in their heads. It is often easier for them to concentrate if they are doodling or doing something with their hands (or feet) while listening. They may need to take frequent breaks while studying to move around, and if they can associate information to be memorized with some physical activity, they will retain it longer.

TK children fair pretty well in preschool and kindergarten where there is lots of action and physical activity. Good teachers recognize that touching is a powerful learning aid. Even in the elementary grades and into junior high, there are usually projects, plays, and other ways to get involved with the subject matter. Science class is good for nature walks, collecting samples, and looking at things through a microscope or telescope; but other subjects become less fascinating to a strong TK child as the work gets more abstract and reading becomes the primary mode of instruction.

Teachers may get frustrated with the TK child's constant need to be in motion, and the students get frustrated and bored with seatwork that becomes the staple of most elementary classes. In high school and college there are more computer, lab, and technical courses that strongly encourage learning by doing. However, to earn a diploma or an Associate in Applied Science Degree, students still must take several general education courses that are seldom taught in a tactile/kinesthetic manner. Therefore, strong TK learners will be at a disadvantage unless they can adapt.

Tactile/Kinesthetic Learners will find these strategies helpful:

- *Sit in the middle of the class where you can be involved in whatever is going on in class.*

- *Ask well-thought-out questions in class.*

- *Participate in class discussions; don't just sit passively.*

- *Take notes and highlight important information as you read the textbook.*

- *Have plenty of paper for taking notes in class to help you concentrate.*

- *Get physically involved as much as possible. Volunteer to assist in a lab demonstration, collect samples, or go to the board to work a problem.*

- *Make charts, models, etc. to bring the content to life.*

- *Work with fellow students in learning teams or study groups.*

- *Use manipulatives (learning aids you can move) whenever possible.*

- *Use interactive computer software when available.*

- *Read while walking on the treadmill.*

■ Academic Strengths and Weaknesses

Everyone does some things well and could improve in other things. By this time in your school experience, you are probably aware of several of your weaknesses. You might think, "I'm not a good test taker," or "I'm not good in math." On the other hand, you should also recognize the abilities, habits, and behaviors you have that make you a good student. It is sometimes easy to overlook your strengths, but acknowledging them can boost your self-confidence and give you ideas about how you can improve your weaknesses.

Let's focus on the positive first and think about the characteristics of successful students. Students who get A's and B's often are no more intelligent than anyone else. However, they practice certain behaviors that give them the edge. Most are not complicated or difficult to implement. You would think that everyone could figure it out, but semester after semester, otherwise bright students earn lower grades or fail because they do not put effort into being successful.

How many of these characteristics do you have? How many could you easily adopt? Use the following chart to identify which positive student behaviors are part of your regular routine and which you need to add.

Characteristic	I do this	I need to do this
I arrive on time for all of my classes. Class attendance is a high priority for me.		
I sit in the front or middle of the class where I can easily see and hear and will not be distracted.		
I pay attention in class. I do not disrupt others by talking, nor do I "space out" and miss important information.		
I come prepared for class. I have read the chapter and my homework is done. I bring my book, notepaper, and pens to class so I am ready to listen and take notes.		
I participate in class discussions. I know I will learn more if I am involved, plus I am contributing to the learning process.		
I ask questions in class, especially if I don't understand or if I want to know more.		
I give the instructor and others positive feedback in class. I make eye contact when someone is talking and express appropriate body language.		
I get to know other students in each class. I have at least one other person I can ask for help or with whom I compare notes. I don't feel like a stranger.		
I contact the instructor if I know I must miss class. I get any hand-outs and information that I missed prior to the next class session whenever possible.		
I develop and use my own, personalized learning tools. I mark my textbooks to suit my needs. I have what I need (calculator, pocket dictionary, planner, etc.) to do my assignments.		
I turn in all assignments on time. I don't lose unnecessary points by turning in late or incomplete work.		
I follow the directions. When I'm doing an assignment, I make sure it is what I'm supposed to do.		
I seek help when I need it. I use the support services the college provides (tutoring, counseling, etc.). I don't let pride keep me from getting tutoring. I would rather pass than fail.		

The chart helped you identify some simple ways to enhance your academic strengths. Now, let's focus on how to overcome your weaknesses. It might be helpful to identify the weakness that you would like to improve. Using the goal setting techniques you learned previously, list your weaknesses in order of importance or difficulty. Then pick out a reasonable number to work on this semester. As you read and study the remaining chapters in this book, you will learn many strategies to help you improve concentration, study skills, note taking, test taking, stress management, and communication.

For each weakness you've committed to strengthen this semester, develop a plan for overcoming it or compensating for it. For example, if your weakness in math is a result of never really learning the multiplication tables in the first place, your plan will include the steps it will take to learn them. If you're a visual learner, make flash cards and drill. If you are an auditory learner, have a friend or family member help or say them out loud over and over every day. If you're a tactile/kinesthetic learner, go to the college's tutoring or computerized learning center and review on the computer for a half hour three times a week, or repeat them over and over while working out. Write out a plan and review it with your instructor or a close friend who will keep you accountable. The best plan in the world won't work unless you put it into action.

■ Eight Ways to Be Intelligent

Dr. Howard Gardner, a psychologist and professor at Harvard University, is one of many researchers who have studied how people learn and what makes them successful in school and in life. His theory that there are multiple ways a person can be intelligent might help you understand your own abilities. While most people have all of the intelligences, a couple of them are usually more developed than the others. Tapping into your strongest intelligences to learn new material will help you understand and master it more readily. Think of them as special talents. If you are talented in a certain area, doesn't that usually mean that it is easier to learn and perform in that area? That's what the multiple intelligence theory is all about. So far Dr. Gardner has identified eight different kinds of intelligence.

Verbal/Linguistic—relates to written and spoken words. People who are good at reading, writing, speaking, debating, or learning foreign languages have a high level of this type of intelligence. The ACT, SAT, IQ tests, and/or other standardized tests taken in school have parts that measure verbal ability. High scores on these tests are considered accurate predictors of college success because verbal ability is one of the two kinds of intelligence emphasized in school. Those who have it fit our traditional notions of "smart."

Logical/Mathematical—has to do with reasoning, critical thinking, problem solving, recognizing patterns, and working with abstract symbols such as numbers or geometric shapes. This is the other type of intelligence that is measured by virtually all standardized tests and is usually the ticket to college success and a good job. Schools place the utmost importance on teaching and developing this in students. Science, math, and computer science majors usually have high levels of logical/mathematical intelligence.

Visual/Spatial—relies on eyesight and also the ability to visualize things/places. It is valued by those in our culture who appreciate the visual arts such as painting, drawing, and sculpture. It is useful in situations where you need to be able to use space or get around somewhere such as in navigation, map-making, architecture, computer-aided drafting, graphic arts, and so forth. It is also an ability that is used in games or puzzles where seeing things from different angles is an advantage. People with strong visual/spatial intelligence can look at something and see how it could be improved or see beyond what *is* to what *could be*. This intelligence is often considered synonymous with a good imagination.

Bodily/Kinesthetic—the ability to express oneself through movement or to do things using the body, or to make things. This intelligence is seen in athletes, dancers, actors/actresses, artists, skilled craftspeople, and inventors. People with this intelligence are often very physically active. The ability to use the capabilities of one's body, sometimes even without conscious thought, is another characteristic of this intelligence.

Musical/Rhythmic—being able to "tune in" to sounds and rhythms and use them to create mood changes in the brain. For example, creating soothing melodies, stirring marches, or stimulating raps requires strong use of this intelligence. Expressing yourself with sounds from nature, musical instruments, or the human voice or being able to differentiate tone qualities are more examples of this intelligence. Often people with this intelligence enjoy listening to music as they work on other things or seem to have an "ear" for it. Unfortunately, this intelligence is often not emphasized in school curriculums and is an "extra" that usually gets cut from tight budgets, even though research has shown that learning to play an instrument stimulates connectors in the brain that enhance other learning. Music and rhythm make up a universal language that can transcend culture and touch people's lives. This can be a powerful intelligence to develop.

Interpersonal—the capacity to communicate effectively with others through verbal and nonverbal expression. Persons who have a high degree of this intelligence can work effectively in groups. They notice and understand things about other people such as their moods, facial expressions, posture, gestures, inner motivations, and personality types. They can also listen to others and make them feel valuable and appreciated. Although teachers like students to get along, children with a naturally high level of interpersonal intelligence may have gotten in trouble for being "too social" in school. Though it is invaluable in many occupations, people who have this talent are often drawn into the helping professions.

Intrapersonal—probably the least understood and/or valued in our educational system, this intelligence deals with knowing and understanding oneself. It involves being able to analyze our own thinking and problem solving processes, being aware of our inner thoughts, feelings, and internal state. It is also a sensitivity to and understanding of spiritual realities, and experiencing wholeness and unity as a person. Being able to anticipate the future and contemplate our unreached potential requires this type of intelligence. Because people with high levels of this intelligence enjoy solitude, meditation, and quiet, their abilities may not be recognized. They probably don't mind, though. Their self-concept and self-confidence does not come from what others think of them. They set their own goals and agendas and know exactly why they do and say the things they do.

Naturalistic—the ability to live in harmony with the natural world and appreciate nature. People who have a "green thumb," or a "way with animals," or who could survive in the wilderness without modern conveniences have naturalistic intelligence. It also includes people who are perceptive about differences in the natural world such as being able to recognize the many kinds of flowers, trees, birds, etc. and can use this ability productively. Farmers, biological scientists, and hunters might utilize naturalistic intelligence. In addition, Dr. Gardner believes that people in our materialistic, consumer culture display naturalistic intelligence when they can distinguish even subtle differences among car styles, athletic shoes, and the like.

■ Multiple Intelligence—What Does It Mean for You?

When you read these descriptions, can you pick out your strongest type of intelligence from Gardner's list? What do you think would happen if our school systems actually taught in ways that emphasized all of the intelligences? Even though the traditional ways of being smart have always been a pathway to success, it is interesting to note that the types of intelligence least emphasized by schools in the United States, when developed fully, provide some of the greatest income potential and social status. Professional athletes, entertainers, musicians, actors, actresses, and artists have a lot more visibility in our society than doctors, judges, scientists, or mathematicians. Think of a few examples of people who achieved fame, fortune, and sometimes even greatness for maximizing their various intelligences.

Let's start with the richest person in the world. Bill Gates's visual/spatial intelligence led him to create a whole new approach to using computers where icons (pictures) replaced typed (verbal) commands. Tiger Woods's bodily/kinesthetic intelligence has made him a legend in the golf world while still in his 20s. Oprah Winfrey and Barbara Walters have used their interpersonal intelligences to pursue lucrative and successful careers in a business that wasn't traditionally open to women (especially women of color) when they began. Mahatma Gandhi in India and later Martin Luther King, Jr. in the United States both used their intrapersonal and interpersonal intelligences to change the course of history.

While you may seem a long way from these examples, recognizing your natural gifts and using the intelligences you have can lead you to a more productive, fulfilling life. If you haven't done so before now, start to appreciate your own ways of being intelligent. Then, use your strengths to help you comprehend new material. For example, if you have great musical/rhythmic intelligence, put your lessons to music. If you excel at interpersonal intelligence, talk to others and learn from the dialogs you initiate. If you have strong intrapersonal intelligence, think through your goals and recognize that doing well in each of your classes will help you achieve them.

Don't ever put yourself down for not being as talented as someone else is. Learn to make the most of what you can do, and always try to do your best. Motivation, desire, and hard work are always the surest pathways to success.

■ Instructional Styles

While it would be wonderful if every teacher were trained to teach to all of the learning styles and to present material that appealed to each of the intelligences, this is the real world, and that isn't going to happen. Just as learners have different styles, your instructors will also have different instructional styles. These styles will be influenced by their personalities, their own learning styles, the intelligences they possess, their education, and/or previous teaching experiences. They may vary their approach, or they may use the same methods semester after semester. The three styles used most often are *Independent, Student Centered/Interactive,* and *Cooperative Learning.* Let's take a look at each one:

Independent—An instructor with an independent style delivers course material primarily by lecturing. S/he may use prepared audio-visual aids or PowerPoint presentations to add a visual component to the auditory delivery. Class sessions are usually formal with little or no input from the students. This style is typically used in large classes such as those at a state university where several hundred students may be seated in a large lecture hall. The instructor is independent of the students, may not take attendance, get to know them personally, or be concerned if they miss class. Therefore, those students must be independent learners. They must motivate themselves to go to class, take notes, read the textbook, do the assignments, prepare for exams and quizzes, and do their own research to get answers to their questions.

Student Centered/Interactive—Instructors using this style are less formal and want students to be involved during class. They may use a lecture/discussion format or prefer questions and answers. They may use the board or an overhead projector to illustrate points but are willing to stop the lecture to field questions and comments. If students don't voluntarily participate, the instructor may call on them. S/he usually tries to get to know each student's name to facilitate this process. Small classes may be asked to move their desks into a circle or semi-circle so students can see each other and discuss issues face-to-face. Class participation and attendance may be part of the final course grade because much of the learning is done in class.

Cooperative Learning—Instructors who break their classes into small groups or learning teams are using a style that places more emphasis on discovery learning and student involvement. Instead of the instructor being the authority figure, imparting wisdom to the class, students are encouraged to take charge of their learning and help each other achieve. With guidance from the instructor, students work together with their teammates to find the information they need. Each person may have a different role (leader, recorder, spokesperson) and is responsible for carrying out his/her portion of the assignment. Team members teach each other, making sure each one has mastered the content. Students are responsible to their teammates to attend class and complete their portion of the assignments. Sometimes they take their exams as a team, or they may all receive the same grade on an assignment.

People in teams who stay together for the entire semester tend to form strong bonds with one another and develop close friendships that last beyond the duration of the course. That is one of the main benefits of this style. Instructors who use cooperative learning point out that it is more like the real world where people have to work together to get a specific job accomplished.

While it's nice to have an instructor whose instructional style matches your learning style, if you don't, you can still achieve satisfaction and success in the course. Use the knowledge you have gained in this chapter to understand what works best for you. Make learning as easy as you can, and use your preferred style and strongest intelligence to master new content. Adapt your class and textbook notes to your style. If the assignments given by the instructor don't get through to you, give yourself additional assignments that will force you to learn thoroughly. Remember that you should always do more than the minimum. This is your education. Take charge of it. As you work from your strength areas, try also to develop and improve your weaker areas. Review previous lessons using a different modality than your preferred one. Explore areas of personal interest/hobbies in one of your less-developed intelligences. College and life are all about learning and growing as a person.

■ Summary

This chapter has focused on three types of learning modes: visual, auditory, and tactile/kinesthetic. It gave you suggested learning strategies to use for each. You were asked to assess your academic strengths and make a list of weaknesses that you plan to improve. In addition, Howard Gardner's theory of multiple intelligence was presented. Gardner maintains that the eight intelligences—verbal/linguistic, mathematical/logical, visual/spatial, bodily/kinesthetic, musical/rhythmic, interpersonal, intrapersonal, and naturalistic are all valuable and useful to people in society. Finally, the three most common teaching styles—independent, interactive, and cooperative learning were discussed. You as the learner can use this information to take charge of your learning and become a more successful student.

■ Journal Assignment

Write at least one paragraph about each course that you are taking this semester.

- ■ Identify the course and the instructor.

- ■ Describe the instructor's teaching style (Independent, Interactive, or Cooperative Learning).

- ■ Does s/he use the same style or a combination of styles?

- ■ To which learning modalities (visual, auditory, tactile/kinesthetic) does this instructor typically teach?

- ■ Does that match your preferred modality?

- ■ How are you doing in this class so far?

- ■ Do you anticipate that it will get harder or easier as the semester progresses?

- ■ What are your academic strengths in this class?

- ■ What are your academic weaknesses?

- ■ What are you planning to do to compensate for your weaknesses?

■ Homework Activity

What's Your Style?

1. What is your preferred learning modality (visual, auditory, or tactile/kinesthetic)?

   _____

2. What learning aids or strategies have you successfully used in the past?

   _____

   _____

   _____

3. Which additional learning aids or strategies discussed in this chapter are you willing to try?

   _____

   _____

   _____

4. Which of Dr. Gardner's Eight Intelligences do you think is your strongest? Why do you think so?

   _____

   _____

   _____

What Should You Do?

Pretend you have a friend in each of the following situations. You are discussing with your friend what s/he should do to achieve the greatest degree of success in each course. Write out at least two recommendations. (Dropping the course is not an option.)

1. The class is Introduction to the Visual Arts. The instructor shows many slides of famous works of art to the class. They are also supposed to look up information on the Internet about the works of art. Tests are based on textbook reading assignments and identifying works of art and the artist from slides. Your friend is not a good visual learner. S/he is more of a tactile/kinesthetic learner.

_____

_____

_____

2. The class is history. The instructor lectures every day. The course grade is determined by two main scores: the mid-term and the final exam, both of which are based on notes from the class lectures. Your friend is primarily a visual learner.

_____

_____

_____

3. The course is computer science. Everything is hands-on and independent learning. The instructor expects the students to look at the book and do the exercises. S/he doesn't fully explain things to the whole group but instead walks around to make sure the students are working. Your friend has never really been a tactile/kinesthetic learner. His/her preferred learning modality is auditory. Besides that, s/he has very little computer experience and is embarrassed to constantly be the one asking the instructor questions. Everyone else seems to enjoy the no lecture/hands-on format of the class.

_____

_____

_____

CHAPTER 11
Learning Strategies for Academic Success

"I am convinced that it is of primordial importance to learn more every year than the year before. After all, what is education but a process by which a person begins to learn how to learn?"

Peter Ustinov

This chapter provides specific strategies to help students learn information at the level required by most college courses. It begins with information about your brain and how you receive and process information. Next, **Bloom's Taxonomy** of Educational Objectives is introduced. This classification system explains levels of thinking and how this relates to learning strategies. The chapter offers specific study strategies and techniques for an effective study session, time management, listening, note taking, memory, concentration, writing, test taking, and textbook reading. Every semester will be a continual process of learning about yourself as a learner. Each course will require that you try different learning strategies that match the level of knowledge required by the course.

■ Understanding How You Learn

Frequently, first-year students enter college classrooms experiencing feelings of apprehension and curiosity. Relatives, friends, and high school teachers may have told you college courses will be vastly different and much harder than high school classes. What is different? What makes college classes so difficult? Why are some classes easier than you expected? What strategies can you learn to cope with new academic challenges? Are you academically ready? Thinking about all these questions can be challenging, confusing, and perplexing.

When you are overwhelmed, the best idea is to take a deep breath and start at the beginning. The first step for assessing your academic readiness is to set aside some time and analyze your **PBID**. What is PBID? Before you begin a new physical activity, such as snowboarding, skiing, or skateboarding, you check your physical readiness. Well, now you need to check four factors, **Purpose, Background, Interest, and Difficulty (PBID)**, that affect your academic readiness; that is, your ability to be successful learning new course information.

Purpose is the reason why you enroll in a course. Why does it matter what your reason is for enrolling in a class? Humans tend to match their behavior to their purpose or goals. Purposes that are unclear (or are based on someone else's goal) may hamper your desire to succeed in the course.

Background knowledge gives you the ability to link new information to previously learned concepts. The more background you have in a subject, the easier it is to make more connections and apply information beyond rote learning. Also, high background knowledge in a subject motivates you to learn more, so your learning can become more purposeful.

Interest is the factor that captures your attention. Think how easily your attention can be caught by the tabloids at the checkout stand! Your lack of interest could be related to a fuzzy purpose for taking the course or even lack of background knowledge in the course. It is difficult to be interested in something you don't know anything about. If your attention is not captured, then you will have to create strategies that involve you in the material.

Difficulty can be a combination of many factors. It could be related to the course content, lack of background, lack of motivation, or the manner in which the course is taught.

Use Figure 1 to assess your PBID. Knowing your PBID and learning about how your brain processes information will help you create the learning strategies you need to be successful.

Learning how individuals receive, store, and retrieve information from the brain is important. This information will help you create strategies to learn material in the most effective manner and then store the facts for future use. Because people make sense of the world based on what they already know, information is learned by connecting new information with the knowledge already in place. How the information travels to the brain, connects with previous information, and then is converted to memory is unique

Assessing Your PBID For Learning Readiness

Purpose: Why are you taking this class?

◆ It is required for my major, for general education.

◆ I need the information to build my background for another subject.

◆ I hope there is information and/or skills I can use to develop my learning skills.

◆ My best friend told me it would be easy.

◆ It was all I could find to fit my schedule.

Background: What do I already know about this subject?

◆ I have had previous classes in this subject.

◆ I have had personal experience with this subject.

◆ I have limited knowledge of the subject.

Interest: Do I like studying this subject?

◆ Other students told me about the class, and I have some questions I hope will be answered by the class.

◆ I really have little interest in this class, but my advisor told me I had to take it.

◆ I am looking at a major related to this subject.

◆ This class will provide information about a hobby that I have.

Difficulty: How difficult do you expect material in the class to be, and how much time do you anticipate you'll have to spend on the class?

◆ I expect the class will be really easy, and I won't have to study much for it.

◆ Studying has always been hard for me, and I don't expect it to be any different in this class.

◆ This particular subject has <u>always</u> been challenging for me.

◆ I have heard this was a very tough class with a difficult instructor.

Figure 1 ■ Assessing Your PBID

for each individual. This is their **learning style**. Most of us prefer learning in the style or format that is easiest for us to comprehend, to store, and retrieve.

Three main sensory paths carry information to the brain: visual, auditory, and kinesthetic. **Visual learners** learn best through visual processing; that is, using their eyes to learn information. To remember information, they need to see it presented visually, as in a chart or diagram or written down. Reading textbooks and obtaining new information in a visual format is the easiest method of learning for these students. They enjoy lecture classes and take many notes to study after class. They often are most comfortable with instructors who use the blackboard to illustrate important concepts or distribute lecture notes or outlines of the lecture.

Auditory learners process information best through their auditory system. They prefer to learn by hearing the information, as in listening to lectures. The auditory learner likes discussion and usually learns well in a study group or with a study partner. Auditory learners often need to hear what a difficult passage sounds like or to talk out a difficult concept before they read the textbook. Their recall is increased when they practice teaching the concept to someone else.

Kinesthetic learners like to associate movement with their learning. They prefer the sense of touch and actually learn better when they are physically involved in what they are studying. They are good at applied, hands-on tasks. They usually find *doing* to be the best way of learning. Strategies that incorporate movement are the most effective for them. Activities such as walking through a demonstration or project, writing down information, and applying it to real-life circumstances are helpful. Movements, such as tapping on the desk, jiggling their legs up and down, and clicking their pens as they study, actually enable them to concentrate and learn. They are most comfortable getting up and walking around while studying, writing lists, outlining chapters, using note cards, and manipulating and moving information around. Strategies that involve music and rhythm, or acting or role playing, may be helpful. (Remember the songs that helped you learn all the names of the fifty states or even the alphabet?)

The sensory path which you tend to use most frequently characterizes your learning style. Most learners make use of all three sensory paths, but many students find themselves relying heavily on one and not always their strongest one. Think of how someone has tried to teach you a skill, such as a new computer program, and you became frustrated that you didn't catch on quickly. Perhaps the instructor explained the process to you, but you needed to read the directions for yourself. When you read the information and then listened to the instructor, you caught on quickly. The strongest learning link occurs when you combine two or more learning styles. It is important to remember that combining your preferred learning style with a different learning style may enhance your learning and increase your retention. This ability to adapt your style will be important as you meet instructors with many teaching styles who use a variety of techniques. The Sensory Modalilty Exercise at the end of the chapter will help you begin to discover what type of learner you are. The chart in Figure 2 outlines strategies for studying based on your learning style preference.

Visual Learners	Auditory Learners	Kinesthetic Learners
Mark important information using a color system.	Lecture to yourself.	Study with another person.
Draw charts, graphs, or diagrams.	Work in study groups.	Have a dialogue with yourself about the material.
Form pictures to which you can attach the information being learned.	Discuss or teach others the material.	Use note cards to record and organize necessary information.
Copy or type notes into an outline format.	Read notes or material aloud.	Match the information to movement (tap a pencil, swing your foot).
	Read notes into a tape recorder, then listen.	Stand up; walk around.
		Demonstrate your knowledge to others.
		Use a hands-on approach.

Figure 2 ■ Learning Style Study Strategies

■ Levels of Thinking

A major distinction between the high school and college class environment is that college faculty expect students to assume responsibility for their own learning of information. Instructors do not check to see if students have purchased textbooks, if they are taking notes, keeping up with the reading assignments, or studying for tests. Attending classes is the responsibility of the student, and many instructors do not penalize students for absences. At first, students may not perceive that the classes are difficult, but this perception often changes after the first exam. College classes often require a level of learning that students may not have incorporated into their previous learning strategies. Most high school courses focus on lower levels of understanding. Often students only needed to recognize the correct answer or restate information. Postsecondary coursework assumes students already know how to do that. They require you to think differently and at higher levels.

Many students find that the self-taught study strategies that enabled them to be successful in high school do not transfer to the college environment. Your high school or job-related experiences developed skills that you can now build upon and expand. Also, your previous study skills can be used as a base to learn more strategies. When you learn more about effective learning and study skills, then you can design your learning time to produce results. *You will not have to work harder, but you will be working smarter.*

Bloom's Taxonomy. Luckily, you already know how to think and are aware that different tasks require different degrees of thinking. The thinking you do when you remember a phone number differs from the thinking you do to solve a math story problem. If you can identify the level of thinking you already do, the level you may need to achieve, then you

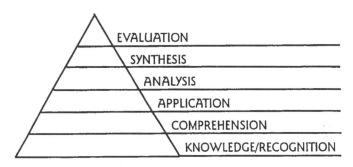

Figure 3

can apply this knowledge to areas involved in studying coursework. Figure 3 shows the levels of thinking according to a system called **Bloom's Taxonomy**. Each level builds on the previous level. That is, students cannot speak and comprehend a foreign language until they have memorized the basic vocabulary. Effective students are aware of learning strategies that incorporate the level of thinking required for success in each course. This chapter uses examples from the Geography 1130 textbook to demonstrate the thinking levels and practical application to studying and learning material.

Knowledge and recognition of information are the first level and form the basis of understanding. It requires you to remember what you heard or read, but not necessarily to understand it. It is as simple as remembering the name of the person you just met or what you need at the grocery store. In coursework, this level is necessary to build information for any subject. Many general education courses you select will require you to learn the basic vocabulary and principles of the course. Memorization can achieve this, but this is not meaningful learning, which requires understanding of the material. In the section from the Geography 1130 textbook (Figure 5), the text discusses climatic classification systems. A student operating at the recognition/knowledge level may memorize the name of "Köppen"and the contribution that he made to science. Possibly, you will form a study group for the course. When you compare your notes for the course, each of you lists Köppen as an important person. You practice asking each other key names and other definitions from that chapter. The Geog 1130 test and the essay question never ask what Köppen did. The test asks you to apply his classification system to describe a particular type of climate. To answer this question, the study group needed to do more processing of information. Simply memorizing the conditions and episodes was not sufficient.

The comprehension level emphasizes studying for an understanding of the material you are trying to learn. In this level of Bloom's taxonomy, you become more focused on what the material is trying to explain to you. During your geography study group time, you may explain to each other the characteristics of each type of climate mentioned in the Geog 1130 lecture. Then you can answer the essay question that asks you to describe the different climatic types. At this level, you can explain information to someone else. You can share the plot of a movie or a novel, report the homework assignment to a roommate who missed class, or explain the course syllabus.

The third level in Bloom's taxonomy is **application**. When you apply what you understand, you begin to link the information you gained to examples in your own life. After seeing a movie or reading a novel, you connect with similar personal experiences. Your ability to see a parallel between the example in the text and the experience in your own life is the thinking skill of application. At this level, math courses require students to solve word problems or solve problems different from those previously seen. You are asked to compare and contrast information on an essay test question. In Geog 1130, an essay test question might ask you to "describe the major differences between the classification systems." Many courses will ask you to provide examples from your own life of the information you study, determine causes and effects, or draw analogies. The more ways you apply the information, the longer you will retain the concepts.

Analysis requires you to break apart and examine the components of a concept in depth. Depth is the key element that true analysis demands. If when discussing a movie or novel with a friend, you discuss the main theme and what made the leading character so evil, then you are using analytical thinking skills. If your friend disagrees with your analysis and questions your theory, the friendly debate that may follow requires additional analytic thinking. In Geog 1130, the instructor may ask you to "calculate the climatic classification based on temperature and precipitation for a particular region." To analyze the problem, you need to gather facts, translate information, look at relationships, and apply rules and principles concerning weather patterns.

Synthesis is the creative level of thinking. You combine different ideas to create a new whole. When you synthesize, you combine your current understanding of concepts with new information that you create. Many instructors assign group projects where students must design, create, or propose a solution to a problem. In Geog 1130, the instructor may require that you work in a group to generate solutions to farming problems that have developed because of global warming. Examples that require that you operate at a synthesizing level include using music or art to express yourself, developing a topic for a research paper, or answering essay questions that ask you to "tie together" all the information you have learned to solve a problem.

Evaluation forms the highest level of thinking in Bloom's taxonomy. At this level, you must use your personal judgment regarding an issue's relevance, depth, value, or other qualities. To do this, you would review all the relevant "facts" and review sources for their contribution to the topic under discussion. You often use evaluation to make judgments and decisions in your personal life. Choosing to attend Utah State University, whether to live on or off campus, or how many hours you can work and still do well in school require evaluation. Coursework may ask you to evaluate decisions in court cases or whether a social policy is adequate in providing aid and assistance to poor people. Geography classes may require you to judge what types of vegetation could adapt to climatic changes.

Although this text describes the levels of Bloom's taxonomy separately, few learning situations depend solely on one level or another. Generally, as the information increases in complexity, the effort needed to learn also increases. Your classes will increase in complexity as will the levels of thinking required, as you specialize in a content area. This information will help you as a learner continually decide what you know, what you still need to learn, and the ways in which you must learn. The study strategies noted in Figure 4, along with examples from the Geog 1130 text and in this chapter, will help you in applying this information as you study.

Level	Skill	Study Strategies
Evaluation	Making judgments about ideas based on previous learning.	Assess, estimate, revise, judge, and critique information. Evaluate plans to advise farmers on planting seasons based on climatic patterns.
Synthesis	Combining ideas to create new connections, summarize, conclude, or predict.	Create, design, organize, manage, and plan using many concepts together. Design solutions to changes in climate that affect farming.
Analysis	Breaking knowledge apart in meaningful ways.	Debate, criticize, question, and solve problems. Given temperature and precipitation data, calculate the annual climate conditions.
Application	Transferring knowledge to new situations.	Practice, apply, or use the information. Using the information on the Köppen System, describe the importance of another classification system for climate.
Comprehension	Trying to understand the information.	Recognize, identify, summarize, or restate the information. Describe the different climates and the characteristics of each.
Knowledge/ Recognition	Learning, storing, and retrieving information— foundation skills for learning any new subject.	Recall, list, state, or define information. Memorize vocabulary definitions in geography (example: "evapotranspiration").

Figure 4 ■ Bloom's Taxonomy of Thinking and Learning

Climate and Climatic Classification 133

The Köppen System

Vladimir Köppen began devising a climatic classification system with his doctoral dissertation and continued to refine it until his death. An ethnic German from Russia, Köppen received formal training as a botanist. His system of climatic classification is based largely on the responses of biological activity to certain critical temperatures and moisture. Köppen reasoned that the world distribution of vegetation closely resembles the world distribution of climates. His attempt was to quantify climatic boundaries evidenced by the global distribution of vegetative groups.

Figure 6.1 illustrates the spatial distribution of global climates according to the **Köppen climatic classification** system. Köppen's labelling system begins at the equator with climates designated with the letter "A" which are macrothermal and humid. Straddling the wet and warm equatorial climates are the dry climates dominated by the subtropical high pressure represented by the symbol "B." Poleward of the B-type climates are the "C" climates characterized by humid, mesothermal atmospheric conditions with mild winters. At higher latitudes, Köppen's "D" climates are mid/latitude humid, mesothermal climates having cold winters. Finally, the "E" climates are those with microthermal characteristics dominated by low temperatures due to polar regions. Sites with climates dominated by altitude are represented by the letter "H." For precise definitions for the Köppen classification system, see End Note 6.

A Geography of Climates

Although a case could be made for 30 to 35 different climatic types, this textbook describes only the climatic types covering significant portions of the earth's surface making them important to an introductory study of climates. Each of the following climatic types are products of earth/atmospheric processes at work in the area. As each climatic region is discussed, some explanation is offered as to the atmospheric mechanism controlling the manner in which the climate behaves. An understanding of various climatic types is basic to a comprehension of the distribution of people, plants, soils, and many other natural phenomena across the surface of the earth.

(Koeppen)

*

Köppen climatic classification: empirical climatic groups based on temperature and precipitation regimes.

$A = tropical$
$B = desert/steppe$
$C = Mediterranean (mild-mes)$
$D = meso-cold$
$E = arctic/polar/tundra$
$H = Highland (altitude)$

Figure 6.1

Figure 5 ■ Geography 1130 Textbook Sample Annotated Page Example

Figure 6.2 Humid tropical climate (Af).

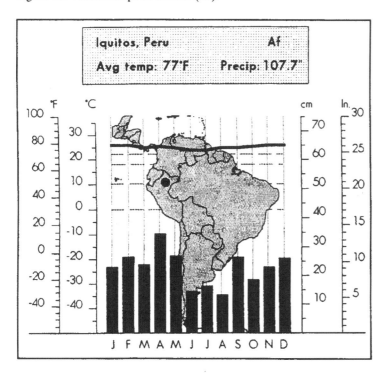

The Humid Tropical Climates

Generally located as a continuous belt near the equator, tropical (A) climates display high daily temperatures and significant annual precipitation. Dominated by proximity to the ITCZ, tropical climates are characteristically humid and warm. With average annual precipitation amounts greater than the annual potential for evapotranspiration, mean monthly temperatures exceed 18 degrees Celsius (64.4 degrees Fahrenheit). High temperatures are a function of the vertical rays of the sun while the high precipitation totals are caused by intertropical convergence.

The **humid tropical climate** (Af) is found in locations where daily, weekly, monthly, and annual conditions are continuously hot and humid. Figure 6.2 is a climograph illustrating the monthly temperature and precipitation of humid tropical climate. Due to the dominance of the ITCZ, precipitation is evenly distributed throughout the year which normally sup-

humid tropical climate: warm and moist year-round

136   *Principles of Physical Geography*

Figure 6.3 Humid wet-dry tropical climate (Aw).

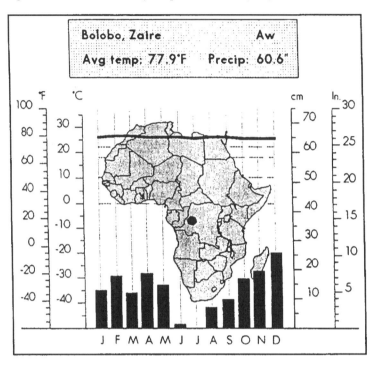

humid wet-dry climate:
warm year-round with
dry winter season

ports large expanses of rainforest accompanied by luxuriant undergrowth. Even though precipitation is received year round, the time of maximum precipitation occurs shortly after the time of the summer solstice. So little change occurs in daily weather patterns that the terms weather and climate are nearly synonymous. Indeed, the daily temperature range typically exceeds those of the annual temperature ranges causing reference to the nighttime as the "winter" of the tropics. Humid tropical climates occur in much of Central America, the equatorial belt of West Central Africa, and Indonesia.

Poleward of the humid tropical climate is the **humid wet-dry tropical climate** (Aw) which displays two distinct seasons of precipitation (Figure 6.3). During the wet season, precipitation rivals that of the humid tropical climate. However, the wet-dry tropical climate has a distinct dry winter during which precipitation is reduced to 30 percent or less of the annual total. The dry season lasts from three to six months and occurs during the time when the sun is not directly overhead, improperly

Climate and Climatic Classification   137

Figure 6.4   Tropical monsoon climate (Am).

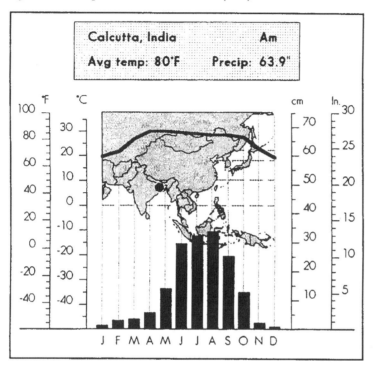

referred to as the tropical "winter." The shifting ITCZ is the climatic control of seasonal precipitation. When the ITCZ is present during the high-sun season, it brings with it abundant precipitation; when the ITCZ is absent during the low-sun season, dryness prevails. During the dry winter season, many of the trees lose their leaves and grasses experience stress. Tropical wet and dry climates are found in South America (central Brazil, Colombia and Venezuela), North and South Central Africa, India and Southeast Asia, Northern Australia, and parts of the Caribbean.

The **tropical monsoon climate** (Am) is characterized by a very short low-sun dry season during which the precipitation is reduced to less than 1/10 of the wet, high-sun season (Figure 6.4). The climate of India is perhaps the best example of a true monsoon. Though not experiencing reversals in regional winds, locations in Northern Brazil, the Guianas, Burma, and much of the Philippines are characterized as having tropical monsoon climates. In order for these locations to experience true mon-

tropical monsoon climate: warm year-round with extremely wet summer season

138 *Principles of Physical Geography*

soonal weather, seasonal reversals of wind must accompany these wet-dry seasons which, in the locations cited above, seldom occurs. Often associated with the mechanisms responsible for the precipitation regime of the true monsoon climate is the presence of high ground (such as a mountain range) located near a coastal plain initiating orographic precipitation.

The Dry Climates

Covering more than a fourth of the total land surface area of the earth, the dry climates are symbolized by the letter "B." Although they can be found at much higher latitudes, the dry climates are concentrated between 20 and 30 degrees north and south latitude (Figure 6.1). A geographic site has a dry climate regime when the annual total precipitation is less than the potential for evaporation from natural surfaces and transpiration (water loss) from plants. The potential for evaporation and transpiration is often combined into one term, **evapotranspiration**. In dry climatic regions, potential evapotranspiration amounts exceed the total accumulations of precipitation. Not only do dry climates experience little precipitation, but they also exhibit great variation in annual precipitation totals and distribution. Because of the general absence of clouds, dry climates receive intense insolation which effectively heats the atmosphere and reduces relative humidity.

The principle controlling mechanisms establishing dry climates on the earth's surface include: (1) high atmospheric pressure caused by the subsidence of air in the subtropical high pressure cells, (2) the rainshadow on the leeward side of the prevailing winds over a major mountain range, and (3) interior continental positions some distance from marine water sources. The dry climates are of two general varieties: the steppe and the desert. The steppe (BS) has a semiarid moisture regime where total annual precipitation is less than potential evapotranspiration but greater than one-half that value making it capable of supporting stumpy woodlands with small communities of grass. Most steppe climates function as transitional zones between humid and arid climates. The desert (BW) has an arid moisture regime with an average annual precipitation less than one-half the annual potential for evapotranspiration.

evapotranspiration: combined water loss by evaporation and transpiration from plants.

■ Study Session Strategies

How much should I study? As a rule of thumb, you will need to plan to study every day for every class. The recommended time is two hours of study for every hour of class. When you set up your study times, be sure to avoid marathon study sessions. Studying for 40–50 minutes and then taking a ten minute break is much more effective than trying to cram for 2–3 hours without stopping. The reason for this is that you remember best what you studied at the beginning and the end of the study session. We most quickly forget material learned in the middle. Therefore, shorter study sessions, with frequent breaks, are recommended. A word of caution—the break should be a non-TV break and should not last longer than the study session itself!

Where should I study? An important part of being successful at studying is setting up the appropriate environment for studying. Do you have a regular place to study? Is that place free of distractions? Does it contain all of the supplies you will need for studying? Is there proper lighting and ventilation? If most of your responses to these questions are "no," then maybe the first thing you need to do is make some changes in your study environment. The following suggestions will help you.

An effective study environment is:

- *A regular place.* By establishing a regular place, you are forming a habit. The habit is "when I sit at this area, I study and learn information." The more you practice that habit, the easier it will become. Think about your behavior. If you continually jump up to find something to eat, that is the habit you are establishing.
- *Free of distractions.* Unfortunately for most of us, a distraction-free environment is not possible. Distractions come in many forms and differ for individuals. Generally, the two greatest distractors are noise and motion. You will want to try to study in a place that is relatively quiet. This might mean that you need to rethink your choice of locations or possibly change your time for studying. Students with families quite often find it easier to stay at school and study in the library or in one of the open study areas in the student center. You will want to explore some options for a study place. The important thing is to find a consistent spot that works for you.
- *Designed to contain all of the supplies you need for studying.* To be most efficient in studying, you should have everything you need in close proximity before beginning. Having your math book in the back of your roommate's car and your roommate on the way to Chicago is not a good way to start a study session. By establishing a regular and consistent place to study, you are also able to make sure that this place contains all the supplies you will be needing: pens, pencils, highlighters, calculators, scrap paper, dictionary, a thesaurus, etc.
- *Properly lit and ventilated.* Lighting is an important part of your learning environment. Students typically spend a great deal of their time reading textbooks. Ideally, your study area should be well lit; otherwise, eye strain from improper lighting may result in decreased concentration. A room that is too hot or too cold will be distracting to you. Rooms that are not properly ventilated tend to get uncomfortable. You may find yourself falling asleep or unable to concentrate if the room is too warm or improperly ventilated. A cold room can make you tense and reduce your ability to concentrate.
- *Not too comfortable.* Many students try to study in bed and then can't figure out why they are always falling asleep. A bed is for sleeping! That is a habit that is well established. If you choose a place that is too comfortable, you will find that you are often unable to stay awake. Students, as a rule, tend to burn the candle at both ends, working, studying, playing, etc., etc. Sleep deprivation appears to be common among students. It is natural that when you finally settle into a comfortable place you begin to nod off.

What should I study? The first step in beginning to study is knowing what to study. Your guideline for knowing what to study will be the class syllabus. The syllabus is an informal contract between you and your professor. The syllabus will usually include a list of course topics, assigned readings, dates of quizzes, exams, and other required assignments. In addition, the syllabus usually provides the instructor's expectations for class participation, attendance, and the grading criteria. You will want to read your syllabus very carefully and make note of all the requirements.

How should I study? Once you know what the course requires, you will need to decide how you are going to study. Your syllabus will be your guide to creating specific study goals. You create study goals by thinking of the product you want at the end of the study session. In addition, the level of knowledge required by the information should guide your studying. Are you aiming for a strict knowledge level where memorization of terms will suffice? What is the testing format of the course? Will there be essay questions on the exam? Does this mean you should comprehend and explain your answers? Setting specific study goals can be difficult. It will take practice for you to be able to distinguish a specific goal from a nonspecific goal. Too often students confuse a broad, general declaration of intent to study with a specific, measurable study goal. The following are examples of specific study goals, based on a desired product.

- ■ I will complete a written outline or summary of the main points in chapter one.
- ■ I will formulate three questions for each major heading in chapter one.
- ■ I will answer the questions at the end of the chapter.
- ■ I will define all of the terms listed in the chapter summary.

By formulating specific, measurable study goals at the beginning of your study session, you then have a way of knowing when you are finished studying, and you have a concrete product. You can create a study guide—a chapter summary, possible test questions, solved problems, or a list of defined terms. These products can be utilized as review tools for future study sessions.

Group and individual studying. Often there are classes with large amounts of information, and knowing what to study or even where to begin can be challenging. If your instructor expects you to comprehend and apply the information, it is wise to practice doing this before an exam. Many students find that studying in a group is a more effective way to organize and learn information. Students benefit from considering information from another point of view or learning style perspective.

To help students in the large University Studies classes, some universities offer **supplemental instruction (SI) sessions,** a group study method. Supplemental Instruction is an enhancement program designed to assist students in mastering course concepts in difficult entry-level courses. Professors of courses with SI have agreed to allow a student (SI leader), who has successfully completed the course, to attend class, take notes, and conduct review sessions for the course. SI leaders schedule weekly review sessions outside of regularly scheduled class time to discuss and explore concepts presented in class and in the assigned readings. During these times, SI leaders guide students to the higher levels of thinking often required to pass a course. The Supplemental Instruction program is a collaborative approach to learning that allows students the opportunity to share and discuss course concepts in a small group setting. Courses with SI provided are designated each semester in the Schedule of Classes.

If you decide that you would benefit from individual tutoring, you can check the free tutoring services offered on campus each semester. Tutoring is available for accounting, math, chemistry, computer science, physics, and writing.

If you need additional tutoring or prefer individual versus drop-in tutoring, you can locate a private tutor.

■ Time Management Strategies

Effective time management will be your most important study strategy. To new college students facing academic, social, and personal demands, there never seems to be enough time. The academic environment presents new opportunities and challenges that appear to demand more time than you may think you have. You can't create more time, but you can become more skilled at how you manage time. Time management involves setting goals, planning, flexibility, commitment, and managing procrastination.

Goal setting. Managing time and setting goals go hand-in-hand. Using your time wisely helps you to achieve what you want, when you want. Knowing what your goals are for college and your future career help guide decisions regarding the use of your time.

There are several types of goals:

- *Short-range or immediate:* Goals you want to achieve tomorrow, next week, or within the semester. (Attend class each week, find a study partner for each class, or locate the free math tutor services.)
- *Mid-range:* Goals you want to achieve within 2–3 years. (Complete all the University Studies requirements.)
- *Long-range:* Goals you want to achieve within 5 years. (Obtain a degree in biology.)

Establishing goals can be difficult. The following guidelines will help you:

- Goals must be related to your **values**. You will find it very difficult to pursue a goal that is not directly linked to something that is important and meaningful for you. For example, if the goal is to pursue a career in social work, but you do not value interpersonal relationships, it will be difficult to succeed in accomplishing it.
- Goals are **specific and concrete**. A goal must state exactly what you are going to do. It can't be some vague, hopeful wish. A goal to stop procrastinating sounds nice, but it is not specific. A specific goal would state, "I will write a study plan by the end of the first week of class so that I can finish my paper in English 1010 by the tenth week of the semester."
- Goals are **measurable**. Progress toward completion of the goal needs to be evaluated. ("I must select my paper topic by the fourth week of class to finish my paper by mid-term. When my paper is typed and bound by the day before it is due, I will have completed my goal.")
- Goals are **realistic**. Your goal must be attainable, taking into consideration personal resources and abilities. (If you have not taken an algebra class in high school, it is not realistic to register for Math 1050, before taking Math 0900 or Math 1010.)
- Goals are **time framed**. Always set a beginning and end date for your goal.
- Goals are **written**. Committing a goal to writing makes it more concrete. It encourages you to be committed to completing it. A goal written on a piece of paper tacked to your bulletin board or written in your daily planner is difficult to ignore.
- Goals are **shared**. Telling someone else of your goals establishes accountability. You will be less likely to procrastinate or waver in your commitment to attaining the goal. Be sure to tell someone who will support you in your efforts to complete your goal.

■ Goals need to be **flexible**. There are many factors that can affect attaining a goal. Rarely is a goal followed through to completion without any problems. Temporary setbacks that will interrupt progress are common. These interruptions do not have to keep you from reaching the goal. Instead, reexamine your plan, revise or make a new one. You may discover that the original time frame is unrealistic. Changing the goal may be necessary (you may have reassessed what is important to you). This is okay, as long as the revisions are a way to ensure success versus avoiding doing something you really don't want to do.

Planning.   Your goals indicate where you want to go. Creating an action plan tells you how to get there. The saying, "if you don't know where you are going, you may end up somewhere else," is a good reminder of what happens without planning. The plan may consist of your "to-do lists," as well as your daily and semester planning schedules. Using these planning tools, write down specifically what you will do, and when and where you will do it. It is through a plan that "time management" becomes tangible and visible. It is no longer a "wish" or a "hope." Plans put you in charge of your time. The time management exercise at the end of this chapter gives you an opportunity to assess your time needs for this semester and create plans that enable you to reach your goals.

Flexibility and commitment.   Students need to allow for changes in schedules and plans. There are students who feel that writing their schedules is too rigid; that a written plan does not allow them to relax and enjoy life. But, in order to achieve a goal, there must be a basic commitment to accomplish what you set out to do. Yes, there should be flexibility and time to relax, but with the dedication to return to the plan. Often students use procrastination as an example of incorporating flexibility into their planning. You need to be honest with yourself and ask if procrastinating will detract from your commitment to accomplishing your goal. For many, procrastination is a barrier to accomplishing their goals. It is important to identify the reasons for procrastination, and then take action to overcome the barrier.

Reasons for procrastination.   Students' causes for procrastination tend to fit under the following categories:

■ *Unrealistic expectations.* Expectations placed upon you by yourself, family, and friends can often result in an overcrowded schedule. You may be able to overdo it for a semester, but over the long haul, it is necessary to realistically define expectations in accordance to personal resources of time, talent, and energy.
■ *Erroneous beliefs about academic work.* Many students believe that it is easy to learn and that smart people don't have to study. This belief leads to the further belief that studying is "unnatural." The truth is that learning anything new takes time and effort. People who appear to know everything without studying have usually spent time and effort in the past learning the information.
■ *Fear of failure.* For some students, the fear of failing is so great that they avoid ever starting a project. Or there is the fear that they are doing the task "wrong." To manage this fear, you will have to face it and separate information about your performance from your feelings or ideas about your own self-worth. In addition, you may need to ask questions and get more information about the task, so that you can begin with more confidence. Information tells you how to improve; it doesn't say anything about whether you're an OK person.
■ *Loss of control.* In the academic world, it is easy to lose control. Other people appear to always be telling you what you must and can do. In many instances, you will have no choices. In response to this lack of control, many students give up or postpone accomplishing required tasks. By identifying what areas of your life you can control, and accepting the others as part of life, you will be better able to handle this feeling of being out of control.

Managing procrastination. You can manage, and in some instances, overcome the procrastination habit. The following strategies may work for you:

- *Pay attention to your excuses (red flags).* "Just this one TV show, and then I'll study." "I work best under pressure." "It's already too late." When you hear yourself saying these things, you know you need to get to work, even if for only five minutes.
- *Optimize your chance for success.* Develop a study routine, including a specific place to study that is conducive to good "brain work." Identify specific goals you want to accomplish during your study session. ("I will read three chapters in Biology 1250." "I will review last week's notes in Math 1010," etc.)
- *Find people who will be supportive.* Find study partners, study groups, or friends who can motivate you to study when you don't feel like it. Attend SI sessions or use the Drop-In tutoring services on campus.
- *Work during your "prime" times.* We all have certain times of the day when we are more energetic and intellectually alert. Do your most difficult work during these hours.
- *Use the "divide and conquer" method.* This involves taking an overwhelming project, like writing a 30-page research paper, and breaking it down into small tasks. Go to the library for 30 minutes to get topic ideas; take an hour to search MERLIN to narrow the topic; take two hours to develop an outline, etc. Breaking a big project into small, manageable tasks creates a sense of accomplishment and control of the task.
- *Don't wait until you feel like it—there is never a "perfect" time.* Tell yourself you will work for just five minutes. Usually, once you start working, it is easier to continue.
- *Reward yourself.* Set up appropriate rewards when you meet your study goals. "If I read all my chapters in English and outline the major points, I will watch my two favorite TV shows."
- *You don't have to be perfect.* The results of your work have nothing to do with who you are as a person. Don't fall into the trap of believing that you need to "do twice as much just to feel half as good."

In summary, how you organize your time will affect your success in the academic environment.

Listening Strategies

Hearing is a physiological, involuntary, natural reaction that does not require interpretation. We know the "muzak" was on in the elevator, but we can't name the song we just heard. In contrast, listening is a psychological, voluntary action that requires interpretation or the assignment of meaning. You must be able to respond to information heard in classes. These are critical skills for a student to develop. Ability in this area will affect your ability to take effective notes that will enhance your success in many classes. Effective listening involves paying attention and concentrating on what the speaker is saying. In order to listen effectively, you must be physically present and mentally alert in class.

Physically present. Being physically present means attending class regularly. If you are not attending regularly, you need to honestly evaluate your situation. Circumstances often necessitate a change in plans. If attending class is not a priority, maybe you need to sit down with an advisor and discuss your academic goals.

Physical presence also means sitting in class where you can hear and see the speaker, focusing on the speaker, and maintaining eye contact. Finding a place to sit where you can see and hear enhances your ability to concentrate. As a general rule, the closer to the front you sit, the more focused and attentive to the lecturer you will remain. In fact, research on college students and academic success has proven that students who sit closer to the instructor achieve higher grades. Those students appear to be more focused on the instructor. From the instructor's perspective he/she may feel that a rapport has been established with those students.

Mentally alert. Being mentally alert means avoiding distractions, thoughts, and behaviors that inhibit or block your ability to listen effectively. Bringing your body to class and allowing your mind to be someplace else sabotages your goals for effective listening. If you are preoccupied, worried, daydreaming, or thinking about something else while trying to listen, you will most likely miss a lot of the information being given. Financial concerns, academic difficulties, family problems, roommates, weekend plans, etc., etc., are all examples of things that compete for a student's attention. For some students, class time is the only quiet time they have. It is during this quiet time that personal problems and concerns begin to enter into consciousness and compete for attention. What can you do when you are sitting in class and your mind begins to wander, or you begin to think about things unrelated to the class?

- Jot down these thoughts on a piece of paper. Tell yourself that you will get back to them later.
- Give yourself permission to attend to these problems at a later time.
- Set aside time during the day to work on problems.

Aside from personal distractions, many students have difficulty listening to lectures because they lack the basic course knowledge. They are unfamiliar with the material being presented and become overwhelmed. This is often the result of failing to do assigned readings or poor class attendance. By attending class regularly, doing supplemental readings to build background, and coming prepared, you are able to keep on top of assignments and avoid being overwhelmed.

Ways to improve listening. There are ways to improve your listening skills. The following is a list of some basic techniques for effective listening in class.

- *Recognize how ideas are organized.* Lectures usually begin with some type of introduction followed by a thesis statement. This statement is what the professor hopes to cover in the day's lecture. The thesis is supported by additional information. Most professors bring closure to their lectures by summarizing what they have covered. Learn to identify the lecture style that is used by your professor.
- *Become involved in what is being said.* If there are prepared notes for the course, read these before coming to class. Think about the purpose of the lecture, identify key points, make connections between ideas, and write down specific examples. Mark possible test questions.
- *Screen out distractions such as:*
  - background noise;
  - unusual accents, dialects, and language mistakes;
  - speaker disorganization, emotion, or habits;
  - superfluous material; and
  - your own inner voice.
- *Organize* statements into main points and supporting reasons. Use an outline form if it is helpful. Add information to prepared notes or outlines.
- *Discriminate* between relevancies and irrelevancies. Remember that not all information is important.

- *Maintain* an active body state. Sit with your back fairly straight and your pen poised to take notes. Sit in front and have eye-contact with the speaker.
- *Develop* a positive attitude about the class. You may have to use "self-talk" statements such as, "I'm going to listen carefully for the key points, so I will be ready for the discussion in my study group."

In order to improve your listening skills, you will need to practice using the suggested techniques for effective listening until they become automatic. There are many situations in which you will have this opportunity—in class, at work, and with friends, family, and strangers.

■ Note Taking Strategies

It is difficult to separate listening and note taking. Note taking actually aids in effective listening. By taking notes, you are forced to listen carefully and critically to what is being said. You can build your interest in a subject through concentrated listening. Note taking provides a written aid for the retention of information. When you take notes in class, you are actively processing information.

Taking notes in class involves more than showing up to class with a pen and a piece of paper. It is an active process that involves three stages: before the lecture, during the lecture, and after the lecture.

Before the lecture. Being prepared to take effective notes involves thinking about the process before the actual class period.

- For each class, use a different standard-sized notebook (8½" x 11") or use colored dividers to create sections in one notebook. The larger size allows you to take notes and jot down questions and comments.
- Read the syllabus and discover the topic for that day. Write the date and the topic at the top of the paper.
- Create a note taking format for that particular class. Formats vary and there is no right way, only the way that works best for you and matches the information in the class. Figure 6 is an example of a popular format called the Cornell method. Divide your paper into separate sections. Choose a main section to take notes and smaller sections for pertinent information, such as key terms, vocabulary, important people, and dates. Include a section for questions and an area to write a short summary in your own words. Additional sections may be added for supplementary information, for example, a comparison with the textbook information or possibly a section on problem solving.
- Be prepared for the class by reading the textbook assignment or reviewing information from the previous class.
- If the instructor has provided prepared notes for the class, read these before coming to class. (See Figure 7.) This will provide you with background knowledge which will increase your understanding of the lecture.

During the lecture. Now that you have prepared yourself for the process, you are ready for the actual recording of the notes.

- Only record the essential points. Instructors usually indicate important material in a variety of ways, such as:
  - Writing important information on the board.
  - Putting important information onto overheads.

- ■ Emphasizing important information through tone or voice level.
- ■ Reviewing or summarizing possible exam material.
- ■ Restating the same material in several ways.

■ Listen for "signal words" from the instructor. These words indicate the direction in which the instructor is headed. (See Figure 11.) Your notes should reflect the signals they gave you such as "There are four important parts of this concept." Then your notes should be labeled accordingly.

■ Write on every other line allowing room for additional material.

■ Skip lines to show the end of one idea and the start of another. Indicate sub-ideas and supporting details with numbers or letters under the major idea.

■ Use abbreviations and symbols when possible. You will want to develop your own personalized vocabulary of symbols that you can use without extra thought. Be careful that you don't use so many types that you can't decipher your notes later. Common symbols are "?" placed by confusing information or "*" by important information to remember. Use abbreviated words such as "i.e." for "in other words" or "ex" for example.

■ Write legibly. Do your notes right the first time. This will save you time, as well as giving you practice in listening and taking effective notes.

■ Purchased notes should also include active processing during the lecture:
  - ■ Add additional examples given by the instructor or classmates.
  - ■ Star important points stressed by the instructor. (Colored pens are a helpful tool.)
  - ■ Mark confusing points with a question mark. Ask instructor or take questions to a SI section or study group.
  - ■ Draw lines to connecting information.
  - ■ Add additional information to charts, graphs, or diagrams.

After the lecture. Even though class time is over, the note taking process continues until you have processed your notes for future study.

■ Review your notes as soon as possible. Read through them, making corrections and filling in information you remember.

■ Depending on your note taking format, list the key concept words, or main dates, people, etc. in a separate column. In the place you left for a summary, write a summary paragraph and possible test questions.

■ Review your notes several times per week, each time adding more information that you remember, or creating more possible test questions.

■ Use different-colored highlighters or pens to mark key terms, definitions, dates, important people, examples, etc.

If you are having trouble taking notes in a particular class, make an appointment to meet with your instructor, and let him/her know that you are having difficulty. Take your notes along, and ask your instructor to go over them with you. You may also want to consider using a tape recorder in class, not as a substitute for note taking, but as a supplement. Continue to take notes as usual, but at the same time record the lecture. When you get behind or miss a point, make a note of where the counter is on the recorder. Later, when you have time, go back to that section on the tape. By doing this, you will be able to fill in any missing information and hopefully clarify any unclear notes.

It may be helpful to share notes with a study partner or study group so you can fill in any information you may have missed. Attending an SI session will help, as the SI leaders demonstrate effective note taking skills for that particular class. And finally, keep in mind that like any skill, learning to take good notes will require practice. Each semester your note taking and listening skills will improve.

Geog	Climatic Classification	September 5
(2 1/2" margin for questions, key words, terms, important dates, or people.)	(6" column for taking notes)	
Köppen	*System of Climatic Classification*	
	-Invented by Wladimir Köppen	
Why is he important?	*-A botanist who saw biological activities as a function of*	
	Climatic characteristics.	
Climograph	*Created a climograph*	
	-Displays monthly temperature and precipitation on one graph	
How do you calculate	*Making it simple: Main Concern*	
problem on a climograph?	*-the relationship between potential evap. & amount of*	
	mois. received at any geog. location.	
What are the characteristics of	*Arctic Climates - Symbols ET and EF*	
E Climates?	*-E climates have aver. monthly temp. <50*	
	ET - Tundra or Continental Subartic	
	Aver temp in warmest month 50 F and <32 F	
	EF - Ice Cap or Arctic	
	Aver. temp in warmest month <32 F	
Boundary calculations?	*The Humid dry boundary*	
	Marks the major difference between a humid and a dry	
	Climate regime	
	Must know how boundary is calculated	
	(2" space for a possible summary, creating test questions,	
	cross reference with other notes or material.)	
	What is the key importance of temperature and precipitation?	

Figure 6 ■ Sample Notes Using the Cornell Format

what you expect = climate

what you get = weather ⟩ *Long-term weather*

Supplement for Physical Geography
SESSION 5
CLIMATIC CLASSIFICATION

H = Highland

to figure out hemisphere =
northern = warm summer months (May/June - Aug/Sep)
southern = warm summer months (Oct/Nov - Mar/Apr)

5.1 <u>Climatic classification</u>. The climate classification system used
but, not the only one!
in this course is the most widely-used and accepted climatic
classification system named after its inventor—Wladimir Koeppen. *(Köppen)*
"Climatologist"
Trained as a (botanist,) Koeppen realized that many biological

<u>activities are a function of climatic characteristics</u>. Beginning

with his doctoral dissertation to his death in 1940, he originated,

revised, and refined his classification system. To aid in the

classification of climates, the climatic diagram (called a

<u>climograph</u>) has been developed which displays the ⟨variables of

<u>monthly temperature and precipitation</u>⟩ on one graphic. The purpose of

any classification system is to make simplicity from complexity;

though the earth/atmospheric energy exchanges with the sun which

create climate variability are extremely complex, we will be simply

concerned with the relationship between potential evaporation and

the amount of moisture received at any geographic location.

5.2 <u>The arctic climates with symbols ET and EF</u>. The E-type climates

are locations where average monthly temperatures are less than 50°

F. Here, precipitation is received, but it comes in the form of snow

and is often not immediately available for biological functions.

E's
all
less
than
50°
ET =
32°-50°
EF =
below

There are two types of E climates; ET (Tundra or Continental

Subarctic) and EF (Ice Cap or Arctic). ⟨ET⟩ climates have average

temperatures of the warmest month between <u>50°F and 32°F</u>, and ⟨EF⟩

climates are those whose average temperatures of the warmest month

are <u>below 32°F</u>.

A's at equator ---- E's at poles

N. pole
E
D
C
B
A
equator
B
C
D
E
S. pole
no D's in Southern!

Figure 7 ■ Instructor-Provided Class Notes

5.3 The humid-dry boundary. Koeppen rationalized that the two most important climatic variables in determining what type of biological activities would take place in any region are temperature and precipitation. He further reasoned that there is a dynamic relationship between these two variables—the hotter the climate, the more the demand placed on water due to greater evaporative potential. To quantify this relationship, the humid-dry boundary was identified, which marked the difference between a humid and dry climate regime. So, perhaps the first step in an understanding of the classification system is to have a knowledge of the manner in which boundary is calculated. For this purpose, all stations (by definition) receive precipitation evenly distributed throughout the year. This is often not the case, but for reasons of simplicity, the humid-dry boundary will be calculated based on that assumption allowing the use of one equation. The humid-dry boundary for any station with even monthly precipitation distribution is determined by

$$r = 0.44T - 8.w \tag{1}$$

where r is the rainfall in inches and T the average annual temperature in °F. Therefore, for a location that has an average annual temperature of 50.0°F, the precipitation necessary for a station to be right on the humid-dry boundary is 13.5" (r = 0.44(50) -8.5). If the station being classified receives more than 13.5" annually, it has a humid climatic regime; and if the station being classified receives less than 13.5" at 50°F annual average temperature, it is considered a dry climatic station site and is symbolized with a letter "B."

Figure 7 ■ *Continued*

■ Memory Strategies

An understanding of how memory works and effective ways to use your memory will increase your ability to memorize information. All incoming information enters the **sensory memory**, which holds an exact copy of everything you see or hear for several seconds. On the way to class, you may notice a squirrel in a tree, but you can't recall that experience several moments later. Generally, your sensory memory will hold information just long enough for your **short-term memory** to register it. Short-term memory is the temporary storehouse for information. If your brain does not identify the information as meaningful or important, it quickly disappears. Your short-term memory lets you concentrate on the task at hand, but prevents you from collecting too much information in temporary storage. You are introduced to several people, but can't use their names in talking with them. You did not retain their names beyond sensory memory. Information that your mind identifies as meaningful or important makes its way into **long-term memory**. In order to enter information into your long-term memory, it must be actively processed through your short-term memory. "Active processing" in short-term memory is the key to the successful transfer of information into long-term memory.

Long-term memory can store an unlimited amount of information for long periods of time. Information is stored in long-term memory on the basis of meaning and importance. Information you don't really understand or consider significant will most likely not find its way into long-term memory. This means that your ability to remember what you study depends on your willingness to make sure you thoroughly understand the material and can relate it to existing information in long-term memory.

Organization. Information learned at the knowledge level of Blooms' Taxonomy of thinking and learning is usually memorized. The key to effective memorizing is to organize information in such a way that you can find it easily. The way you organize information will determine how the information is remembered and retrieved. In deciding how to organize information for later recall, you need to ask yourself: "How will I be asked to recall this information?" The answer to this question will determine how you input the information. Memorizing something by rote, means to "regurgitate" the information in the exact same way it is learned. For this type of memorization, you will be able to make use of mnemonic techniques. These techniques serve as a link between the new information and your memory. You have been making many of these links for years, but may not have known that they are called mnemonics.

- *Acronyms* are words created by the first letters of a series of words. For example: FBI, CIA, IRS, USU. By using acronyms, you can create your own cues for recalling a series of facts or words. Be sure to create an acronym that is simple enough to not be forgotten or confused.
- *Acrostics* are creative sentences that help you remember a series of letters that stand for something. You can create acrostics to remember a specific item, such as the planets in our solar system in sequence (Mercury, Venus, Earth, Mars, Jupiter, Saturn, Uranus, Neptune, and Pluto.) Taking the first letter of each word, you would have m, v, e, m, j, s, u, n, and p. Make up a nonsensical phrase to help you remember the exact order, such as, "My very elegant mother just served us nine pies." A good sense of humor will help you remember your sentence.
- *Rhymes and Songs.* Rhymes are used to help remember facts. For example: "In fourteen hundred and ninety-two, Columbus sailed the ocean blue." "Fifty Nifty United States" is an example of a song that helps us to remember many isolated facts, such as the names of all the states.
- *Loci and Peg Systems.* Loci is a strategy where you associate a concept with a place. This includes where you were when you heard the concept, how it looked in your notes, which graphics were on the page containing the information, etc. You can

create a visual association between the material to be learned and a familiar place or routine. For instance, suppose you want to learn a list of chemical elements. You choose a familiar route, such as the route from the TSC to the Business Building. As you pass each building along the way, you assign it a chemical element. Later in your class, you visualize your route. As you "see" each place, you recall the element it represents. The method of loci helps you to remember things in a particular order. This is especially helpful when trying to remember steps in a process. Peg systems work by visualizing pegs or hooks in a closet. You hang information on each peg, and then recall what's on each one.

Mnemonic devices have some limitations. First, the technique is often difficult to learn and remember. You may forget the technique. Second, mnemonic techniques don't work well for remembering technical terms in math and science. And third, mnemonic techniques won't necessarily help you get beyond the knowledge level of thinking. You won't necessarily understand or comprehend the material you are trying to recall.

Association. When asked to recall information that requires that you comprehend and apply the information, you will need to practice effective memory techniques that go beyond rote memorization. The understanding of new material is aided by associating it with other ideas. New information is learned in small related units. These units of knowledge are interrelated with previously learned material. The goal is to establish a chain of relationship and, through related organization, master the new material. The more associations you can create from an idea, the more meaning the new idea will have, and the more likely the material will be retained. Try to associate the information with personal experiences, and see how the information could affect your life. In addition, the more background you have on a subject the easier it is to form these associations and to discern relationships. To gain more background, you may need to reference other textbooks, seek help from your instructor, join a study group, attend Supplemental Instruction (SI) sessions, or hire a tutor.

Selection. When trying to remember information, be selective. First, survey what is to be covered. Concentrate on the most significant things to remember. Give most of your attention to that which is new and difficult to understand, yet necessary to remember. Decide on the order of importance, and organize the material into a framework. If available, attend the SI sessions as the SI leaders often give examples of the most important information to remember.

Review. Study often. The best review is immediate use of the information. Test yourself by making up illustrations of the material. Use flash cards, outlines, and practice tests to help check your ability to recall the information. Research has demonstrated that a daily short review is likely to increase your success on tests.

Rehearsal. Refresh your memory by allowing time between review sessions. Time between practice sessions allows your mind time to organize and make connections with the new information. Use the rehearsal time to practice using what you have learned. Experiments indicate that the very rapid forgetting, which is so common after a reading session, can be significantly reduced by spaced verbal or written recitation of the material. Rephrase and explain new information to yourself. Talk to someone else or yourself about the topic you've been studying. If you can't explain something, you really haven't learned it.

It is easy to be fooled into believing you know something and then, when asked to recall that piece of information, be unable to do so. For instance, have you ever been reading along in your textbook and come across information that you knew, and therefore skipped it, only to be unable to remember it for a test the next day? You probably did know that information. However, the knowledge you had of it was "recognition knowledge" not "recall knowledge." Recognition knowledge is a surface knowing, a recognizing of certain information as being familiar. Recall or retrieval knowledge is the ability to access that information and to recall it. One way to check whether you have recognition knowledge or retrieval knowledge of a subject is to try to explain that information to someone else. Being able to verbalize new information or to summarize it in writing is usually a sign that you possess sufficient recall knowledge.

Overlearning. Reviewing something that has already been learned sufficiently for still one more time is called overlearning. Anything you can recall instantly without effort has been overlearned. The more important and the more difficult the learning, the more you should reinforce it with frequent practice.

Sleep. Freshly learned material and material that is reviewed is better remembered after a period of sleep than after an equal period of daytime activity when interference may take place. There is some truth to the old adage to "sleep on it." This does not mean placing the textbook under your pillow.

Forgetting. Forgetting is the result of either failing to adequately input information or failing to recall or access the information once it has been input. Often students comment that they got to an exam and "forgot" the information. Unfortunately, their study method may have never put the information beyond a recognition level. Other factors can also affect the input and recall of information. The very nature of memory itself affects the storage of information and its later recall. First, memory is subjective. We tend to remember things that are more favorable to ourselves. The need to feel positive about ourselves causes us to remember things in a positive way (or inversely, in a negative way). Second, memory is interpretive. As we input information into our memory, we interpret and read meaning into the information. Our memory of a fact or an event is then a combination of the original information plus our perceptions and feelings. Third, memory is constructive. We are continually taking bits and pieces of information and putting them together to construct memory. Fourth, memory serves our emotional needs. Stress and emotions can affect memory. Often we remember only what is meaningful to us, or what captures our attention. Competing demands for our attention can interfere with the retrieval of information.

Millions of dollars have been earned by the creators of memory improvement tapes, videos, kits, and workshops. Strategies for increasing the power of your memory can be found on every bookstore shelf. As a student, you will certainly want to develop your memory skills. The ability to accurately recall the information you have read or heard will be vital to your success.

■ Concentration

Students often cite lack of concentration as a major barrier to learning information. Some common laments are "I can only concentrate for a few minutes." "Studying is boring." Some common concentration problems include: fatigue, distractions, and poor time management.

Distractions are those things in the environment that compete for attention. These distractions may be external or internal. An inappropriate learning environment will definitely decrease your ability to concentrate. Learning new material requires your complete and focused attention. Being distracted by personal problems and frequent daydreaming divides your attention and causes a decrease in your ability to concentrate.

Concentration strategies. Concentration is giving material your complete and focused attention. This focus is necessary to store information. Without concentration and focus, information is not put into long-term memory for later recall. Often, knowing that we are not concentrating begins a cycle of frustration. "Tomorrow is the test. I don't want to sit here and read this. I can't think at all. I'm going to fail." The fear of failure adds an additional barrier to concentration. Knowing the common causes of poor concentration may help you to focus during your study time. Ineffective time management has a great deal to do with concentration. By setting goals and establishing priorities, you will be better able to schedule time for studying. Procrastination causes stress, which in turn affects your ability to concentrate. Knowing how to pace yourself and prioritize your commitments will directly increase your ability to concentrate.

Barriers to concentration. The major barriers to concentration come under four main categories: distractions, attitude, poor time management, and fatigue. Knowing what is causing your inability to focus may aid you in choosing strategies to solve the problem.

Distractions are those things in the environment that compete for our attention. Minor distractions can be small environmental problems that are simple to control: the phone ringing, the noise of the TV, roommates chattering, the room too hot or too cold, a great view, being hungry, tired, or thirsty. Major distractions absorb your thoughts and are more difficult to manage. Anticipating an upcoming vacation is just as distracting as worrying about relationships or financial problems. Major or minor distractions can make it difficult to remember what you just read in U.S. History.

Strategies to eliminate distractions:

- Be physically prepared to study. Are you sleepy? Hungry?
- Find a place to study that is free of distractions.
- Deal with personal problems before or after studying.
- Write down your problem and set it aside for later.
- Study with a partner to increase motivation.
- Practice increasing your "focused" concentration time. Set a timer and start with short times that will bring you success.
- Practice effective time management strategies, such as creating a study schedule and daily "to-do" lists.

Students often confuse "concentration" problems with "interest and attitude" problems. The reality is that not every course will be on a favorite subject. Having a negative attitude about a course creates a concentration barrier. To the extent that you can convince yourself that there is something of interest in each of your classes, you will find that you can concentrate at a higher level. You may have to create a reward system for yourself to overcome an attitude. Rewards can vary from candy bars to time with friends, but many students find they work effectively.

Strategies to overcome attitude problems:

- Accept your responsibility for learning the information.
- Accept your instructor's limitations. He/she does not have to "entertain" you.
- Relate the course to your goals. "After this class, I can take a class in my major."
- Break long assignments into smaller parts.
- Set specific study goals for a time block. (For example: finish reading three sections of chapter seven in the history text, or complete two math problems.)
- Study the least interesting subject first.
- Promise yourself a small reward for your concentrated study time.
- Talk about the problem with a friend or professional counselor.

Proper rest, exercise, and nutrition are essential to maintaining a healthy body. Inattention to any of these three areas may result in fatigue and the decreased ability to concentrate. Eat well-balanced meals, include exercise as part of your daily routine, and allow enough time for rest and recreation.

Strategies to prevent fatigue:

- Schedule study times when you are not tired.
- Eat well so you won't be hungry.
- Sign up for a physical education course.
- Exercise with a partner to increase motivation.
- Take advantage of the University exercise facilities.

Causes of poor concentration can also include lack of academic, listening, or note taking skills. In this text, we list many suggestions to help you in these areas. If you identify your problem area, you can then decide to make changes. Start with a small change. Perhaps you will decide to study longer on a difficult subject. Start with a manageable time to give you success, then increase the time gradually. Be sure to reward yourself for each gain.

■ Writing Strategies

Writing to inform. University students will, on the average, write five major papers per school year and many more shorter papers. That's a lot of writing! And every assignment will be different, requiring different kinds of thinking and organization. Regardless of the details of any particular assignment, there are three factors which must always be considered as you begin.

Format. How should the information be presented? Did your professor ask for a one-page critique, an essay that summarizes the positive and negative aspects of a particular topic, a five-page annotated bibliography? If you are unsure about the format for an assignment—ask!

Audience. Obviously your professor will read your assignment, but some students make the mistake of not including enough information because their teacher "already knows everything about it." While this might be true, writing assignments are given not only to encourage your original ideas, but to test your understanding of a subject. Write for your professor, but your writing should be clear enough that any other college student could pick it up and make sense of your ideas, even if he or she were unfamiliar with the assignment itself.

Purpose. Every writing assignment has a purpose. Your job is to understand what that purpose is and then adjust the content and the tone of your paper to meet that purpose. Every writing assignment, from a lab report to a critical analysis of Romeo and Juliet, should make a point. If your writing assignment doesn't make a clear and original point, you should revise it so it does.

Not every writing assignment is the same—know what is expected of you and then write, format, and polish your paper in such a way that your purpose and message are clear. To evaluate the quality and effectiveness of your writing, consider these five criteria:

- Completeness—did you expand on the ideas, or just think superficially about the topic?
- Support—did you back up your ideas and opinions with reasons or proof so that your knowledge of the subject matter is evident? Did you use specific examples, whether from your textbook, lab experiments, class discussion, outside reading, etc.?

■ Organization—is your paper easy to read? Is there an adequate introduction and conclusion as well as transitions between parts?
■ Authority—does your paper reflect a depth of thought and commitment that a critically thinking student should exhibit? (Do not mistake this for conformity to concepts or ideals that sound good but that you really don't believe in.)
■ Correctness—have you proofread your paper sufficiently so that spelling, punctuation, and grammar errors do not interfere with its readability?

The best writing is usually not done in isolation. We all need help generating ideas, organizing our thoughts, or evaluating the effectiveness of our writing.

Writing to learn. Most students think of writing only in terms of completing papers assigned for class. But writing can also be a learning tool; writing to learn can enable you to organize your thinking, increase your understanding, and make personal connections to the material. All of these processes will increase learning and help you remember the material. Below are some ideas for using writing as a tool for learning. These writing activities range from the knowledge/memorization level of thinking to the evaluation level, as discussed in Bloom's Taxonomy of Educational Objectives, and can be adapted to any class—from physics to philosophy to family science.

Keep a class journal. In it you could:

■ summarize the main points from lectures in your own words.
■ keep a list of questions you need answered.
■ write down your goals for that particular class.
■ summarize the main ideas in the text chapters.
■ summarize sub-sections if the chapters are quite long.
■ define terms or concepts in your own words.
■ critique the ideas presented in class or the way they are presented by the teacher.

Use writing as a learning activity in study groups or with a study partner. You could:

■ exchange chapter or lecture summaries to get a different perspective on the same topic.
■ write and exchange sample essay questions and then practice answering them.
■ write and exchange sample test questions and then try answering them.

Think up your own ways to use writing to help you learn. Remember, writing isn't just for showing others what you know. It can also be a valuable tool to help you better understand what you know or think or even discover what it is you don't know.

■ Test Taking Strategies

Most course tests measure your ability to remember many facts and figures, as well as your understanding of the course materials. These tests are designed to make you think beyond the knowledge/recognition level of learning. The factors which contribute to good test scores can be summarized in two words: preparation and strategies. Successful preparation for an exam starts at the beginning of each semester and continues throughout. Prepare yourself for higher-level thinking as you study.

Preparation. This activity includes mental and physical readiness.

- *Make a semester study plan.* At the beginning of each semester, develop a daily schedule that allows time for class preparation, study, review, recreation, eating, and sleeping. Be sure you have clearly marked the dates of all exams.
- *Use good review techniques.* Study and review differ from each other. Study refers to learning new material for the first time. Review is critical because it strengthens the retention of new knowledge. Because forgetting takes place most rapidly immediately after learning, it is more effective to review soon after studying or after each class. Your review should include strategies that incorporate the level of thinking required for that class. Do you need to apply the information as well as comprehend the concept? Will you have to solve a problem in your social work class?
  - Review notes and text(s)—list the major concepts that have been covered.
  - Highlight topics that were emphasized in class or on handouts.
  - Concentrate on the vocabulary of the course. Identify words used to represent specific concepts (i.e., the word "mesothermal" in geography) and treat them as you would a foreign language. Make flash cards for drills and try to use these words whenever you review the course materials.
  - Construct diagrams, charts, tables, or lists to summarize relationships.
  - Review and recite often. Try to say or write out complete ideas or facts. Try to be detailed and precise so you are not relying on just recognition of the information when you see the test.
- *Develop a confident attitude.* Your attitude toward exams can make a difference. Tests do serve a good purpose. They give you an opportunity to check your progress. Students who have formed good study habits throughout the semester should be confident.
- *Organize pre-exam hours.* The day before an important exam, plan to review a maximum of three hours, interspersed with pace-changing breaks. Question yourself, recite the main points to yourself, and reread the passages only when you are having difficulty remembering them. Eat and sleep well to avoid rushing on the morning of the test. Stay calm. Be sure you have all the supplies you need before leaving your room. Arrive on time in order to get a good seat.
- *Attend any study groups or Supplemental Instruction sessions.* Sometimes these are a supplement to the course. They can be offered by an instructor—or form a group of your own.

Test preparation also includes finding out what will be covered on the test, what kind of test it will be (i.e., objective, essay, or both), and knowing what you are allowed to bring into the testing room. You learn about these things by asking your professor. If you are afraid or embarrassed to ask during class, then schedule an appointment with him/her to find out this important information.

Test day strategies. Some general strategies for taking tests include:

- *Get off to a good start.* Arrive early for the exam, and sit near the front or in a well-lighted, quiet spot. Avoid friends and panic stricken people. Listen carefully to any instructions.
- *Look over the entire exam.* Pay attention to point values, and figure out a rough time allowance for each section of the exam. Get an idea about what the exam is covering. By reading over the entire exam, you will build confidence in your ability to do well.
- *Read all directions.* Underline all significant words in the directions. Be sure you understand what is asked.
- *Begin to work.* Tackle questions in the order that appeals to you, as this builds confidence. Keep in mind the point values, and use the entire time!

■ *Learn to relax.* If you find yourself becoming tense or anxious, stop, take deep breaths, close your eyes, and visualize yourself succeeding. Simple relaxation exercises such as flexing and relaxing your muscles will help relieve your stress.

■ *Learn from the test.* Go over the test results, and use the information to help you prepare more adequately for the next exam.

Each type of test requires different test-taking skills. It is wise to be aware of reasons students have difficulty with these tests and the strategies for success.

The multiple choice test. Students typically have a difficult time with taking multiple choice tests. Some reasons for this are:

■ Imprecise knowledge.
■ Incomplete or sloppy reading of the question.
■ Limited ways to trigger memory.

Imprecise knowledge. Because students often study by "looking over" the material, rather than actively processing, they have an imprecise memory of its meaning (recognition knowledge vs. recall knowledge). Although multiple choice questions are used most often to test your memory of details, facts, and relationships, they are also used to test your comprehension and your ability to solve problems or the application and analysis learning levels. Students are easily confused by the choices or alternative answers. Some ways to counter this problem are to make up practice tests, make study notes, use 3 x 5 cards, and review daily. Also discuss the concepts with a study partner or study group. Attempting to verbalize the information in your own words increases your comprehension level and the ability to recall the information. The Practice Multiple Choice Exercise allows you the opportunity to decide what level of knowledge of information is required to answer the geography multiple choice questions correctly.

Incomplete or sloppy reading of the question or item. If you don't know what decision you are asked to make about the topic, it will be hard to select the correct answer. Some students read questions without attention or without thinking, and jump to the alternative choices without really knowing what has been asked. When you wind up trying to find the correct answer without really knowing what was asked, you can become confused. Sometimes the choices which you are given muddle your thinking. The following suggestion may be useful. Read the question or the item as if it were an independent free-standing statement. Do not look at answers. Think of the answer. Only then should you look for a MATCH among the given answers. READ . . . THINK . . . MATCH. For example:

"Horse" is to "animal" as "ivy" is to _____.

Stop! Think of the answer! Then find a match to your thoughts.

Limited ways to trigger memory. Some students study by using one word to act as a cue to the memory. If the professor doesn't use this word in the test question, these students are lost. Without that limited one word, they cannot find the information in memory. If students have stayed at the knowledge or recognition level of learning, by reciting the answer using textbook words or the exact words used by the professor instead of thinking about the meaning and relationship of the ideas, then different wording in the answer may not result in recall.

Expand your cues to trigger memory by studying for understanding. Try to explain what you have learned by using your own words (but check to ensure your own words are accurate). Go over your notes and practice questions and substitute synonyms wherever possible.

Students often ask: "What if I read the question carefully and find no match among the alternative answers?" Then GUESS! The following suggestions are helpful hints for educated guessing and eliminating some of the options.

- If two answers are similar, except for one or two words, choose one of these answers.
- If two answers have similar sounding or looking words, choose one of these.
- Look for answers that are grammatically correct.
- If two quantities are equal, choose one of them.
- If there is a wide range, choose a middle value.
- Look for root words in the answers that are similar to words in the item or the question.
- Look for answers within the test itself.
- Watch out for words like *always, never,* and *only.* They must be interpreted as meaning all of the time, not just 99% of the time. These choices are frequently incorrect.

The essay exam. The other type of exam that some students have problems with is the essay exam. Preparation for an essay test, as for any test, requires close and careful review, and possible rereading of textbooks and class notes. Many professors will announce in advance the general area the test will cover, the concepts, issues, controversies, theories, etc. Reviewing your lecture notes will also reveal which broad areas have been central to class discussion and are therefore likely to appear on the test. The following suggestions may be helpful in preparing for an essay exam.

Anticipation. Anticipate questions that are likely to be on the test. Use previous tests and your class notes as your basic source material for this task. Ask yourself, "What are the concepts and relationships involved in the material?" Review notes, omitting detail. Review major headings and chapter summaries in the text.

Condensation. Organize all of your material into principal groups. Identify the major concepts, the main subordinate concepts under each one, and the critical details. Now, summarize the material in your own words. Boil down the material to a rather tight outline form. Fit the necessary details into the concepts.

Practice. Some students profit by making up sample questions and then practicing answering them. It is important to note that mastery of a course's special vocabulary is essential groundwork. You will frequently be required to manipulate terminology. Getting this done is like tying your shoes before running. Failure to do it will most likely weaken your performance. So practice using the vocabulary of the course by making flash cards and keeping word lists. If the course has a Supplemental Instruction (SI) section, the SI leader will model effective essay test writing and provide opportunities to practice this skill.

Strategies for the completion of the essay exam. Having a plan for taking an essay test will help you with the organized thinking that is required.

- Read the directions carefully. Notice whether you must answer all essay questions or whether you may choose which ones to answer.
- Read every question before beginning—clarify any unclear questions. Select those questions for which you are best prepared, and begin with the easiest one. This will score quick points for you, inspire confidence, and promote clear thinking. It will also enable you to avoid content overlap by making you aware of information that could be better used in answering another question. After each answer, leave enough space to add further ideas that may come to mind as the exam proceeds.

- ■ Make a "brain dump." Jot notes alongside each question. Quickly (in about 5 minutes) note a few key words and phrases alongside each question. List technical terms and names that are right on the tip of your tongue. This will keep them available later, when pressures and anxiety may otherwise block them off.
- ■ Calculate and budget time for each question. Budget time according to the point value of each question. Questions worth more points should be given more time.
- ■ Answer the easy questions first. These are the questions you are certain you can answer correctly. This develops a confident attitude and helps you feel more at ease. After each answer, leave enough space to add further ideas that may come to mind as the exam proceeds.
- ■ Don't get bogged down. Do not hesitate too long on a difficult question. Inaction may block your thinking. Forcing yourself to write increases your chances of recalling the answer. "Free association" or freely jotting down on a piece of scrap paper words that come to mind as you think about the answer may help you overcome blocking and remind you of new ideas to be organized into your answer.

Essay exam key words. When thinking about the content of your essay, remember to note the key instruction words. In answering an essay question, you want to be sure that you are answering the question that has been asked, and not the question which you think has been asked. The Essay Exam Key Word exercise asks you to apply your knowledge of clue words to practice essay test questions.

The words in Figure 8 are commonly found in essay test questions. Understanding them is essential to success in answering such questions. If you want to do well on essay tests, then study this page thoroughly. Know these words backwards and forwards. To heighten your awareness of them, underline the words when you see them in a test question.

Before you even begin to write, you should make a skeletal outline. This is not a "doodle." It is a brief, informative summary of the information which you will cover in your answer. It will save you time and stress by providing direction and helping you avoid repetition. In addition, if you don't have time to finish, you can include your outline and maybe gain some partial credit.

Your instructor is greatly influenced by the compactness and clarity of an organized answer. To begin writing in hopes that the right answer will somehow turn up is time consuming and usually futile. To know a little and present it well is, by and large, superior to knowing much and presenting it poorly. Therefore, be concise and to the point. Think more and write less. Avoid flowery language. Instructors are usually impressed by directness, brevity, conciseness, organization, and accuracy.

A common problem that students have in writing short-answer and essay exams is in being direct. One mark of a good answer is directness in responding to the question. In a sociology course, the essay question may ask you to "describe the major differences between patrilineal, matrilineal, and bilateral societies." You answer the question directly and forcefully in the first sentence. "The major differences between the patrilineal, matrilineal, and bilateral societies are. . . ." Expand your first sentence according to your skeletal outline, supporting the main idea with facts, illustrations, and reasons, using the technical terms and references from your textbooks and lectures.

Essay Exam Word	Answer should:
Analyze	Break into several parts; and discuss, examine, or interpret each part.
Compare	Examine two or more things. Identify similarities and differences.
Contrast	Show differences. Set in opposition.
Criticize	Make judgments. Evaluate comparative worth. Criticism often involves analysis.
Define	Give the meaning; usually a meaning specific to the course or subject determine the precise limits of the term to be defined.
Describe	Give a detailed account. Make a picture with words. List characteristics, qualities, and parts.
Discuss	Consider and debate or argue the pros and cons of an issue. Write about a conflict.
Enumerate	List several ideas, aspects, events, things, qualities, reasons, etc.
Explain	Make an idea clear. Show logically how a concept is developed. Give the reasons for an event.
Evaluate	Give your opinion or cite the opinion of an expert. Include evidence to support the evaluation.
Illustrate	Give concrete examples. Explain clearly by using comparisons or examples.
Interpret	Comment upon, give examples, describe relationships. Explain the meaning. Describe, then evaluate.
Outline	Describe main ideas, characteristics, or events. (Does not necessarily mean — "write a Roman numeral/letter outline.")
Prove	Support with facts (especially facts presented in class or in the text).
Relate	Show the connections between ideas or events. Provide a larger context.
State	Explain precisely.
Summarize	Give brief, condensed account. Include conclusions. Avoid unnecessary details.
Trace	Show the order of events or progress of a subject or event.

Figure 8 ■ Essay Exam Key Words

In conclusion, writing essay answers may take practice. Be sure to reread your corrected test and learn from the comments written by the instructor. Keep the following points in mind as you develop this skill.

- *Always write something.* If you do not know the answer to a question, try to reason it out. Sometimes, just getting your thoughts on paper will help you make connections with the ideas. You may get partial credit; you will never get credit for empty space.
- *Summarize and conclude.* The introduction will be the "thesis" or the main point to be made. The summary is simply a rephrasing of the introduction.
- *Be sure you leave enough time to reread your answer.* Check your answer and correct any errors in spelling, grammar, sentence structure, or penmanship. Be sure you haven't left out any words, parts of words, or parts of answers.

■ Test Anxiety

Test anxiety has two components: a mental component and a physical component. The mental component consists of your beliefs, ideas, and concerns regarding exams. The physical component includes a variety of physical symptoms: tightening of the neck/back muscles, sweating, increased heart rate, increased blood pressure, feelings of irritability and frustration, shaking hands, stomachache, or headache. The list goes on. Fifteen to twenty-five percent of all students suffer moderate cases of test anxiety. A little bit of anxiety may be necessary to motivate you to do well. The difference between test anxious and non-test anxious students is in their focus. Non-test anxious students think only about the exam and getting it done. They are extremely well focused on the task of taking the exam. Test-anxious students perform badly, because their attention is not focused solely on the exam. Test-anxious students divert their attention from the exam to the mental and physical sensations which they are experiencing.

It is accurate to say that too little anxiety inhibits performance, and too much hinders it. As with many stress-related conditions, the causes are varied: parents and teachers expecting too much, fear of failure, feeling of having to please others, fear of not getting accepted to certain schools or programs, fear of damaging an academic record, or having a perfectionistic attitude. Anxiety is learned; it grows and snowballs as students push themselves and try harder. Students who find themselves dealing with intense feelings of anxiety and worry need to seek help.

Most students who work to eliminate test anxiety are very successful. A word of caution. Test anxiety is not the same as **test stupidity**! If you have missed class, not taken notes, neglected to read the text, didn't have time to study—you are not anxious—you are underprepared! Don't confuse inadequate preparation, and the normal anxiety that accompanies it, with the irrational fear that many students have about taking tests.

"I FORGOT!" The jolt of going "blank" on a test can raise beads of perspiration on the most experienced test taker. It happens. The term or idea, which you knew minutes before the test, is suddenly locked tight in your memory. During the exam, if you blank out, don't fight it, accept it. Shrug it off, and go on with the test. Otherwise, your anxiety increases and absorbs all of your attention. If instead, you switch your attention to other questions, your memory will continue to search for the answer automatically. With less anxiety, you may recall the answer before the end of the test, instead of 12 hours later!

When you return to the skipped items, think methodically. Systematically search for your memory of them. Pay attention to key words in the question, and recall synonyms for them. Losing something in your memory is like losing your car keys. Ask questions of yourself that lead you to the lost memory, just like you ask questions that lead you to the lost set of car keys.

■ College Reading Strategies

You may have arrived on campus feeling confident in your academic reading skills. Having a reading section in this book may appear unnecessary to you. Reading in your high school courses may have varied, from being able to pass the class without looking at the text, to required reading of several texts, novels, or supplemental readings. You may have heard rumors that college reading is "different," however, the only problem you currently anticipate is the expense of the text.

Often, by mid-semester, students realize why college reading may require more skills than they previously had to demonstrate. This section, "College Reading," explains active study/reading approaches to textbooks that will involve you in using your textbooks to gain information. College classes usually require a text, often expensive, and reading assignments that must be completed in order to pass the class. You may find the text difficult to comprehend. The reading assignments contain more facts and ideas per page and are written at a higher reading level than high school texts. In fifteen weeks, you may have to be responsible for the amount of information you covered in an entire year in high school. The chart in Figure 9 lists common reading problems and suggested study strategies to help you with this area.

Active study reading is not "speed-reading." Research has shown that speed-reading is only effective when you are reading information that you already know and understand. What students do need are active reading/study strategies and a flexible reading rate. In some instances, you will be able to speed up your reading, but often new information requires more than one reading and an interactive approach. Active reading strategies involve you in the reading process, so that you are able to effectively read and comprehend the material in the textbook. With the use of time management skills, concentration techniques, and study strategies, you can feel in charge of all the reading required in college.

What affects reading comprehension? At the beginning of this chapter, you were introduced to the strategy of PBID to check your academic readiness. Similarly, you should check your readiness to comprehend textbook material by identifying your **Purpose, Background, Interest, and Difficulty (PBID).** Assessing yourself in each area, then developing strategies to improve each area, will help you read effectively. You will be able to recall and use the information from the textbook.

Purpose. Students often sit down to read with only the thought that they have to "study" this chapter and hopefully retain "something." Take a minute to identify the purpose of the reading, that is, what is your reason for reading the textbook? Textbooks are read for different reasons:

- ■ To build background knowledge so you can understand the lecture.
- ■ To add supplemental information to your class notes.
- ■ To learn details, such as the classification of types of rock or the time sequence of events that led up to the Civil War.
- ■ To be prepared for a class discussion: the causes of the Civil War and the effect it had on the future politics of the South.
- ■ To understand principles, processes, and concepts, such as Mendel's Law of Genetics, Newton's Three Laws of Motion, or the properties of real numbers.

Causes of Reading Problems	Active Reading Strategies
1. Lack of motivation.	• Evaluate your reading purpose, your background knowledge, your interest in the material, and the difficulty of the reading. • Do the most difficult reading first. • Arrange your schedule so that you read at your most productive study time. • Find a way to personalize the information. • Join a study group, divide the reading responsibility so that each person creates a summary and study guide for the group.
2. Lack of background knowledge and understanding of the subject.	• Skim the chapter headings, pictures, charts, graphs, and diagrams. • Read the summary or conclusion first. • Get a tutor to explain difficult concepts. • Form a study group to discuss topics. • Allow additional time to reread the text 2-3 times.
3. Inability to concentrate.	• Formulate a purpose for reading. • Practice a study strategy such as SQ3R. • Annotate the text. • Look for signal words to follow the organization of the text. • Break the reading time into manageable blocks.
4. Frustration with inability to recall the information.	• Make connections between old and new information. • Review the main concepts daily. • Create study guides that reflect the type of test for that class.
5. Course and textbook contain difficult vocabulary and terminology.	• Make a course vocabulary notebook or 3x5 card system, listing new words and definitions. • Review the vocabulary daily. • Learn common prefixes, suffixes, and root words to help you build your vocabulary. • Use color to highlight similarities and differences in word parts.

Figure 9 ■ Reading Comprehension Problems and Strategies

How do you know the purpose of the text for each class?

1. Read the syllabus, and pay careful attention to the relationship between the reading assignments and the class topics.

2. Talk to the instructor.

3. Talk to other students who have had the class or are in class with you. Find out how they used, or are using, the text for the class.

4. If Supplemental Instruction sessions are available for the class, attend, and the SI leader will model how to use the textbook.

Background. Your reading comprehension is strongly affected by your background knowledge or what you already know about the subject. This is why:

- If you have high knowledge of the subject, it may be easier for you to read the material. You will be able to meet your purpose quicker than if the information is totally new to you.
- If your knowledge of the subject is low, you will have to build up your knowledge base. Some lectures are intended to build background before attempting textbook reading. However, you will often be expected to do this on your own. Time management becomes a factor, as you may have to reread your text three times to build up enough knowledge to comprehend the information.

How do you check your background for reading?

1. Before reading the chapter, skim the chapter headings, pictures, charts, graphs, and diagrams.

2. Read the summary and think about what you know about the subject.

3. Read the syllabus, and mark the topics that you know something about.

4. Review your notes, and look for connections between the lecture and the reading.

5. Discuss new information with other students in a study group or at an SI session. This will enhance your knowledge base and help you comprehend the information.

Interest. Students often complain that they don't like to read the text because it is not interesting. In many cases this is a true statement, but it doesn't remove the fact that in many classes, if you do not read the text, you will not pass the class. If you avoid the text because of lack of interest, then you need to take some action to make the reading bearable for that semester.

How do you create interest in what you need to read?

1. Break your reading session into small time units: twenty minutes of concentrated reading, then a small break, then twenty minutes more of focused reading.

2. Create questions before you read. Pretend they are real test questions, and you must know the answers to pass the class.

3. Use a specific reading strategy, such as SQ3R, to keep focused.

4. Do something with the information as you read the text. Write lists or notes in the margins. Create a picture of the information in your mind. Write an outline or draw pictures of the process.

5. Share the reading with study partners. Divide up the chapter into sections, and make each student responsible for reading and teaching the concepts from their section to the other members of the group. Be aware that the section you learn best will be the one that you teach.

6. Talk to the instructor and ask questions about the subject matter. Ask him/her for advice about how to read and comprehend the text. The instructor may say something to spark your interest.

7. Reward yourself for reading and studying material that is not interesting to you.

Difficulty. The difficulty of the reading material can encourage or discourage a student from reading and studying the text. Sometimes the format of the text is more difficult than the actual course material. You have little control over the choice of the text, but you do have options if the reading is difficult.

How do you cope with difficult reading material?

1. Think again about your purpose for reading, your prior knowledge of the subject, and your interest in the course and material. Are any of these factors making the reading difficult? Reread the suggestions in this section and the reading solutions chart in Figure 9.

2. Get a tutor for the class or attend Supplemental Instruction sessions. At these sessions, difficult information is explained and discussed. This may make the reading less complex and more interesting.

3. Read another text that is on the same subject, but is written in a different style or at a different reading level. You can check out textbooks at the library.

The SQ3R Reading Strategy.

After you have evaluated your purpose, background, interest, and difficulty, then you are ready to begin the reading/study session. Just as when you begin a journey to a new destination, you follow a map or plan, so should your reading session have a plan. SQ3R is a basic reading system that is often used by college students to improve their reading and studying.

How Do I Use SQ3R?

S = Survey. (Gather the information necessary to focus and formulate reading goals.)

- Read the title, headings, and subheadings of the chapter or the article. This helps your mind prepare to receive the information.
- Read the introduction and summary to get an overview of the main ideas. This will familiarize you with the concepts and how the chapter fits the author's purposes.
- Notice the graphics—charts, maps, diagrams, etc. are there to make a point—don't miss them.
- Pay attention to reading aids—italics, bold face print, chapter objectives, and end-of-chapter questions are all included to help you sort, comprehend, and remember information.

Q = Question. (Question as you survey. This helps your mind engage and concentrate as you actively search for answers to questions.)

■ Ask yourself what YOU already know about the subject.
■ As you read each of the above parts, ask yourself what is meant by the title, headings, subheadings, and captions. One section at a time, turn the bold face headings into as many questions as you think will be answered in that section. Write these down on 3 x 5 cards or create a study guide.
■ Add further questions as you proceed through the section.
■ Ask yourself, "What did the instructor say about the assignment in class? What handouts support the reading? What is the purpose of the reading assignment?"

R = Read. (Read and think actively. Fill in the information around the questions and structure you have been building.)

■ Look for main ideas and supporting details. Use outlining, underlining, and text-marking skills. Read to answer the questions that were raised in the question step.
■ Read carefully all of the underlined, italicized, and bold face words or phrases.

R = Recite. (Recite right after reading an assignment. This trains your mind to concentrate and learn as it reads.)

■ Use good judgment about places to stop and recite.
■ Use outlining and underlining skills. (Do not underline long passages. Use a pencil to first underline important information. Only mark after you have read a passage AND understood it.)
■ Write a summary statement of each section.
■ Quiz yourself on the main points. See if you can answer from memory. If not, look back again, and don't go on to the next section until you can recite.
■ Connect new material with what you already know about the subject.
■ Write questions about any material you do not understand, and ask your instructor to explain it.
■ Write the answers to the questions you created.

R = Review. (Review after you recite: daily, weekly, and before a test. This refines your mental organization and puts information into long-term memory.)

■ Look over your outlines, underlining, and any notations you made in your textbook.
■ Recite briefly the main ideas to keep the information fresh in your mind.
■ Make practice test questions from review notes.
■ Relate the textbook information to the Levels of Knowledge in Bloom's Taxonomy. Can you use the information beyond the basic knowledge level?

How to adapt the SQ3R Study System. There is not one study system that works for everyone all the time. Finding a study system that helps you read, understand, and remember the information depends on many factors that have been discussed in this book. For each class, you will have concepts to learn that are presented in distinct formats. Your commitment to identify the concepts, then create and practice a study system you choose, is more important than the type of system used.

Course	Concepts	Study System May Include:
Social Sciences	Major theorists in the field. Theories and principles of behavior.	Underlining and marking as you read. Making charts to compare theories. Attending SI sessions.
Foreign Languages	Vocabulary words, meanings, pronunciations, and tenses.	Practicing translation and pronunciation at the language lab. Adding flash cards and conjugation charts to your review step.
Literature	Elements of writing: plot, characters, point of view, theme, style, and tone.	Interpreting, evaluating, and writing about the selection.
Math	Formulas to learn, Sample problems and exercises.	Practice for solving problems; a math tutor.

Figure 10 ■ Adapt the SQ3R Study System

When creating a study system, SQ3R can be a starting point. You can then adapt the steps to fit the concepts in the class and your preferred way to learn. Your system may include outside resources, such as a tutor, study group, or a Supplemental Instruction (SI) section. Figure 10 summarizes suggested ways to adapt your study system.

Using signal words and phrases. Signal words can help you understand relationships between ideas. They can guide you through a textbook passage, showing where you need to concentrate more, or where you may speed up on your reading. The words will help you anticipate where the author will lead the discussion. If you observe the words carefully, they can be a useful tool in marking a text for main ideas. Figure 11 lists some commonly used signal words and their meanings in a textbook pattern.

Read the following paragraph. As you read, identify each signal word and think about its meaning in the sentence. How does the word guide you in following the author's thoughts? What do you think will be the main subject of the next paragraph?

"Geography is what geographers do." This statement by A.E. Parkins is an effort to define the discipline of geography. The word geography comes from Greek "geo" meaning "earth" and "graphicus" meaning "to write a description." Geography, therefore, deals with descriptions of the earth, especially how space is occupied on our earth. It is concerned with the investigation of spatial variations of people, places, things, or any other observable phenomena on earth. As a discipline, geography is divided into two main areas of focus, i.e., human and physical. Human geography is concerned with global cultures, histories, economics, and politics, to name a few areas of study. Physical geography, on the other hand, deals with the interrelations of the atmosphere, hydrosphere, biosphere, and lithosphere. Due to the vastness of each of these natural spheres, it is helpful for the physical geographer to have a working knowledge of scientific notation.

1. **Example Words: To indicate that another point or an example follows**:
to illustrate	for example	for instance	another
also	furthermore	moreover	specifically
such as			

2. **Emphasis Words: To indicate that the next information is important**:
most important	remember that	pay attention to	above all
a key idea	the main point	most significant	of primary concern

3. **Cause and Effect Words: Check to be sure you know the cause for each effect word**:
because	since	due to	consequently
as a result	effect	cause	for
accordingly	if....then	therefore	thus, so

4. **Summary Words: To indicate that a conclusion follows**:
therefore	finally	consequently	in conclusion
so	to conclude	in a nutshell	to sum up

5. **Time Words: To indicate that a time relationship is being established**:
numbers	steps	stages	next
finally	first, second, etc.	the four steps...	

6. **Compare/contrast Words: To indicate concepts are to be looked at from more than one angle:**
similar	like	disadvantages	different
pros and cons	in contrast	equally	contrary to
conversely	on the other hand		

7. **Swivel Words: To indicate an exception to a stated fact:**
however	although	but	nevertheless
though	except	yet	still

Figure 11 ◼ Signal Words for Note Taking and Reading

Reading and marking textbooks. When you read a chapter in a textbook, the quickest way to focus on the information that you need to learn is to mark the information. Information that is marked in an organized format will be learned in an organized manner. You may have mastered the use of colored highlighters to mark information, but that doesn't organize the information for later study and review.

Annotate means to add marks. By using a system of symbols and notation, not just colored highlighters, you mark the text after the first reading so that a complete rereading will not be necessary. The marking should include important points that you will need to review for an exam.

When should you annotate your text? Annotating should be done after a unit of thought has been presented, when the information can be viewed as a whole. This may mean marking after only one paragraph or after three pages, as what you mark will depend a great deal on your purpose, background, interest and the difficulty of the text. If you mark as you read, too much may be marked and you may be unable to see the "big picture" or main concepts. It takes time for the brain to organize information; so if you read, think, and then mark, the main points will develop and you can decide what you need to mark to remember later.

How do you annotate your text? These signals should be marked:

- Underline all the headings, key terms, and definitions.
- Add important information to illustrations. Explanations are usually given on the same page as the illustrations. Write your title near the illustration.
- Highlight or underline important people, dates, or time sequences.
- Turn the heading into a question by writing a question phrase in front of the heading. Use who, how, why, what, or when to start your question.
- Read the section to find the answer to your question.
- Underline or circle the answer. In the margin, write ANS and a few words to answer the question. Most texts are dense with facts and dates and there may be several parts of the answer to your question. Mark and number each part that answers your question.

To mark terms and definitions: Note how your text prints key terms. They are usually printed in italics or bold, but the definitions that follow appear in regular print.

- Underline or circle a key term and its definition.
- In the margin, write the key terms.
- If the key term is also an answer to a question, write ANS above the words in the margin.

To mark important information signaled by lists:

- Circle the words that tell you what a list is about.
- Number the items in the list, if they do not already have numbers and letters.
- In the margin, write what the list is about in a word or two. Then, list the points in an abbreviated format.
- If the list is also an answer to your question phrase, write ANS in the margin next to the words which introduce the list.

Figure 7 shows an example of an annotated page in a Geog 1130 textbook.

◼ Exercise 1. Learning Styles: Sensory Modality Inventory

There are eleven incomplete sentences and three choices for each. Some choices contain more than one option. If any one of the options seems typical of you, score that answer. All of the options do not have to apply to you. Score the three choices by rating:

3 = to the answer most typical of you
2 = to your second choice
1 = to the one least like you

1. When I want to learn something new, I usually:

   _____ a. want someone to explain it to me.

   _____ b. want to read about it in a book or magazine.

   _____ c. want to try it out, take notes, or make a model of it.

2. At a party, I usually like to:

   _____ a. listen and talk to two or three people at once.

   _____ b. watch the people to see how everyone looks.

   _____ c. dance, play games, or take part in activities.

3. If I were helping with a musical show, I would most likely:

   _____ a. write the music, sing the songs, or play the accompaniment.

   _____ b. design the costumes, paint the scenery, or work the lighting effects.

   _____ c. make the costumes, build the sets, or take an acting role.

4. When I am angry, my first reaction is to:

   _____ a. tell people off, laugh, joke, or talk it over with someone.

   _____ b. blame myself or someone else, daydream about taking revenge, or keep it inside.

   _____ c. make a fist or tense my muscles, take it out on something else, hit or throw things.

5. A happy experience I would like to have is:

   _____ a. hearing thunderous applause for my speech or music.

   _____ b. photographing the prized picture of a sensational newspaper story.

   _____ c. achieving the fame of being first in a physical activity, such as dancing, acting, surfing, or a sports event.

6. I prefer a teacher to:

   _____ a. use the lecture method with informative explanations and discussions.

   _____ b. write on the chalkboard, use visual aids, and assign readings.

   _____ c. require posters, models, hands-on practice, and class activities.

7. I know that I talk with:

_____ a. different tones of voice.

_____ b. my eyes and facial expressions.

_____ c. my hands and gestures.

8. If I had to remember an event so that I could record it later, I would choose to:

_____ a. tell it aloud to someone, or hear an audio tape recording or song about it.

_____ b. see pictures of it, or read a description.

_____ c. replay it in a practice rehearsal using movements such as dance, play acting, or drill.

9. When I cook something new, I like to:

_____ a. have someone tell me the directions (a friend or TV show).

_____ b. read the recipe.

_____ c. use many pots and dishes; stir often and taste-test.

10. In my free time, I like to:

_____ a. listen to the radio, talk on the telephone, or attend a musical event.

_____ b. go to the movies, watch TV, or read a magazine or book.

_____ c. get some exercise, go for a walk, play games, or make things.

11. If I am using equipment, such as a VCR, camcorder, or computer, for the first time I want:

_____ a. someone to tell me how to use it.

_____ b. to read the directions or watch someone else do it.

_____ c. to jump right in and do it; I'll figure it out sooner or later.

To interpret your sensory modality, add up your score for each letter.

Total number: a._____   Auditory

b._____   Visual

c._____   Kinesthetic or Tactual

If your highest score was:

a — you learn best through listening.
b — you learn best by seeing it in print or other visual modes.
c — you learn best by getting physically involved.

Learning Styles
"Learning Style Preferences" by Adele Ducharme and Luck Watford.

Exercise 2. Determining Your Course PBID

Behind every class you are taking this semester is a **Purpose** (the reason why you are taking the class). You also bring to each class a different **Background** (past experiences and coursework) and level of **Interest** (some subjects you simply enjoy more than others). In addition, your classes will vary in terms of the level of **Difficulty** each represents to you (some subjects just seem to be easier or harder for you). The same study method may not work for each course you are taking.

At the beginning of each semester, "study smart" students do a PBID assessment of each class. Based on that assessment, the student develops his/her strategies for tackling each class. Using your course schedule for this semester, assess your PBID for each class. Why are you taking the class? What is your background and interest in the class? Then, assess the difficulty the class will pose to you. Finally, create study strategies that match your abilities and the demands of the course.

Semester Courses	Purpose	Background	Interest	Difficulty	Academic Strategies
Example: USU 1300 Amer. Institu.	**Example:** Fulfill Gen. Ed. Requirement.	**Example:** Had this course in high school.	**Example:** Moderate, good instructor.	**Example:** A lot of reading. Essay exams are a challenge.	**Example:** Attend the SI sessions, read text before the lecture, create essay question.

■ Exercise 3. Goal Planning Sheet

Academic Area	Today's Date	Final Target Date	Date Achieved

Set an academic goal for the semester. (Be sure the goal is specific, concrete, measurable, and flexible.)

_____

_____

_____

_____

How does this goal relate to your values and what are the benefits from achieving this goal?

_____

_____

Specific Action Steps for Achieving this Goal	Target Date	Date Shared and Reviewed	Date Completed
1. _____ _____			
2. _____ _____			
3. _____ _____			
4. _____ _____			

■ Exercise 4. Time Management

Part A. Conduct a Time Audit

Do you ever find yourself wondering, "Where has the time gone?" Well, now is your chance to find out. In this assignment you are to observe and record how you "spend" your time in a given week. Here's how you do it:

1. Your instructor will assign you a specific week for observation. (Put the date above the appropriate day on the Time Audit form.)

2. Carry the Time Audit with you during the target week. Don't forget and leave it in your room.

3. Every half hour, or when it is reasonable after an activity, record what you have done during that half hour. Be specific in describing what you did—don't just say studied; note subject studied, pages read/written, problems worked, etc.

4. Note what you *did*, not where you were. That is, note that you studied USU 1300 not that you were at the Library.

5. Don't break down the time into less that a half-hour.

Part B. Analyze Your Time Audit

1. Indicate the number of class hours (credits you're taking this semester). _____

2. How many hours did you study during the week? _____

3. How many hours did you spend on exercise or other stress reduction activities? _____
    Do you need to plan for more or less time in this area? More _____ Less _____

4. Are you working? Yes _____ No _____ If yes, how many hours do you work? Did the number of hours you work conflict with your studies? Yes! _____ No! _____

5. How much time did you waste? _____

6. Did you get enough sleep? Yes! _____ No! _____ Did you eat regular balanced meals?
    Yes! _____ No! _____ Can you realistically keep up this pace? Yes! _____ No! _____

7. Was the week you audited: Typical _____ or Unusual _____ ?
    If it was unusual, in what ways did this unusual week affect your time?

Part C. Make a Plan

Use the sheet called "Daily Planning Calendar." Indicate how you plan to use your time during the week. Consider these points:

1. How many hours have you planned for studying? _____ Does your planned study time equal approximately 2 hours of study for each hour of credit? Yes! _____ No! _____

2. Highlight areas that you will use for short periods of study. (Going over class notes, reviews, studying note cards, etc.)

3. What major areas of your schedule are you changing because of your time audit? (i.e., less time for TV, more time for class study, consider my job load, etc.)

_____

_____

_____

Part D. Semester Planning Calendar

Fill in the semester, year and monthly dates in each box on the calendar. Obtain a course syllabus from each of your instructors. All examinations and due dates of major assignments, projects and papers should be entered on the calendar to assist you in planning your course of study each week throughout the quarter. Make two copies; keep one in your room in a clearly visible place and keep the other copy in your notebook.

Part E. Summary

1. What are the benefits to you of planning your time?

2. What problems or time conflicts do you foresee in this semester? Example: Do you have two or more tests on one day? Do you have a paper and a test due on the same day?

3. Using colored highlighter: —highlight your tests

   —highlight your papers

   —highlight your busy times

Time Audit

Directions: Beginning on the day of the week given by your instructor, keep a record of how you spend your time for the next week. Record what you did (behavior) not where you were. Record your activities every half hour or as soon as possible.

Time	Mon	Tues	Wed	Thur	Fri	Sat	Sun
5:30							
6:00							
6:30							
7:00							
7:30							
8:00							
8:30							
9:00							
9:30							
10:00							
10:30							
11:00							
11:30							
12:00							
12:30							
1:00							
1:30							
2:00							
2:30							
3:00							
3:30							
4:00							
4:30							
5:00							
5:30							
6:00							
6:30							
7:00							
7:30							
8:00							
8:30							
9:00							
9:30							
10:00							
10:30							

Daily Planning Calendar							
Directions: Map out a routine week this semester. Schedule your fixed time first. Schedule study time at times you know you are likely to study (usually not Friday night). Remember all the little blocks of time. Allow for "Reasonable" R&R time.							
Time	Mon	Tues	Wed	Thur	Fri	Sat	Sun
5:30							
6:00							
6:30							
7:00							
7:30							
8:00							
8:30							
9:00							
9:30							
10:00							
10:30							
11:00							
11:30							
12:00							
12:30							
1:00							
1:30							
2:00							
2:30							
3:00							
3:30							
4:00							
4:30							
5:00							
5:30							
6:00							
6:30							
7:00							
7:30							
8:00							
8:30							
9:00							
9:30							
10:00							
10:30							

Semester Planning Calendar

_____ _____ to _____
(Semester)   (Months)

Sunday	Monday	Tuesday	Wednesday	Thursday	Friday	Saturday

■ Exercise 5. Applying Bloom's Taxonomy to Multiple Choice Questions

Indicate the level(s) of thinking required to answer each multiple choice question correctly:

Examples:

A. Which of the following is an enzyme?
   A. a carbohydrate   B. a protein
   C. a nutrient   D. a starch

   Level(s) of Thinking: *Knowledge/Recognition*

B. At present growth rates, which of the following countries will have a larger human population than the U.S. in twenty years?
   A. Canada   B. Brazil
   C. Mexico   D. Germany

   Level(s) of Thinking: *Knowledge/recognition, comprehension, application*

1. Which of the following is likely to be found growing in a desert?

   A. xerophyte   B. epiphyte
   C. hydrophyte   D. mesophyte

   Level(s) of Thinking: _____

2. The variety of species of terrestrial life-forms generally _____with increasing latitude.

   A. increases   B. gets structurally larger
   C. decreases   D. grows more rapidly

   Level(s) of Thinking: _____

3. Which of the following would result in an increase in the red fox population?
   A. fewer rabbits   B. more grass
   C. drought   D. more demand for rabbit stew

   Level(s) of Thinking: _____

4. Which of the following plant associations has the least percent of its biomass in stem tissue?
   A. coniferous forest   B. tropical rainforest
   C. desert   D. grassland

   Level(s) of Thinking: _____

■ Exercise 6. Essay Exam Key Words

See Figure 8 Essay Exam Key Words, for definitions.

1. Test your knowledge of essay exam key words by matching terms to definitions.

   a. analyze   _____   to support or deny by showing evidence or facts.

   b. criticize   _____   break into parts and explain parts and their importance.

   c. trace   _____   to make clear or comprehensible.

   d. evaluate   _____   to show the order of events or development.

   e. prove   _____   list several ideas, events, aspects, etc., briefly.

   f. enumerate   _____   to point out both good and bad characteristics.

   g. explain   _____   to point out both good and bad features, along with a statement or comment or opinion.

   h. summarize   _____   report various sides of an issue and relationships between points.

   i. discuss   _____   point out characteristics two or more items have in common and their differences.

   j. outline   _____   present main points and major subpoints in an organized fashion.

   k. interpret   _____   present main point in general sentences.

   l. compare   _____   explain by using examples or demonstrations.

2. The following essay questions relate to the information from the Geog 1130 textbook selection. Outline answers to these questions. Be sure you read the question carefully.

   A. Explain the Köppen system of climatic classification.

   B. Create a comparison chart showing the characteristics of the humid tropical climate, the humid wet-dry climate, and the tropical monsoon climate.

   C. Analyze the differences between the humid-dry boundary and the dry climates with a "B" symbol.

■ Exercise 7. Practice Using SQ3R

DIRECTIONS: The following exercise is designed to give you practice in the steps of SQ3R.

Section I. Survey

1. Name of textbook:

2. List at least two questions or thoughts which the title suggests to you:

   _____

   _____

3. List at least two major points the author makes in the Preface:

   _____

   _____

4. List at least two major points the author makes in the Introduction:

   _____

   _____

5. Take at least three chapter titles listed in the Table of Contents and turn them into questions:

   _____

   _____

   _____

6. If there is an Appendix, what does it contain?

   _____

7. Does the book contain a Glossary? Yes _____ No _____ An Index? Yes _____ No _____ If the answers are yes, look over the Glossary and/or thumb through the Index looking for familiar names, places, or terms. How much do you think you are going to know about the contents?

8. Look through the first two chapters of the book and check any of the following aids used in them.

   ___ headings   ___ footnotes   ___ pictures

   ___ subheadings   ___ bibliography   ___ graphs

   ___ italics   ___ study questions   ___ bold vocabulary words

   ___ summary   ___ assignments   ___ other

Section II. Question

Use the textbook you surveyed. Pick one chapter.

Title of Chapter: _____

1. What do you think is the main idea of the chapter?

    _____

    _____

2. Turn three headings into questions.

    _____

    _____

    _____

3. Write the answer to one of the questions in your own words. Use a format that will help you remember the information: an outline, list, drawing, diagram, etc.

    _____

    _____

    _____

Section III. Read, Recite, Review

Now, think about how you will actively **Read** the text, **Recite** the information, and **Review** the material.

1. Describe your active reading techniques. (Did you annotate, answer questions, etc.?)

    _____

    _____

2. Describe what you will do when you review the material. (Will you create an outline, study sheets, study cards, etc.?)

    _____

    _____

3. Attach a photocopy of a page from your textbook and show how you annotated the important information.

Section 5

Planning for Success

CHAPTER 12
Planning Your Career and Education

Chapter Focus

Read to answer these key questions:

- What are some employment trends for the future?
- What are work skills necessary for success in the 21st Century?
- How do I research a career?
- How do I plan my education?
- How can I make good decisions about my future?
- How can I obtain my ideal job?
- What is a dangerous opportunity?

It is always easier to get where you are going if you have a road map or a plan. To start the journey, it is helpful to know about yourself, including your personality, interests, talents, and values. Once you have this picture, you will need to know about the world of work and job trends that will affect your future employment opportunities. Next, you will need to make decisions about which road to follow. Then, you will need to plan your education to reach your destination. Finally, you will need some job-seeking skills such as writing a resume and preparing for a successful interview.

■ Employment Trends

The world is changing quickly, and these changes will affect your future career. To assure your future career success, you will need to become aware of career trends and observe how they change over time so that you can adjust your career plans accordingly. For example, recently a school was established in our area for training bank tellers. The school quickly went out of business and the students demanded their money back because they were not able to get jobs. A careful observer of career trends would have noticed that bank tellers are being replaced by automatic teller machines (ATM's) and would not have started a school for training bank tellers. Students observant of career trends would not have paid money for the training. It is probably a good idea for bank tellers to look ahead and plan a new career direction.

How can you find out about career trends that may affect you in the future? Become a careful observer by reading about current events. Good sources of information include

- Your local newspaper, especially the business section
- News programs
- Current magazines
- Government statistics and publications
- The Internet

When thinking about future trends, use your critical thinking skills. Sometimes trends change quickly or interact in different ways. For example, since we are using e-mail to a great extent today, it might seem that mail carriers would not be as much in demand in the future. However, since people are buying more goods over the Internet, there has been an increased demand for mail carriers and other delivery services. Develop the habit of looking at what is happening to see if you can identify trends that may affect your future. The following are some trends to watch that may affect your future career. As you read about each trend, think about how it could affect you.

Baby Boomers, Generation X, and the Millennial Generation

About every twenty years, sociologists begin to describe a new generation with similar characteristics based on shared historical experiences. Each generation has different opportunities and challenges in the workplace.

The Baby Boomers were born following World War II between 1946 and 1964. Four out of every ten adults today is in this Baby Boom Generation.[1] Because there are so many aging Baby Boomers, the average age of Americans is increasing. Life expectancy is also increasing. In 2000, the average life expectancy was 76.9 years.[2] In the new millennium many more people will live to be 100 years old or more! Think about the implications of an older population. Older people need such things as health care, recreation, travel and financial planning. Occupations related to these needs are likely to be in demand now and in the future.

Those born between 1965 and 1977 are often referred to as Generation X. They are sometimes called the "baby bust" generation because fewer babies were born during this period than in the previous generations. There is much in the media about this generation having to pay higher taxes and social security payments to support the large number of aging Baby Boomers. Some say that this generation will not enjoy the prosperity of the Baby Boomers. Those who left college in the early nineties faced a recession and the worst job market since World War II.[3] Many left college in debt and returned home to live with their parents. Because of a lack of employment opportunities, many in this generation became entrepreneurs, starting new companies at a faster rate than previous generations.

Jane Bryant Quinn notes that in spite of economic challenges, Generation Xers have a lot going for them:[4]

- They have record-high levels of education, which correlate with higher income and lower unemployment. In 1993, 47 percent of 18- to 24-year-olds had at least some higher education. Also high school dropout rates were down.
- There is a demand for more skilled workers, so employers are more willing to train employees. Anthony Carnevale, chairman of the National Commission for Employment Policy, "sees a big demand for 'high-school plus'—a high school diploma plus technical school or junior college."
- Generation Xers are computer literate, and those who use computers on the job earn 10 to 15 percent more than those who don't.
- This group often has a good work ethic valued by employers. However, they value a balanced lifestyle with time for outside interests and family.
- As Baby Boomers retire, more job opportunities are created for this group.
- Unlike the Baby Boomers, this generation was born into a more integrated and more diverse society. They are better able than previous generations to adapt to diversity in society and the workplace.

Many of today's college students are part of the Millennial Generation born between 1977 and 1995. This generation is sometimes called Generation Y or the Echo Boomers since they are the children of the Baby Boomers.[5] This new generation of approximately 60 million is three times larger than Generation X and will eventually exceed the number of Baby Boomers. By 2010, they will become the largest teen population is U.S. history. As the Millennials reach college age, they will attend college in increasing numbers. In the next ten years, college enrollments will increase by approximately 300,000 students per year. Colleges will find it difficult to accommodate rapidly increasing numbers of students and as a result, the Millennial Generation will face increasingly competitive college admissions criteria.

Millennials are more ethnically diverse than previous generations with 34 percent ethnic minorities. One in four lives with a single parent. Three in four have working mothers. Most of them started using computers before they were five years old. Marketing researchers describe this new generation as "technologically adept, info-savvy, a cybergeneration, the clickeratti."[6] They are the connected generation, accustomed to cell phones, chatting on the Internet, and listening to downloaded music.

Young people in the Millennial Generation share a different historical perspective from the Baby Boom Generation. Baby Boomers remember the Viet Nam War and the assassinations of President John F. Kennedy and Martin Luther King. For Millennials school shootings such as Columbine and acts of terrorism such as the Oklahoma City bombing and the 9-11 attack on New York City stand out as important events. The Millennial Generation will see their main problems as dealing with violence, easy access to weapons, and the threat of terrorism.

Neil Howe and William Strauss paint a very positive picture of this new generation in their book *Millennials Rising: The Next Great Generation:*

- Millennials will rebel by tearing down old institutions that do not work and building new and better institutions. The authors share a quote from Shansel Nagia: "I like to think of my generation, the Class of 2000, as the Millennial Generation. We are the kids who are going to change things."
- Surveys show that this generation describes themselves as happy, confident, and positive.
- They are cooperative team players.
- They generally accept authority and respect their parents' values.
- They follow rules. The rates of homicides, violent crime, abortion, and teen pregnancy are decreasing rapidly.
- The use of alcohol, drugs, and tobacco is decreasing.
- Millennials have a fascination with and mastery of new technology.
- Their most important values are individuality and uniqueness.[7]

It is predicted that the world of work for the Millennials will be dramatically different. Previous generations anticipated having a lifetime career. By the year 2020, many jobs will probably be short-term contracts. This arrangement will provide cost savings and efficiency for employers and flexibility for employees to start or stop work to take vacations, train for new jobs, or meet family responsibilities. One in five people will be self-employed. Retirement will be postponed as people look forward to living longer and healthier lives.[8]

What generation are you in and how might this affect your future?

A Diverse Workforce

The workforce in the United States is becoming increasingly more diverse. Diversity includes many demographic variables such as race, religion, color, gender, national origin, disability, sexual orientation, age, education, geographic origin, and skill characteristics. Having an appreciation for diversity is important in maintaining a work environment that is open and allows for individual differences. Increasing diversity provides opportunities for many different kinds of individuals and makes it important to be able to have good working relationships with all kinds of people.

The U.S. Department of Labor[9] and the Bureau of Labor Statistics[10] have described some trends affecting the workplace:

- From 1998 to 2008, total employment is projected to increase from 140.5 million to 160.8 million. This is an increase of 14.4 percent.
- Because of the aging of the Baby Boomers, the average age of workers will rise. The median age for workers in 2000 was 39.
- More women will be in the workforce. Women now comprise 47 to 50 percent of the workforce. Because women are still concentrated in traditionally women's jobs, they still earn only 76 cents for every dollar earned by a man.
- One third of new workers will be from minority populations. Hispanics and African Americans will continue to increase their representation in the workforce.
- There will be more immigrants than at any time since World War I.

How might these trends affect your future?

Impact of the Internet

The Internet is having a profound effect on the way we communicate, work, and do business. Microsoft CEO Bill Gates has predicted that business will change more in the next ten years than in the last fifty years. In his book, *Business @ the Speed of Thought*[11], he summarizes the kinds of changes happening to businesses because of the Internet. These changes will affect the kinds of jobs that exist in the future.

E-mail. The 2000s will be an age of speedy communication. Bill Gates predicts that within five years businesses will use the Internet more than the telephone. This rapid communication will help businesses to deliver goods and services faster.

E-commerce. E-commerce is business conducted over the Internet. Department of Labor statistics show that e-commerce more than doubled between 1996 and 1997 from $15.5 billion to $38.8 billion. By 1998, sales exceeded $300 billion. By 2005, e-commerce is expected to reach $1 trillion.[12] Bill Gates describes Dell computers as an example of the most successful businesses using e-commerce:

> *Dell was one of the first major companies to move to e-commerce. A global computer supplier with more than $18 billion in revenue, Dell began selling its products online in mid-1996. The company's online business quickly rose from $1 million a week to $1 million a day. Soon it jumped to $3 million a day, then $5 million. It's now risen to $14 million.*[13]

Businesses that do not use the Internet will be missing out on opportunities and may not be able to compete with businesses using e-commerce. Gates says that online sales will increase 45 percent per year, changing the nature of the way we do business. Online commerce will be increasingly used in finance, insurance, travel, online auctions, and computer sales. The increase in e-commerce may reduce the use of conventional stores, increase mail delivery services, and reduce inventory.

The paperless office. In the future, businesses will increasingly use an intranet to take the place of numerous forms and papers. An intranet works much the same way as the Internet. It is a network used to share information within a company and is accessible only to those within the company. Using an intranet helps employees to access, organize, and file information in a fast and efficient way. There will be no more searching through piles of paper to find needed information.

Friction-free capitalism. Bill Gates uses the term "friction-free capitalism" to describe a marketplace in which buyers and sellers can find each other easily. Consumers can use the Internet to find any product, and businesses can use it to find consumers interested in purchasing their products. Consumers can also gather information about products and find the best prices using the Internet.

Customer service. The Internet will increasingly be used to provide customer service. For example, hotels can use the Internet to process reservations anywhere in the world. The consumer can access a digital photo of the hotel and room options. Many hotel rooms feature modem connections. Since the computer handles the details of the reservation, clerks will have more time for personal service.

The Web lifestyle. Gates refers to the Web lifestyle as new hardware and software that will change the way we live. Because of rapid communication through the Internet, the people of the world will be drawn closer together. Personal computers and access to the Internet are becoming less expensive. More and more people will use the Web to get information, learn, and communicate.

One of the biggest changes is that consumers will shift to managing their finances online. Many will bank and pay bills electronically. When consumers pay bills online, the U.S. Commerce Department estimates that processing costs will drop more than $20 billion annually.[14] This will mean fewer people will be involved in the bill-paying process, and those who work in this area will be using a computer to do their jobs.

The Web workstyle. Digital tools will change the roles and skills required of many workers in the future. Many workers will become freelancers, or free agents who work on a project basis. When a project is completed, they will move on to a different project, possibly in a different company. Because of the Web, workers can live in one place and work in another. Workers in the future will need to be more highly skilled.

> *The Web lifestyle will increasingly equalize opportunities for skilled people around the world. If you had to guess someone's approximate income today and were limited to a single polite question, a good one would be: "What country do you live in?" The reason is the huge disparity in average wages from country to country. In twenty years, if you want to guess somebody's income, the most telling question will be: "What's your education?"*[15]

Gates thinks positively and says that these changes will empower people. People will be shifted from routine nonthinking work to more productive thinking work. He does not see people being replaced by computers. He states, "A good knowledge worker will add value to the computer." When workers are freed from the routine work, they can provide the human touch where it is important. "Workers are no longer a cog in a machine but rather are an intelligent part of the overall process."[16]

How might the above trends affect your future?

The Microprocessor

The microprocessor is a silicon chip containing transistors that determine the capability of a computer. In the past twenty years, the power of the microprocessor has increased more than one million times. In the next twenty years, the power will increase a million times again.[17] Because of the increased power of the microprocessor, it will be used in new ways and with new devices. Consider the "smart home" of the future:

> *At home, you'll be able to operate your PC by talking to it. It will automatically back up all your information, update its own software and synchronize itself with your TV, cell phone, handheld, and all the devices on your home network. The refrigerator in your kitchen will know how well stocked it is, suggest recipes based on what's available, and order more food from your online grocer. Your TV will double as an interactive shopping mall, letting you buy advertised products or clothes you saw in a sitcom. And if you don't want to watch TV, you'll be able to read an electronic book that knows your favorite authors and automatically downloads their latest novels. If you decide to read one of them, your bank account will be debited.*[18]

The microprocessor is increasingly available to all and for less cost. The personal computer that I have on my desk would have occupied an entire building 35 years ago. Today we have access to powerful computers that will play an ever greater role in our daily lives.

> *It's remarkable how we now take all that power for granted. Using a basic home PC costing less than $1,000, you can balance your household budget, do your taxes, write letters to friends and fax or e-mail them over the Internet, listen to CDs or the radio, watch the news, consult a doctor, play games, book a vacation, view a house, buy a book or a car. The list is endless.*[19]

How might access to more powerful computers affect your future?

New Advances in Technology

It is interesting to note new advances in technology and what might be possible in the future. One interesting development to watch is artificial intelligence software, which enables computers to recognize patterns, improve from experience, make inferences, and approximate human thought. Scientists at the MIT Artificial Intelligence Lab have developed a robot named Cog. Here is a description of Cog and its capabilities:

> *We have given it a multitude of sensors to "feel" and learn what it is like to be touched and spoken to. Cog's ability to make eye contact and reach out to moving objects is also meant to motivate people to interact with it. These features have taught Cog, among other things, to distinguish a human face from inanimate objects (this puts its development at about a 3-month-old's). It can also listen to music and keep rhythm by tapping on a drum (something a 5-year-old can do). One of the most startling moments in Cog's development came when it was learning to touch things. At one point, Cog began to touch and discover its own body. It looked so eerie and human, I was stunned.*[20]

In addition to artificial intelligence, look for new developments in biotechnology and medicine. We can probably look forward to new kinds of foods, new medications, and cures for diseases. Watch the news for future developments that will affect how we all live and work.

How might new advances in technology affect your future?

The Middle Class as an Endangered Species

Author Joyce Lain Kennedy believes that the middle class is becoming an endangered species.[21] She states that many jobs traditionally held by the middle class have been "dumbed down," making them so simple that anyone can do them. These jobs pay very little and offer no benefits, no employment stability, and little opportunity for advancement. Young people often hold these jobs in their teens and twenties. Individuals who do not go on for education or training after high school often become stuck in these low-paying jobs.

One of the reasons for making these lower-level jobs simpler is that employers are concerned about the lack of skills of their employees. Kennedy states, "One third of today's workers will be unable to read well enough to qualify for entry-level jobs. Almost half of the firms in a recent survey say that between 15 percent and 35 percent of their current employees aren't capable of handling more complex tasks; about 10 percent say that up to half of their current workers do not have the skills needed for promotion."[22]

At the other end of the job continuum are jobs requiring a college education or training beyond high school. These high-end jobs often require technical or computer skills. These are the jobs that pay better and offer benefits. It seems that we are becoming a nation of haves and have-nots who are separated by their education and technical skills.

How might this trend affect your future?

Moving from Goods to Services and Technology

Human society has moved through several stages. The first stage, about 20,000 years ago, was the hunting and gathering stage. During this time, society depended on the natural environment for food and other resources. When natural resources were depleted, the community moved to another area. The second stage, some 10,000 years ago, was the agricultural stage. Human beings learned to domesticate animals and cultivate crops. This allowed people to stay in one place and develop more permanent villages. About 200 years ago, industrial societies came into being by harnessing power sources to produce goods on a large scale.

Today in the U.S. we are evolving into a service, technology, and information society. Fewer people are working in agriculture and manufacturing. More people are working in service, technology, and information occupations. Futurists John Naisbitt, Patricia Aburdeen, and Walter Krechel note that we are moving toward a service economy based on high technology, rapid communications, biotechnology for use in agriculture and medicine, health care, and sales of merchandise.[23] Four out of five new jobs are in the service area.[24] Service occupations include health care, business, education, wholesale and retail trade, finance, insurance, real estate, transportation, communication, public utilities, and government.

The Department of Labor reported that most job growth since 1970 has been in the service area.[25] These are some service areas that are projected to increase in the coming decades:

- Health-care-related occupations will increase faster than any other service occupation. Two factors will contribute to this growth: an aging population has greater need for health services, and advances in technology and medication provide services and treatments that result in improved health care.
- Contracted-out business services will continue to increase. Businesses contract out services to operate more efficiently at a lower cost. These services include data processing, advertising, and security services.
- There will be a shift in work usually done in the home to outside service agencies. For example, people are increasingly eating out or eating prepared foods. As a consequence, jobs will increase in restaurants and related food industries.
- There will be increasing demand for child care, nursing homes, and home health care services.

■ The fastest growing occupations between 1998 and 2008 are expected to be computer related: computer engineers, computer support specialists, computer systems analysts, database administrators, and desktop publishers.[26]

The Need for Lifelong Education

In the past, the life pattern for many people was to graduate from school, go to work, and eventually retire. Because of the rapid changes in technology and society today, workers will need additional training and education over a lifetime. Education will take place in a variety of forms: community college courses, training on the job, private training sessions, and learning on your own. Those who do not keep up with the new technology will find that their skills quickly become obsolete. Those who do keep up will find their skills in demand.

While most of the fastest growing jobs will require at least an associate's degree, three out of four U.S. workers are in jobs that do not require a bachelor's degree. These workers will rely on short-term and on-the-job training. They will need good skills in reading, communication, and math to take advantage of these training opportunities.[27]

How might this trend affect your future?

Nontraditional Workers

Unlike traditional workers, nontraditional workers do not have full-time, year-round jobs with health and retirement benefits. Employers are moving toward using nontraditional workers, including multiple jobholders, contingent and part-time workers, independent contractors, and temporary workers. Nearly four out of five employers use nontraditional workers to help them become more efficient, prevent layoffs, and access workers with special skills. There are advantages and disadvantages to this arrangement. Nontraditional workers have no benefits and risk unemployment. This arrangement can also provide workers with a flexible work schedule in which they work during some periods and pursue other interests or gain new skills when not working.

Companies Say No to Drugs and Alcohol

Problems related to drug and alcohol abuse in the workplace are widespread and costly. Drug and alcohol abuse result in decreased productivity, injuries, and fatalities in the workplace, higher unemployment, and lower income. Many employers screen applicants and employees for drug and alcohol abuse. Employers reject applicants who show evidence of drug abuse. In some cases, employees are directed to rehabilitation programs, which are costly to administer. Here are some interesting statistics related to drug and alcohol abuse in the workplace:

■ 63 percent of firms responding to a 1991 survey were engaged in some sort of drug testing, a 200 percent increase since 1987.[28]
■ Shortfalls in productivity and employment among individuals with alcohol or other drug-related problems cost the American economy $80.9 billion in 1992, of which $66.7 billion is attributed to alcohol and $14.2 billion to other drugs.[29]

- Although 70 percent of all current adult illegal drug users are employed,[30] use of most illicit drugs is substantially higher among the unemployed. The use of crack cocaine is ten times higher among unemployed persons than those with jobs.[31]
- Up to 40 percent of industrial fatalities and 47 percent of industrial injuries can be linked to alcohol consumption and alcoholism.[32]
- 60 percent of alcohol-related work performance problems can be attributed to employees who are not alcohol dependent but who occasionally drink too much on a work night or drink during a weekday lunch.[33]
- 21 percent of workers reported being injured or put in danger, having to redo work or to cover for a coworker, or needing to work harder due to others' drinking.[34]
- Workers who report having three or more jobs in the previous five years are about twice as likely to be current or past-year illicit drug users as those who have had two or fewer jobs.[35]
- Workers in the following occupations report the highest rates of current and past-year illicit drug use: construction, food preparation, and waiters and waitresses. Heavy alcohol use followed a similar pattern, although auto mechanics, vehicle repairers, light truck drivers, and laborers also have high rates of alcohol use.[36]
- The lowest rates of illicit drug use are found among workers in the following occupations: police and detectives, administrative support, teachers and child care workers. The lowest rates of heavy alcohol use are among data clerks, personnel specialists, and secretaries.[37]
- Individuals with drinking problems or alcoholism at any time in their lives suffer income reductions ranging from 1.5 percent to 18.7 percent, depending on age and sex, compared with those with no such diagnosis.[38]

How might this trend affect your future?

_____

_____

■ Work Skills for the Twenty-First Century

Because of rapid changes in technology, college students of today may be preparing for jobs that do not exist right now. After graduation, many college students find employment that is not even related to their college major. One researcher found that 48 percent of college graduates find employment in fields not related to their college major.[39] More important than college major, however, are the general skills learned in college that prepare students for the future.

To define skills needed in the future workplace, the U.S. Secretary of Labor created the Secretary's Commission on Achieving Necessary Skills (SCANS). Based on interviews with employers and educators, the members of the commission outlined foundation skills and workplace competencies needed to succeed in the workplace in the twenty-first century.[40] The following skills apply to all occupations in all fields and will help you to become a successful employee, regardless of your major. As you read through these skills, think about your competency in these areas. Then complete "Rate Your Skills for Success in the Workplace."

Foundation Skills

Basic Skills
- Reading
- Writing
- Basic arithmetic
- Higher level mathematics
- Listening
- Speaking

Thinking Skills
- Creative thinking
- Decision making
- Problem solving
- Mental visualization
- Knowing how to learn
- Reasoning

Personal Qualities
- Responsibility
- Self-esteem
- Sociability
- Self-management
- Integrity/honesty

Workplace Competencies

Resources
- Time—Selects relevant goals, sets priorities, follows schedules
- Money—Uses budgets, keeps records, and makes adjustments
- Materials and facilities—Acquires, stores, and distributes materials, supplies, parts, equipment, space, or final products
- Human resources—Assesses knowledge and skills, distributes work, evaluates performance, and provides feedback

Interpersonal
- Participates as a member of a team—Works cooperatively with others and contributes to group efforts
- Teaches others—Helps others learn needed skills
- Serves clients/customers—Works and communicates with clients and customers to satisfy their expectations
- Exercises leadership—Communicates, encourages, persuades, and convinces others; responsibly challenges procedures, policies, or authority
- Negotiates to arrive at a decision—Works toward an agreement involving resources or diverging interests
- Works with cultural diversity—Works well with men and women and with people from a variety of ethnic, social, or educational backgrounds

Information
- Acquires and evaluates information—Identifies the need for information, obtains information, and evaluates it
- Organizes and maintains information—Organizes, processes, and maintains written or computerized records

- Uses computers to process information—Employs computers to acquire, organize, analyze, and communicate information

Systems

- Understands systems—Knows how social, organizational, and technological systems work and operates efficiently within them
- Monitors and corrects performance—Distinguishes trends, predicts impacts of actions on systems operations, takes action to correct performance
- Improves and designs systems—Develops new systems to improve products or services

Technology

- Selects technology—Judges which procedures, tools, or machines, including computers, will produce the desired results
- Applies technology to tasks—Understands the proper procedures for using machines and computers
- Maintains and troubleshoots technology—Prevents, identifies, or solves problems with machines, computers, and other technologies

Because the workplace is changing, these skills may be more important than the background acquired through a college major. Work to develop these skills and you will be prepared for whatever lies ahead.

How to Research Your Career

After you have assessed your personality, interests, values, and talents, the next step is to learn about the world of work. Try to find a match between your personal characteristics and the world of work. To learn about the world of work, you will need to research possible careers. This includes reading career descriptions, and investigating career outlooks, salaries, and educational requirements.

Career Descriptions

The career description tells you about the nature of the work, working conditions, employment, training, qualifications, advancement, job outlook, earnings, and related occupations. The two best sources of job descriptions are the *Occupational Outlook Handbook* and *Occupational Outlook Quarterly*. The *Handbook*, published by the Bureau of Labor Statistics, is like an encyclopedia of careers. You can search alphabetically by career or by career cluster.

The *Occupational Outlook Quarterly* is a periodical with up-to-date articles on new and emerging occupations, training opportunities, salary trends, and new studies from the Bureau of Labor Statistics. You can find these resources in a public or school library, college career center, or on the Internet.

Career Outlook

It is especially important to know about the career outlook of an occupation you are considering. Career outlook includes salary and availability of employment. How much does the occupation pay? Will the occupation exist in the future, and will there be employment opportunities? Of course you will want to prepare yourself for careers that pay well and have future employment opportunities.

You can find information about career outlooks in the sources listed above, current periodicals, and materials from the Bureau of Labor Statistics. The table below, for example, lists the fastest growing occupations, occupations with the highest salaries, and occupations with the largest job growth. Information from the Bureau of Labor Statistics is also available online.

Employment Projections, 1998–2008		
Ten Fastest-Growing Occupations	**Ten Industries with the Fastest Wage and Salary Employment Growth**	**Ten Occupations with the Largest Job Growth**
Computer engineer Computer support specialist Systems analyst Database administrator Desktop publishing specialist Paralegals and legal assistant Personal care and home health aid Medical assistant Social and human service assistant Physician's assistants	Computer and data processing services Health services Residential care Management and public relations Personnel supply services Equipment rental and leasing Museums, botanical and zoological gardens Research and testing Transportation services Security and commodity brokers	Systems analyst Retail salesperson Cashier General managers or top executive Truck driver Office clerk, general Registered nurse Computer support specialist Personal care and home health aide Teacher's assistant

Source: Bureau of Labor Statistics, 1999.

Internet Resources

There are many other sources of career information available over the Internet. This information is often more up-to-date than printed material. There are many helpful sources of online information in the "Success over the Internet" section at the end of this chapter.

■ Planning Your Education

Once you have assessed your personal characteristics and researched your career options, it is important to plan your education. If you have a plan, you will be able to finish your education more quickly and avoid taking unnecessary classes. You can begin work on your educational plan by following the steps below. After you have done some work on your plan, visit your college counselor or advisor to make sure that your plan is appropriate.

■ Steps in Planning Your Education

_____ 1. **Take your college entrance or assessment tests before you apply to colleges.** Most colleges require the Scholastic Aptitude Test (SAT) or their own local placement tests in order for you to be admitted. You can find information about these tests from your high school or college counseling center or online at http://www.ets.org/ or http://cbweb1.collegeboard.org/index.html.

_____ 2. **Take English the first semester, and continue each semester until your English requirement is complete.** English courses provide the foundation for further college study. Your SAT or college placement test will determine what level of English you need to take. As a general rule, community colleges require one semester of college-level English. Four-year colleges and universities generally require two semesters or three quarters of college-level English. If your placement scores are low, you may be required to take review courses first.

_____ 3. **Start your math classes early, preferably in the first semester or quarter.** Many high paying careers require a long series of math classes, particularly in the sciences, engineering, and business. If you delay taking math courses until later, you may limit your career options and extend your time in college.

_____ 4. **Take the required general education courses.** Find out what your college requires for general education and put these classes on your plan. You will find this information in the college catalog. Be careful to select the correct general education plan. In community colleges, there are different plans for transfer and associate's degree students. At a university there may be different plans for different colleges within the university. Check with a college counselor or advisor to make sure you have the correct plan.

_____ 5. **Prepare for your major.** Consult your college catalog to see what courses are required for your major. If you are undecided on a major, take the general education courses and start working on a decision about your major. If you are interested in the sciences or engineering, start work on math in the first semester. Start on your major requirements as soon as possible so that you do not delay your graduation.

_____ 6. **Check prerequisites.** A prerequisite is a course that is required before taking a higher-level course. The college catalog lists courses offered and includes prerequisites. Most colleges will not let you register for a course for which you do not have the prerequisite. It is also difficult to succeed in an advanced course without taking the prerequisite first.

_____ 7. **Make an educational plan.** The educational plan includes all the courses you will need to graduate. Again, use the college catalog as your guide.

_____ 8. **Check your plan.** See your college counselor or advisor to check your plan. He or she can save you from taking classes that you do not need and help you to graduate in the minimum amount of time.

Use the educational planning forms at the end of this chapter to complete your educational plan.

■ Making Good Decisions

Knowing how to make a good decision about your career and important life events is very important to your future.

How to Make a Career Decision

Sometimes people end up in a career because they simply seized an opportunity for employment. A good job becomes available and they happen to be in the right place at the right time. Sometimes people end up in a career because it is familiar to them because it is a job held by a member of the family or a friend in the community. Sometimes people end up in a career because of economic necessity. The job pays well and they need the money. These careers are the result of chance circumstances. Sometimes they turn out well, and sometimes they turn out miserably.

Whether you are male or female, married or single, you will spend a great deal of your life working. By doing some careful thinking and planning about your career, you can improve your chances of success and happiness. Use the following steps to do some careful decision making about your career. Although you are the person who needs to make the decision about a career, you can get help from your college career center or your college counselor or advisor. To evaluate your career options, use the "Checklist for a Satisfying Career."

Steps in Making a Career Decision

1. **Begin with self-assessment.**
   - What is your personality type?
   - What are your interests?
   - What are your talents, gifts, and strengths?
   - What is your learning style?
   - What are your values?
   - What lifestyle do you prefer?

2. **Explore your options.**
   - What careers match your personal characteristics?

3. **Research your career options.**
   - Read the job description.
   - Investigate the career outlook.
   - What is the salary?
   - What training and education is required?
   - Speak with an advisor, counselor, or person involved in the career that interests you.
   - Choose a career or general career area that matches your personal characteristics.

4. **Plan your education to match your career goal.**
   - Try out courses in your area of interest.
   - Start your general education if you need more time to decide on a major.
   - Try an internship or part-time job in your area of interest.

5. **Make a commitment to take action and follow through with your plan.**

6. **Evaluate.**
   - ■ Do you like the courses you are taking?
   - ■ Are you doing well in the courses?
   - ■ Continue research if necessary.

7. **Refine your plan.**
   - ■ Make your plan more specific to aim for a particular career.
   - ■ Select the college major that is best for you.

8. **Change your plan if it is not working.**
   - ■ Go back to the self-assessment step.

The Decision-Making Process

Dependent decisions. Different kinds of decisions are appropriate in different situations. When you make a dependent decision, you depend on someone else to make the decision for you. The dependent decision was probably the first kind of decision that you ever made. When your parents told you what to do as a child, you were making a dependent decision. As an adult, you make a dependent decision when your doctor tells you what medication to take for an illness or when your stockbroker tells you what stock you should purchase. Dependent decisions are easy to make and require little thought. Making a dependent decision saves time and energy.

The dependent decision, however, has some disadvantages. You may not like the outcome of the decision. The medication that your doctor prescribes may have unpleasant side effects. The stock that you purchased may go down in value. When students ask a counselor to recommend a major or a career, they are making a dependent decision. When the decision does not work, they blame the counselor. Even if the dependent decision does have good results, you may become dependent on others to continue making decisions for you. Dependent decisions do work in certain situations, but they do not give you as much control over your own life.

Intuitive decisions. Intuitive decisions are based on intuition or a gut feeling about what is the best course of action. Intuitive decisions can be made quickly and are useful in dealing with emergencies. If I see a car heading on a collision path toward me, I have to swerve quickly to the right or left. I do not have time to ask someone else what to do or think much about the alternatives. Another example of an intuitive decision is in gambling. If I am trying to decide whether to bet a dollar on red or black, I rely on my gut feeling to make a choice. Intuitive decisions may work out or they may not. You could make a mistake and swerve the wrong way as the car approaches or you could lose your money in gambling.

Planful decisions. For important decisions, it is advantageous to use what is called a planful decision. The planful decision is made after carefully weighing the consequences and the pros and cons of the different alternatives. The planful decision-making strategy is particularly useful for such decisions as

- ■ What will be my major?
- ■ What career should I choose?
- ■ Whom should I marry?

The steps in a planful decision-making process.

1. **State the problem.**
   When we become aware of a problem, the first step is to state the problem in the simplest way possible. Just stating the problem will help you to clarify the issues.

2. **Consider your values.**
   What is important to you? What are your hopes and dreams? By keeping your values in mind, you are more likely to make a decision that will make you happy.

3. **What are your talents?**
   What special skills do you have? How can you make a decision that utilizes these skills?

4. **Gather information.**
   What information can you find that would be helpful in solving the problem? Look for ideas. Ask other people. Do some research. Gathering information can give you insight into alternatives or possible solutions to the problem.

5. **Generate alternatives.**
   Based on the information you have gathered, identify some possible solutions to the problem.

6. **Evaluate the pros and cons of each alternative.**
   List the alternatives and think about the pros and cons of each one. In thinking about the pros and cons, consider your values and talents as well as your future goals.

7. **Select the best alternative.**
   Choose the alternatives that is the best match for your values and helps you to achieve your goals.

8. **Take action.**
   You put your decision into practice when you take some action on it. Get started!

Practice this decision-making strategy by completing "The Planful Decision Strategy" exercise.

The Resume and Job Interview

After investing your time in achieving a college education, you will need some additional skills to get a job. Having a good resume and knowing how to successfully interview for a job will help you to obtain your dream job.

Your Resume

A resume is a snapshot of your education and experience. It is generally one page in length. You will need a resume to apply for scholarships, part-time jobs, or find a position after you graduate. Start with a file of information you can use to create your resume. Keep your resume on file in your computer or on a disk so that you can revise it as needed. A resume includes the following:

- Contact information: your name, address, telephone number, and e-mail address
- A brief statement of your career objective
- A summary of your education:
  - Names and locations of schools
  - Dates of attendance
  - Diplomas or degrees received

- A summary of your work and/or volunteer experience
- If you have little directly related work experience, a list of courses you have taken that would help the employer understand your skills for employment

- Special skills, honors, awards, or achievements
- References (people who can recommend you for a job or scholarship)

Your resume is important in establishing a good first impression. There is no one best way to write a resume. Whatever form you choose, write clearly and be brief, neat, and honest. If your resume is too lengthy or difficult to read, it may wind up in the trash can. Adjust your resume to match the job for which you are applying. This is easy to do if you have your resume stored on your computer. Update your resume regularly.

Ask for a letter of reference from your current supervisor at work or someone in a position to recommend you, such as a college professor or community member. Ask the person to address the letter "To Whom It May Concern" so that you can use the letter many times. The person recommending you should comment on your work habits, skills, and personal qualities. If you wait until you graduate to obtain letters of reference, potential recommenders may no longer be there or may not remember who you are. Always ask if you can use a person's name as a reference. When you are applying for a job and references are requested, phone the persons who have agreed to recommend you and let them know to expect a call.

Print your resume so that it looks professional. Use a good-quality white, tan, or gray paper.

You will probably need to post your resume online to apply for some scholarships and job opportunities. Having your resume in written form will make this task easier.

Complete the "Resume Worksheet for Your Ideal Career" after reviewing the sample resume at the end of this chapter.

The Cover Letter

When you respond to job announcements, you will send a cover letter with your resume attached. Address your letter to a specific person at the company or organization and spell the name correctly. You can call the personnel office to obtain this information. The purpose of the cover letter is to state your interest in the job, highlight your qualifications, and get the employer to read your resume and call you for an interview. The cover letter should be brief and to the point. Include the following items:

- State the job you are interested in and how you heard about the opening.
- Briefly state how your education and experience would be assets to the company.
- Ask for an interview and tell the employer how you can be contacted.
- Attach your resume.
- Your cover letter is the first contact you have with the employer. Make it neat and free from errors. Use spell check and grammar check and read it over again.

The Job Interview

Knowing how to be successful in an interview will help you to get the job that you want. Here are some ideas for being prepared and making a good impression.

Learn about the job. Before the interview, it is important to research both the company and the job. This research will help you in two ways: you will know if the job is really the one you want, and you will have information that will help you to succeed at the interview. If you have taken the time to learn about the company before the interview, you will make a good impression and show that you are really interested in the job. Here are some ways that you can find this information:

- Your college or public library may have a profile describing the company and the products it produces. This profile may include the size of the company and the company mission or philosophy.
- Do you know someone who works for the company? Do any of your family, friends, or teachers know someone who works for the company? If so, you can find out valuable information about the company.
- The personnel office often has informational brochures that describe the employer.
- Visit the company website on the Internet.

Understand the criteria used in an interview. The interviewer represents the company and is looking for the best person to fill the job. It is your job to show the interviewer that you will do a good job. Of course you are interested in salary and benefits, but in order to get hired you must first convince the interviewer that you have something to offer the company. Focus on what you can offer the company based on your education and experience and what you have learned about the company. You may be able to obtain information on salary and benefits from the personnel office before the interview.

Interviewers look for candidates who show the enthusiasm and commitment necessary to do a good job. They are interested in hiring someone who can work as part of a team. Think about your education and experience and be prepared to describe your skills and give examples of how you have been successful on the job. Give a realistic and honest description of your work.

Make a good impression. Here are some suggestions for making a good impression:

- Dress appropriately for the interview. Look at how the employees of the company dress and then dress a little better. Of course your attire will vary with the type of job you are seeking. You will dress differently if you are interviewing for a position as manager of a surf shop or an entry-level job in an engineering firm. Wear a conservative, dark colored or neutral suit for most professional positions. Do not wear too much jewelry, and remove excess body piercings (unless you are working at a piercing shop).
- Relax during the interview. You can relax by preparing in advance. Research the company, practice interview questions, and visualize yourself in the interview room feeling confident about the interview.
- When you enter the interview room, smile, introduce yourself, and shake hands with the interviewer. If your hands are cold and clammy, go to the restroom before the interview and run warm water over your hands or rub them together.
- Maintain eye contact with the interviewer and sit up straight. Poor posture or leaning back in your chair could be seen as a lack of confidence or interest in the job.

Anticipate the interview questions. Listen carefully to the interview questions. Ask for clarification of any question you do not understand. Answer the questions concisely and honestly. It helps to anticipate the questions that are likely to be asked and think about your answers in advance. Generally, be prepared to talk about yourself, your goals, and your reasons for applying for the job. Here are some questions that are typically asked in interviews and some suggestions for answering them:

1. *What can you tell us about yourself?*
   Think about the job requirements, and remember that the interviewer is looking for someone who will do a good job for the company. Talk about your education and experience as it relates to the job. You can put in interesting facts about your life and your hobbies, but keep your answers brief. This question is generally an ice breaker that helps the interviewer get a general picture of you and help you relax.

2. *Why do you want this job? Why should I hire you?*
Think about the research you did on this company and several ways that you could benefit the company. A good answer might be, "I have always been good at technical skills and engineering. I am interested in putting these technical skills into practice in your company." A not-so-good answer would be, "I'm interested in making a lot of money and need health insurance."

3. *Why are you leaving your present job?*
Instead of saying that the boss was horrible and the working conditions were intolerable (even if this was the case), think of some positive reasons for leaving such as:

- I am looking for a job that provides challenge and an opportunity for growth.

- I received my degree and am looking for a job where I can use my education.

- I had a part-time job to help me through school. I have graduated and am looking for a career.

- I moved (or the company downsized or went out of business).

Be careful about discussing problems on your previous job. The interviewers might assume that you were the cause of the problems or that you could not get along with other people.

4. *What are your strengths and weaknesses?*
Think about your strengths in relation to the job requirements, and be prepared to talk about them during the interview. When asked about your weaknesses, smile and try to turn them into strengths. For example, if you are an introvert, you might say that you are quiet and like to concentrate on your work, but you make an effort to communicate with others on the job. If you are an extrovert, say that you enjoy talking and working with others, but you are good at time management and get the job done on time. If you are a perfectionist, say that you like to do an excellent job, but you know the importance of meeting deadlines, so you do the best you can in the time available.

5. *Tell us about a difficulty or problem that you solved on the job.*
Think about some problem that you successfully solved on the job and describe how you did it. Focus on what you accomplished. If the problem was one that dealt with other people, do not focus on blaming or complaining. Focus on your desire to work things out and work well with everyone.

6. *Tell us about one of your achievements on the job.*
Give examples of projects you have done on the job that have turned out well and projects that gave you a sense of pride and accomplishment.

7. *What do you like best about your work? What do you like least?*
Think about these questions in advance and use the question about what you like best to highlight your skills for the job. For the question about what you like the least, be honest but express your willingness to do the job that is required.

8. *Are there any questions that you would like to ask?*
Based on your research on the company, think of some specific questions that show your interest in the company. A good question might be, "Tell me about your company's plans for the future." A not-so-good question would be, "How much vacation do I get?"

Write a thank you note. After the interview, write a thank you note and express your interest in the job. It makes a good impression and causes the interviewer to think about you again.

■ Life Is a Dangerous Opportunity

Even though we may do our best in planning our career and education, life does not always turn out as planned. Unexpected events happen, putting our life in crisis. The crisis might be loss of employment, divorce, illness or death of a loved one. How we deal with the crisis events in our lives can have a great impact on our current well-being and the future.

The Chinese word for crisis has two characters: one character represents danger and the other represents opportunity. Every crisis has the danger of loss of something important to us and the resulting emotions of frustration, sorrow, and grief. But every crisis also has an opportunity. Sometimes it is difficult to see the opportunity because we are overwhelmed by the danger. A crisis, however, can provide an impetus for change and growth. A crisis forces us to look inside ourselves to find capabilities that have always been there but we just did not know it. If life goes too smoothly, there is no motivation to change. If we get too comfortable, we stop growing. There is no testing of our capabilities. We stay in the same patterns.

To find the opportunity in a crisis, focus on what is possible in the situation. Every adversity has the seed of a greater benefit or possibility. Expect things to work out well. Expect success. To deal with negative emotions, consider that feelings are not simply a result of what happens to us but of our interpretation of events. If we focus on the danger, we cannot see the possibilities.

As a practical application, consider the example of someone who has just lost a job. John had worked as a construction worker for nearly ten years when he injured his back. His doctor told him that he would no longer be able to do physical labor. John was 30 years old, had two children and large house and truck payments. He was having difficulty finding a job that paid as well as his construction job. He was suffering from many negative emotions resulting from his loss of employment.

John decided that he would have to use his brain rather than his back. As soon as he was up and moving, he started taking some general education courses at the local college. He assessed his skills and identified his strengths. He was a good father and communicated well with his children. He had wanted to go to college but got married early and started to work in construction instead. John decided that he would really enjoy being a marriage and family counselor. It would mean getting a bachelor's and a master's degree, which would take five or more years.

John began to search for a way to accomplish this new goal. He first tackled the financial problems. He investigated vocational rehabilitation, veteran's benefits, financial aid, and scholarships. He sold his house and his truck. His wife took a part-time job. He worked out a careful budget. He began to work toward his new goal with a high degree of motivation and self-satisfaction. He had found a new opportunity.

■ Notes

1. Gail Sheehy, *New Passages* (New York: Random House, 1995), 34.
2. U.S. Department of Health and Human Services, Centers for Disease Control and Prevention, National Center for Health Statistics, 2003. Available at www.cdc.gov/nchc/fastats/lifexpec
3. Jeff Giles, "Generalization X," *Newsweek*, June 6, 1994.
4. Jane Bryant Quinn, "The Luck of the Xers, Comeback Kids: Young People Will Live Better Than They Think," *Newsweek*, 6 June 1994, 66–67.

5. Ellen Neuborne, http://www.businessweek.com, 1999.

6. Claudia Smith Brison, http://www.thestate.com, 14 July 2002.

7. Neil Howe and William Strauss, *Millennials Rising: The Next Great Generation* (New York: Vintage Books, 2000).

8. Neuborne, www.businessweek.com, 1999.

9. U.S. Department of Labor, *Outlook 2000* (Washington, DC: U.S. Government Printing Office 1990).

10. Douglas Braddock, "Occupational Employment Projection to 2008," *Monthly Labor Review*, November 1999.

11. Bill Gates, *Business @ the Speed of Thought: Using a Digital Nervous System* (Warner, 1999). Excerpts available at www.speed-of-thought.com .

12. "Futurework, Trends and Challenges for Work in the 21st Century," an adapted excerpt from a U.S. Department of Labor Report, *Occupational Outlook Quarterly*, Summer 2000.

13. http://www.speed-of-thought.com.

14. Ibid.

15. Ibid.

16. Ibid.

17. Bill Gates, "Microprocessors Upgraded the Way We Live," *USA Today*, 22 June 1999.

18. Ibid.

19. Ibid.

20. Anne Foerst, "A New Breed of 'Replicants' Is Redefining What It Means to Be Human," *Forbes ASAP*, 1999.

21. Joyce Lain Kennedy, *Joyce Lain Kennedy's Career Book* (Chicago, IL: VGM Career Horizons, 1993), 32.

22. Ibid.

23. John Naisbitt, Patricia Aburdeen, and Walter Kiechel III, "How We Will Work in the Year 2000," *Fortune*, 17 May 1993, 41–52.

24. Susan Sears and Virginia Gordon, *Building Your Career* (Englewood Cliffs, NJ: Prentice-Hall, 1998), 100.

25. "Futurework, Trends and Challenges for Work in the 21st Century," an adapted excerpt from a U.S. Department of Labor Report *Occupational Outlook Quarterly*, Summer 2000.

26. "Futurework, Trends and Challenges for Work in the 21st Century," an adapted excerpt from a U.S. Department of Labor Report *Occupational Outlook Quarterly*, Summer 2000.

27. American Management Association, *AMA Survey on Workplace Drug Testing and Drug Abuse Policies*, 1991, 1.

28. National Institute on Drug Abuse and National Institute on Alcoholism and Alcohol Abuse, 1990, *The Economic Cost of Alcohol and Drug Abuse*, 1992, 1–5.

29. NIDA, *Research on Drugs and the Workplace*, NIDA Capsules, 1990, 1.

30. NIDA, *National Household Survey on Drug Abuse: Race/Ethnicity, Socioeconomic Status, and Drug Abuse*, 1991, 19.

31. M. Bernstein and J.J. Mahoney, "Management Perspectives on Alcoholism: The Employer's Stake in Alcoholism Treatment," *Occupational Medicine*, 2, (1989): 223–32.

32. TW Mangione et al., *New Perspectives for Worksite Alcohol Strategies: Results from a Corporate Drinking Study*, JSI Research and Training Institute, 1998, 1.

33. Ibid., 2.

34. USDHHS, SAMHSA, *Drug Use among U.S. Workers: Prevalence and Trends by Occupation and Industry Categories*, 1996, 1.

35. Ibid.

36. Ibid.

37. NIAAA, *Eighth Special Report to U.S. Congress on Alcohol and Health*, 1993, 256.

38. T. J. Grites, "Being 'Undecided' Could Be the Best Decision They Could Make," *School Counselor* 29 (1981): 41–46.

39. Secretary's Commission on Achieving Necessary Skills (SCANS), *Learning a Living: A Blueprint for High Performance* (Washington, DC: U.S. Department of Labor, 1991).
40. Quoted in Rob Gilbert, ed., *Bits and Pieces*, 7 October 1999.

■ Sample Resume for a Recent College Graduate

Sara Student
222 College Avenue; San Diego, CA 92019
(619) 123-4567
saraengineer@aol.com

OBJECTIVE	Electrical Engineer
HIGHLIGHTS	Recent degree in Electrical Engineering Specialized coursework in electromagnetism, photonics and lasers, biomedical imaging devices, and experimental techniques
EDUCATION	B.S., Electrical Engineering, University of California, San Diego, CA, 2003 A.S. with Honors, Cuyamaca College, El Cajon, CA, 2000

KEY RELATED COURSES

- **Circuits and systems:** solving network equations, Laplace transforms, practical robotics development
- **Electromagnetism:** Maxwell's equations, wave guides and transmission, electromagnetic properties of circuits and materials
- **Experimental techniques:** built and programmed a voice processor; studied transducers, computer architecture, and interfacing; applied integrated construction techniques
- **Photonics and lasers:** laser stability and design, holography, optical information processing, pattern recognition, electro-optic modulation, fiber optics
- **Biomedical imaging devices:** microscopy, x-rays, and neural imaging; designed an optical prosthesis
- **Quantum physics:** uncertainty principle, wave equation and spin, particle models, scattering theory and radiation

SKILLS	**Computer Skills:** PSpice, Matlab, Java, DSP, Assembly Language, Unix, Windows, Microsoft Word, Excel, and PowerPoint **Technical Skills:** Microprocessors, circuits, optical components, oscilloscope, function generator, photovoltaics, signal processing, typing, SQUID testing **Personal Skills:** Leadership, good people skills, organized, responsible, creative, motivated, hard-working, good writing skills
EMPLOYMENT	Intern, Quantum Design, La Jolla, CA, Summer 2002 Computer Lab Assistant, UCSD, La Jolla, CA, 2000–2003 Teacher's Aide, Cuyamaca College, El Cajon, CA, 1998–2000 Volunteer, Habitat for Humanity, Tijuana, Mexico, 1996–1999
INTERESTS	Optics, computing, programming, physics, electronic music, sampling, marine biology, and scuba diving
ACHIEVEMENTS	Advanced Placement Scholar Golden State Award, High Honors in Biology Girl Scout Silver Award Dean's List, Phi Theta Kappa Honor Society Provost's Honors List

■ Sample Cover Letter

Sara Student
222 College Avenue
San Diego, CA 92019
(619) 123-4567

June 20, 2003

Mr. John Smith
Director of Human Resources
Future Technology Company
111 Technology Way
La Jolla, CA 92111

Dear Mr. Smith:

At our college job fair last week, I enjoyed speaking with you about some new engineering jobs available at Future Technology Company. As you suggested, I am sending my resume. I am interested in your opening for an electrical engineer. Is there anything else I need to do to apply for this position?

While at UCSD, I gained experience in laboratory projects, writing scientific reports and preparing technical presentations. Some engineering projects that I completed relate to work done at your company:

■ Constructed a programmable robot with motor and sensors

■ Worked with a group of students on the design of a satellite communications system

■ Completed lab projects on innovative fiber-optic fabrication techniques

■ Proposed a design for a prosthetic device to help the visually impaired

For my senior design project, I used my knowledge of digital signal processing and systems integration to design and construct a voice modulator. This project involved applying theory to hardware and understanding information processing as well as the relation of a computer to its controlled devices.

I am excited about the possibility of continuing work in this field and would enjoy the opportunity to discuss my qualifications in more detail. I am available for an interview at your convenience. I look forward to hearing from you.

Sincerely,

Sara Student
Encl.: Resume

Name: _____ Date: _____

■ Resume Worksheet for Your Ideal Career

Use this worksheet to prepare a resume similar to the sample. Assume that you have graduated from college and are applying for your ideal career.

1. What is the specific job title of your ideal job?

2. What are two or three qualifications you possess that would especially qualify you for this job? These qualifications can be listed under Highlights on your resume.

3. List your degree or degrees, major, and dates of completion.

4. List five courses you will take to prepare for your ideal career. For each course, list some key components that would catch the interest of your potential employer. Use a college catalog to complete this section.

5. List the skills you would need in each of these areas.

   Computer skills:

   Technical or other job-related skills:

   Personal skills related to your job objective:

6. List employment that would prepare you for your ideal job. Consider internships or part-time employment.

7. What are your interests?

8. What special achievements or awards do you have?

■ Interview Worksheet

Answer the following questions to prepare for the interview for your ideal job. If you do not know what your ideal job is, pretend that you are interviewing for any good job. You may want to practice these questions with a classmate.

1. What can you tell us about yourself?

2. Why are you leaving your present job?

3. What are your strengths and weaknesses?

4. Tell us about a difficulty or problem that you solved on the job.

5. Tell us about one of your achievements on the job.

6. What do you like best about your work? What do you like least?

7. Are there any questions that you would like to ask?

■ Rate Your Skills for Success in the Workplace

Read each statement relating to skills needed for success in the workplace. Use the following scale to rate your competencies:

5 = Excellent   4 = Very good   3 = Average   2 = Needs improvement   1 = Need to develop

_____ 1. I have good reading skills. I can locate information I need to read and understand and interpret it. I can pick out the main idea and judge the accuracy of the information.

_____ 2. I have good writing skills. I can communicate thoughts, ideas, and information in writing. I know how to edit and revise my writing and use correct spelling, punctuation, and grammar.

_____ 3. I am good at arithmetic. I can perform basic computations using whole numbers and percentages. I can make reasonable estimates without a calculator and can read tables, graphs, and charts.

_____ 4. I am good at mathematics. I can use a variety of mathematical techniques including statistics to predict the occurrence of events.

_____ 5. I am good at speaking. I can organize my ideas and participate in discussions, and group presentations. I speak clearly and am a good listener. I ask questions to obtain feedback when needed.

_____ 6. I am a creative thinker. I can come up with new ideas and unusual connections. I can imagine new possibilities and combine ideas in new ways.

_____ 7. I make good decisions. I can specify goals and constraints, generate alternatives, consider risks, and evaluate alternatives.

_____ 8. I am good at solving problems. I can see when a problem exists, identify the reasons for the problem, and devise a plan of action for solving the problem.

_____ 9. I am good at mental visualization. I can see things in my mind's eye. Examples include building a project from a blueprint or imagining the taste of a recipe from reading it.

_____ 10. I know how to learn. I am aware of my learning style and can use learning strategies to obtain new knowledge.

_____ 11. I am good at reasoning. I can use logic to draw conclusions and apply rules and principles to new situations.

_____ 12. I am a responsible person. I work toward accomplishing goals, set high standards, and pay attention to details. I usually accomplish tasks on time.

_____ 13. I have high self-esteem. I believe in my self-worth and maintain a positive view of myself.

_____ 14. I am sociable, understanding, friendly, adaptable, polite, and relate well to others.

_____ 15. I am good at self-management. I know my background, skills, and abilities and set realistic goals for myself. I monitor my progress toward completing my goals and complete them.

_____ 16. I practice integrity and honesty. I recognize when I am faced with a decision that involves ethics and choose ethical behavior.

_____ 17. I am good at managing my time. I set goals, prioritize, and follow schedules to complete tasks on time.

_____ 18. I manage money well. I know how to use and prepare a budget and keep records, making adjustments when necessary.

_____ 19. I can manage material and resources. I can store and distribute materials, supplies, parts, equipment, space, or products.

_____ 20. I can participate as a member of a team. I can work cooperatively with others and contribute to group efforts.

_____ 21. I can teach others. I can help others to learn needed knowledge and skills.

_____ 22. I can exercise leadership. I know how to communicate, encourage, persuade, and motivate individuals.

_____ 23. I am a good negotiator. I can work toward an agreement and resolve divergent interests.

_____ 24. I can work with men and women from a variety of ethnic, social, or educational backgrounds.

_____ 25. I can acquire and evaluate information. I can identify a need for information and find the information I need.

_____ 26. I can organize and maintain information. I can find written or computerized information.

_____ 27. I can use computers to process information.

_____ 28. I have an understanding of social, organizational, and technological systems and can operate effectively in these systems.

_____ 29. I can monitor and correct performance in a system. I can use trends to figure out how to achieve the best performance.

_____ 30. I can improve the design of a system to improve the quality of products and services.

_____ 31. I can select the appropriate tool, procedure, machine, or computer to do the desired task.

_____ 32. I can use machines and computers to accomplish the desired task.

_____ 33. I can maintain and troubleshoot machines and computers.

_____ **Total**

Score your skills for success in the workplace

165–133	Excellent
132–100	Very good
99–67	Average
66–34	Need improvement
Below 34	Need to develop skills

■ Analyze Your Workplace Skills

If you need to improve or develop skills for success in the workplace, many are covered in this text. Use this text to learn about creative thinking, decision making, problem solving, mental visualization, learning style, reasoning, time management, money management, communications, and self-esteem. Other skills can be improved by taking courses in computer use and general education courses such as English, math, and speech.

From the previous list of workplace skills, make a list of five of your strong points. What do you do well?

From the list of workplace skills, make a list of five areas you need to improve or develop.

Think about how you can improve or develop the skills you listed above. Write your ideas here.

◼ Checklist for a Satisfying Career

Read each statement and think about your current career choice or the options you are considering. Place a checkmark next to the items that are true about your career choice. Before you begin, you may want to review the self-assessment exercises that you have completed in this book and as part of this course.

My career choice (or tentative career choice) is _____.

_____ 1. My career matches the natural preferences of my personality type.

_____ 2. This career matches my interests. I would enjoy doing this type of work.

_____ 3. This career will allow me to live the lifestyle that I want.

_____ 4. This career matches my values (what I think is important).

_____ 5. This career matches my skills, aptitudes, talents, intelligences, and learning style.

_____ 6. I have the skills necessary to be successful in this career or I am willing to obtain these skills.

_____ 7. This career provides the kind of salary I need to live the way I want.

_____ 8. This career has a positive outlook for the future. The career will exist in the future and there will likely be job openings in this area.

_____ 9. I am willing to complete the education or training required to enter this career.

_____ 10. This career choice will help me to accomplish my lifetime goals.

Look at the items you have not checked above. Sometimes a career does not allow us to achieve everything we hope to do in our lives. Hobbies or recreational interests are important to satisfaction with life. Does your career choice give you the opportunity to pursue your hobbies and interests? Does it give you time for relaxation and recreation? Will you have time to spend with the people who are important in your life? Write your thoughts here.

Name: _____ Date: _____

■ Educational Planning Form (One Semester or Quarter)

Student ID or SSN _____

Class Section	Course Number	Course Title	Units	Days	Times

Weekly Class Grid

Time	Mon.	Tues.	Wed.	Thurs.	Fri.	Sat.

Note: Include general education courses, preparation for your major, and English and math classes if needed. Check to make sure you have met the course prerequisities.

Counselor signature _____ Date _____

Name: _____ Date: _____

■ Educational Planning Form (Semester System)

Student ID or SSN _____

Fall	Spring	Summer
Total units	Total units	Total units
Fall	**Spring**	**Summer**
Total units	Total units	Total units
Fall	**Spring**	**Summer**
Total units	Total units	Total units
Fall	**Spring**	**Summer**
Total units	Total units	Total units

Total units _____ Date of graduation _____

Counselor signature _____

Comments _____

Name: _____ Date: _____

◼ Educational Planning Form (Quarter System)

Student ID or SSN _____

Fall	Winter	Spring	Summer
Total units	Total units	Total units	Total units
Fall	**Winter**	**Spring**	**Summer**
Total units	Total units	Total units	Total units
Fall	**Winter**	**Spring**	**Summer**
Total units	Total units	Total units	Total units
Fall	**Winter**	**Spring**	**Summer**
Total units	Total units	Total units	Total units

Total units _____ Date of graduation _____

Counselor signature _____

Comments _____

The Planful Decision Strategy

Read the following scenario describing a college student in a problem situation. Then, answer the questions that follow to practice the planful decision strategy. You may want to do this as a group activity with other students in the class.

Rhonda is an 18-year-old student who is trying to decide on her major. She was a good student in high school, earning a 3.4 grade point average. Her best subjects were English and American history. She struggled with math and science but still earned good grades in these subjects. While in high school she enjoyed being on the debate team and organizing the African American Club. This club was active in writing letters to the editor and became involved in supporting a local candidate for city council.

Rhonda is considering majoring in political science and has dreams of eventually going to law school. Rhonda likes being politically involved and advocating for different social causes. The highlight of her life in high school was when she organized students to speak to the city council about installing a traffic light in front of the school after a student was killed trying to cross the street. The light was installed during her senior year.

Rhonda's family has always been supportive, and she values her family life and the close relationships in the family. She comes from a middle-income family that is struggling to pay for her college education. Getting a bachelor's degree in political science and going to law school would take seven years and be very expensive. There is no law school in town, so Rhonda would have to move away from home to attend school.

Rhonda's parents have suggested that she consider becoming a nurse and attending the local nursing college. Rhonda could finish a bachelor's degree in nursing in four years and could begin working part-time as a nurse's aide in a short time. A cousin in the family became a nurse and found a job easily and is now earning a good income. The cousin arranged for Rhonda to volunteer this summer at the hospital where she works. Rhonda enjoys helping people at the hospital. Rhonda is trying to decide on her major. What should she do?

1. State the problem.

2. Describe Rhonda's values, hopes, and dreams.

3. What special interests, talents, or aptitudes does she have?

4. What further information would be helpful to Rhonda in making her decision?

5. What are the alternatives and the pros and cons of each?

Alternative 1	
Pros:	Cons:
Alternative 2	
Pros:	Cons:
Alternative 3 (be creative!)	
Pros:	Cons:

6. Only Rhonda can choose what is best for her. If you were Rhonda, what would you do and why? Use a separate piece of paper, if necessary, to write your answer.

Section 6

Looking Toward
the Future

CHAPTER 13
In Hot Pursuit of Happiness

Happiness is a butterfly, which, when pursued, is always just beyond your grasp, but which, if you will sit down quietly, may alight upon you.

—Nathaniel Hawthorne

The Constitution only gives people the right to pursue happiness. You have to catch it yourself.

—Ben Franklin

Pause, take a deep breath, and circle the number corresponding to your feelings about the following question: *How satisfied are you with your life as a whole these days?*

| / | 0 | / | 1 | / | 2 | / | 3 | / | 4 | / | 5 | / | 6 | / | 7 | / | 8 | / | 9 | / | 10 | / |

Completely   Neutral   Completely
Dissatisfied   Satisfied

What did you put? Do you think you are about average in life satisfaction? Are you about the same as your friends? What about other college students? What about people world-wide? Do you think pre-college adolescents would give the same ratings?

This question has actually been asked of individuals many times in a multitude of situations across diverse backgrounds. Two investigators of happiness, David Myers and Ed Diener (1996), combined data from 916 surveys of 1.1 million people in 45 nations representing most of the world. They found the *average* individual's rating of satisfaction was *6.75*. We found virtually the same scores in our research involving college students (Starks, Astor-Stetson, Beck, Jara, & Zarecky, 1998), high school students (Beck & Scott, 1996), and middle school students (Beck, Jara, Astor-Stetson, Zarecky, & Starks, 1998; Beck, Zarecky, Astor-Stetson, Jara, & Starks, 1998).

Surprised? It seems that most people think that others are less happy than they really are. The nightly news shows many unhappy people in horrible circumstances. Is that an accurate reflection of society? If we can believe what people say, it appears that it is not. From published reports (e.g., Myers, 2000), more than 90% of individuals indicate that they are somewhat or very happy. So what is responsible for all this happiness? What are the characteristics and situations that lead to happy lives? Before continuing, complete the following writing assignment on what it takes to be really happy.

◼ Writing Activity 1

Key questions to ask yourself about how to be really happy. Answer each question about how you *personally* feel.

What are you doing when *"time flies"*?

_____

_____

What would you do *if money were no object*? Would you do this for a *short time* or *permanently*? Why?

_____

_____

How would you feel in 5 years if you were doing *exactly* the same things you are doing right now? What is *the one thing* you would most like to be different 5 years from now?

_____

_____

What kind of people bring out "the best" in you—make you feel good about the situation *and yourself*?

_____

_____

Right now *and* on a day-to-day basis, how can you get more pleasant activities and more stimulating people into your life? What would be your *first* step toward this change?

_____

_____

For you, what would characterize a depressed, unfulfilling life? A fulfilling, exciting life?

_____

_____

What would be a *first* step to make your life more fulfilling and exciting *right now*?

_____

_____

What is *really* possible for you to become? What are *your* real expectations for yourself? How high a price are you willing to pay for what you want to become? What are you *not* willing to "pay" or give up?

_____

_____

■ Core Dimensions of Happiness

Any insights? What does it take to be truly happy and satisfied with one's life? There has been a recent movement toward the scientific understanding of life satisfaction and happiness (also known as ***subjective well-being***). Some of the findings from this research may surprise you. When we ask students what they think brings happiness, they often respond, *"Health and Wealth!"* Sounds reasonable, but is this accurate? Scientific results suggest that the answer is *"NO!"* For example, when we reported at the first of the chapter that most people around the world were happy (Myers & Diener, 1996), this actually included many who were poor, unemployed, elderly, or disabled. For example, Diener and Diener (1996) found that people with spinal cord injuries were only slightly less satisfied with life than others and that over 90% of individuals with spinal cord injuries said they were happy to be alive.

Maybe *money* is the key to happiness. Wouldn't it be great to win that big lottery or inherit a fortune so that life would be easy and stress-free? Wealthy people must be happier than the average person—what do they have to worry about? Interestingly, a study of the richest people in America (Diener, Sandvik, Seidlitz, & Diener, 1993) showed that they are only slightly happier than the average person. In addition, Myers (2000) reports that today's college-aged individuals are much wealthier than their grandparents. Has this resulted in increased levels of happiness? As a matter of fact, it has not. If anything, today's college students have a slightly *decreased* level of happiness and a much greater risk of depression and other psychological problems. *Stunning!* We are not saying that it is great to be poor. Extreme poverty is associated with lower levels of happiness and with more life difficulties. However, the research literature suggests that once your basic needs are met, money has very little correlation with happiness.

So, what *is* the key? Many people from various disciplines have weighed in on this question. In fact, entire books have been written on happiness. We don't want to force entire books on you; we think that might be associated with unhappiness! However, we do want to give you some things to think about and inspire you to do some research on your own. A nice framework on happiness has been provided by the psychologist Carol D. Ryff (1995). From reading the research literature, she has identified *six core dimensions of subjective well-being*. These are *self-acceptance, positive relations with other people, autonomy, environmental mastery, purpose in life*, and *personal growth*. Let's explore each area in greater detail.

Self-Acceptance

In terms of happiness, accepting yourself for who you are is very important. This is easier said than done. This does not mean that you don't continue to strive for additional learning or self-improvement; rather you need to realize you are a worthy person just because you are a human being. And as a human being, you realize that you are continually in the process of realizing your potential. *Self-acceptance refers to owning all your qualities, good and bad.* You are aware of negative aspects of yourself and don't have to vehemently deny them to others. You are okay with being less than perfect. You are okay with past experiences. The next **Activity** is related to the idea of "fooling yourself." See if you can find times in the past when you have done this and assess whether you are comfortable with your poor judgment.

Writing Activity 2. Fooling Yourself

Write about an experience when you felt one way at one time, but later realized it wasn't that way at all. Were there people you met or felt one way about, but you later realized your feelings had changed or been hidden? Did a situation itself seem good or bad, but later you realized it was the opposite? Did you think you could or couldn't do something, but then you found out differently when you tried?

Now read some actual reports of such incidents from students in our courses.

Response number one. "My senior year in high school, I met my first boyfriend. He was my complete opposite. He did not go to high school anymore because he was kicked out for hitting a teacher. He also drank and dealt drugs, which I had never even been related to. He was sweet to me and eventually said the three magical words, I love you. I was hooked for some reason. We thought we would be together forever, and I thought I could change his ways. I was way off on that one. I stuck by him for too long. It was so hard for me to break up with him because I thought I loved him and I thought I could change him. However, it was me in the end that was hurt the most. I fell head over heels for him. When we broke up, I swore I would never love anyone ever again. I would never let myself get hurt like that again. After my first semester at college, I was completely convinced that all men were jerks. I cannot state that more emphatically. I hated men in a relationship. I turned down a few guys who could have been good guys, but I would not even give them the chance. I was bitter. Even though my father is a wonderful man, I still found flaws that supported my feelings toward men. I swore I would make my own money and live the single life. I was never interested in children, especially having my own. So my life was set. I was going to work and make lots of money. I would be an aunt to my sister's children once she settled down. Not until my second semester junior year did I allow myself to have another boyfriend. He was a good friend of mine. We started seeing each other casually. I was enjoying myself. I had dates to my date parties and hayrides. I still did not want to let myself get too close to him. It was like that for a while. We both just liked hanging out with each other. Before I realized it, I actually had feelings for him. I was angry with myself for caring too much. Before long, I realized this guy is a good guy. What can I say but I fell in love with him. He's my best friend and my confidant. I would like to have his children one day. I know he would be a great father. Whether we take our relationship to the next stage of getting engaged or not, I still do not worry about it. I realized that I cannot rely on wishes. I take this relationship day by day. Whether he's 'the one' or not, I now know there are good guys out there. Men are not all bad. I am glad I realized this and that I was wrong."

Response number two. "Well, being a person who is rarely wrong (ha, ha), it is not often that I fool myself into thinking otherwise. Seriously, I tend to look at the world in a fairly realistic manner. Everyday, usual occurrences I tend to deal with very well. In female/male relationships, on the other hand, I have often had a problem seeing what is right in front of me. The incidence that is freshest in my mind is the situation that brought about my marriage. My spouse previously was a co-worker of mine. I had recently gotten out of a horrible relationship. (I use the word 'horrible' because certain expletives are inappropriate to use in a paper that is to be handed in to a professor. I will simply say I was lucky to get away with my life.) This person I worked with was the most supportive, most wonderful, most anything I have ever known. He became my best friend, and we spent much time together. He proposed that we take our relationship to another level. I felt slightly uncomfortable about that, so much so that I cut off ties with this person. He was in love with me. I rationalized the ideas I had of what I wanted, who he was, and what I was to do. I am very good at rationalizing. I told myself that this individual has all of the qualities of the individual you want to marry—he is honorable, trustworthy, loving, romantic . . . I could go on and on. I do not want you to puke or anything, so I will stop now. Coming to this realization, I cut all ties with him for a period of five months! Then, one day it struck me. I love this person. I want to be with him. I will be with him. After all those months of denying how I felt and what I wanted, I realized, virtually in seconds, what I was going to do. It was like this incredible weight was lifted off of my shoulders. I knew what I needed to do. I did it. I am now married to the most wonderful person in the world."

Response number three. "The most recent 'fooling myself' episode I had was the 'unwanted, but needed' break up with my boyfriend. Have you ever had a friend that you knew deserved better, but was just hanging on to a relationship for security's sake? Well, that friend was me. Deep down inside I knew that I deserved better, but was not doing anything about it. I kept telling myself and everyone else, 'No, it will get better; he really does love me.' All the signs of a terrible relationship were right in my face: the mistrust (I didn't trust him), the extreme selfishness on his part, and the emotional abuse. Then finally one day my 'knowing' self came into contact with my 'reality' self and all things I knew in my head filled my heart too. It was like a barrier from my head to my heart was finally broken. I finally admitted to myself that he didn't really care because if he did, he would not be treating me this way and I would not always feel so awful about the relationship. And finally I ended it, and it actually felt good. Sometimes reality does feel good."

So how about it? Were you able to identify situations in which you "fooled yourself?" Looking back on it, are you able to accept your errors in judgment? Could you *accept* the errors made by the students in the vignettes? Part of happiness is giving up the irrational need to be perfect. We all are fallible human beings who make many errors and grow personally from hard life experiences. *Come join the rest of us morons!*

Positive relations with others

> *A friend is one who knows us, but loves us anyway.*
>
> —Fr. Jerome Cummings

The importance of close friends is an idea that goes back through history. In recent scientific research, few variables have proved as powerful in alleviating the effects of stressful events and aiding psychological well-being as has social support from others. All three authors have performed numerous research studies in which social support was investigated to see if it served as a buffer for negative life events. *The variable has been important every single time!* One of the authors had an amusing interaction with a psychologist at a national convention. The psychologist said she thought she had run the only study in history in which social support was found unimportant. *It is just that powerful!*

Happy, healthy people cultivate friendships. In these interactions they can experience trust, respect, admiration, affection, and regard. The noted psychologist Irv Yalom (1985) stated that friends help us experience *universality*—the idea that we are all experiencing the same issues in life. Myers (2000) provided substantial experimental support for the idea that having friends is one of the biggest predictors of individual well-being. If you don't believe us, take this **Quiz**, currently circulating on the Internet, on the importance of friends.

■ Friendship Quiz

This isn't like other quizzes, so don't bother getting a pen and paper . . . just read:

- ■ Name the five wealthiest people in the world.
- ■ Name the last five Heisman trophy winners.
- ■ Name the last five winners of the Miss America contest.
- ■ Name ten people who have won the Nobel or Pulitzer prize.
- ■ Name the last half dozen Academy Award winners for Best Actor and Actress.
- ■ Name the last decade's worth of World Series Winners.

How did you do? The point is, none of us remembers the headliners of yesterday. These are no second-rate achievers. They're the best in their fields. But the applause dies. Awards tarnish. Achievements are forgotten. Accolades and certificates are buried with their owners. Now, here are some more questions. See how you do on them:

- ■ List a few teachers who aided your journey through school.
- ■ Name three friends who have helped you through a difficult time.
- ■ Name five people who have taught you something worthwhile.
- ■ Think of a few people who have made you feel appreciated and special.
- ■ Think of five people you enjoy spending time with.
- ■ Name a half dozen "heroes" whose stories have inspired you.

Easier?

The lesson? The people who make a difference in our lives aren't the ones with the most credentials, the most money, or the most awards. They are our friends and others who care.

Intimate Relationships with Others

Our students often ask us the secrets about romantic, intimate relationships with others. How do you find, maintain, and manage that relationship with a special someone? This certainly has a correlation with happiness, doesn't it? Of course, it does! In fact, most of the art, music, and literature of our civilization has been devoted to this topic. So, we don't hold any delusions that we are going to give you the ultimate answers in a couple of pages. We thought it might be helpful to give you some advice from people with four years of experience in college relationships—our senior teaching assistants. Here is advice from our TA's on relationships.

■ Senior TA's Dish the Dirt on Relationships

Initiating a Relationship

- Go to activities on and off campus.
- Talk to other people in your classes.
- Get to know other people on your floor in your dorm.
- Practice: "Don't I know you from General Psychology?"
- Don't try too hard and be wary of bars.
- Share commonalities and join clubs (e.g., major, interests).
- Use basic flirting and flattery.
- Stay alert for opportunities (e.g., laundry, grocery store, gym, Wal-Mart).
- Introduce yourself to as many people as possible (particularly if you are shy!).

Maintaining a Relationship

- Don't spend all of your time together!
- Keep your own interests and hobbies.
- Do something other than having sex.
- Plan fun outings (e.g., skiing, picnics, concerts, hikes).
- Be realistic in your expectations, say what you mean, and don't be dramatic.
- Keep communicating so you can deal with inevitable conflicts.
- Be unpredictable (but not too much so); appreciate the other person (and say so!).
- Cook dinner together; study together.
- Maintain a sense of humor about things.
- Sometimes you need to walk away when you are angry.
- Try to see problems from the other person's point of view.

Ending a Relationship

- Don't keep calling the other person.
- Be honest (every TA said this!).
- Tell them immediately and give an adequate explanation for why.

The Web site for the Student Counseling and Resource Center at the University of Chicago (cited at the end of this chapter) has many more ideas for each of these situations.

■ Autonomy

> ***Thoughts from the Internet***—*Happy people are usually happy throughout life. As discussed earlier, neither age nor debilitating illness nor disability predicts degree of happiness over time. Here is a message circulating on the Internet that illustrates the attitude of a happy person.*
>
> *"The 92-year-old well-poised and proud woman, who, despite her being legally blind, is dressed each morning by 8:00 with her hair fashionably coifed and makeup perfectly applied, moved to a nursing home today. Her husband of 70 years recently passed away, making the move necessary. After many hours of waiting patiently in the lobby, she smiled sweetly when told her room was ready. As she maneuvered her walker to the elevator, the nurse provided a visual description of her tiny room, including the eyelet sheets that had been hung on her window.*
>
> *"I love it," she stated with the enthusiasm of an 8-year-old having just been presented with a new puppy.*
>
> *"Mrs. Jones, you haven't seen the room—just wait."*
>
> *"That doesn't have anything to do with it," she replied. "Happiness is something you decide on ahead of time. Whether I like my room or not doesn't depend on how the furniture is arranged. It's how I arrange my mind. I already decided to love it. It's a decision I make every morning when I wake up. I have a choice; I can spend the day in bed recounting the difficulty I have with the parts of my body that no longer work or get out of bed and be thankful for the ones that do. Each day is a gift, and as long as my eyes open, I'll focus on the new day and all the happy memories I've stored away—just for this time in my life. Old age is like a bank account—you withdraw from what you've put in."*

Students often say to us, "Isn't happiness just about being lucky enough to have good things happening to you?" In other words, is it more the good fortune of avoiding environmental disasters? Well, interestingly enough, there is little evidence to suggest that positive life events are a major force related to depression. We mentioned earlier the fact that most people who suffered debilitating injuries or were disabled reported that they were happy. Although people's happiness or unhappiness is disrupted by positive and negative life events (e.g., marriage, widowhood), both formerly happy and unhappy people rebound toward their prior level of happiness (e.g., Lucas, Clark, Georgellis, & Diener, 2003; Suh, Diener, & Fujita, 1996).

If good fortune isn't the answer, what is? Well, it seems that independently choosing one's activities and goals is partly the answer. ***Happy people are self-directed and autonomous.*** They are not easily swayed by what is politically correct at the time or by current trends. While not exactly arrogant, they do have a good sense of their values and are not easily influenced to follow the opinions of the group. Once they act, they take ownership for their behavior. Consider the following guidelines and *assess how autonomous you are in **your** decision-making.*

■ I Am Responsible for the Choices in My Life

- Your past is PAST—don't moan about what "might have been." You are who you are *right now*, including the coping skills developed through the experiences.
- Develop a complex self-concept—don't be a "one-trick pony." Value yourself for *all* your skills and characteristics—you won't be as disappointed when you aren't doing well in one area because you can still see how well you are progressing in another! Such a complex self-concept helps you cope better with stressful events, *and* you will be less likely to get bored since you have many interests and abilities.
- Avoid excusing, blaming, or punishing yourself—use positive self-talk instead.
- But remember to be *realistic* about why an event occurred—don't blame another person or the situation if YOU were responsible—this includes the *mood* you are in (e.g., "you make me angry" is really "I get angry when you . . .").
- Respect yourself and your opinions—*but* remain open-minded to new information from all sources. Self-confidence reduces a tendency to be defensive!
- *Be enthusiastic!*—not only will you find you are more motivated in *any* situation— you will also be *more attractive* to other people!
- Know your strengths, abilities, possibilities, and preferences *before* you enter a new situation—and stay focused on them when you become frustrated (and you will!).
- Frustration is a sign of "work in progress" and that you may have overestimated your skill-level or the difficulty of the task. You may become frustrated because you went into the task unmotivated or pessimistic. If so, use positive self-talk to get yourself back on task! Think of a situation in which you worked hard for extended periods of time—a sport? a hobby?—and you will realize the power of motivation!
- Remember the self-fulfilling prophecy—if you believe you can, you will work harder to make it happen. If you believe you can't, your motivation will be compromised.
- It is also important to admit your weaknesses, unpracticed and unlearned skills, and nonmotivating situations because they will guide you in your life choices, show you what still needs to be worked on in your development, and alert you about situations during which you need to be more patient with yourself and ask for help!
- Regardless of circumstances, it is the way you look at a situation that affects how hard you try and what you say to yourself about both your effort and its outcomes.
- Remember that your thoughts and emotions are your most powerful assets—and they are the only things in a situation that you can always control!

Environmental mastery

Happy people do have some skills in coping with environmental difficulties. Sometimes, however, it is not so much that they are so accomplished in problem-solving, but rather they set the situation so that they are more likely to succeed. We are amused at the students who come to us to discuss their plans to make changes in their lives. They confidently assert that they are going to quit smoking, lose weight, get along better with their parents, and study more *ALL AT THE SAME TIME!* And they tend to want to see results by the end of the week! This is just a recipe for failure (think: New Year's Resolution!). Happy people are much better at choosing *realistic* goals and actually accomplishing them. *This is what makes them happy!* One of the best boosters to self-esteem is actually accomplishing something. It doesn't help much that people try to comfort you by telling you what a good person you are—it helps to be able to *do* something! **Happy people are much better at structuring the situation to ensure success.**

Along with showing environmental mastery, **happy people are able to manipulate their internal voices to turn obstacles into opportunities.** That is, they are able to appraise the situation as a *challenge* rather than another chance for failure. Below, we have examples of the types of self-talk that differentiate happy people from the rest.

■ Self-Talk: It *Will* Affect Your Motivation

HELPLESSNESS	POWER
I can't (or shouldn't).	I won't.
I should (or must) . . .	I could, but don't have to . . .
It's not my fault.	I'm responsible for . . .
It's a problem.	It's hard, but it's an opportunity.
Why can't I just be satisfied? It's safer to stick with my old habits and roles.	I'm curious—I want to learn and grow.
Life is a struggle and often out of my control.	Life is an adventure—a chance to explore, to try out new roles.
I hope (or wish) it would happen.	I will work toward . . .
If only *things* had gone differently . . .	Next time *I* will . . .
Oh, what can I do?	I can handle it—I can stand it.
It's terrible! I can't stand it!	I have a chance to learn.
Oh, poor me!	It's OK to be disappointed.

Purpose in life

Happiness . . . proceeds from the achievement of one's values.

—*Ayn Rand*

A strong indicator of happiness is whether one has a purpose in life—a sense of meaning about the past, present, and future. Myers (2000) presented some interesting data from 6.5 million U.S. college students on this variable. Since 1965, the percentage of college students reporting that it is "very important" or "essential" to "develop a meaningful philosophy of life" has dropped from over 80% to roughly 40%. At the same time, the percentage of college students reporting that it is "very important" or "essential" to "be very well off financially" has risen from about 40% in 1965 to 74% in 1998. *For happiness, this is disastrous.* We discussed earlier that money is very minimally associated with happiness—and remember that putting financial well-being ahead of friends/family, helping the world, and self-knowledge is related to maladjustment (Kasser & Ryan, 1993). However, our culture's rampant focus on material goods has convinced many young people that this must be the path to well-being. In addition, what seems to have been sacrificed is the idea of the importance of developing a *sense of purpose* in one's life. Research suggests that they may pay a high price for these misaligned priorities.

Myers (2000) found **a number of correlations of well-being with active religiosity.** Active religiosity is not merely identifying with a religion; rather, it is frequently participating in it. Actively religious people are less likely to experience common mental health problems. They tend to be physically healthier and live longer. They report *higher levels of happiness.* Finally, they tend to bounce back better after suffering negative life events, such as, unemployment, divorce, serious illness, or loss of a loved one. While the mechanism for this resilience is not exactly clear, we certainly could speculate that actively religious people receive a high degree of social support and have a stronger sense of purpose in life.

How About You? *Close your eyes for a minute and think about what your purpose in life is. What are your top two or three goals? Then, look at your daily activities for the past week. Are they consistent with these life goals? Keeping your daily rituals in line with your overall purpose can go a long way toward increasing your happiness!*

Personal growth

Freedom is what you do with what's been done to you.

—Jean-Paul Sartre

Finally, happy people see themselves as continually growing and expanding. As mentioned earlier, they have a sense of self-acceptance about their present and past. But they also have an orientation toward the future. **Happy people interpret life's experiences as an opportunity for learning and personal growth.** They also take active steps toward ensuring that their lives, values, and relationships are not stagnant. The following are some suggestions for how to facilitate personal growth in your own life, along with some common fears that inhibit this growth. While reading these items, honestly assess your capacities and tendencies in each area. Then, we encourage you to set some realistic goals for improvement.

■ You Are a Work in Progress: Suggestions for Getting There!

Adventure isn't hanging on a rope off the side of a mountain. Adventure is an attitude that we must apply to the day-to-day obstacles of life: facing new challenges, seizing new opportunities, testing our resources against the unknown, and, in the process, discovering our own unique potential.

—John Amatt, Organizer of/participant in Canada's first successful expedition up Mt. Everest

When making *any* change (a new relationship, a new major or job, a lifestyle change), you will face self-doubts and remarks from even those with your "best interest" in mind. Here are some common reactions to expect. After these, we offer ideas to help you *go for it.*

External factors that may be hindering your choices for or attempts to change:

- family obligations, real or imagined
- stereotyping others hold about you (e.g., age, gender, ethnicity, personality)
- financial obligations or limitations
- regional limitations (partly due to unwillingness to leave family or friends)

Internal factors that may be limiting your possibilities for change:

- ■ lack of skills, education, or credentials (e.g., degrees, licenses)
- ■ lack of willingness to ask for or accept help
- ■ lack of knowledge of how to work with others (interpersonal skills)
- ■ limiting your choices due to your own stereotypes of yourself (may include false beliefs about what a choice requires—how hard it will be, what skills are required)
- ■ beliefs that your personality, motivation, temperament, or past limit your choices
- ■ lack of knowledge of available choices (e.g., what a major or career really is, how to find out about options or careers, where to get information, how to get started)

Some common fears that may be "roadblocks" for you:

- ■ fear of change
- ■ fear of failure
- ■ fear of making a "wrong" choice
- ■ fear of not having enough confidence, motivation, or skill to pursue a choice
- ■ fear of adverse impact on present relationships (e.g., loss due to move, time pressures, "growing apart")
- ■ fear of rejection, disapproval, or ridicule
- ■ fear that it really won't make life better—or that things aren't better anywhere else
- ■ fear of making a fool of yourself or of embarrassment while learning a new path
- ■ fear of losing security—of abandoning a "safe," familiar behavior, situation, or person

Ideas for coping with real or imagined fears or limitations:

- ■ *Take one step at a time* (break large steps into smaller ones *or* ask for help!).
- ■ Minimize risk by taking a "practice tour" of a choice you *might* make. Sample rather than making a complete change—*reality test* rather than burning that bridge!
- ■ Sometimes you think you need change when you're just bored! Examine your current life. Would a small change do the trick? Could an acquaintance become a friend? Could a friend become a romantic interest? Could your major or job be enhanced or redirected?
- ■ Realize that feeling shaky and uncertain about change is *normal*—fear occurs *naturally* when making a choice and when experiencing change:
  - ■ Fear is what any *sensible* person feels—you *don't* know what will happen, if you can *handle* it, if the *costs* will be too large. Talk back to negative, derogatory self-talk.
  - ■ Being nervous is a sign you are *aroused*—not that you are "chicken." It is a *survival state*, energizing your body—our ancestors wouldn't have lived long enough to reproduce if they hadn't had this feeling in their more physically dangerous world!
  - ■ Don't try to *suppress* your arousal—these attempts take too much effort (one reason why the shakes and headaches often occur *after* an emergency passes).
  - ■ If you get overaroused facing change (e.g., nausea, hyperventilation, weakness), use a relaxation technique to help you "tone down" the arousal.
- ■ For major or long-term changes, self-help groups can be very useful. You can also look on the internet, and some self-help books can help with ideas and techniques.

- If you can, talk to someone who has already made the change you are planning. Get advice and ask about pitfalls so you can anticipate and prepare for them. If the change is a skill, watch a model perform the behavior. Self-help groups (or books) may also be helpful.

- Role models can provide tips on how to proceed, but *do not* measure your current state against the success they have already reached or think it was "easy" for them!

- *Visualize* yourself coping successfully with the next step of your "project." Picturing yourself actually *doing* what you have chosen to do will help you "practice" how to proceed *and* increase motivation. Try rehearsing in front of a mirror or with a friend too.

- Use positive self-talk—"psych" yourself up, be optimistic. Remember, you have control over *how you react mentally*, even if you can't control the situation! Look for the good side of situations—but don't deny *real* costs and pitfalls.

- Avoid self-limiting talk (. . . too old . . . too young . . . too shy . . . too unlovable . . . too afraid . . . too inexperienced). Creative, enthusiastic people change and grow throughout life.

- Realize you have *many* options and choices available—even if things initially look bleak or too difficult. Expect *gradual* change toward a goal—and occasional road blocks. Keep your eye on your goal during difficulties and times of frustration.

- Redefine change as an *evolving lifestyle*—some of the changes will be unpleasant but will *lead to* pleasant goals you are working toward. Don't always choose the "easy" way. Try to see the harmony and coherence of your life. Don't feel "at the mercy of" life.

- Allow time for change to become "natural." Any new behavior or situation feels strange at first, even if you don't have to learn how to do it—it will disrupt the pattern of your day, whether the change is adding or subtracting something from your life. Be patient and the change will become a habit—as natural as the old one you chose to leave behind.

- Realize that *persistence* is more useful than *mere confidence* when making changes! Change attempts are often abandoned because of frustration and lack of a skill. Think of something that was very hard for you to learn to do, *but* that you worked on until you "got it right." Remind yourself of that experience when your spirit lags.

- Realize that life is sometimes boring. And stimulation and excitement are stressful—but welcomed—changes *at times*. Balancing between too much security and too much adventure will make you happier than striving for just one of these all the time!

- Don't undertake changes you do not "own." Doing something just because others want you to or because you won't make the effort to explore other options will end either in failure due to lack of motivation or unhappiness because of not following a path you love.

- A further warning—thinking you can accomplish *anything* by working hard enough is a myth! Some people won't like you no matter how nice you are, some won't love you even if you dedicate your life to them, and some careers and behaviors just don't fit you due to physical, mental, emotional, or temperament limitations! There is no *one, perfect* friend, lover, career, or job for you—there are *many* that can lead to your being a happy, contented person! *Make choices with your dreams, abilities,* **and** *limitations in mind!*

- When making changes, be honest about the costs *and* rewards for a change. Giving up smoking is a very costly change—but the rewards easily outweigh the costs! However, "winning" some friendships, lovers, grades, or jobs may tempt you to endure costs far beyond the rewards you will reap. *Don't compromise your values and self-worth!*

- Rewards from others are *least likely* early in a lifestyle change or new activity.
    - Even if the change was their idea or had their blessing, they will worry that a change will threaten their place and power in your life! Their fears may lead them to punish, or attempt to sabotage, your efforts. Especially beware if the person has been possessive or overprotective of you in the past.
    - Recognize that external sources of recognition, security, and reward are fickle—learn to reinforce yourself for making the changes you know are best for you.
    - Forming or joining a support group of others currently changing will give you social support when motivation lags—and you can celebrate their small victories too!
    - Cultivate friends, a mentor, or a counselor to cheer progress and soften setbacks.
- In times of stress and negative events, promise yourself that you will work *at least one* good experience or reward into each day—you deserve a reward for coping!
- Beware of **entrapment**, the tendency to think you must continue toward a selected goal *just because you have invested so much and worked so hard to get this far.* You have a right to change your mind—the goal may turn out to be unsuitable or too costly, you may have changed in ways that make the goal less appealing, or you may have found a more attractive or currently available goal. Keep in mind that the more you have *invested* in the process, the stronger will be the feeling that you *must* continue—that it *must* be a "good" project for you to have invested so much effort. Needs and interests change.
- Confronting a challenge or working for change will increase your self-worth and the skills you will need to cope with future stressors. This is true *regardless* of whether you meet your original or an altered goal—or stop short of what you originally defined as "success." The *process* can be more important than the product! You learn tolerance for change and more about your life goals, current skill levels, *and* limitations. This insight will help you make *better* choices and *better* plans for accomplishing them in the future.

Once you make a decision, the universe conspires to make it happen.

—*Ralph Waldo Emerson*

■ An Ending That Is Really a Beginning

The doors we open and close each day decide the lives we live.

—*Flora Whittemore*

We've given you a lot of information about ways to live your life to *maximize* your chances for happiness and *minimize* choices that won't be particularly fulfilling. *It is your job to take this information and make modifications in your daily rituals that will let you reach your goals **and** win that pursuit of happiness.* We thought we would finish this chapter by reminding you of a song from that happiness sage, Bobby McFerrin. Surely you remember the words and tune from his classic song, "Don't Worry, Be Happy!" We hope it runs happily through your head all day long!

References

Kasser, T., & Ryan, R. M. (1993). A dark side of the American dream: Correlates of financial success as a central life aspiration. *Journal of Personality and Social Psychology, 65,* 410–422.

Diener, E., & Diener, C. (1996). Most people are happy. *Psychological Science, 7,* 181–185.

Diener, E., Sandvik, E., Seidlitz, L., & Diener, M. (1993). The relationship between income and subjective well-being: Relative or absolute? *Social Indicators Research, 28,* 195–223.

Myers, D. G. (2000). The funds, friends, and faith of happy people. *American Psychologist, 55,* 56–67.

Myers, D. G., & Diener, E. (1996, May). The pursuit of happiness. *Scientific American, 274,* 54–56.

Ryff, C. D. (1995). Psychological well-being in adult life. *Current Directions in Psychological Science, 4,* 99–103.

Suggested Web Sites

www.psych.upenn.edu/seligman/teachinghighschool.htm Site for Positive Psychology.

http://www.psych.uiuc.edu/~ediener/index.html This is Dr. Ed Diener's home page. It contains links to information on subjective well-being (happiness).

http://counseling.uchicago.edu/vpc The site for the Student Counseling and Resource Center at the University of Chicago. They have excellent virtual pamphlets on dealing with relationships.

CHAPTER 14

Looking Toward the Future

◼ Chapter Focus

Read to answer these key questions:

- ◼ What is my life stage?
- ◼ How does positive thinking affect my future success?
- ◼ What are some beliefs of successful people?
- ◼ What are some secrets to achieving happiness?

Psychologists have identified life stages that we all go through. Knowing about life stages can help you to understand where you are now and where you might be in the future. Positive thinking is also a powerful tool for achieving life goals. Learn to use your attitudes and beliefs to enhance your future success. Many of you have happiness as one of your lifetime goals. This chapter ends with some useful ideas about how to achieve happiness in your life.

■ Life Stages

A number of researchers believe that adults progress through a series of orderly and predictable stages in which success or failure at each stage has an influence on later stages. Understanding these stages can help you to understand where you are now and where you are headed in the future. Life stage theorists include Erik Erikson and Daniel Levinson. Gail Sheehy, author of *Passages* and *New Passages,* is a journalist who has summarized and popularized current research on life stages.[1]

Erik Erikson

Philosophy is perfectly right in saying that life must be understood backward. But one forgets the other clause—that it must be lived forward.

Soren Kierkegaard

Erik Erikson proposes that human beings progress through eight stages of psychosocial development in a fixed order.[2] These stages are turning points, or crises, and the outcome of each turning point will determine future personality development. Each crisis has two possible outcomes; one is negative and the other positive. For example, the first turning point happens during the first year of life. He titles this stage trust vs. mistrust. If the infant's parents and caregivers provide consistent, caring, and adequate treatment, the infant learns to trust the world as a safe place. If the infant is abused or not cared for adequately, he or she will learn that the world is an unsafe place. The sense of trust or mistrust is carried with the individual throughout life. Erickson identifies seven stages, which range from ages zero to age 65 and beyond.

1. **Basic trust vs. mistrust (age 0–1)**
   Based on the parents' care, the infant learns to trust others and feel comfortable in the world or learns to distrust a world that is perceived to be unsafe.

2. **Autonomy vs. shame and doubt (age 1–3)**
   Between the ages of one and three children learn to feel competent by feeding themselves, learning to use the toilet, and playing alone. If they do not accomplish these tasks successfully, children learn to doubt their own abilities.

3. **Initiative vs. guilt (age 3–5)**
   During this stage, children learn to plan their own activities within the parents' guidelines. If the children do not learn these tasks, they develop guilt over their misbehavior.

4. **Industry vs. inferiority (age 5–11)**
   In this stage children learn to meet the demands of parents, teachers, and peers. They learn to clean their rooms, do their homework, and ride a bike, for example. If they accomplish these tasks successfully, they learn that their effort (industry) leads to success. If they do not learn these tasks, Erikson believes that they develop a lifelong feeling of inferiority.

5. **Identity vs. role confusion (age 11–18)**
   During this stage the child develops his or her identity. It is also during this stage that the child starts to prepare for work by gaining insights into personality, interests, and values as well as learning about the world of work. If these tasks are not successfully accomplished, the result is confusion over his or her role in life.

6. **Intimacy vs. isolation (age 18–40)**
   This is an adult stage of development in which relationships are formed with a partner. The task is to develop loving and committed relationships with others that partially replace the bonds with parents. If this task is not completed, the adult remains isolated from others and has difficulty establishing meaningful relationships. He or she is less capable of full emotional development.

7. **Generativity vs. stagnation (age 40–65)**

   During this adult stage, the person contributes to future generations through raising children, helping others, developing products, or coming up with creative new ideas. At this time, the person puts unfulfilled dreams aside and finds meaning in work and family and continues to grow and produce. If this task is not accomplished, growth is stopped and the person becomes stagnant and self-centered.

8. **Integrity vs. despair (age 65 plus)**

   At this stage, people reap the benefits of all that they have done during their life and accept the fact that life is temporary. If this task is not accomplished, the individual is in despair and struggles to find meaning in life.

OURNAL ENTRY #1

What is your life stage according to Erik Erikson?

Write your Journal Entry on page 381.

Daniel Levinson

The research and writing by Daniel Levinson has been very useful in understanding adult development and career development.[3] Levinson proposes four stages in adult development:

1. Pre-adulthood

2. Early adulthood (age 17–45)

3. Middle adulthood (age 40–60)

4. Late adulthood (age 60–65)

Each of these stages of adulthood alternates between stable and transitional periods. Stable periods last six to seven years, during which people pursue their goals and create a desired structure in their lives. Transitional periods last four to five years, during which people question and reappraise the structure and consider making changes. These transitional periods provide the opportunity for growth and reflection.

These stable and transitional periods are related to age. Levinson's research showed that people do vary a little on the onset or termination of each stage, but generally by not more than two years. He also believes that people go through these stages in a fixed sequence during which certain developmental tasks present themselves in a fixed order. How a person deals with these developmental tasks has a big impact on later life. Transitional and stable periods, including developmental tasks, are summarized below. As you read each description, think about your life stage and where you may be headed in the future.

■ **Age 17–22 Transitional Period**
The task here is to move from adolescence to young adulthood and to separate from parents.

■ **Age 22–28 Stable Period**
This is a period of settling down and creating life structure, while still keeping the options open to explore jobs and relationships.

■ **Age 28–33 Transitional Period**

During this period, adults reappraise their current life structure. There is the feeling that if a change is to be made, it must be made before it is too late.

■ **Age 33–40 Stable Period**

During this time, adults build clear work, family, and leisure roles. The need to attain one's dream is powerful and intense. Levinson says that this stage ends with a BOOP (Becoming One's Own Person). Women often have the challenge of balancing work and family roles at this time.

■ **Age 40–45 Transitional Period**

This is a time of turmoil. Up to 80 percent of men and 85 percent of women experience a moderate to severe crisis at this time.[4] At this point there is an awareness of human mortality and the feeling that half of life is now over. There is often a generational shift at this point; adults may have teenage children, and their parents are getting old or have passed away. At this point adults assess their progress toward accomplishing their dream. If the dream has not been accomplished, there is a sense of failure. If the dream has been accomplished, the person considers whether it was worth the effort and wonders, "Is this all there is?" Women are often juggling three roles: career, marriage, and motherhood. Only 4 percent of women manage to have it all: marriage, motherhood, and a full-time career.[5] Efforts to combine these roles often do not provide the satisfaction that women expect.

■ **Age 45–50 Stable Period**

During this period, adults work on stable life structures for the middle years. They often have more autonomy and flexibility in choosing roles.

■ **Age 50–55 Transitional Period**

Adults continue to work on questions raised during the midlife crisis.

■ **Age 55–60 Stable Period**

Adults work on stable life structures.

■ **Age 60–65 Transitional Period**

Adults deal with retirement transitions.

JOURNAL ENTRY #2

What is your life stage according to Daniel Levinson?

Write your Journal Entry on page 381.

Gail Sheehy

Gail Sheehy is a journalist who became famous in 1976 for her book *Passages*. She continued to survey current research on life stages in her 1995 book, *New Passages*. In her later book she looks at the research as well as historical events to describe some new trends in adult life stages. She notes that because of increasing life spans, earlier theories of life stages need to be updated. Previous theories of life development covered a life span to age 65. Sheehy notes that women today who reach 50 (without developing cancer or heart disease) can expect to live to be 92 years old. Men who are healthy and live to age 65 can expect to live until the age of 81.[6] She quotes the president of a nursing home: "Twenty years ago I'd see forty-year-olds bringing in their sixty-year-old parents. Now I'm seeing seventy-year-olds bringing in their ninety-year-old parents."[7]

The good news is that we will all be living longer and healthier lives in the years to come. In terms of life stages, Sheehy states that "the territory of the mid-forties, fifties and sixties and beyond is changing so fundamentally it now opens up whole new passages and stages of life." She asks us to "stop and recalculate. Imagine the day you turn 45 as the infancy of another life . . . a second adulthood in middle life."[8] She divides adult life stages into the stages:

- provisional adulthood (18–30)
- first adulthood (30–45)
- second adulthood (45–85)

Provisional Adulthood and the Try-Out Twenties (age 18–30)

This stage is traditionally characterized by two opposing goals: a desire for exploration and a desire for stability. Historically this was a time to finish one's education move away from the parents' home to start a career and family. Young people are now living at home longer, and the period of adolescence has been extended. The author notes that of unmarried American men between 25 and 34, more than one third are still living at home.[9] She describes a dramatic shift that occurs around the age of 30. "Before the shift men and women feel unable to make clear choices or cope with life's vicissitudes without expecting some help from parents. After the shift they feel confident enough in their own values to make their own choices and competent enough in life skills to set a course."[10]

Some challenges for the Try-Out Twenties include coping with a rapidly changing world:

- Views on marriage are changing. Young women have seen their mothers struggling to balance career, marriage, and children. Many young people are delaying marriage into the 20s or 30s or are deciding not to get married at all.
- Sheehy notes that in previous generations the enemies were external: wars, communism, and the nuclear bomb. Today for many young people, the enemies are internal: drugs, guns, and violence.
- The world has become more unpredictable and violent. Many teenagers do not feel safe in their schools or communities.
- There is a growing gap between the rich and poor.
- There is increased competition for jobs.
- There is an epidemic of adolescent suicide, teenage pregnancy, and AIDS.
- Young people have to reassess their morals, as they become full of fear and anxiety about sex outside of marriage.
- Many worry that they are being educated for jobs that no longer exist.

Some positives include the following:

- This group is becoming more educated: by age 20 to 24, 58 percent of women and 53 percent of men have some college education or have graduated from college.
- Since this age group is smaller than preceding generations, there will be less competition as older workers retire.
- Because of increased education, this group will be better able to adapt to change and to do freelance or free-agent work.
- This generation is becoming more ethnically diverse and is more receptive to multiculturalism.
- They will participate in great advances in technology and biotechnology.
- This group will use the Internet to conduct business in a more efficient way than ever before.
- Since young people are waiting longer to marry, they may have fewer divorces.[11]

First Adulthood: The Turbulent Thirties and the Flourishing Forties

Thirty-year-olds step into first adulthood with questions about who they are and what life is all about. They pay the rent or mortgage, make the car payment, and take care of the children. Maybe they used to say that someone over 30 could not be trusted. Now they are 30 themselves and become conscious that they are getting older. At age 35, they take inventory and ask, "Is half of my life over? Is this what it is all about?" These questions are the beginning of a mid-life crisis. Since people are living longer, half of their life is not over at age 35. The mid-life crisis used to happen around age 38–43. Gail Sheehy suggests that the mid-life crisis is now often delayed until the mid-40s.

A **mid-life crisis** is a major transition in life in which we question what we did during the first half of our life. The central issue in mid-life is dealing with growing older and our own mortality. During this time adults make major changes in their lives. They may start a new hobby, change careers, go back to school, start a new business, get a divorce, or buy a new sports car. During this transition adults often go through what Gail Sheehy calls middlescence, which she defines as adolescence the second time around. She gives this example:

> "At forty-eight I lost forty pounds, looked younger than I did at forty and took up a long-repressed passion—music," says a typical homemaker. Jeannie enrolled in music school to study electric bass and drums. She now plays in a garage rock band with 18-year-old boys. She already has planned her antidote to "hardening of the attitudes." After 65 she plans to launch a heavy metal band called Guns and Geezers.[12]

Men and women are often at a crossroads going in different directions during this mid-life transition. If women married and had children, their children are often grown, and there is a void in their lives. This is called the "empty nest" syndrome. At this stage in life, women may look to a career and work as a source of fulfillment and motivation. At the same point many men think about future retirement and spending more time in leisure activities. They often become more interested in family. They realize that no one ever wished on his deathbed that he had put in more time at the office. Because men and women are struggling with their identity and often have different goals in life during this period, divorce is often the outcome. One research study showed a divorce rate of 36 percent for women between the ages of 40 and 44.[13]

While the mid-life crisis can be dangerous, it can have some positive outcomes. Adults look at their lives and make changes that lead to continued growth and enjoyment of life. The mid-life crisis is a gateway to a new beginning or second adulthood. Half of life is not over; half of life lies ahead, and adults can take advantage of their experiences in the first half of life to find exciting new opportunities in the second half.

Reprinted with Special Permission of King Features Syndicate.

Second Adulthood: The Ages of Mastery and Integrity

The second adulthood begins with the resolution of the mid-life crisis at around age 45 and goes to age 85 or longer. We expect that people will be living into their eighties and nineties and leading healthy and productive lives. Sheehy divides the second adulthood into two stages: the Age of Mastery (45–65) and the Age of Integrity (65–85 or beyond).[14]

The Age of Mastery (45–65) marks the apex of life in which people have a stable psychological sense of mastery. People face the second half of life with fifty years of experience in living. Sheehy states that "45 represents the old age of youth, while 50 initiates the youth of Second Adulthood." She compares life to watching a play:

It's as though when we are young, we have seen only the first act of the play. By our forties we have reached the climactic second-act curtain. Only as we approach fifty does the shape and meaning of the whole play become clear.[15]

People in their fifties are more serene about their mortality. At age 35, our mortality becomes a realization and at age 40, it becomes a terrifying idea. We try to turn back the clock. At age 50, we are better able to accept the aging process. We have had experience with life and have successfully dealt with many challenges. At this age, many may even feel physically fit and devote time to exercise and better health. The question is, "How long do I want to live and how can I invest my time in my mental and physical health?"

Successful aging does not happen automatically. To age successfully, people need to look at their priorities and determine what is most important in life. Successful aging means taking an active part in life rather than being sedentary and inactive. The central question of this age is a search for the meaning of life. People find meaning by searching for their passion. They need to find what they really enjoy and do it.

Many Baby Boomers (born between 1946 and 1965) are now approaching this age. Sheehy notes that one-third of all women in the United States today have passed their fiftieth birthday. At this age, women are independent, enjoy learning new skills, start new careers, and begin new adventures. They enjoy greater well-being than at any other time in life. Sheehy found that education is a key factor to well-being and happiness at this age. Of the women she surveyed, those who measured near the top on the scale of well-being had completed college or earned a graduate degree.[16] She also reports that women who are age 50 say that this age feels like "an optimistic, can-do stage of life."[17]

Men face more difficult times in their fifties. Men frequently base their identity on their career; and many men in their fifties are unemployed, underemployed or hate their jobs. They are often the victims of an economy that is downsizing.[18] Sheehy believes that men at this age need to move from competing in the workplace to connecting with people who are important to them. Men may try to connect with children and family, but the children may have already left home. She also notes that men from age 45 to 64 who live with their wives live ten years longer than their unmarried counterparts.[19] One of the male participants in Sheehy's surveys states that he had to come to realize that "a lot of good friendships is better than a lot of money."[20]

The Age of Integrity (65–85 and beyond) is a new life stage resulting from the extended average life span. In the "serene sixties," only ten percent of Americans 65 and older have a chronic health problem that restricts them from carrying on a major activity. Those who do have chronic health problems are often suffering as a result of neglecting their health at earlier ages.[21] In the sixties, most people are healthy and looking forward to using their experience with life to make contributions to their families and community. An example of a woman in the "serene sixties" is Deborah Szekely, a pioneer in creating fitness spas. She says that life can be divided into three parts:

The first third of life is devoted to being a child, learning in school and at home. The next third is spent working as hard as you're able and being rewarded for it. The final third is perhaps the most important: taking a role in making the world better for the next generation.[22]

People who have lived to the Age of Integrity have learned to deal with life. They have passed through many stages and dealt with many crises. They have learned how to put life into perspective. Gail Sheehy cites a study of Harvard men done over a period of years in which it was found that "even the most painful and traumatic events in childhood had virtually no effect on the well-being of these men in their mid-sixties."[23] It takes about sixty-five years for human beings to finally figure it all out and to be happy with their lives!

Retirement is one of the most difficult transitions in the Age of Integrity. It used to be that people worked for about thirty years and then retired. However, if a person retires at age 65, there are still twenty to thirty years of life to live. A new idea is serial retirement. A person retires from one career and enters a new career and retires again. This happens because of the need to stay active and involved as well as the need to extend financial resources over a longer life span. It is difficult to predict how much money will be needed to retire twenty or thirty years into the future. To successfully move through the retirement transition, people need to continue to grow and learn how to play after a life of work.

Gail Sheehy summarizes some of the research on factors contributing to health and well-being in the sixties and beyond.[24]

- Having mature love (a wife, husband, partner) is more important than money or power.
- Continued growth experiences and feeling an excitement about life help people to feel happy.
- It is important to find your passion and pursue it.
- Exercise is the most important factor in retarding the aging process. It was found that men and women who walk a half-hour a day cut their mortality rates in half.[25]

Many people are living to the age of 90 to 100. Gail Sheehy describes the **characteristics of successful centenarians**:

> *Characteristics of healthy centenarians, garnered from a number of studies, are these: most have high native intelligence, a keen interest in current events, a good memory, and few illnesses. They tend to be early risers, sleeping on average between six and seven hours. Most drink coffee, follow no special diets, but generally prefer diets high in protein, low in fat. There is no uniformity in their drinking habits, but they use less medication in their lifetimes than many old people use in a week. They prefer living in the present, with changes, and are usually religious in the broad sense. All have a degree of optimism and a marked sense of humor. Life seems to have been a great adventure.*[26]

Sheehy defines successful aging as "sageing." Sageing is defined as "the process by which men and women accumulate wisdom and grow into the culture's sages."[27] The stages of our lives are like a spiral pattern. We move through successive stages gaining understanding and experience. Erik Erikson and his wife, Joan, wrote a book in their eighties titled *Vital Involvement in Old Age*, in which they described the patterns of the life cycle and how we learn from experience:

> *The life cycle does more than extend itself into the next generation. It curves back on the life of the individual, allowing . . . a reexamination of earlier stages in a new form.*[28]

Writer F. Scott Fitzgerald said that we need to learn "to accept life not as a series of random events but as path of awakening."[29] We learn and grow and develop over a lifetime. Knowing about the stages of our lives helps us to realize that as long as we continue to grow and develop, we can awaken to each new day with the prospect of continued satisfaction and enjoyment of life.

OURNAL ENTRY #3

What is your life stage according to Gail Sheehy?

Write your Journal Entry on page 382.

Quiz—Understanding Life Stages

Test what you have learned by selecting the correct answer to the following questions.

1. *Erik Erikson believes that all human beings pass through eight stages of development*
   A. *that last ten years for each stage.*
   B. *in a random pattern.*
   C. *in a fixed order.*

2. *According to Erikson, the main task of the identity vs. role confusion stage (age 11–18) is*
   A. *learning to follow the rules of society.*
   B. *discovering personality and interests in preparation for work.*
   C. *forming intimate relationships.*

3. *Daniel Levinson says that stages of adult development alternate between*
   A. *stable and transitional periods.*
   B. *calm and stressful periods.*
   C. *integrity and despair.*

4. *The midlife crisis is defined as*
   A. *a brief period of insanity.*
   B. *a major transition in which we question what we did in the first half of life.*
   C. *the realization that half of life is over.*

5. *Factors contributing to successful aging include*
   A. *increasing time for relaxation.*
   B. *continuing exercise throughout life.*
   C. *reflecting on past accomplishments.*

How did you do on the quiz? Check your answers: 1. C, 2. B, 3. A, 4. B, 5. B

■ Thinking Positively about Your Life

Thinking positively about yourself and your life is one of the most important skills you can learn for your future success. Following are some ways to practice positive thinking.

Believe in Yourself

Anthony Robbins defines belief as "any guiding principle, dictum, faith, or passion that can provide meaning and direction in life . . . Beliefs are the compass and maps that guide us toward our goals and give us the surety to know we'll get there."[30] The beliefs that we have about ourselves determine how much of our potential we will use and how successful we will be in the future. If we have positive beliefs about ourselves, we will feel confident and accomplish our goals in life. Negative beliefs get in the way of our success. Robbins reminds us that we can change our beliefs and choose new ones if necessary.

> *The birth of excellence begins with our awareness that our beliefs are a choice. We usually do not think of it that way, but belief can be a conscious choice. You can choose beliefs that limit you, or you can choose beliefs that support you. The trick is to choose the beliefs that are conducive to success and the results you want and to discard the ones that hold you back.*[31]

The Self-Fulfilling Prophecy

The first step in thinking positively is to examine your beliefs about yourself, your life, and the world around you. Personal beliefs are influenced by our environment, significant events that have happened in life, what we have learned in the past, and our picture of the future. Beliefs cause us to have certain expectations about the world and ourselves. These expectations are such a powerful influence on behavior that psychologists use the term "self-fulfilling prophecy" to describe what happens when our expectations come true.

For example, if I believe that I am not good in math (my expectation), I may not try to do the assignment or may avoid taking a math class (my behavior). As a result, I am not good in math. My expectations have been fulfilled. Expectations can also have a positive effect. If I believe that I am a good student, I will take steps to enroll in college and complete my assignments. I will then become a good student. The prophecy will again come true.

Psychologist Robert Rosenthal has done some interesting research on the self-fulfilling prophecy. He describes the following experiment:

> *Twelve experimenters were each given five rats that were taught to run a maze with the aid of visual cues. Six of the experimenters were told that their rats had been specially bred for maze-brightness; the other six were told that their rats had been bred for maze-dullness. Actually, there was no difference between the rats. At the end of the experiment, researchers with "maze-bright" rats found superior learning in their rats compared to the researchers with "maze-dull" rats.*[32]

Rosenthal also did experiments with human subjects. Students in an elementary school were given an IQ test. Researchers told the teachers that this was a test that would determine "intellectual blooming." An experimental group of these students was chosen at random and teachers were told to expect remarkable gains in intellectual achievement in these children during the next eight months. At the end of this time, researchers gave the IQ test again. Students in the experimental group in which the teachers expected "intellectual blooming" actually gained higher IQ points than the control group. In addition, teachers described these students as more "interesting, curious and happy" than the control group. The teachers' expectations resulted in a self-fulfilling prophecy.

If I believe I cannot do something, it makes me incapable of doing it. But when I believe I can, then I acquire the ability to do it, even if I did not have the ability in the beginning.

Mahatma Gandhi

To think positively, it is necessary to recognize your negative beliefs and turn them into positive beliefs. Some negative beliefs commonly heard from college students include the following:

> I don't have the money for college.
> English was never my best subject.
> I was never any good at math.

Human beings can alter their lives by altering their attitude of mind.

William James

When you hear yourself saying these negative thoughts, remember that these thoughts can become self-fulfilling prophecies. First of all, notice the thought. Then see if you can change the statement into a positive statement such as:

> *I can find the money for college.*
> *English has been a challenge for me in the past, but I will do better this time.*
> *I can learn to be good at math.*

If you believe that you can find money for college, you can go to the financial aid office and the scholarship office to begin your search for money to attend school. You can look for a better job or improve your money management. If you believe that you will do better in English, you will keep up with your assignments and ask the teacher for help. If you believe that you can learn to be good at math, you will attend every math class and seek tutoring when you do not understand. Your positive thoughts will help you to be successful.

Positive Self-Talk and Affirmations

Self-talk refers to the silent inner voice in our heads. This voice is often negative, especially when we are frustrated or trying to learn something new. Have you ever had thoughts about yourself that are similar to these:

> *How could you be so stupid!*
> *That was dumb!*
> *You idiot!*

■ Activity

What do you say to yourself when you are angry or frustrated? Write several examples of your negative self-talk.

_____

_____

_____

_____

_____

_____

_____

_____

_____

_____

_____

_____

_____

_____

_____

_____

_____

_____

Negative thoughts can actually be toxic to your body. They can cause biochemical changes that can lead to depression and negatively affect the immune system.[33] Negative self-talk causes anxiety and poor performance and is damaging to self-esteem. It can also lead to a negative self-fulfilling prophecy. Positive thoughts can help us build self-esteem, become confident in our abilities, and achieve our goals. These positive thoughts are called affirmations.

We are what we think. All that we are arises With our thoughts. With our thoughts we make the world.

Buddha

If we make the world with our thoughts, it is important to become aware of the thoughts about ourselves that are continuously running through our heads. Are your thoughts positive or negative? Negative thoughts lead to failure. What we hear over and over again shapes our beliefs. If you say over and over to yourself such things as, "I am stupid," "I am ugly," or "I am fat," you will start to believe these things and act in a way that supports your beliefs. Positive thoughts help to build success. If you say to yourself, "I'm a good person," "I'm doing my best," or "I'm doing fine," you will begin to believe these things about yourself and act in a way that supports these beliefs. Here are some guidelines for increasing your positive self-talk and making affirmations:

1. Monitor your thoughts about yourself and become aware of them. Are they positive or negative?

2. When you notice a negative thought about yourself, imagine rewinding a tape and recording a new positive message.

3. Start the positive message with "I" and use the present tense. Using an "I" statement shows you are in charge. Using the present tense shows you are ready for action now.

4. Focus on the positive. Think about what you want to achieve and what you can do rather than what you do not want to do. For example, instead of saying, "I will not eat junk food," say, "I will eat a healthy diet."

5. Make your affirmation stronger by adding an emotion to it.

6. Form a mental picture of what it is that you want to achieve. See yourself doing it successfully.

7. You may need to say the positive thoughts over and over again until you believe them and they become a habit. You can also write them down and put them in a place where you will see them often.

Here are some examples of negative self-talk and a contrasting positive affirmations:

Negative: I'm always broke.
Affirmation: I feel really good when I manage my finances. See yourself taking steps to manage finances. For example, a budget or savings plan.

Negative: I'm too fat. It just runs in the family.
Affirmation: I feel good about myself when I exercise and eat a healthy diet. See yourself exercising and eating a healthy diet.

Negative: I can't do this. I must be stupid.
Affirmation: I can do this. I am capable. I feel a sense of accomplishment when I accomplish something challenging. See yourself making your best attempt and taking the first step to accomplish the project.

Activity

Select one example of negative self-talk that you wrote earlier. Use the examples above to turn your negative message into a positive one and write it here.

_____

_____

_____

_____

_____

_____

_____

_____

_____

_____

_____

_____

_____

_____

_____

_____

_____

_____

Visualize Your Success

Visualization is a powerful tool for using your brain to improve memory, deal with stress, and think positively. Coaches and athletes study sports psychology to learn how to use visualization along with physical practice to improve athletic performance. College students can use the same techniques to enhance college success.

If you are familiar with sports or are an athlete, you can probably think of times when your coach asked you to use visualization to improve your performance. In baseball, the coach reminds players to keep their eye on the ball and visualize hitting it. In swimming, the coach asks swimmers to visualize reaching their arms out to touch the edge of the pool at the end of the race. Pole-vaulters visualize clearing the pole and sometimes even go through the motions before making the jump. Using imagery lets you practice for future events and pre-experience achieving your goals. Athletes imagine winning the race or completing the perfect jump in figure skating. In this way they prepare mentally and physically and develop confidence in their abilities.

> The future first exists in imagination, then planning, then reality.
>
> R.A. Wilson

Just as the athlete visualizes and then performs, the college student can do the same. It is said we create all things twice. First we make a mental picture, and then we create the physical reality by taking action. For example if we are building a house, we first get the idea; then we begin to design the house we want. We start with a blueprint and then build the house. The blueprint determines what kind of house we construct. The same thing happens in any project we undertake. First we have a mental picture and then we complete the project. Visualize what you would like to accomplish in your life as if you were creating a blueprint. Then take the steps to accomplish what you want.

As a college student, you might visualize yourself in your graduation robe walking across the stage to receive your diploma. You might visualize yourself in the exam room confidently taking the exam. You might see yourself on the job enjoying your future career. You can make a mental picture of what you would like your life to be and then work toward accomplishing your goal.

Hope for the Best

Believing that you will accomplish your goals and build a good future for yourself can help you to be successful. One research study showed that for entering college freshmen, level of hope was a better predictor of college grades than standardized tests or high school grade point average.[34] Students with a high level of hope set higher goals and worked to attain those goals. Hopeful people use positive self-talk and believe that the future will be good. They change goals and plans when necessary. People who are not hopeful about the future use negative self-talk and become victims of the negative self-fulfilling prophecy.

■ Successful Beliefs

Steven Covey's book, "The 7 Habits of Highly Successful People" has been described as one of the most influential books of the 20th century.[35] In 2004 he released a new book called "The 8th Habit, From Effectiveness to Greatness."[36] These habits are based on beliefs that lead to success.

1. **Be proactive.**
   Being proactive means accepting responsibility for your life. Covey uses the word "response-ability" for the ability to choose responses. The quality of your life is based on the decisions and responses that you make. Proactive people make things

happen through responsibility and initiative. They do not blame circumstances or conditions for their behavior.

2. **Begin with the end in mind.**
Know what is important and what you wish to accomplish in your life. To be able to do this, you will need to know your values and goals in life. You will need a clear vision of what you want your life to be and where you are headed.

3. **Put first things first.**
Once you have established your goals and vision for the future, you will need to manage yourself to do what is important first. Set priorities so that you can accomplish the tasks that are important to you.

4. **Think win-win.**
In human interactions, seek solutions that benefit everyone. Focus on cooperation rather than competition. If everyone feels good about the decision, there is cooperation and harmony. If one person wins and the other loses, the loser becomes angry and resentful.

5. **First seek to understand, then to be understood.**
Too often in our personal communications, we try to talk first and listen later. Often we don't really listen; we use this time to think of our reply. It is best to listen and understand before speaking. Effective communication is one of the most important skills in life.

6. **Synergize.**
A simple definition of synergy is that the whole is greater than the sum of its parts. If people can cooperate and have good communication, they can work together as a team to accomplish more than each individual could do separately. Synergy is also part of the creative process.

7. **Sharpen the saw.**
Covey shares the story of a man who was trying to cut down a tree with a dull saw. As he struggled to cut the tree, someone suggested that he stop and sharpen the saw. The man said that he did not have time to sharpen the saw, so he continued to struggle. Covey suggests that we need to take time to stop and sharpen the saw. We need to stop working and invest some time in ourselves by staying healthy physically, mentally, spiritually, and socially. We need to take time for self-renewal.

8. **Find your voice, and inspire others to find theirs.**
Believe that you can make a positive difference in the world and inspire others to do the same. Covey says that leaders "deal with people in a way that will communicate to them their worth and potential so clearly that they will come to see it in themselves." Accomplishing this ideal begins with developing one's own voice or "unique personal significance."[37]

Successful Beliefs

- Be proactive
- Begin with the end in mind
- Put first things first
- Think win-win
- First seek to understand, then to be understood
- Synergize
- Sharpen the saw
- Find your voice, and inspire others to find theirs

Quiz—Positive Thinking

Test what you have learned by selecting the correct answer to the following questions.

1. *When teachers were told to expect "intellectual blooming" in their students,*
   A. *students gained IQ points at the end of the year.*
   B. *students had the same IQ at the end of the year.*
   C. *students became frustrated because of high teacher expectations.*

2. *Positive self-talk results in*
   A. *lower self-esteem.*
   B. *over confidence.*
   C. *higher self-esteem.*

3. *The statement, "We create all things twice," refers to*
   A. *doing the task twice to make sure it is done right.*
   B. *creating and refining.*
   C. *first making a mental picture and then taking action.*

4. *A win-win solution means*
   A. *winning at any cost.*
   B. *seeking a solution that benefits everyone.*
   C. *focusing on competition.*

5. *The statement by Steven Covey, "Sharpen the saw," refers to*
   A. *proper tool maintenance.*
   B. *studying hard to sharpen thinking skills.*
   C. *investing time to maintain physical and mental health.*

How did you do on the quiz? Check your answers: 1. A, 2. C, 3. C, 4. B, 5. C

■ Secrets to Happiness

> The three grand essentials of happiness are: something to do, someone to love, and something to hope for.
>
> *Thomas Chalmers*

Many of you probably have happiness on your list of lifetime goals. It sounds easy, right? But what is happiness, anyway?

Psychologist Martin Seligman says that real happiness comes from identifying, cultivating, and using your personal strengths in work, love, play, and parenting."[38] You have identified these strengths by learning about your personality type, learning style, interests, and values.

Seligman contrasts authentic happiness with hedonism. He states that a hedonist "wants as many good moments and as few bad moments as possible in life."[39] Hedonism is a shortcut to happiness that leaves us feeling empty. For example, we often assume that more material possessions will make us happy. However, the more material possessions we have, the greater the expectations, and we no longer appreciate what we have.

> *Suppose you could be hooked up to a hypothetical "experience machine" that, for the rest of your life, would stimulate your brain and give you any positive feelings you desire. Most people to whom I offer this imaginary choice refuse the machine. It is not just positive feelings we want, we want to be entitled to our positive feelings. Yet we have invented myriad shortcuts to feeling good: drugs, chocolate, loveless sex, shopping,*

masturbation, and television are all examples. (I am not, however, suggesting that you should drop these shortcuts altogether.) The belief that we can rely on shortcuts to happiness, joy, rapture, comfort, and ecstasy, rather than be entitled to these feelings by the exercise of personal strengths and virtues, leads to the legions of people who in the middle of great wealth are starving spiritually. Positive emotion alienated from the exercise of character leads to emptiness, to inauthenticity, to depression, and as we age, to the gnawing realization that we are fidgeting until we die.[40]

Seligman provides a formula for happiness:[41]

$$Happiness = S + C + V$$

In the formula *S* stands for set range. Psychologists believe that 50 percent of happiness is determined by heredity. In other words, half of your level of happiness is determined by the genes inherited from your ancestors. In good times or bad times, people generally return to their set range of happiness. Six months after receiving a piece of good fortune such as a raise, promotion, or winning the lottery, unhappy people are still unhappy. Six months after a tragedy, naturally happy people return to being happy.

The letter *C* in the equation stands for circumstances such as money, marriage, social life, health, education, climate, race, gender, and religion. These circumstances account for 8 to 15 percent of happiness. Here is what psychologists know about how these circumstances affect happiness:

- Once basic needs are met, greater wealth does not increase happiness.
- Having a good marriage is related to increased happiness.
- Happy people are more social.
- Moderate ill health does not bring unhappiness, but severe illness does.
- Educated people are slightly happier.
- Climate, race, and gender do not affect level of happiness.
- Religious people are somewhat happier than nonreligious people.

The letter *V* in the equation stands for factors under your voluntary control. These factors account for approximately 40 percent of happiness. Factors under voluntary control include positive emotions and optimism about the future. Positive emotions include hope, faith, trust, joy, ecstasy, calm, zest, ebullience, pleasure, flow, satisfaction, contentment, fulfillment, pride, and serenity. Seligman suggests the following ideas to increase your positive emotions:

- Realize that the past does not determine your future. The future is open to new possibilities.
- Be grateful for the good events of the past and place less emphasis on the bad events.
- Build positive emotions through forgiving and forgetting.
- Work on increasing optimism and hope for the future.
- Find out what activities make you happy and engage in them. Spread these activities out over time so that you will not get tired of them.
- Take the time to savor the happy times. Make mental photographs of happy times so that you can think of them later.
- Take time to enjoy the present moment.
- Build more flow into your life. Flow is the state of gratification we feel when totally absorbed in an activity that matches our strengths.

David Myers, a professor of psychology at Hope College in Michigan, is a leading researcher on happiness. He says that 90 percent of us are naturally happy. He adds that if most of us "were characteristically unhappy, the emotional pain would lose its ability to alert us to an unusual and possibly harmful condition."[42]

Just as you have made a decision to get a college degree, make a decision to be happy. Make a decision to be happy by altering your internal outlook and choosing to change your behavior. Here are some suggestions for consciously choosing happiness.

1. Find small things that make you happy and sprinkle your life with them. A glorious sunset, a pat on the back, a well-manicured yard, an unexpected gift, a round of tennis, a favorite sandwich, a fishing line cast on a quiet lake, the wagging tail of the family dog, or your child finally taking some responsibility—these are things that will help to create a continual climate of happiness.[43]

2. Smile and stand up straight. Michael Mercer and Maryann Troiani, authors of *Spontaneous Optimism: Proven Strategies for Health, Prosperity and Happiness,* say that "unhappy people tend to slouch, happy people don't. . . . Happy people even take bigger steps when they walk."[44]

3. Learn to think like an optimist. "Pessimists tend to complain; optimists focus on solving their problems."[45] Never use the word "try"; this word is for pessimists. Assume you will succeed.

4. Replace negative thoughts with positive ones.

5. Do things that use your skills.

6. Fill your life with things you like to do.

7. Get enough rest. If you do not get enough sleep, you will feel tired and gloomy. Sleep deprivation can lead to depression.

8. Exercise. Twenty minutes of exercise produces endorphins that help you feel good and cope with anxiety.

9. Learn from your elders. Psychologist Daniel Mroczek says that "people in their sixties and seventies who are in good health are among the happiest people in our society. . . . They may be better able to regulate their emotions, they've developed perspective, they don't get so worried about little things, and they've often achieved their goals and aren't trying to prove themselves."[46]

10. Reduce stress.

11. Take charge of your time by doing first things first.

12. Close relationships are important. Myers and Mroczek report higher levels of happiness among married men and women.[47]

13. Keep things in perspective. Will it matter in six months to a year?

14. Laugh more. Laughter produces a relaxation response.

Keys to Success: You Are What You Think

Sometimes students enter college with the fear of failure. This belief leads to anxiety and behavior that leads to failure. If you have doubts about your ability to succeed in college, you might not go to class or attempt the challenging work required in college. It is difficult to make the effort if you cannot see positive results ahead. Unfortunately, failure in college can lead to a loss of confidence and lack of success in other areas of life as well.

Henry Ford said that "what we believe is true, comes true. What we believe is possible, becomes possible." If you believe that you will succeed, you will be more likely to take actions that lead to your success. Once you have experienced some small part of success, you will have confidence in your abilities and will continue on the road to success. Success leads to more success. It becomes a habit. You will be motivated to make the effort necessary to accomplish your goals. You might even become excited and energized along the way. You will use your gifts and talents to reach your potential and achieve happiness. It all begins with the thoughts you choose.

> *Watch your thoughts; they become words.*
> *Watch your words; they become actions.*
> *Watch your actions; they become habits.*
> *Watch your habits; they become character.*
> *Watch your character; it becomes your destiny.*[48]

—Frank Outlaw

To help you choose positive beliefs, picture in your mind how you want your life to be. Imagine it is here now. See all the details and experience the feelings associated with this picture. Pretend it is true until you believe it. Then take action to make your dreams come true.

 OURNAL ENTRY #4

Write five intention statements about increasing your future happiness. I intend to . . .

Write your Journal Entry on page 382.

Success over the Internet

Visit the College Success website at www.cuyamaca.edu/collegesuccess/

The College Success website is continually updated with new topics and links to the material presented in this chapter. Topics include

- *Adult development*

- *Happiness*

- *Self-improvement*

- *Self-esteem*

- *Sports psychology*

- *How to be successful*

Contact your instructor if you have any problems in accessing the College Success website.

Endnotes

1. Gail Sheehy, *Passages* (New York: E.P. Dutton, 1976) and *New Passages* (New York: Random House, 1995).
2. Erik H. Erikson, *Childhood and Society* (New York: W.W. Norton, 1963).
3. D. J. Levinson and J. D. Levinson, *Seasons of a Woman's Life* (New York: Knopf, 1996). D. J. Levinson, C. N. Darrow, E. B. Klein, M. H. Levinson, and B. McKee, *Seasons of a Man's Life* (New York: Knopf, 1978).
4. D. J. Levinson, "A Conception of Adult Development," *American Psychologist* 41 (1986): 107.
5. Levinson and Levinson, *Seasons of a Woman's Life*, 372.
6. Sheehy, *New Passages*, 5–6.
7. Ibid., 7.
8. Ibid., 6.
9. Ibid., 49.
10. Ibid., 52.
11. Ibid., 43–53.
12. Ibid., 140.
13. Ibid., 91.
14. Ibid., 145.
15. Ibid., 150.
16. Ibid., 189.
17. Ibid., 191.
18. Ibid., 264.
19. Ibid., 335.
20. Ibid., 277.
21. Ibid., 351.
22. Ibid., 395.
23. Ibid., 356.
24. Ibid., 384.
25. Ibid., 426.
26. Ibid., 427.

27. Ibid., 420.

28. Erik Erikson, *Vital Involvement in Old Age* (New York: Brunner/Mazel, 1974), 112.

29. Sheehy, *New Passages*, 429.

30. Anthony Robbins, *Unlimited Power* (New York: Fawcett Columbine, 1986), 54–55.

31. Ibid., 57.

32. Robert Rosenthal, "Self-Fulfilling Prophecy," *Psychology Today*, September 1968.

33. Joan Smith, "Nineteen Habits of Happy Women," *Redbook Magazine*, August 1999, 68.

34. Daniel Goleman, "Hope Emerges a Key to Success in Life," *New York Times*, 24 December 1991.

35. Stephen R. Covey, *The Seven Habits of Highly Effective People* (New York: Simon and Schuster, 1989).

36. Stephen R. Covey. *The 8th Habit, from Effectiveness to Greatness* (New York: Free Press, 2004).

37. Ibid

38. Martin Seligman, *Authentic Happiness, Using the New Positive Psychology to Realize Your Potential for Lasting Fulfillment*. New York: Free Press, p. xiii.

39. Ibid, p. 6.

40. Ibid, p. 8.

41. Ibid, p. 45.

42. Quoted in Joan Smith, "Nineteen Habits of Happy Women," *Redbook Magazine*, August 1999, 66.

43. Boal, "Happy Daze."

44. Quoted in Smith, "Nineteen Habits of Happy Women."

45. Ibid.

46. Ibid.

47. Ibid.

48. Rob Gilbert, ed., *Bits and Pieces* (Fairfield, NJ: The Economics Press), Vol. R, No. 40, p. 7, copyright 1998.

■ Looking Toward the Future Journal Entries

1   What is your life stage according to Erik Erikson?

_____

_____

_____

_____

_____

_____

_____

_____

_____

_____

2   What is your life stage according to Daniel Levinson?

_____

_____

_____

_____

_____

_____

_____

_____

_____

_____

3   What is your life stage according to Gail Sheehy?

_____

_____

_____

_____

_____

_____

_____

_____

_____

_____

4   Write five intention statements about increasing your future happiness. I
    intend to . . .

_____

_____

_____

_____

_____

_____

_____

_____

_____

_____

_____

■ Measure Your Success

Now that you have finished the text, complete the following assessment to measure your improvement. Compare your results to the assessment taken at the beginning of class.

Directions: Read the following statements and rate how true they are for you at the present time.

5 Definitely true
4 Mostly true
3 Somewhat true
2 Seldom true
1 Never true

_____ I am motivated to be successful in college.

_____ I know the value of a college education.

_____ I know how to establish successful patterns of behavior.

_____ I can concentrate on an important task until it is completed.

_____ I am attending college to accomplish my own personal goals.

_____ I believe to a great extent that my actions determine my future.

_____ I am persistent in achieving my goals.

_____ Total points for Motivation

_____ I have a list or mental picture of my lifetime goals.

_____ I know what I would like to accomplish in the next four years.

_____ I spend my time on activities that help me accomplish my lifetime goals.

_____ I effectively use priorities in managing my time.

_____ I can balance study, work, and recreation time.

_____ I generally avoid procrastination on important tasks.

_____ I am good at managing my money.

_____ Total points for Managing Time and Money

_____ I know memory techniques and can apply them to my college studies.

_____ I can read a college textbook and remember the important points.

_____ I know how to effectively mark a college textbook.

_____ I can quickly survey a college text and select the main ideas.

_____ I generally have good reading comprehension.

_____ I can concentrate on the material I am reading.

_____ I am confident in my ability to read and remember college level material.

    _____ Total points for Memory and Reading

_____ I know how to adequately prepare for a test.

_____ I can predict the questions that are likely to be on the test.

_____ I know how to deal with test anxiety.

_____ I am successful on math exams.

_____ I know how to make a reasonable guess if I am uncertain about the answer.

_____ I am confident of my ability to take objective tests.

_____ I can write a good essay answer.

    _____ Total points for Test Taking

_____ I know how to listen for the main points in a college lecture.

_____ I am familiar with note-taking systems for college lectures.

_____ I know how to review my lecture notes.

_____ I feel comfortable with writing.

_____ I know the steps in writing a college term paper.

_____ I know how to prepare a speech.

_____ I am comfortable with public speaking.

    _____ Total points for Taking Notes, Writing, and Speaking

_____ I can describe my personality type.

_____ I can list careers that match my personality type.

_____ I can describe my personal strengths and talents based on my personality type.

_____ I understand how my personality type affects how I manage my time and money.

_____ I know what college majors are most in demand.

_____ I am confident that I have chosen the best major for myself.

_____ Courses related to my major are interesting and exciting to me.

_____ Total points for Personality and Major

_____ I can describe my learning style.

_____ I can list study techniques that match my learning style.

_____ I understand how my personality affects my learning style.

_____ I understand the connection between learning and teaching style.

_____ I understand the concept of multiple intelligences.

_____ I can list my multiple intelligences.

_____ I create my own success.

_____ Total points for Learning Style and Intelligence

_____ I can describe my vocational interests.

_____ I can list careers that match my vocational interests.

_____ I can list my top five values.

_____ I generally consider my most important values when making decisions.

_____ My actions are generally guided by my personal values.

_____ My personal values motivate me to be successful.

_____ I can balance work, study and leisure activities.

_____ Total points for Interests and Values

_____ I understand how current employment trends will affect my future.

_____ I know what work skills will be most important for the 21st century.

_____ I have an educational plan that matches my academic and career goals.

_____ I know the steps in making a good career decision.

_____ I have a good resume.

_____ I know how to interview for a job.

_____ I know how to choose a satisfying career.

_____ Total points for Career and Education

_____ I understand how my personality affects my communication style.

_____ I know how to be a good listener.

_____ I can use some basic techniques for good communication.

_____ I can identify some barriers to effective communication.

_____ I know how to deal with conflict.

_____ I feel confident about making new friends in college and on the job.

_____ I am generally a good communicator.

_____ Total points for Communication and Relationships

_____ I have the skills to analyze data, generate alternatives, and solve problems.

_____ I can identify fallacies in reasoning.

_____ I can apply the steps of critical thinking to analyze a complex issue.

_____ I am willing to consider different points of view.

_____ I can use brainstorming to generate a variety of ideas.

_____ I am good at visualization and creative imagination.

_____ I am generally curious about the world and can spot problems and opportunities.

_____ Total points for Critical and Creative Thinking

_____ I understand the basics of good nutrition.

_____ I understand how to maintain my ideal body weight.

_____ I exercise regularly.

_____ I avoid addictions to smoking, alcohol, and drugs.

_____ I protect myself from sexually transmitted diseases.

_____ I generally get enough sleep.

_____ I am good at managing stress.

_____ Total points for Health

_____ I understand the concept of diversity and know why it is important.

_____ I understand the basics of communicating with a person from a different culture.

_____ I understand how the global economy will affect my future career.

_____ I understand how the concept of the electronic village will affect my future.

_____ I am familiar with the basic vocabulary of diversity.

_____ I am aware of some of the myths about sexual orientation.

_____ I try to understand and appreciate those who are different from me.

    _____ Total points for Diversity

_____ I understand the theories of life stages.

_____ I can describe my present developmental stage in life.

_____ I have self-confidence.

_____ I use positive self-talk and affirmations.

_____ I have a visual picture of my future success.

_____ I have a clear idea of what happiness means to me.

_____ I usually practice positive thinking.

    _____ Total points for Future

_____ I am confident of my ability to succeed in college.

_____ I am confident of my ability to succeed in my career.

_____ Total additional points

Total your points:

_____ Motivation

_____ Time and Money

_____ Memory and Reading

_____ Test Taking

_____ Taking Notes, Writing, and Speaking

_____ Personality and Major

_____ Learning Style and Intelligence

_____ Interests and Values

_____ Career and Education

_____ Communication and Relationships

_____ Critical and Creative Thinking

_____ Health

_____ Diversity

_____ Future

_____ Additional Points

_____ Grand Total Points

If you scored

450–500   You are very confident of your skills for success in college.
          Maybe you do not need this class?

400–449   You have good skills for success in college. You can always improve.

350–399   You have average skills for success in college. You will definitely
          benefit from taking this course.

Below 350 You need some help to survive in college. You are in the right place
          to begin.

Name: _____   Date: _____

■ Chart Your Succecss

Use your scores from "Measure Your Success" to complete the following chart.

College Success

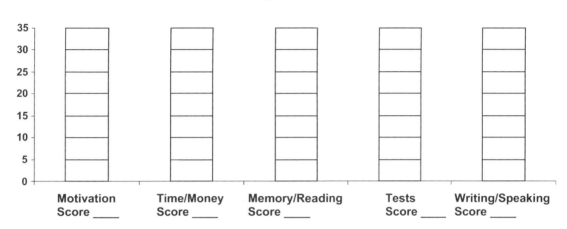

Motivation Score ____   Time/Money Score ____   Memory/Reading Score ____   Tests Score ____   Writing/Speaking Score ____

Career Success

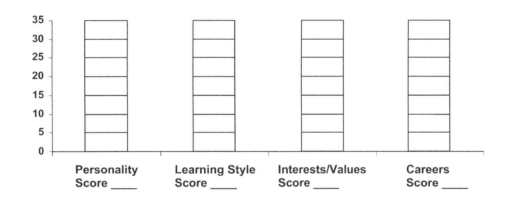

Personality Score ____   Learning Style Score ____   Interests/Values Score ____   Careers Score ____

Lifelong Success

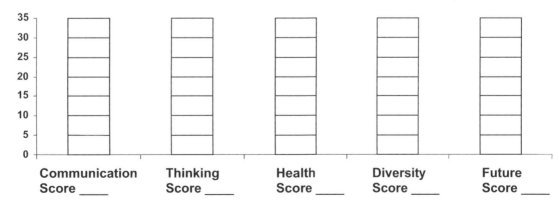

Communication Score ____   Thinking Score ____   Health Score ____   Diversity Score ____   Future Score ____

What areas do you need to improve?

■ Thinking about Your Life Stage

1. According to Erikson's seven life stages, what is your life stage? _____

   _____

   _____

2. What is your next life stage? _____

   _____

   _____

3. According to Levinson, are you in a stable or transitional period? _____

4. How do Gail Sheehy's ideas about life stages differ from those of Erik Erikson and Daniel Levinson?

   _____

   _____

5. According to Gail Sheehy, what is your life stage?

   _____

   _____

6. What is a mid-life crisis? Can you avoid one?

   _____

   _____

7. What are some ideas for successful aging?

   _____

   _____

◼ Positive Thinking

Below are some negative thoughts. Transform each negative statement into a positive statement that could help a student to be successful. You may want to do this exercise as part of a group in your classroom.

Example: Negative thought: I have never been any good in math.
Positive thought: I have had difficulty with math in the past, but I can do better this time.

1. I can't find a job.

   _____

2. I can never manage to save any money.

   _____

3. I hate physical education. Why do I have to take that class anyway?

   _____

4. I'm not very good at job interviews.

   _____

5. I'll never pass that test.

   _____

6. I'll never finish my college degree.

   _____

7. I was never good in school. I just want to play sports.

   _____

8. I'm not smart enough to do that.

   _____

9. Some people have all the luck.

   _____

Visualize Your Success

To be successful, you will need a clear mental picture of what success means to you. Take a few minutes to create a mental picture of what success means to you. Include your education, career, family life, lifestyle, finances, and anything else that is important to you. Make your picture as specific and detailed as possible. Write about this picture or draw it in the space below. You may wish to use a mind map, list, outline, or sentences to describe your picture of success.

■ Happiness Is . . .

Think of small things and big things that make you happy. List or draw them in the space below.

■ Intentions for the Future

Look over the table of contents of this book and think about what you have learned and how you will put it into practice. Write ten intention statements about how you will use the material you have learned in this class to be successful in the future.

1.

2.

3.

4.

5.

6.

7.

8.

9.

10.

◼ Course Evaluation

1. What did you think of this course?

   _____ A. This was one of the best courses I ever had.

   _____ B. This course was excellent.

   _____ C. This course was very good.

   _____ D. This course was satisfactory.

   _____ E. This course was not satisfactory.

2. How helpful was this course in choosing a major or career or confirming you choice of a major or career?

   _____ A. Extremely helpful

   _____ B. Very helpful

   _____ C. Helpful

   _____ D. Not helpful

   _____ E. Unknown

3. How helpful was this course in improving your chances for success in college?

   _____ A. Extremely helpful

   _____ B. Very helpful

   _____ C. Helpful

   _____ D. Not helpful

   _____ E. Unknown

4. How helpful was this course in improving your chances for success in your future career?

   _____ A. Extremely helpful

   _____ B. Very helpful

   _____ C. Helpful

   _____ D. Not helpful

   _____ E. Unknown

5. How helpful was this course in building your self-confidence?

   _____ A. Extremely helpful

   _____ B. Very helpful

   _____ C. Helpful

   _____ D. Not helpful

   _____ E. Unknown

6. Please rate the textbook used for this class.

_____ A. Outstanding

_____ B. Excellent

_____ C. Satisfactory

_____ D. Needs Improvement

7. Please rate the instructor in this class.

_____ A. Outstanding

_____ B. Excellent

_____ C. Satisfactory

_____ D. Needs Improvement

8. Would you recommend this course to a friend?

_____ A. Yes

_____ B. No

9. Do you plan to continue your college studies next semester?

_____ A. Yes

_____ B. No

10. Please tell what you liked about this class and how it was useful to you.

11. Do you have any suggestions for improving the class or text?

Appendix A

Going Global

The Office of Global Learning at Fairleigh Dickinson University

Fairleigh Dickinson University opened its doors at the start of World War II with an innovative and ambitious goal: to provide its students with an education "of and for the world." Today, our University considers its founding mission more relevant and urgent than ever before, and our mission is to be "a center of academic excellence dedicated to the preparation of world citizens through global education."

The Office of Global Learning is a central university office that coordinates and initiates various programs and events designed to promote the Global Mission of Fairleigh Dickinson University. The Office works closely with many units at the University to provide international experiences for students:

1. UNITED NATIONS PATHWAYS program: Lectures by UN Ambassadors followed by formal dinners take place every semester on both campuses; interactive videoconferences from the Ambassador's Club at the UN are designed for our students twice/semester and are broadcast to the ITV rooms on both campuses; tours and NGO briefings of the UN are available year round; UN internships, alliances and conferences are facilitated for our students; UN student Clubs exist on each campus. Videos and learning resources of all UN events are available in video streaming format on the Global Issues Gateway website www.gig.org

2. GLOBAL VIRTUAL FACULTY and GLOBAL VIRTUAL CLASSROOM programs: FDU students might enroll in courses that include a "guest lecturer" from another country who provides a global perspective through online interaction with the students. In some courses, FDU students can engage with an entire classroom in an international setting.

3. GLOBAL ISSUES GATEWAY website: This extensive gig.org website offers internship and training opportunities for students; provides forums and resources for student learning; and offers new spaces for student creative and intellectual contributions, including the Global Virtual Classroom.

4. INTERDISCIPLINARY AREA STUDIES: FDU offers academic courses and co-curricular programs intended to further students' global education. Besides the University Core program and the internationalized courses within traditional majors, FDU now offers a Middle East Studies and an African Studies minor on each Campus, hosted a major *Symposium on Human Rights & Conflict Resolution* in the Fall of '06, supports a dynamic *Institute for Sustainable Enterprise*, and regularly provides

lectures and activities that support the global mission. These include: *Interrogating Boundaries* lecture series, *Green Day* event, *Hot Topics* forums on the College at Florham Campus. *Human Rights* mini-lecture series, Africa Week, and *Rock for Human Rights* event at the Metropolitan Campus.

5. LIVE AND LEARN OPPORTUNITIES: The Global Scholars Program on the Metro Campus and the Florham Scholars in Global Studies at the College at Florham are both designed to offer academic, residential and global extra-curricular experiences for FDU students.

6. LANGUAGES: Both Campuses offer select language courses in Spanish, French, German, Italian, Arabic, Japanese, and Chinese. Students can also take a foreign language abroad or at an accredited institution and may also demonstrate proficiency on a placement test, or by taking the CLEP or NYU language exams for credit. The Metro Campus also offers English instruction within the Program in Language, Culture, and Professional Advancement (PLCPA) for International Students.

7. STUDENT CLUBS: Both campuses offer International Student organizations, Indian and Latin American associations, chapters of Amnesty International and United Nations Clubs. Additionally, the Metro Campus includes the following clubs: Multi-Cultural Council, Asian Club, Organization for African Unity, Nubian Ladies Making Vital Programs, Chinese Student Assoc., Haitian Cultural Assoc., Caribbean Connection Club, Islamic Society, and Interfaith Campus Ministry. The College at Florham includes the Student Volunteer Association, the Green Club, Japanese Club, and Voices of Peace.

8. EMPLOYMENT: The Office of Global Learning provides work opportunities for students on both campuses. Whenever possible, we look to create relevant academic internships in the following areas: information technology, graphic design, journal editing, event planning, public relations and advertising, education, and global studies.

Please take the time to browse our site, globaleducation.edu, to learn more about our Office and the many opportunities available for students. We appreciate your contributions and feedback and look forward to meeting, and working with, as many of you as possible.

■ Becoming a World Citizen through Travel

Study abroad and extend your intellectual horizons while gaining firsthand experience in our global society. Fairleigh Dickinson University's campus in England, Wroxton College, promises the journey of a lifetime. At Wroxton College, you will experience the majestic aura of the 17th-century Jacobean mansion that houses the College, the breathtaking splendor of the surrounding English countryside and the profound educational offerings and cultural excursions. As one alumnus has said, "It was the highlight of my life. In no other time or place have I learned, grown and been exposed to so much." The program is open to all students, eligibility requires that you be at least a second semester sophomore with a GPA of 3.0 or better.

The University has also recently opened summer courses at our new campus in Vancouver, British Columbia. These courses are also open to all students.

During spring, fall and summer intersessions there are a number of faculty-led, short term programs open to all students that travel to a variety of locations. A list of current offerings can be found in the study abroad section of FDU's website.

For a list of currently running programs or if a student is interested in attending a particular program or would like to study abroad in a particular country they are advised to contact Brian Swanzey in the Office of Study Abroad to set up a meeting. He can be reached at 973-443-8086 or via email at Brian_Swanzey@fdu.edu

■ Getting Involved—Become a Campus Citizen

Service Organizations

ASC-US

The ASC-US committee is responsible for representing and voicing the students' needs regarding auxiliary services such as Gourmet Dining food services, the bookstore, laundry rooms, and the mail room. It coordinates with the director of auxiliary services in order to voice students' concerns regarding these essential issues.

Colleges Against Cancer (CAC)

CAC is a program created to help eliminate cancer by initiating and supporting the programs of the American Cancer Society on college campuses. It is a program designed and administered by college students from across the country and is supported by the American Cancer Society. The program is designed to allow students and staff to work through many different channels to eliminate cancer. These channels are our strategic directions—advocacy, cancer education, Relay For Life, and survivorship.

Commuter Council

This organization is a representative body for commuter students. This group also plans events that relate to the social life and welfare of commuter students and resident students.

FDU Green Team

This organization provides a platform for people interested in making the world a better place by recycling, creating, and administering green initiatives, and being a platform for change.

MultiCultural Council

The MultiCultural Council serves as the umbrella organization for all cultural student organizations on the Metropolitan Campus. The organization provides cultural student organizations with a voice in critical campus issues, a forum for discussion of cultural issues concerning all students, and a vehicle for effecting change on campus.

Residence Hall Association

The purposes of the Residence Hall Association are to identify and address the needs of resident students; to serve as a liaison between resident students and the rest of the FDU community; and to create, develop, and maintain a setting of community living that is educational, stimulating, comfortable, and secure.

Student Government Association (SGA)

The SGA acts as the liaison between the University administration and the student body. It supports, encourages, and seeks student input in all levels of governance and coordinates the recognition and disbursement of funds to clubs and organizations.

Student Programming Board

This organization coordinates and implements social, cultural, intellectual, recreational, and educational events for all students. The board provides an outlet for creative and entertaining programs, ranging from comedians and musicians, to lecturers, performers, day trips, and leadership activities.

The Film Movement

This club creates a greater sense of unity by providing a voice for the activities of the various groups on campus through entertainment such as news programs, talk shows, interviews, and public service material.

MultiCultural Clubs and Organizations

African Heritage Society

The purpose of this organization is to create awareness of African culture, society, people, and places in order to diminish the stereotypes associated with the African continent.

Asian Club

This organization brings together students from many different Asian backgrounds to share information about themselves and their cultures to foster a greater understanding of this ethnic group.

BARKADA Filipino Club

The goals of the BARKADA Filipino Club are to stimulate the academic, cultural, and social interests of Filipino-Americans and introduce the Philippine culture to the campus community.

Black Men Alliance

The purpose of this organization is to promote an environment that encourages achievement and stresses the importance of academics within the black community, and to provide and recognize positive role models for minority students.

Caribbean Connection

This organization aims to educate all students by developing a better understanding of Caribbean culture, topics, issues, and diversity.

Chinese Students Friendship Association (CSFA)

This organization promotes Chinese culture at FDU and enhances a mutual understanding among students from different cultural and ethnic backgrounds. The organization brings together Chinese students as well as alumni to develop constructive and cooperative relations and support dialogues with local communities.

Francophone Club

Featuring an environment to speak French, learn about Francophone countries, and eat food from around the world, the Francophone Club is open to any student interested in learning more about Francophone countries and their heritage.

Haitian Cultural Association

This club's main purpose is to increase awareness and educate the campus about Haitian culture, and to increase awareness of issues in the Caribbean in general.

Indian Cultural Experience

This organization aims to promote Indian culture, heritage, and unity through interaction with Indian students and the general campus community by sponsoring a wide variety of events and programs.

International Student Association (ISA)

The purpose of the ISA is to spread, develop, and carry out—in a spirit of fraternity, equality, and collaboration—all cultural expressions of the countries it represents.

MultiCultural Council

The MultiCultural Council serves as the umbrella organization for all cultural student organizations on the Metropolitan Campus. This organization provides cultural student organizations with a voice in critical campus issues, a forum for discussion of cultural issues concerning all students, and a vehicle for effecting change on campus.

Muslim Educational and Cultural Association

The main purpose of this organization is to bring together the Muslim community at FDU in celebration of Islam and to provide an outlet for a better understanding of the Islamic faith.

Latin Exchange Organization

The purposes of this organization are to promote the cultural exchange and integration among the FDU students and the Morris County community about the rich culture and traditions of the South American continent, as well as to serve as a support organization for the students from different countries.

Nubian Ladies Making Vital Progress

The main purpose of this club is to support, encourage, enlighten, and praise all women no matter what race. It provides a forum for open and systematic group activities that allow the members to open up their horizons about a wide variety of topics.

Organization of Latin Americans (OLA)

This organization was established to raise awareness of Latin American heritage and influence in the community and around the world. It strives to reach out to many groups through the Metropolitan Campus by creating a wide range of programs and service projects.

PISA Italian-American Club

The goal of the Proud Italian Students Association's (PISA) is to spread both the Italian language and culture on and off campus. It works closely with many other collegiate Italian clubs throughout the northern and central New Jersey areas, including but not limited to Rutgers University, William Paterson University, Drew University, Montclair State University, and FDU's College at Florham. PISA members regularly attend meetings and functions of those other clubs. PISA is a member of Amici Della Cultura Italiana (Friends of the Italian Culture), a foundation started by Joseph Coccia, a generous benefactor who wishes to see the Italian culture passed on to this and future generations.

Fine and Performing Arts

Knightscapes

Knightscapes is the Metropolitan Campus' art and literary magazine. Published every semester, *Knightscapes* strives to enhance and showcase the University's artistic and literary community by offering readings, discussions, and writing workshops. For information: knightscapes54@gmail.com.

Motion Defined

Through the integrated teaching of ballroom, step, Latin, and R&B dance, Motion Defined provides students with a forum for dance in both teaching and learning capabilities.

Pri'sizhen

This club provides students with the opportunity for creative expressions through dances, step, and stroll.

The University Players (TUP)

TUP is the student theater group of the Metropolitan Campus. Membership in TUP is open to all students, faculty, and staff who present theatrical performances for the campus community and the public.

Organizations of Faith

Hillel-Jewish Student Union

This group strives to celebrate Jewish heritage and culture. The organization creates programs throughout the academic year, from movie nights to Sabbath dinners and holiday parties.

Interfaith Campus Ministry

Sharing together in God's work, this group brings together the many different faiths to work for the betterment of all peoples.

University Christian Fellowship

This group strives to deepen and strengthen the spiritual lives of members by Bible study, prayer, fellowship, and services in which students can apply Christian faith to all areas of their lives.

Inspirational Gospel Ensemble

The Inspirational Gospel Ensemble allows all FDU students to exhibit and exercise their vocal, instrumental, and other musical talents. It works with the Christian Fellowship to bring awareness of God through music and songs.

Fraternities

Alpha Phi Alpha Fraternity, Inc.

Alpha Phi Alpha Fraternity, Inc., the first intercollegiate Greek letter fraternity established for African-Americans, was founded at Cornell University in Ithaca, New York on December 4, 1906, by seven college men who recognized the need for a strong bond of brotherhood among African descendants in this country. The visionary founders, known as the "Jewels" of the fraternity, are Henry Arthur Callis, Charles Henry Chapman, Eugene Kinckle Jones, George Biddle Kelley, Nathaniel Allison Murray, Robert Harold Ogle, and Vertner Woodson Tandy.

The fraternity initially served as a study and support group for minority students who faced racial prejudice, both educationally and socially, at Cornell. The Jewel founders and early leaders of the fraternity succeeded in laying a firm foundation for Alpha Phi Alpha's principles of scholarship, fellowship, good character, and the uplifting of humanity.

Alpha Phi Alpha chapters were established at other colleges and universities, many of them historically black institutions, soon after the founding at Cornell. The first Alumni Chapter was established in 1911. While continuing to stress academic excellence among its members, Alpha also recognized the need to help correct the educational, economic, political, and social injustices faced by African-Americans. Alpha Phi Alpha has long stood at the forefront of the African-American community's fight for civil rights through leaders such as W.E.B. DuBois, Adam Clayton Powell, Jr., Edward Brooke, Martin Luther King, Jr., Thurgood Marshall, Andrew Young, William Gray, Paul Robeson, and many others. True to its form as the "first of firsts," Alpha Phi Alpha has been interracial since 1945.

The objectives of Alpha Phi Alpha Fraternity, Inc. are to stimulate the ambition of its members; to prepare them for the greatest usefulness in the causes of humanity, freedom, and dignity of the individual; to encourage the highest and noblest form of manhood; and to aid down-trodden humanity in its efforts to achieve higher social, economic, and intellectual status.

Website: http://www.alpha-phi-alpha.com/index.php

Lambda Theta Phi Latin Fraternity, Inc.

On December 1, 1975, history was made–Lambda Theta Phi was founded on the campus of Kean College in Union, New Jersey. In 1975, there were no Latino fraternities in existence in the United States. The Greek-letter organizations of the time primarily catered to Anglo and African-American students and graduates. Lambda's founders, as men of vision, realized there was a need to unite the Latino students, develop their leadership skills, impart upon them the value of an education, and instill in them a commitment to their community and culture. The traditional student club would not suffice to accomplish such lofty goals. Hence, Latino unity and brotherhood would be achieved through a long recognized institution—the fraternity. This newest addition to the Greek system would be the first in the nation, by identity and by name: Lambda Theta Phi Latin Fraternity, Inc.

The ideals of this brotherhood are the following: academic excellence, brotherhood, leadership, Latino unity, and service. On a daily basis, our brothers live up to these ideals, as set forth by 14 young Latino men decades ago.

At the undergraduate level, our brothers are active within the fraternity and in other student organizations. As a result of their active participation in every aspect of college life, our undergraduates are developing their organizational, communication, and leadership skills, all while pursuing the coveted diploma. Our younger Lambdas are receiving the training and competence to serve as the future leaders of our brotherhood, community, and nation.

At the professional level, among our ranks you will find attorneys, doctors, engineers, educators, dedicated fathers, law enforcement, the armed forces, entrepreneurs, coaches, mentors, community activists, elected officials serving on city councils, boards of education, the U.S. House of Representatives, and the U.S. Senate. In short, Lambdas are contributing and excelling in every facet of human endeavor.

Since our founding, our brotherhood continues to provide the necessary skills and resources for the advancement and empowerment of our people and for the betterment of this nation. Our illustrious history is not only our past but also our guiding light to the future. As the first, we overcame many obstacles. Not having much guidance in our formative stages, we persevered and became stronger. Lambda is the product of vision, strength, and unity. Our history serves as a legacy and testament to our accomplishments and greatness.

Website: http://www.lambda1975.org/

Omega Psi Phi Fraternity

Omega Psi Phi is the first African-American national fraternal organization to be founded at a historically black college. On Friday evening, November 17, 1911, three Howard University undergraduate students, with the assistance of their faculty adviser, gave birth to the Omega Psi Phi Fraternity. This event occurred in the office of biology in the Science Hall. The three students were Edgar Amos Love, Oscar James Cooper, and Frank Coleman, and their faculty adviser was Dr. Ernest Everett Just. From the initials of the Greek phrase, meaning "friendship is essential to the soul," the name Omega Psi Phi was derived. The phrase was selected as the motto. Manhood, scholarship, perseverance, and uplift were adopted as cardinal principles.

Each of the founders graduated and went on to have distinguished careers in their chosen fields. Bishop Edgar Amos Love became Bishop of the United Methodist Church; Dr. Oscar James Cooper became a prominent physician, who practiced in Philadelphia for over 50 years; Professor Frank Coleman became the Chairman of the Department of Physics at Howard University for many years; and Dr. Ernest Everett Just became a world-renowned biologist.

On November 23, 1911, in Thirkield Hall, Love became the first Grand Basileus (National President). Cooper and Coleman were selected to be the Grandkeeper of the Records (National Secretary) and Grandkeeper of Seals (National Treasurer), respectively. Eleven Howard University undergraduate men were selected to be the charter members.

The fraternity has worked to build a strong and effective force of men dedicated to its cardinal principles of manhood, scholarship, perseverance, and uplift. In 1927, at the urging of fraternity member Carter G. Woodson, the fraternity made National Negro Achievement Week an annual observance, and it continues today as Black History Month.

Omega continued to flourish, largely because founders Love, Cooper, Coleman, and Just were men of the very highest ideals and intellect. The founders selected and attracted men of similar ideals and characteristics. It is not by accident that many of America's great black men are/were Omega Men. To this date, there are very few Americans whose lives have not been touched by a member of the Omega Psi Phi Fraternity. Omega has a rich heritage to be protected, celebrated, and enhanced!

Website: http://www.omegapsiphifraternity.org/

Sigma Lambda Beta International Fraternity, Inc.

During the fall of 1985, Baltazar Mendoza-Madrigal began to explore the idea of establishing a Latino-based fraternity at the University of Iowa. After months of intensive research, a special meeting was called on March 7, 1986, with some of the Latino students at the University of Iowa. The purpose of the meeting was to discuss the need and feasibility of creating a new social fraternity with an emphasis on the Latino culture. At that point in time, the student body at the University of Iowa was predominantly Caucasian. In addition, the Latino community on campus was divided into different social groups. As a result, the students who attended the first meeting wanted to solidify and unify the Latino community. Furthermore, the students wanted to promote a positive image of Latinos at the University.

After the first meeting, the enthusiasm in favor of the fraternity was so encouraging that the word spread throughout the University. Everyone knew that something special was about to take place. On Friday, April 4, 1986, the members finalized the philosophy and ideology of the organization. The 18 founding fathers established Sigma Lambda Beta with the following principles in mind: BROTHERHOOD, SCHOLARSHIP, CULTURAL AWARENESS, and COMMUNITY SERVICE.

Our founding fathers had a dream and VISION that our honorable fraternity could promote a positive image of the Latino community at the University of Iowa and other universities located throughout the nation by scholastic achievements, eternal brotherhood, the dissemination of our unique and rich culture, and service to our community. Furthermore, as our honorable fraternity expanded and grew in the late 1980s, the new and younger brothers worked hard by trying their best to carry out the founding principles of our organization. Current brothers are keeping the light shining and working hard to promote a positive image of our people and our community throughout the nation.

The organization is committed to create and expand multicultural leadership, promote academic excellence, advance cultural awareness and service, while influencing its mission among all dedicated collegiate men worldwide. Our motto is "Opportunity for Wisdom, Wisdom for Culture." Dare to be different and hold yourself to one of the most prestigious, gentlemanly, and educated standards.

Website: http://www.sigmalambdabeta.com/

Sigma Pi Fraternity, International

Sigma Pi is a social fraternity, founded in 1892 at Vincennes University. From the beginning, the fraternity has undergone several name changes. February 11, 1907, is a significant date in the fraternity history. It was then the members last assembled as Tau Phi Delta and first assumed the name of Sigma Pi Fraternity of the United States. Tau Phi Delta had had limited ambitions for expansion. Soon after the name change, Sigma Pi embarked on a program of establishing chapters on other campuses.

In 1984, the fraternity again changed its name. At the 37th Biennial Convocation, Sigma Pi became an international fraternity by accepting its first Canadian chapter. This international status required the fraternity to become Sigma Pi Fraternity, International. Today, Sigma Pi is comprised of 124 active chapters, seven colonies, over 90,000 alumni, and continues to grow each year.

The mission of Sigma Pi Fraternity, International, is to build and support chapters and alumni organizations for the purpose of maintaining a fellowship of kindred minds united in brotherhood. To advance truth and justice; to promote scholarship; to encourage chivalry; to diffuse culture; and to develop character . . . in the service of God and man.

Sigma Pi Fraternity is the leading, international men's collegiate fraternal organization that provides training, guidance, and innovative opportunities for leadership development, social and personal development, academic achievement, community service, and heightened moral awareness for its brothers throughout their lives.

The Epsilon Xi chapter was re-colonized at the Metropolitan Campus on January 30, 2005, by a group of gentlemen looking for a "new kind of fraternity." This strong group of young men, united in brotherhood, continues to cultivate their fraternal bond and represent the ideals/ethics/principles of Sigma Pi.

Website: http://www.sigmapi2.org/

Phi Beta Sigma Fraternity

Phi Beta Sigma Fraternity was founded at Howard University in Washington, DC, on January 9, 1914, by three young African-American male students. The founders, Honorable A. Langston Taylor, Honorable Leonard F. Morse, and Honorable Charles I. Brown, wanted to organize a Greek letter fraternity that would truly exemplify the ideals of brotherhood, scholarship, and service.

The founders deeply wished to create an organization that viewed itself as "a part of" the general community. They believed that each potential member should be judged by his own merits, rather than his family background of affluence . . . without regard to race, nationality, skin tone, or texture of hair. They desired for their fraternity to exist as part of an even greater brotherhood that would be devoted to the "inclusive we" rather than the "exclusive we."

From its inception, the founders also conceived Phi Beta Sigma as a mechanism to deliver services to the greater community. Rather than gaining skills to be utilized exclusively for themselves and their immediate families, they held a deep conviction that they should return their newly acquired skills to the communities from which they had come. This deep conviction was mirrored in the fraternity's motto: "Culture For Service and Service For Humanity."

Today, Phi Beta Sigma has blossomed into an international organization of leaders. No longer a single entity, members of the fraternity have been instrumental in the establishment of the Phi Beta Sigma National Foundation, the Phi Beta Sigma Federal Credit Union, and the Sigma Beta Club Foundation. Zeta Phi Beta Sorority, founded in 1920 with the assistance of Phi Beta Sigma, is the sister organization of the fraternity.

Website: http://www.pbs1914.org/

Sororities

Alpha Epsilon Phi Sorority

Alpha Epsilon Phi Sorority was founded by seven Jewish women, Helen Phillips, Ida Beck, Rose Gerstein, Augustina "Tina" Hess, Lee Reiss, Rose Salmowitz, and Stella Strauss, at Barnard College in New York City on October 24, 1909. Their goal was to foster lifelong friendship and sisterhood, academics, social involvement, and community service, while providing a home away from home for their members. "It was her [Helen Phillips'] idea and her persistence more than anything else that brought Alpha Epsilon Phi into existence," one founder wrote. "I sometimes think that some of those ties were more necessary to Helen than to the others in this group because Helen had no mother and no sisters or brothers, and to her a group of adopted sisters was more of a need and had more significance."

The dream that was born in a dorm room at Barnard College in 1909 continues to succeed, prosper, and thrive on over 50 college and university campuses nationwide. AEPhi welcomes with open arms hundreds of new members each year, and seeks not only to live up to the ideals and goals of its original founders, but also to exceed them.

The beliefs and goals of Alpha Epsilon Phi and our members are best stated in our Core Values Statement: "Above all else, Alpha Epsilon Phi inspires exemplary women who are: enriched by sisterhood and unconditional friendships, dedicated to selfless service and inspiring others, and committed to intellectual growth and personal development. As a lifelong member of Alpha Epsilon Phi, I will: respect our shared heritage and traditions, exhibit high ideals and moral character, fulfill expectations and responsibilities of membership, and continually exemplify the values of beauty, strength and wisdom as embodied by the three columns of our insignia."

Members of Alpha Epsilon Phi have continued to make the vision of our founders a high priority, as seen in AEPhi's commitment to community service and philanthropy since our earliest days, our members' continued academic excellence, and our ongoing leadership training and development.

At FDU's Metropolitan Campus, we stay true to AEPhi's ideals with a diverse group of women from all over the country and the world. The Phi Xi chapter of AEPhi at FDU was founded on campus September 26, 1987, and has been going strong for 23 years- giving us the honor of being the oldest continually active sorority on this campus! We encourage our members to be active in all aspects of college and Greek life, including community service and philanthropic activities. We have two national medical philan- thropies: Sharsheret, a national breast cancer organization, and The Elizabeth Glaser Pediatric Aids foundation, founded by an AEPhi member to promote awareness and educate people on the special issues concerning children with the AIDS virus.

Website: http://www.aephi.org/

Alpha Sigma Tau

For over 100 years, Alpha Sigma Tau has been an active presence at universities and col- leges across the country. From its beginnings in 1899 to today, the purpose of the soror- ity has been to promote the ethical, cultural, and social development of its members, and members have maintained high standards of scholarship, friendship, and social grace.

The establishment of sororities on college campuses that addressed themselves to the education of teachers led to the formation of those sororities into the Association of Edu- cation Sororities (AES). One of the goals of Alpha Sigma Tau was to become a national sorority, and to achieve membership in AES.

Alpha Sigma Tau's first 10 years was a period of establishing an appropriate founda- tion to move toward the structure needed to develop a national organization. In April 1905, a group of women at Central Michigan Normal School (now Central Michigan University), in Mt. Pleasant, joined Alpha Sigma Tau as a Beta Chapter. Other chapters soon affiliated, and by April 1926, the sorority had achieved membership in AES. The sorority's first convention was held in Detroit, Michigan, where the sorority magazine, *The ANCHOR*, was established.

In December 1951, the AES merged with the National Panhellenic Conference (NPC), and Alpha Sigma Tau began its long and active association with the NPC. AST Cynthia Peckhart McCrory served on the Executive Committee of the NPC from 1979 through 1985, and was elected to the first Executive Board of the National Panhellenic Confer- ence Foundation.

The Alpha Sigma Tau National Foundation was incorporated in 1982 to promote and expand the educational and charitable activities of the sorority. The major milestone has provided Alpha Sigma Tau with the means to make stronger philanthropic contributions and to more readily provide academic scholarships to sisters.

In 1995 Alpha Sigma Tau established its new building for the Alpha Sigma Tau national headquarters in Birmingham, Alabama. This office serves as the clearinghouse for most sorority information, and as the sorority's "home."

From the beginning, alumnae involvement has been an important part of membership in Alpha Sigma Tau. Alumnae have been instrumental in the expansion and growth of the sorority, providing guidance and support to collegiate chapters, and taking leader- ship roles in Greek organizations. They have also staffed headquarters, coordinated con- ventions, and funded major sorority projects.

Today, collegiate and alumnae sisters continue to form strong and lasting bonds in Alpha Sigma Tau. The sorority's programs and social service projects continue to enrich the lives of many, helping sisters contribute our share to the progress of man- kind. We welcome new sisters and help each other grow to be contributing mem- bers of our community.

Website: http://www.alphasigmatau.org/

Lambda Tau Omega Sorority, Inc.

Lambda Tau Omega Sorority, Inc., was founded in 1988 by 16 young, intelligent, and energetic women at Montclair State College, now known as Montclair State University.

The overall membership of Lambda Tau Omega Sorority, Inc., reflects diversity; we are a myriad of ethnic, political, and religious backgrounds. With the belief in mind that education equals women's empowerment, we were founded on superior scholarship, and we vow to advance our academic ideals at every college and university that we may reach.

Our sisterhood also serves as a common social ground that encourages close friendships among our sisters, other respective Greeks, and the community. And in carrying out that purpose of Lambda Tau Omega Sorority, Inc., we inspire sisters to disseminate "Excellence Through Unity, Knowledge and Dedication"; hence our motto.

Today, more than ever, Lambda Tau Omega Sorority, Inc., serves as an integral and functional part of college and university experience; we encompass various fields of higher education.

Moreover, we are a sisterhood of young, energetic, and strong minded women with the courage to thrive on innovation, while never losing sight of our main philanthropic focus—children. We believe that children are a powerful means of fostering a productive future for all. Therefore, children's guidance, education, and health must be a leading concern for all Lambda Tau Omega Sorority, Inc. sisters. Also, even though our philanthropic focus is the overall welfare of children, we are open to other causes as well.

From the inception, Lambda Tau Omega Sorority, Inc., began her journey alone. Over a decade later, we continue to pride ourselves on being independent women who will ALWAYS be independent women. We are women who search for quality as opposed to quantity. We welcome all women who share our beliefs, determination, discipline, and dedication to the challenge . . . the challenge of pledging . . . Lambda Tau Omega Sorority, Inc. A Sisterhood to Last a Lifetime!

Website: http://www.lambdatauomega.org/

Lambda Theta Alpha Latin Sorority, Inc.

The year 1975 saw the birth of what started as a vision—an idea of an organization, a sisterhood that would cater to the needs of Latinas and the universal woman. Thanks to the tremendous strides made by our 17 founding mothers, this dream was realized, and took form as the entity Lambda Theta Alpha Latin Sorority, Inc., the first Latina sorority in the nation.

There were several causes leading to the realization that such an organization was necessary. Traditionally, the role of the Latina woman was that of maintaining the family institution and falling into the realm of the machismo stigma. As the Latino migration to the United States increased, so did the emergence of independent Latina women, eager to be at the forefront of an era of a new educational, political, and social consciousness. In the early 1970s, colleges and universities experienced an influx of Latino enrollment. With this growth, the need for support groups and outreach programs were at an all-time high, primarily for the low percentage of Latina women in higher education institutions.

In 1975, Kean University in Union, New Jersey, introduced and began to implement bilingual studies, as well as a Latino and Caribbean studies department. Women of Latin descent were now able to embark in higher education, even if English was not their native language. Although this enabled and facilitated the educational advancement of the Latina woman, a huge void was yet to be filled—still missing was support and equality; a constant reminder to these women that they were still the minority, and that their struggle for equality on every level had just begun. It was at this university, in this historic time period, that a group of women convened to discuss the formation of a sorority for Latina women. Its focus would be to actively integrate itself into the social, political, and community service arena that other students had been involved with. Together, as a united front they could compete, collaborate, and assist with any student-run programs, thus making their voices as loud and profound as the majority voice; their concerns equally as important.

Lambda Theta Alpha was recognized at Kean University as the first Latina sorority founded in the United States. This organization was the first to recognize the need for a support system, thus creating one. The desire to progress, dedication to their community, and the aspiration for the advancement of the Latina women marked the beginning of Lambda Theta Alpha. It allowed the independent Latina woman of a new era to have a sense of belonging, and with that, achieve her highest potential. It would define a new role for the Latina woman; one with education, goals, and vision in hopes of great success.

Now, 34 years later, we have seen the outcome of such an organization. Lambda Theta Alpha has contributed to the advancement of all people by helping to produce educated women of many races, ethnicities, and creeds. These women are political leaders, doctors, lawyers, teachers, accountants, etc. LTA has also paved the way for many other Latina organizations, which would later pursue the empowering movement that we set the trend for. From 1975 to date, Lambda Theta Alpha has upheld its purpose and mission, each day realizing the founder's dream—that it may serve as a quintessential trailblazer for all women.

Website: http://www.lambdalady.org/

Omega Phi Chi Sorority, Inc.

Omega Phi Chi is a multicultural sorority that was established on November 9, 1988, at Rutgers University in New Jersey by eight women of Asian, African-American, and Latina descent. Our eight founding mothers were an active group of young women leaders who felt the absence of any organization on the Rutgers campus that spoke to their needs across diverse backgrounds, distinct cultural roots, and a commitment to womanhood. They came together to found a multicultural sorority; a different type of organization that would not be categorized by ethnicity or culture.

The overall purpose of Omega Phi Chi is to generate unity among all women. We believe that we can promote ethnic diversity by integrating women across all boundaries and cultures. Through the common bond of womanhood, we are then able to nurture our ideals of sisterhood. Among our ideals of sisterhood are the concepts of love, honesty, loyalty, mutual respect, and the responsibility of one another. After unity, the main objectives of this organization are academic excellence and involvement in community affairs. Education plays a vital role throughout the course of one's lifetime; therefore, through the aid of donations, scholarships, and the shared efforts of our sisters, we can propel one another toward various career goals and aspirations. We aim to promote positivity and an improved outlook on life, as well as foster opportunities to improve one's standard of living.

Omega Phi Chi is above the stereotypical notions of sorority as a purely social endeavor. We have created a space for women to come together as a true sisterhood and support system that is strong and empowering. Our sisterhood cultivates leaders backed by the support of an entire organization of women committed to making sure we each have a voice and place at the table in a society where women and minorities continue to be underrepresented across all fields. While undergraduate sisters are provided with support and encouragement during their college years, they are welcomed into a network of professionals upon graduation, willing to mentor and offer guidance as they move into the real world.

Omega Phi Chi recognizes that academic excellence is significant in building a foundation of knowledge to support future individual growth and aspiration. In addition to organizational and leadership skills building, Omega Phi Chi instills in each sister a commitment to high academic standards. As a result of our emphasis on academics, which is implemented by providing scholarships, holding study sessions, tutoring, and counseling, we have among our ranks: scholars, honor society members, high honor graduates, graduate and doctoral students, as well as doctors, lawyers, and business executives.

Omega Phi Chi recognizes the challenges women face as professionals, from unequal pay to breaking through the glass ceiling to balancing a career and family, and is also cognizant of how these obstacles differ across race, class, and sexuality. Our alumni will get together informally and formally throughout the year, either during small personal gatherings or planned networking events, to make connections, build relationships, or share ideas and advice. The sisterhood is always present for each individual throughout various stages of life and personal growth.

Website: http://www.omegaphichi.org/

Zeta Phi Beta, Sorority, Inc.

The year was 1920. It was the start of the decade, shortly after World War I, and a time of great prosperity for the country. Women were called dames, dolls, or the cat's meow. At the beginning of the decade, women still wore long skirts, but the "Roaring 20s" brought a new look of short skirts and smartly coiffed shorter hair. Racial tensions were high, and quotas set for immigrants coming into America. The Klan was very active during this period. The Harlem Renaissance was acknowledged as the first important movement of black artists and writers in the U.S. On January 16, 1920, the Volstead Act became effective, heralding the start of Prohibition, and on August 18th of the same year, Tennessee delivered the crucial 36th ratification necessary for the final adoption of the 19th Amendment, giving women the right to vote. The worst and longest economic recession to ever hit the United States would define the end of the decade—the Great Depression.

It was within this environment that Zeta Phi Beta Sorority was founded. Zeta Phi Beta Sorority was founded on the simple belief that sorority elitism and socializing should not overshadow the real mission for progressive organizations—to address societal mores, ills, prejudices, poverty, and health concerns of the day. Founded on January 16, 1920, Zeta began as an idea conceived by five coeds at Howard University in Washington, DC: Arizona Cleaver, Myrtle Tyler, Viola Tyler, Fannie Pettie, and Pearl Neal. These five women, also known as our Five Pearls, dared to depart from the traditional coalitions for black women and sought to establish a new organization predicated on the precepts of Scholarship, Service, Sisterly Love, and Finer Womanhood. It was the ideal of the founders that the sorority would reach college women in all parts of the country who were sorority minded and desired to follow the founding principles of the organization. Founder Viola Tyler was oft quoted to say "[In the ideal collegiate situation] there is a Zeta in a girl regardless of race, creed, or color, who has high standards and principles, a good scholarly average and an active interest in all things that she undertakes to accomplish."

Since its inception, the sorority has chronicled a number of firsts. Zeta Phi Beta was the first Greek letter organization to charter a chapter in Africa (1948); to form adult and youth auxiliary groups; to centralize its operations in a national headquarters; and to be constitutionally bound to a fraternity, Phi Beta Sigma Fraternity, Inc.

Zeta's national and local programs include endowment of its National Educational Foundation, community outreach services, and support of multiple affiliate organizations. Zeta chapters and auxiliary groups have given untold hours of voluntary service to educate the public, assist youth, provide scholarships, support organized charities, and promote legislation for social and civic change. A nonprofit organization, Zeta Phi Beta, is incorporated in Washington, DC, and in the state of Illinois. The dues and gifts of its members support the sorority.

Over the years since the sorority's inception, Zeta Phi Beta has chartered hundreds of chapters and initiated thousands of women around the world. Zeta has continued to thrive and flourish, while adapting to the ever-changing needs of a new century. Despite the Great Depression, discrimination and segregation, and a host of other challenges, Zeta has continued to hold true to its ideals and purpose, for, as stated by one of the sorority's founding members: " . . . I believe that no [other] organization could have been founded upon principles that were so near and dear to all of our hearts." (Founder Myrtle Tyler)

Website: http://www.zphib1920.org/

Chi Upsilon Sigma National Latin Sorority, Inc. (PETITIONING)

Corazones Unidos Siempre, Chi Upsilon Sigma National Latin Sorority, Inc. (C.U.S.), is an organization founded on the principles of integrity, respect, and accountability. Today, we have created a solid foundation and a structure for ourselves that will ensure our longevity among Greek organizations. Not only have we increased our membership intake, but we also continue to increase the active level among our undergraduates and alumnae through new programs, training, and mentoring.

The sisterhood is unique in its capabilities to draw in new members who embrace our appreciation for family, individuality, and collaboration with each other. Our members take their dedication to new levels by creating bonds with members across chapters and regions. Our sisters are women who not only exemplify and embody the essence of our organization, but also educate themselves and others about societal current events that enlighten their understanding of the world and their communities. They recognize this lifelong membership as a highly rewarding experience, in which they impart knowledge and wisdom throughout their encounters with one another.

C.U.S. has been in existence as a diverse organization for over 30 years. Today, we are present in over 12 states expanding over 40 schools. We continuously recruit women who are leaders in their communities, and increase our communication with other organizations on their campuses with the goal of servicing the community, and creating educational, cultural, political, and social programming with them. We provide the platform for our undergraduates and alumnae to excel in their own right as individuals, hence the phrase, "Women So Strong, We Need No Brothers." Yet, at the same time, we embark upon opportunities to build relationships with other organizations.

Website: http://www.justbecus.org/

Lambda Pi Upsilon Sorority Latinas Poderosas Unidas, Inc.

(PETITIONING)

The State University of New York at Genesee, otherwise known as S.U.N.Y. Genesee is an extraordinary university locale. To some individuals, this location is a tiny spot on a New York State map, possibly having little importance. However, to the members of this organization, S.U.N.Y. Genesee has great significance; it is our birthplace. A predominantly Caucasian campus with a diminutive minority population was the driving force behind our Six Pillars of Strength: to eagerly seek commonality, cultural identity, and growth of mind. They aspired to address, combat, and earnestly attempt a resolution to the increasing complexity and seriousness of womanhood problems; particularly those of Latinas. Their desires lead them the Lambda Way to experience the unknown. They had a great deal of faith, vision, and ambition in their capabilities, and believed that as a closer support system they would provide others, especially Latinas, with the strength to succeed. Through sacrifices and struggles they confronted challenges of women of color by providing a sisterly network of strength, substantiality, and empowerment.

Defying social and political boundaries, on November 6, 1992, they succeeded in creating a new path in which women of all walks of life can follow. Members of Lambda Pi Upsilon Sorority, Latinas Poderosas Unidas, Inc., uphold the following six founding principles: Family, Advancement, Education, Motivation, Learning, and Exposure. Throughout the years, we have maintained such dedication to these principles and earnestly seek quality members to develop the organization at various universities and colleges.

Lambda Pi Upsilon Sorority, Latinas Poderosas Unidas, Inc., is proud to be one of the youngest Latina-based, all-inclusive Greek letter organizations in the country. We recognize and appreciate that our Six Pillars of Strength created the foundation for our Hermandad to be everlasting, which is why it is a special relationship that must always be nurtured. Our commitment to education, cultural awareness, family, and above all, each other guarantees our Legacy . . . Hermanas Para Siempre Con Amor, Dignidad Y Orgullo!

Website: http://www.lpiu.com/version1/

Academic and Professional Clubs and Organizations

Accounting Society

This organization's main goal is focused toward informing students about current accounting topics and enhancing professional and career development skills. In addition, the society promotes friendly relations among faculty, students, and alumni as they work with other organizations within FDU.

ASCD Student Chapter

The FDU chapter of the Association for Supervision and Curriculum Development (ASCD) brings together students focusing on education. Its programs include lectures, trips, and conferences.

Business Leaders of Tomorrow

Through the use of interactive social, community service, and networking events, the Business Leaders of Tomorrow prepare all students of FDU to enter into the business world and to begin in progressive careers as thoughtful, creative, and compassionate leaders in a fun, open, and friendly environment. For information: blt.fdu@gmail.com.

Campus Health and Public Safety Team (CHAPS)

The purpose of CHAPS is to provide certified emergency medical services training to members of the campus community. The organization offers CPR training, wellness seminars, and other health-related educational programs.

Communication Honor Society

The purposes of this honor society are to recognize, foster, and reward outstanding scholastic achievement in communication studies; stimulate interest in the field of communication by promoting and encouraging professional development among communication majors; to provide an opportunity to discuss and exchange ideas in the field of communication; and to establish and maintain closer relationships and mutual understanding between communication studies faculty and students.

Computer Science Information Technology Club

The purpose of this club is to provide FDU students with a formal venue to gather and work in groups to receive assistance in computer-related technology.

Criminal Justice Club

This club is committed to education, excellence, and civic service. It is committed to helping students interested in criminal justice build strong networks in the field, providing educational and training opportunities, and giving back to students' communities.

Hotel, Restaurant, and Tourism Management Society

This professional organization of inn-keeping and restaurant students engaged in industry, government, and education aims to foster the individual welfare of its members, both individually and as a group, and to advance the theory of scientific management, wherever it may apply, through research, education, and discussion.

Institute of Electrical and Electronics Engineers (IEEE)

The IEEE student branch provides an opportunity for men and women studying in the field of engineering and technologies to network among their peers, develop social skills for community relations, and work on projects together in an academically challenging and friendly environment.

Math Club

This club enables students to further explore mathematical topics with their peers and to provide help for struggling students.

National Society of Black Engineers

This society provides an outlet for students of color whose career focus is engineering. The group's portfolio of activities includes guest lectures, field trips, and engineering and leadership conferences.

Pre-Health Professional Club

The main purpose of this club is to provide information and guidance to students of the FDU community who desire to learn about any of the health professions. It offers a wide range of programs, from guest speakers, to field trips, to professional schools. For information: phpfdu@gmail.com.

Psychology Club

The purposes and objectives of the Psychology Club are to foster awareness for the students; to promote participation in the field of psychology; to provide information about the field of psychology; to promote academic achievement in the field of psychology; and to encourage participation in activities involving psychology.

Society of Women Engineers (SWE)

The SWE provides an outlet for women studying in the field of engineering and technologies. Networking, information sessions, lectures, and conferences are just a few of the opportunities the organization offers its members.

Student-Athlete Advisory Committee

This organization is a communication vehicle where FDU student-athletes and the athletic administration discuss the student-athlete experience, while encouraging the involvement and unification of the campus community and the surrounding communities.

Tri-Beta Biological Honor Society

This honor society brings together science majors who share a common interest in the biological field. For information: bbbfdu@gmail.com.

Political Clubs and Organizations

Amnesty International

Amnesty International's mission is to undertake research and action focused on preventing and ending grave abuses of the rights to physical and mental integrity, freedom of conscience and expression, and freedom from discrimination, within the context of its work to promote all human rights. Amnesty International is independent of any government, political ideology, or religious creed. It does not support or oppose the views of the victims whose rights it seeks to protect. It is concerned solely with the impartial protection of human rights.

Young Democrats

The purpose of this organization is to unite politically oriented students in an open and intellectual organization. They create awareness of the Democratic campaign on campus, and are committed to increasing political awareness in the surrounding community. They run workshops, lectures, and bring speakers from political parties to campus, and are open to any political affiliation.

FDU College Republicans (FDU-CR)

The FDU-CR is comprised of students who are dedicated to fostering awareness and allegiance to American principles of government and public service, and opposed to political corruption, and who want to promote honest and free electoral methods, encourage public attention to the discussion of government and civic concerns, and engage the interest and activity of young voters. For information: fducollegerepublicans@gmail.com.

UNA-USA

UNA-USA promotes the University's ties with the United Nations on campus by providing the student community with both academic and social activities relating to the international system, and the United Nations as a whole, as well as encouraging learning that focuses on global issues.

Sport Clubs

Bowling Club

This club is committed to fostering integrity and excellence in academic, social, recreational, and competitive atmospheres through participation in the game of bowling.

Crew Club

This club practices regular crew races against other schools and universities in the area on the Hackensack River.

Cricket Club

This club is open to all FDU students interested in the sport of cricket. Instruction is provided for new players as well as opportunities for experienced players to further improve their skills.

FDU Soccer Club

The aim of this club is to contribute to the healthy practice of soccer in a friendly and organized way, as well as to create diverse activities to broaden students' perspective about this beautiful game.

FDU Rugby Club

Our mission is to manage, serve, and promote the game of rugby for all levels of play. We will teach the proper way to play the game by adhering to the laws of the game, while developing new friendships that may last a lifetime.

FDU Fencing

The goals of the club are to teach the rules of the sport and conduct lessons on the proper techniques used in the art of fencing. We will use the nationally renowned FDU Knights fencing team to assist with education in a fun, non-competitive environment.

Roller Hockey Club

The purpose of this club is to broaden the horizons of the athletic programs offered at the Metropolitan Campus by increasing the athletic interest among current and future students in the field of roller hockey.

Tae Kwon Do Club

Our mission is to teach the art of Tae Kwon Do, following the principles used by the World Martial Arts Association (WMAA) to the FDU students, faculty and alumni. FDU Tae Kwon Do teaches self-defense, but also helps students build strong character and enhance their overall wellness in a supportive, non-judgmental, collegial environment. Classes are open to all abilities and fitness levels.

Media Organizations

The Equinox Student Newspaper

This bi-weekly student-run, edited, and printed newspaper provides a means of mass communication and dissemination of student-related news, features, entertainment, and opinion, from and throughout the University campus, and serves as a forum for varying ideas and opinions of the Metropolitan Campus community. For information: equinoxfdu@gmail.com.

Knightscapes

Knightscapes is the Metropolitan Campus' art and literary magazine. Published every semester, *Knightscapes* strives to enhance and showcase the University's artistic and literary community by offering readings, discussions, and writing workshops. For information: knightscapes54@gmail.com.

WFDQ-92–FM Radio Station

The radio station serves the Metropolitan Campus community by broadcasting cultural, informational, and other programs and materials for the entertainment and profit of the public, as well as to educate its members in the policies and procedures used in professional radio broadcasting. For information: wfdq91_9@hotmail.com.

Index

Page numbers followed by f *indicate a figure*
Page numbers followed by t *indicate a table*